The Literary Work of Art

Northwestern University
STUDIES IN *Phenomenology &*
Existential Philosophy

Roman Ingarden

Translated, with an Introduction, by

The Literary Work of Art

An Investigation on the
Borderlines of Ontology, Logic,
and Theory of Literature

With an Appendix on the Functions
of Language in the Theater

GEORGE G. GRABOWICZ

NORTHWESTERN UNIVERSITY PRESS

EVANSTON   1973

The Literary Work of Art is a translation of the third edition of *Das literarische Kunstwerk,* copyright © 1965 by Max Niemeyer Verlag, Tübingen.

To Nuna

Contents

[ix]

Foreword
by David Michael Levin

IF THERE BE a peculiarly modern sensibility, I would incline to describe it as especially vulnerable to the conceits of subjectivism: especially unprepared, in fact, to resist the variously argued skeptical conclusion. In the contemporary world of art, anarchy prevails, confusion spreads. Where are the models of taste, the canons and conventions for the production and judgment of art? Our age, it seems, has no authoritative past to live by: neither perception nor judgment can take comfort in ready-made rules or in some tacit *sensus communis*. It is not only that we find it difficult to say whether, and why, this or that is a superior work of art; it is, or seems to have become, much more difficult to say whether, or why, this or that should be approached as (say) a painting rather than a sculpture (or an instance of theater rather than dance), or indeed, whether, and why, something should be regarded as a work of art at all. The products of the imagination, no longer easily subsumed under the rules of an accepted model, seem thus to propose themselves to us, in many cases, as altogether *problematic*. In the eighteenth century, for example, it was generally possible to recognize at once the genre, the style, and the model of principles informing a given work of art. It was generally possible, in other words, to give the work its authoritative place on the ontological map and thus approach it in the appropriate canonical way. But it has become necessary, in our century, that we approach the works which artists present without any a priori notions, and with an open, but especially acute consciousness, so that we can *discover* what makes them works of art and, in effect, *discover* what principles inform them: an accomplishment which must emerge within the process of constituting them as unique objects peculiarly accommodating to the play and the pleasure of the aesthetic mode of consciousness.

Contemporary works of literature have not, perhaps, so noticeably refused their place in a continuous history of literary conventions. Poetry, certainly, has asserted its vitality in a discontinuous form; but the novel and the theater have maintained, on the whole, a more conventional—and less perplexing—originality. Even so, it is not altogether easy to find and defend the principles of criticism which a profound appreciation of many original literary works now seems to demand. Consequently, it is fitting to raise the question: Is there a hidden unity, a thread of invariant principles, which underlies the apparent diversity of literary works, literary genres, literary styles? Are there, in other words, any invariant, or necessary, principles constitutive of all literary works of art as such and constitutive, correlatively, of every instance of an aesthetic consciousness which has, for its object, the literary work?

What we wish to know is whether or not every entity which is to count as a literary work, however innovative or however experimental it may be, exhibits a certain objective structure, the rules of which we can articulate and indeed decisively ground in the unquestionable sense of our literary experience. Roman Ingarden, addressing himself to these and other, related questions, has answered them in the affirmative. In *Das literarische Kunstwerk,* translated for the first time, here, into English, Roman Ingarden has employed the powerful method of phenomenology in order to penetrate the underlying ontological essence, or mode of being, of the literary work and to make explicit the corresponding side of subjectivity, within whose structures the underlying modes of givenness peculiar to the literary entity are lawfully established.

I have said that Ingarden's chosen method is that of phenomenology. What does this mean? It means, first of all, that his approach to literature will be strictly determined in accordance with the investigatory possibilities peculiar to the phenomenological method. Inside this special framework, however, he wants to pursue a line of reflection that we still may properly call ontological. For his fundamental guiding question is certainly: *What are the essential properties, the invariant logical conditions, of that mode of being which the literary work of art uniquely possesses?* And, for him, the very *sense* of this question will be constituted as an ontological one through his phenomenologically oriented course of reflection. At the same time, of course, Ingarden is interested in making explicit the particular modes of givenness or the particular and altogether unique structures of consciousness in virtue of which this mode of being of the literary work is possible. And the *test* for the truth of his account is always to be our literary experience just as it is lived in unquestionable awareness.

Since Ingarden's project represents a specific demonstration of the phenomenological approach rather than a theoretical exposition or a critique of that approach as such, I would like to offer, here, a brief introduction to the Husserlian method of phenomenology and its primary concepts; and I would like to provide the reader with some perspicuous illustrations, not only of these concepts, but also of such specialized concepts as Ingarden himself had to originate in the process of his thinking.

Let me begin with the concept of a mental act. Suppose I ask: What is the most striking, and most fundamental, logical feature of most, if not all, mental acts (acts of consciousness)? Consider, for example, the following sorts of consciousness: desirings, fearings, broodings, acts of believing, acts of knowing, acts of imagining, and acts of supposing. In each of these instances, it is evident that the act exhibits a certain directedness (or, in other words, a certain intentionality). Thus, one doesn't desire *simpliciter;* one is always desiring some *x* (say a piece of fruit), or one desires *that* a certain *state of affairs* should obtain (say, that nations finally cease their hostilities toward one another). Nor does one just brood; one always has *something,* whether it be real or imaginary, *over which* to brood. And one doesn't just *know;* one knows, rather, *of* some event or state of affairs (say, the parade down Main Street on Thanksgiving Day), or one knows *how* to do something (say, how to repair a broken watch), or one knows *that* something is (or is not, or could be, should be, or will possibly be) the case (say, one knows that inflation will probably persist, despite all measures to halt it). And the same is true, *mutatis mutandis,* for most of the other sorts of consciousness: each one exhibits its own logically distinctive directedness. (Kinaesthetic consciousness, though, seems to be a notable exception to this intentional characterization.)

Now it would seem, since I have spoken of directedness, that for every act there must be a corresponding object (or state of affairs). But it is crucial to note that the *object* of an intentional act need not exist in the spatiotemporal world; it may be the ideal object of a theoretical consciousness (such as one of the natural numbers or a certain mathematical set), or it may be the sort of ideal object which is the product of imagination (a purely fictional object, such as a troll or Maggie Verver), or it may be an absurdity (such as the notions "mauve belief" and "round square"). If the intentional act, with its own logically unique directedness, should fail to refer (i.e., if it should lack a reference) to something which exists in the spatiotemporal world, then we would have to say that there is an intentional act and a *merely intentional* object: the intentional act is not referring, through its intentional object, to any real object in the spatiotemporal world. Thus, when we characterize something (say, Bucephalus) as an intentional object, we are not saying that it does (or could possibly) exist. Rather, we are saying only that there are (or could be) certain acts of consciousness (say, acts of imagining, acts of remembering, and acts of wishing) which would have to be described as acts of imagining *Bucephalus,* acts of remembering (something about) *Bucephalus,* acts of wishing something to be true of *Bucephalus,* and so forth.

What do we find, when we reflect in a phenomenologically disciplined way upon the intentional act as such? We shall note, on the one hand, (1) the real traits of the real (really occurring) mental act (e.g., that it is an act of pure conception taking place at exactly 1:30 on the afternoon of October 10, 1972) and, on the other hand, (2) the purely *logical* features that it possesses simply by virtue of the fact that it serves as the carrier of some logically *distinct* meaning, or sense (e.g., if the mental act is an act of imaginatively presenting Cerberus, then Cerberus, and not any other thing—not Bucephalus, not my shoes, not this manuscript, and not the outcome of the war in Indo-China—is precisely what I mean, precisely what the logical sense, or logical content, of my act uniquely discriminates).

Let us consider more closely, now, this logical dimension of the intentional act. First of all, we can see that it is *in virtue of* a logical content, or sense, that the mental act is *uniquely* directed upon its object. In other words, when we bracket the question of the act's success or failure in existential reference, reflecting solely on the *sense* of a mental act, and then proceed to explicate its particular content, we invariably find something that shows us precisely *which* (or, if you wish, precisely *what*) intentional object it is that the mental act is occupied with. Second, we see that the logical content contains exact information about the *kind* of object intended: whether the object is (meant as) a perceptual object, for example, or whether it is (meant as) an object of volition or perhaps (meant as) an object of conceptual supposition. And, *finally,* we see that the logical content tells us precisely what particular properties (aspects) of the intended object have been discriminated by, and made present to, the mental act in question.

This *third* component of the logical sense of a mental act, which we might describe as telling us in what *way* (in what respect) the object is made present to consciousness, is, of course, extremely important. For, as we have noted, it is of the essence of an object that it is logically distinct from (i.e. logically irreducible to) the mental act that is occupied with it. The mental act is one thing, after all, and the intended object is quite another. (This is not to deny, however, that the intentional object is dependent on the act, both in regard to its being and in regard to its aspects, or properties, which are limited to what the act in question actually intends.)

Every object, whether real or merely intentional, is such that it can become *the self-same* object of an infinite number of mental acts. Consider, for example, the object which is *this* manuscript. It can become the object not only of *my* mental acts, but in fact of an entire community's mental acts. It can become the object of a mental act right this minute and the object of a mental act tomorrow morning or, for that matter, ten years hence. And, too, it can become the *object* not only of perceptual acts (e.g., noticing the printed marks) but also, indeed, of intentionally founded verbal utterances (when, e.g., someone reads this introduction out loud), acts of phantasy (for instance, when I imagine the possibility that this manuscript is utterly destroyed in a fire), acts of desire (if, for example, a reader should someday entertain the wish to read it), acts of recollection, and so forth. Whatever the intentional act happens to be, here, *one and the same* object, namely, *this* manuscript, is in question. So the manuscript, we may say, is *transcendent* with respect to the multiplicity of its logically possible correlative intentional acts.

Furthermore, the transcendence of the object is such that it is never accessible in its absolute totality of properties. The object of an intentional act can be present, for *that* act, only in respect of some particular, uniquely unified *discrimination* of its aspects. Consequently, just as one and the same object can be the theme of a multiplicity of intentional acts (and, often, of different *kinds* and *modalities* of acts), so, too, one and the same object can be present to consciousness in respect of a multiplicity of different aspect (or property) conjunctions. (Each such ideal conjunction, defined as what is lived as present to consciousness at any given time and as that in virtue of which the act is uniquely directed or has a unique sense, is what Husserl called the "noema." A *system* of noemata, then, constitutes the so-called intentional object.) Indeed, one and the same object can be present in terms of the very same conjunction of properties, or aspects, to *different* intentional acts at *different* times. It follows from the essence of objectivity that one and the same object, given as something transcendent and ontologically distinct from all the conscious acts that intend it, cannot possibly reveal itself in the absolute plenitude of *its virtual contexts and relationships*. (This is true of the "object" in question, regardless of whether it be a real object or a merely intentional object.)

The material objects with which we are acquainted in perception readily illustrate this point: this book on my desk, for example, is a salient object (figure) that I have variously differentiated from its enveloping, and constantly changing, background; and, as I move around the desk, different properties, or aspects, of the book come into a partially prefigured prominence. But even such fleeting and ephemeral objects as images will elude one's efforts at totalization. To be sure, the image of the Parthenon that I now behold has precisely the number of columns that I happen to give it; and that image, once gone, can never be said to endow the Parthenon with any *more* (or any fewer) columns. Still, that image *is* certainly available for numerous subsequent intentional acts—acts of purely private reminiscence, acts of public discourse (including, for example, the occasions when others, having been informed of my experience, should choose to discuss it), acts of doubting (perhaps I can't clearly remember just how *many* columns I actually saw and am inclined now to doubt that I could really have seen as many as I seem to *remember* having seen), acts of supposition (I may now entertain the playful supposition, for example, that my image showed not six columns but eight), and so forth.

In brief, then, a *complete* explication of the logical sense of an intentional act must include: (1) a mere mention, phenomenologically empty, of its *what* component (just *which* object it is that the act is occupied with: *this* X or *that* Y), (2) a description of its *how* component (the phenomenological *kind* of object, or *kind* of properties, in question, e.g., perceptual, imaginary, linguistic, etc.), and (3) a description of the *aspect* component (*which* actual properties of the object itself and which potentially immediate properties of its intentionally co-present background, or horizon, are the properties the act has discriminated and occupied itself with).

When, in the course of time, a multiplicity of intentional acts is variously directed upon one and the same real (existing) object, then the different noemata, or meanings, each one of which is carried by just one temporally individuated act, constitute a phenomenologically lived *and* logically interwoven *system* of noemata—the livingly present intentional object itself—in virtue of which the different acts refer to (are directed upon) the real object. On the other hand, when there exists no (real) object (suppose you are reading about Othello's jealousy of Desdemona), then the different intentional acts (those, for example, which occur during the time of your reading *Othello*) are logically describable in terms of a system of noemata which constitutes an intentional, or ideal, object; but this intentional object has no reference beyond itself. And, in this latter sort of case, the intentional object is the temporally unified and unifying transcendent pole of the various subjective intentional acts.

One's consciousness of a work of art is a temporally constituted flow of intentional acts, each one of which is directed, in some manner or other, upon the work in question. The work of art has real being, of course, for it always has a certain *material* stratum (the literary work, for example, consists of a string of word sounds). But the unique object of *aesthetic* consciousness —that is to say, of a consciousness modalized in the appropriate ways as, among other things, a fiction-positing, or imaginative, consciousness "playing" with the aspectival possibilities of organizing the work of art—is finally an *intersubjective* intentional object constituted into an aesthetically satisfying noematic unity on the basis of a constant and faithful intentional reference to some given real object which is the work of art itself.

In view of the fact that the literary work is a narrative form which is experienced as unfolding noematically in time, it is of the utmost importance, if we would understand the essence of the literary work and, of course, the essence of the appropriate aesthetic experience, that we make explicit the phenomenology of literary time-consciousness and that we illuminate, on the corresponding side of the literary work itself, the various possible ways in which its given structures (such as long and short syllables, rhythmic lulls and contractions in syntactic spacing, rising and falling lines of sound, and oblique and metaphorical presentations of meaning) can serve to *modulate* the lived time of an inevitably temporalizing—and always already temporalized—consciousness. And furthermore, it is important that we make explicit the phenomenology of intentional act and noema so that we can fathom how a fictional world comes into being as an aesthetically perfect unity through the narrative unfolding of its manifold and yet simultaneously present aspects. It is, then, about these and many other important topics (topics important for a philosophically complete ontology and, no less so, for a guiding theory of literary criticism) that Roman Ingarden writes, illuminating them to a remarkable degree through an investigation uniquely suited to the disclosure of the essential literary work.

These, I think, are the most fundamental concepts of Husserlian phenomenology. And inasmuch as these are the same concepts in use throughout this book, Ingarden is certainly entitled to consider himself an orthodox Husserlian phenomenologist. (I don't mean to deny, though, that there are some significant points of disagreement between Husserl and Ingarden. But, since Ingarden is explicit and clear enough as to the nature of these differences, I shall let him speak for himself.)

In any case, it is not merely his conceptual framework that is, on the whole, quite orthodox. His methodology, too—his particular way of *approaching* the literary work of art—is likewise rigorously phenomenological. What does his adherence to this methodology entail? Certainly, the principal fact to note is that his approach is faithfully and scrupulously *descriptive*. Ingarden carefully avoids the common temptation to take any evaluative stands: he neither appraises the aesthetic worthiness of the literature he considers nor attempts to judge this literature from a moral, social, historical, or political standpoint. Obviously, his avoidance of such stands *within* the framework of his study in no sense constitutes a repudiation of the possibility of taking some stand outside this framework; nor does it mean that he thinks this to be generally undesirable or pointless. Indeed, it may well be imagined that, in his private life, so to speak, he is himself disposed to make any number of evaluative judgments and to believe that this is sometimes a proper and desirable thing to do. But his investigations of the literary work of art are guided by a very special methodological intention—an intention that he thinks would be fatally compromised were he to allow himself the privilege of normative judgments. If he is to be absolutely faithful to the particular objects of his concern, he must not exclude in advance, because of his own preferences or because of those dominant in his social and cultural milieu, such works of art as belong no *less* to the muses of art on account of their apparent inferiority. Moreover, he is quite willing to recognize that evaluative judgments, and the value qualities residing in the work of art that are claimed as their ground, can likewise be subject to an appropriately geared phenomenological description. Ingarden eschews this sort of position, too; not for the reason that it falls outside the proper purview of his method, but rather for the reason that it would extend unduly the already ambitious scope of his project.

Descriptive phenomenological fidelity to the literary work itself also accounts for Ingarden's avoidance of explanatory schemes. In this case, too, it must be observed that his exclusion of explanations, be they causal or noncausal, does not in any way impugn the possibility or the desirability of such an approach. Freud's psychoanalytic explanations, Jung's reference to the explanatory mechanisms of a phylogenetic symbolism, Tolstoi's historical speculations, and Lucien Goldmann's studies of the origins of literature in the sociopolitical dialectic are certainly *possible* approaches to the literary work of art. And there can be little doubt that each of them has yielded its own treasures of insight. But this concession, if not altogether beside the point, can only provide *further* support for Ingarden's original contention that phenomenological description is able to render its own special insights only by virtue of its adherence to a rigorous and *exclusive* method. Explanatory approaches cannot avoid being speculative: since their aim is to explain something X by reference to some other thing Φ, rather than simply to describe X itself, they are logically committed to a sort of oblique, or mediated, approach to the object, the literary work itself, and they cannot avoid having, therefore, a hypothetical and provisional status. By contrast, the concepts of phenomenological theory are themselves directly drawn from the world of its concern. For the phenomenologist, it can never be a matter of establishing some external connection between, on the one side, a ready-made, autonomous network of concepts and, on the other side, the objects themselves. No, his phenomenologically exacting method will tolerate only those concepts whose fidelity can be assured by an evident origination, and a primitive presence, *within* the renderings of perception.

When Ingarden originates his inquiry with the leading question, *What is the literary work of art?*, what he has in mind, then, is, first, a descriptive analysis of the *mode of being* (the ontological status) peculiar to the literary work as such; second, a descriptive exhibition of the *properties* without which no artificial object could be truly regarded as a *literary* work of art; and third, a description of the *modes of givenness* of the literary work, insofar as these are essential to the possibility of a distinctively *literary* experience. In this sense, therefore, his project is at once a study in ontology and a study of essence. But we must be very clear about the sense in which his investigations are to be called "ontological"; and, of course, we must be no less sure about the purport of this notion of "essence."

In regard to the first term, we must note that Ingarden's assertions about the mode of being in literature, and about the properties which distinguish literary works of art from all other entities in our universe, are constrained by his intention to remain entirely faithful to the ways in which literary works are naturally experienced. Let me put the issue thus: Ingarden's ontological descriptions are required to have their foundation, their justified and compelling sense, in the phenomenologically unquestionable evidence of our universal literary experience. This requirement certainly does not entail a *reduction* of the ontological dimension to the being of transcendental subjectivity (a point on which Ingarden explicitly takes issue with Husserl); for, on the contrary, our literary experience clearly *shows* the ontological transcendence of the literary work. (Ingarden's word for this fact is "heteronomy.") So it means, rather, that his ontological descriptions must be confirmed solely by reference to the genuine evidences of our experience: every ontological statement must be accounted for in terms of its appropriate phenomenological fidelities. The point of such a phenomenological accountability, of course, is that it precludes the usual philosophical temptations to engage in unwarranted metaphysical speculations.

And, in regard to the other key term, the notion of "essence," it should be observed that Ingarden has not at all smuggled in, through the back door, some altogether queer metaphysical entity. After all, his search for the literary essence is likewise constrained by the rigors of the phenomenological method—and in precisely the same way, in fact, as were Husserl's own eidetic investigations. The essence of the literary work is to be sought, simply, in the logically necessary and sufficient conditions that constitute our perfectly ordinary (but also, to be sure, our perfectly clearheaded) recognition of the literary work of art as being the sort of thing that it is: but sought, it should be added, with the intention of showing that, and how, these logical conditions are *phenomenologically grounded* in our literary experience. (It is certainly possible that no such essence, strictly speaking, can be established; but for every philosopher worth his salt, the venture is worth his effort. In regard to the distinctions of literary modes and genres, though—I am thinking, here, of the problems that emerge when we try to differentiate comedy and romance—it is rather doubtful that any tidy essences are to be gathered by an entirely *descriptive* method. On the other hand, of course, we can always provide a phenomenological description of our historical conventions and even our normative delineations.)

Numerous ontological perplexities come to mind once the leading question has been posed. Each one of them challenges us to decide its fate in keeping with our phenomenological sense of our envisaged object, the literary work of art. The challenge is both a logical and a phenomenological one: logical, in that our task is to articulate the logic of the relevant concepts and map their logical interdependencies; and also phenomenological, in that everything we say must be perspicuously exhibited and fully grounded in the relevant structures of our literary experience.

Is the literary work just a physical thing? Henry James's novel *The Golden Bowl*, for example, is an item of so many pages of print; and the copy I own is something I can weigh and touch and see. Moreover, the story itself, as well as my particular copy, can be assigned a specific date of origin, a date of entry into the world; both have a history, just like every other physical thing. So the literary work certainly satisfies at least *some* of the conditions peculiar to physical thinghood. Yet its printed or spoken sentences, in themselves simply physical (as visible marks on the page or as patterns of sound), are also the vehicles of the author's intended meanings. And I can hardly claim to "know" the work if all that I know is its physical properties (its weight, the color of its binding, its date of publication, the number of pages it contains, the style of its print, etc.).

When I consider that the novel is a tissue of meanings, and indeed, something which, as we say, *creates* a fictional world of scenes and characters, I am naturally inclined to assert that the work itself, the thing that grips me and moves me while I read it, the thing that haunts me long after I have put it back on the shelf, cannot possibly be strictly identical with a set of physical properties (however large) and that, really, the work can only be identical with its meanings. In that case, then, the work would be "located," not in this spatiotemporal world, but in the ideal world of pure sense.

Pure sense? Then are we to suppose that the work is nothing but the reader's experience of it? *That* seems to suggest that there are as many distinct works called *The Golden Bowl* as there are different readings. And that *seems* to be, in a sense, quite true but also, in another sense, utterly false. For we surely *want* to say that there is just *one* work called *The Golden Bowl*. Then, too, it seems somewhat odd to hold that Maggie Verver, or the gardens she and the Prince stroll in, are just meanings. There are all sorts of properties that are true of Maggie, and all sorts of things that are said of the gardens, that could never be thought true of the ideal entities we call "meanings." *Is* the novel a tissue of meanings, after all? Or is it identical, rather, with the *world* that James has represented? And what should we say of the characters and scenes that compose this represented world? If we hold that Maggie does not exist (she *is*, of course, a merely fictitious character), then how can we maintain that the novel is "about" Maggie Verver or "about" (say) her movement from the solipsism of innocence to the solipsism of self-damnation? On the other hand, if the novel is *not* about *her*, what *else* could it possibly be about? It certainly is not a novel about the Napoleonic Wars, or about Emma Wodehouse, or about the life of Bertrand Russell!

Suppose we do conclude that, since intentional acts *can* be directed upon nonexistent objects, James's sentences are indeed "about" Maggie Verver. Does it follow that all the sentences are true? Could *some* be true, on this account, while others are false? If that seems impossible, then are they, one and all, *necessarily* true? And just what does our immersion in the Jamesian world amount to? Does our "faith" in James's descriptions, our believing or accepting them, mean that we believe in their *truth*? What could be the logical status of our belief in their truth? We could never be tempted to *act* on our belief, the way we would, or might, if we believed the same things to be true of some real friend of ours.

It is to the settling of all these, and many other, perplexities that Roman Ingarden has devoted his vast and insightful study of the literary work of art. In particular, he discusses the ontological conditions of *truth* in literary works and the correlative mode of consciousness through which truth and its epistemic (or doxic) variants are posited.

In an excitingly fruitful way, his answer to the fundamental ontological question (Is the literary work a physical thing, or is it, instead, something ideal?) *cuts right across* the traditional ontological dualism; and, in so doing, it helps us to understand just how, and why, we are strongly pulled in two apparently *opposite* directions whenever we try to resolve it.

First of all, he distinguishes, in good phenomenological fashion, between the work of art *itself* and the work as an aesthetic object constituted (or, in his own terms, "concretized") through the various intentional acts of reading or performing it. The intentional act–intentional object correlation enables him not only to sharpen *this* ontological distinction (it is an entailment of the fact that the work, as an identity through time, is accessible to a multiplicity of intentional acts) but also to distinguish the multiplicity of aesthetically constituted renderings of the work itself from the subjective *processes* of interpretation (i.e., the acts of reading and performing, as such). This latter distinction is no less essential than the former, inasmuch as we must recognize, among other things, that every literary work allows a *manifold* of interpretations and that each such interpretation has, as it were, a public life of its own. So we see, already, that the propriety of the either/or conditions, implicit in our originally natural ontological questions ("Is the literary work one thing, or is it *many* things?"), should itself be a subject for investigation.

Second, an advantage of the phenomenological approach is that Ingarden can account, not merely for those properties which are "contained" strictly within the *objective* structure of the work itself, but also, indeed, for those properties, generally ascribed to the work, which acquire their ontological origin within the *subjective* conditions of our mode(s) of access. (I have in mind, here, such matters as the way a novel's objective ordering of sentences can create suspense and prepare for a moment of "revelation" and the ways in which an objective ordering of words and sentences will be preadjusted to the temporal conditions of its readings, so that the experience itself will assume a certain aesthetic structure and receive thereby a qualitative texture and rhythm that live and fade with the receding of the moment.) Again, we should note how Ingarden's analysis erodes our faith in the old ontological mapping of things.

Third, Ingarden takes over the notion of a *hylē/morphē* structure—something we first encounter in Husserl's analysis of perception in *Ideas;* and he borrows from Husserl, but for his own original purposes, the astonishingly fruitful notions of *founding acts* (or, correlatively, founding sense) and *founded acts* (or, correlatively, founded sense). It will be recalled that in his *Logical Investigations* Husserl had already applied these notions to the phenomenological description of speech (and other language-using) acts. Together, these notions, suitably modified, enable Ingarden to construe the literary work of art as an onto-logical item that is at one and the same time an absolute aesthetic *unity* and also a logically differentiated *composite.* The literary work of art is a composition, or structural formation, the different "strata" of which, when they are properly adjusted to one another, can constitute a symphonic totality of great power and beauty.[1] What we might call the original "material" of the literary work—its most fundamental, founding stratum—is simply the total syntactically ordered sequence of word sounds. (In Massenet's opera *Werther,* Act III, Werther says: "Oui! Je vois ... . Ici, rien n'a changé ... que les coeurs! Toute chose est encore à la place connue." And then Charlotte echoes his final sentence; she repeats it word for word. But note how her repetition of an

---

1. Aristotle's *Poetics* is, I believe, the ultimate source of inspiration for Ingarden's theory of stratification. If we attempt to transpose the Aristotelian categories and place them within the Ingarden framework, we get a symphony of hierarchic strata, perhaps of the following sort: *melos* (word sounds, syntactically spaced), *lexis* (the syntax, or medium of meanings), *opsis* (the noematic exhibition, the progressively unfolding spectacle, of the world represented), and, finally, *dianoia* (the represented world itself, a noematically constituted unity of *ethos* and *mythos,* and the revelation of character through the narrative construction). These strata are so ordered that the first (*melos*) constitutes the essential founding matter for the founded second (*lexis*), the second for the founded third, and the third for the founded fourth, a final and consummate form, the represented world itself. *Melos,* of course, being a "first matter," can exist, as such, apart; the other strata plainly cannot exist in this mode. Still, it is only in *lexis* that *melos* attains fulfillment and a metamorphosis in its being. Likewise, *opsis,* dependent upon *lexis* and *melos* for the possibility of its being, can attain fulfillment and a metamorphosis in its being only insofar as the world it details, aspect by aspect, is an autonomous presence, rendered through the narrative structure. But the aesthetic object is an indivisible whole, a quite special unity, so that each of the strata—including *melos,* which can exist, as such, apart from the others—must be construed as a function whose particular being modifies and, in turn, is modified by the other strata functions. The possibilities, here, are indeed without limit; such limits, therefore, as we are wont to find simply indicate the limits or conventions of the human imagination. The main text of this introduction will examine some of the possible ways such interanimation of strata, such polyphony and counterpoint, can take place in the process of reading.

identical *sentence* [an identical "matter"] is *not* a repetition of the original animating *meaning:* it is a purely literal sense that animates Werther's words [the "material stratum"], since he is referring to the objects which surround his beloved; whereas *her* sense, dramatically counterbalancing his, somehow makes the words pronounce metaphysical sentence on the impossibility of their love, the inexorable truth of which is fatally revealed by this very placement of familiar objects. Everything still in its proper place: this is the furniture world of the mannered bourgeoisie, whose proprieties and repetitions exchange the shafts of ardor for the bolts of order.)

This stratum of word sounds then serves as the material foundation for such formations of meaning as the reader's intentional acts of reading may constitute, either on the basis of the sensuous qualities of these sounds or on the basis of the cognitive rules of his natural language (or on account of both of these). And it is this stratum, of course, the dimension of pure meaning, which provides the "materials" for the gradual representation of an imaginary "world," a world whose "scenes" and "episodes" are inhabited by fictitious characters. But this stratum, that of the imaginary world itself, in fact rests upon, and is obliquely revealed through, the immediately "lower" stratum of schematic *aspects.* (In *The Wings of the Dove,* for example, the city of Venice is variously presented through the eyes and actions of several different characters and, indeed, by means of a large number of descriptive sentences, each one of which introduces the city in a certain schematic perspective.) Finally, these strata can provide the material foundation for a formally synoptic interpretation of the world so represented (e.g., the "metaphysical" sense that our human condition is an unending tragedy, or the sense that neither war nor peace can alter very much the intractable facts and forms of everyday human life).

Should we say, then, that this entity, the literary work of art, has the ontological status of a simple reality? Or should we say, rather, that a literary work is a merely ideal entity? We certainly feel torn, as I said, between these two ontological polarities. But, if Ingarden be right that the literary work is a stratified formation, that it is something material which the profound complicity of author and reader variously animates for the ends of form and order and fictional representation, then we shall have to say that the being of the literary work truly *cuts across* the old ontological distinction and that it insists on being understood *outside* our very crude binary logic. Yes, when we consider the "materials" of (in) the work—the sequence of words printed on paper—it makes perfect sense to say that literature is a spatiotemporal reality. But when we consider the transformed materials of the work, the work as a tissue of meaning units through which a certain fictional world has been created, it makes equally good sense to shift the literary work into the timeless realm of pure consciousness.

Ingarden's study carefully accounts for our helpless equivocations, our conceptual confusion; in addition, however, it calls out attention to the numerous dangers, well camouflaged, that stand in the way of easy and simple answers. It is at this point that Ingarden's careful and penetrating analysis of the modes of givenness of the literary work proves its immense utility. The work of literature is given, phenomenologically, as something transcendent, but transcendent in a rather complicated way. It is an entity which has, to begin with, a certain physical reality, since it is a syntactic construction of word sounds. But the literary work which is constituted through various acts of consciousness (for example, the time-constituting process of reading) as an aesthetic object is finally a formation of *meanings* on the basis of which a fictional world is imagined and brought into transcendent being. Thus, the aesthetic object, as constituted through the appropriate modalities of consciousness, belongs, from an ontological point of view, in the domain of *ideal* transcendence (the quasi-belief of fiction). Meanings, after all, are ideal, or intensional entities; and the constitution of the literary work as a literary work, which occurs by way of the stratum of meaning units, requires the animating intentional experience of a reader or an audience. It is only in virtue of a reading (or a performance) that the founding physical stratum can be animated and the higher, founded strata brought into the transcendence of ideal being.

In fact, as we shall see, intentional experience serves not only to bring the higher strata into being but also (and simultaneously) to put the different strata into aesthetically commodious points of interaction: for it is only through (say) the reading of the sentences of a novel that, for example, the given word sounds and the sense they convey touch one another in a playful dialectic.

Perhaps it is appropriate, at this point, to say something about the difference between the phenomenological and the structuralist approaches. Structuralism is an important and fruitful method; but its one fatal weakness, so far as I can tell, is that it tends to be a one-sided approach; it concentrates, that is, on the formal structures of the literary work itself, while ignoring the distinctive structures and modalities of the aesthetic consciousness *for which* the work is an intentional object and *through which* the work is constituted as a unique aesthetic object. Structuralism, therefore, tends to miss—or at least, it cannot fully account for—such latent or dispositional properties of the work of art as come into being only through the constitutive intentionalities of an animating and reflective consciousness. Moreover, the one-sided object orientation which characterizes the method of structuralism means that structuralism cannot, as such, *show the ground* of the structures it has discerned in principles of the aesthetic consciousness. For, as Kant understood so well, the possibility of grounding objective structures *presupposes* the possibility of demonstrating how these structures "accommodate" the aesthetic capacity of the human consciousness.

Ingarden's commitment to a *phenomenological* analysis of the literary work is not to be dismissed, then, as an expression of his temperament or private preference. It is, rather, the consequence of a genuinely *philosophical* conviction that certain features of the literary work of art—certain features of it as a *distinctive kind of being* with quite distinctive modes of givenness—and certain features of the *experience* of such objects (certain features, for example, intrinsic to the temporal process of reading a novel) cannot be noticed and rendered explicit *outside* the focus of a phenomenological illumination.

We have seen, thus, that Ingarden's study provides, in the first place, a powerful framework of conceptual and methodological tools which make it possible for reader and critic alike to gain a more aesthetically rewarding, more reflectively illuminated access to the literary work. Second, his study truly *accounts* for aesthetic perceptions and sensibilities, in that it enables one to trace very precisely the phenomenological genesis (Husserl's term would be *Sinnesgenesis:* the logic of the genesis of meaning) of such modalities of consciousness, and, correspondingly, of the aesthetic object formed and constituted thereby, to the given structural properties of the work itself. Considered from this standpoint, then, Ingarden's study of the literary essence directly contributes to the higher-order critical insight we plainly require in order to establish sound principles of confirmation for aesthetic judgment.[2] Finally, too, we should recognize that it is unquestionably the unique merit of Ingarden's phenomenology to reveal, with an exceptional force and articulation, the elements of that wondrous process through which the literary work is constituted as an aesthetic object and renders accordingly, from the gift of its materials, some quite special fictitious instance of a possible world. I mean, simply, that Ingarden's phenomenology assists the reader in his critical, or reflective, reconstruction of the objective details—details of structural texture, of sound, of pace and rhythm, of sculptural phrasing, of conjunctions and incongruities in the aspects of a thing, and so forth—in terms of which the fictional world is brought into being, composed and presented.

I would like now, in the remaining space of this foreword, to provide some examples of the strata differentiations which Ingarden has made. My aim is to show that the several

2. It might still be wondered *why* the very elaborate *theoretical* framework of phenomenology is indispensable for good literary criticism. Does it not seem possible for literary critics to exhibit the literary text as an aesthetic object in accordance with a sensibility that is naturally, or merely intuitively, phenomenological? I can, indeed, think of critics who have done just this, without resort to the forbidding technical terminology of phenomenological theory. Just as Monsieur Jourdain could be speaking prose without knowing it, so, too, there have been literary critics who, without knowing it, somehow approached the literary work in a genuinely phenomenological manner. My reply, briefly rendered in four parts, is this. (1) In science, as we know, it is the ascent to theory which makes possible the articulation, or discovery, of new and unnoticed phenomena. Likewise, the native phenomenological insights of literary criticism will acquire vital power and scope when they are projected *through the map of theory* onto their literary objects. (2) A knowledge of phenomenological theory provides the literary critic who wants to be doing phenomenology with some explicit controls, or guidelines, for his chosen approach. Without such knowledge, the critic's approach will the more easily go astray, confusing phenomenological descriptions of consciousness just as it is lived, for example, with the hypothetical descriptions of consciousness determined through the methods of empirical psychology or psychoanalysis. (3) A knowledge of phenomenological theory enables the naïve phenomenological critic to understand more profoundly what he is doing, much as one's learning the *principles* of mathematics enables one to *understand* what one is doing when one manipulates quantities and equations. (4) Finally, a knowledge of the theoretical framework of phenomenology is necessary, not only for the tasks of phenomenological criticism, but also for the difficult tasks fundamental to a *philosophy* of art. For there are certain questions, certain problems, which are central to the philosophy of art and which a phenomenological approach can handle, but only insofar as the *theoretical framework* of phenomenology (its method, its basic concepts, and its aims) is clearly articulated and itself subject to the constant critique of use.

strata are constituted not only in terms of the founding/founded relationship but also, indeed, in terms of an impressive number of more specific interdependencies. With each example, then, I shall attempt an analysis which both elicits the specific principle (or principles) of the stratum interaction I have chosen to illustrate and clarifies, at the same time, the constitutive acts of consciousness which are the corresponding source of this interaction. Ingarden's analysis tends to be theoretical and rather free-floating. Perhaps my illustrations will make it easier for the reader to grasp the precise concrete sense, the vital issue, of Ingarden's subtle thought; and perhaps, too, they will facilitate the reader's ultimate task of confirming, for himself, the positions of an otherwise abstruse theory.

1. Consider, first, the *sensuous* stratum of the literary text—its most fundamental, founding material resources. Literary texts quite naturally treasure the device of mimesis through word sounds and patterns of sound. (Onomatopoeia is a common mode of such mimesis, but it is by no means the only mode.) Mime's sinister words in Act I of *Siegfried* ("Fühltest du nie / im finst'ren Wald . . .") echo and reverberate like sounds in a steep canyon and all together produce a frightening envelope of sounds which, so to speak, *make true* the sense of his words.[3] In Desdemona's "Willow Song" in Act IV of *Otello* ("Salce, Salce . . ."), the word sounds seem to weep in a mimesis, not only of the willows about which she is singing, but also of the unfathomable sadness which has invaded her. There is a mimesis of Antigone's mood and character in her opening declamation (I refer to the original Greek of Sophocles' play *Antigone*), for the dominant sounds ("t," "k," "kt," "ch") are biting and harsh and bitter. And there is mimesis, too, in the episode from the tenth canto of Dante's *Inferno*, where Farinata degli Uberti cries out, in dark and dolorous tones, "O Tosco che per la città del foco / vivo ten vai così parlando onesto, / piacciati di restare in questo loco. . . ."

---

3. Shakespeare's dramatic verse contains a remarkable number of echoings and mirrorings at the primary level of word sounds. However, this musical quality does not have the *symbolic* function of, say, the Wagnerian leitmotiv, but rather the aim of establishing certain appropriate *moods:* the comic, or ironic, or romantic, for example. These are the qualities that Northrop Frye has called "humours." Thus it is less a question of Shakespeare's adding what we might call special cognitive information to the stratum of meaning than a question of his inducing, through sound, and solely in this stratum, a sort of magical hypnosis through poetic incantations.

What such literary moments show is how it happens that, through the intentional acts of reading, the *different* strata of the literary work are simultaneously constituted into a *unity* within which they can interact and, as it were, comment upon one another. Such interaction *may* be one in which—as it is in all the cases that I have just cited—the strata reinforce or amplify one another. But it is also possible for a certain stratum to conflict with another stratum (irony and ambiguity), or to defeat the effect of some other stratum (as in my Nabokov examples, discussed below), or to call another stratum into question (as in the Robbe-Grillet example, interpreted below). Moreover, because the reading (or performance) of a narrative structure is a linear, sequential process in time, it is possible for one stratum (or perhaps more) to provide certain anticipatory materials—intimations—of the subsequent data introduced in other strata and to develop or explode the data projected from the earlier data of other strata. Obviously, there will be a complicated and subtle modification of consciousness corresponding to each possibility of interaction among certain elements or aspects of the various strata; and the mode of givenness of the literary work itself, as an aesthetic object constituted in a temporal unity, will be altered in correspondingly subtle and complicated ways. In the examples that follow, we will indeed observe some of these things happening.

2. The literary work is constituted as an aesthetic object within the process of a dialectical encounter between the objective structures of the work of art and the subjective structures of an aesthetic (aesthetically modalized) consciousness. More particularly, the literary work is constituted by a consciousness which is situated, and which correspondingly situates the literary work, within the coordinates of (at least) three different fields of temporality. These fields are, first, the conventional orders of our clocks and watches; second, the subjectively lived time vectors of a primordial, temporalizing consciousness; and third, the time orders which compose the unfolding fictional world itself. Thus, for example, it is possible for the timing of the narrative reading, a result of the unique spacing which consciousness of word sounds and syntax has composed, to amplify and heighten, in a dramatic mimesis, the temporalization of the narrated (fictionally represented) world.

Consider the closing section of Chapter III of Thomas Mann's novel, *Buddenbrooks*. Mann has found a way to indicate the passage of time so that his readers will apprehend the interval between the final episode of Chapter III and the opening episode of Chapter IV as a continuity whose untold events we do not at all miss. Chapter III concludes with a vignette: Young Christian, at table, puts back on his plate the peach he has just bitten into, and he vows never again to risk the possibility of swallowing the stone. Here is the paragraph:

> The Consul has been pale with fright, but he recovers and begins to scold. Old Johann bangs his fist on the table and forbids any more of these idiotic practical jokes. But Christian, for a long, long time, eats no more peaches.

There are two key linguistic factors, here, that constitute the quasi-illusion of a temporal continuum. One is Mann's use of the present tense, which usually is employed simply for the sake of pictorial vividness, whereas here it is used in order to constitute the specific illusion of a *forward-flowing* "present" and, especially in the last sentence, to endow the future, as future, with a substantial presence. And the second factor is the phrase "for a long, long time," which in a perfectly literal sense simply states a certain *fact* about Christian but which here, by virtue of its somewhat fairy-tale and hypnotic word repetition, functions primarily in a symbolic manner to represent (or stand in for) the passage of time itself. The repetition of the word "long," moreover, serves to *stretch out* the real time that is involved in one's reading of the passage, thus putting the reader through an experience that truly duplicates, in miniature, the untold but still intended passage of time. The author has very skillfully prepared us, then, for the time of the situation that opens Chapter IV:

> It was not simply weakness of age that made Madame Antoinette Buddenbrooks take to her lofty bed in the bedchamber of the entresol, one cold January day after they had dwelt some six years in Meng Street. . . .

3. Consider some literary devices that modalize our quasi-belief in the "reality" of the world represented. (*a*) In Gogol's *Dead Souls*, the narrator's occasional interventions modalize our consciousness in such a way that what we would otherwise read as "serious" we read, instead, as the comic adventures of a not too credible rogue. The interventions block our "quasi-belief" (as Ingarden calls it) in the characters and events presented in the novel, and this belief, deflected, turns back, dramatically, upon

itself; but there is a further movement of consciousness once the reader reflects that these disruptive interventions are themselves rendered "false" and "suspicious" since they, too, belong to the fiction of a literary text. Thus, a mere sentence, indicating that it comes from the narrating author himself (also a fiction created by the still hiding author?), can so twist and perplex the reader's reading consciousness that it will create a dramatic tension, a movement and play of mind, the structural origin of which is quite independent of the events belonging to the novel's fictional world.[4] (This sort of device is not new, of course. In *Peace*, Aristophanes has the Athenian farmer Trygaeus beseech the stagehands to give him a safe journey as he starts his flight, on the back of a dung beetle, to address the gods on high. And in Plautus' *Casina*, the wife relents and forgives her husband— only, as she says, "to keep an already long play from being still longer.") (*b*) In Mann's novel *Doctor Faustus*, the diary form, though itself explicitly the product of a fictitious character, nevertheless changes the modality of our reading consciousness from a state of resistance and disbelief ("I'm reading a work of fiction; Adrian Leverkühn does not really exist, and his torments and final damnation are impossible forgeries. . . .") into a state of feigned, or quasi-, belief, a state of spiritual consent and participation. We know, of course, that the narrator is himself a character in Mann's fiction; but this character persuades us at once that he is altogether a model of conventional bourgeois sanity, a character who, were he to exist in our real world, would be counted as "one of us," and that, in short, *his* perceptions can be trusted. So we are disposed to accept as "true" (true, that is, within the fictional world, which of course *includes* the narrator) the terrible drama of Leverkühn's soul.[5]

---

4. In "The Man on the Threshold," a story by Borges, just a few words from the narrator suffice not only to suspend the belief modality of the reader's consciousness but also to render altogether problematic the reader's reliance on certain conventions about the time order of the narrated events—and even his reliance on conventions about the time of the narration itself: "The old man did not understand me (*perhaps he did not hear me*), and I had to explain that Glencairn was a judge and that I was looking for him. I felt, on speaking these words, the pointlessness of questioning this old man *for whom the present was hardly more than a dim rumor.*" (My italics.) Thus, the narrator of the story, who himself suffered a deception and, too late, a rude awakening in his encounter with the old man, brings it about that the reader of his story suffers a similar deception and, indeed, that the reader's moment of *anagnōrisis* is simultaneous, in narrative time, with his own.

5. In Max Ophuls' film *La Ronde*, the regular intervention of the director, "playing" himself on screen, arrests the progress of each of the

4. Here is the last paragraph from Jane Austen's *Mansfield Park:*

> On that event they removed to Mansfield, and the parsonage there, which under each of its two former owners, Fanny had never been able to approach but with some painful sensation of restraint or alarm, soon grew as dear to her heart, and as thoroughly perfect in her eyes, as everything else, within the view and patronage of Mansfield Park, had long been.

Let us note, first, the very deliberate, measured *tempo* of this sentence: neither fast nor too slow, but simply exquisitely controlled, this particular tempo conveys, entirely by itself, and thus quite apart from the *meaning* of the chosen words, the sense that, henceforth, Fanny Price's life will be—cannot, indeed, be other than—one of perfect contentment and tranquillity, exactly the life, in fact, to which she had always patiently aspired. And now attend to the mood and tense of the verb phrase that concludes the entire novel. These final words, "had long been," are so positioned that they can convey, simply through their grammatical form, a certain very specific summary condensation of the sense of the novel's development. Since the verb phrase points backward and refuses to invent a future, we know that Fanny's inner life, in the future, will be little different from what it always in fact had been. Her constancy and patience—her own peculiar sort of psychic *passivity,* perfectly mirrored by the mood of the verb itself—will indeed be finally rewarded; the time of testing and striving is decisively behind her, a part of the absolutely *irreversible* past. The tense of the verb, of course, precludes the possibility of a truly *open* future; insofar as there is a "future," it cannot be imagined to allow any events whose existence would necessitate a reinterpretation of the past. Thus, the human universe we are shown, through this tense information, is an inherently stable, well-ordered one, in which virtue must triumph and the past must attain the expected fulfillment. With the time that marks the conclusion of the telling of her story, then, the time of the fictional world is arrested, and there is, as it were, a perfect sphere of time, such that past and future coincide. Sel-

---

futile love affairs and serves just the opposite end: it negates our originally feigned but increasingly less disengaged belief in the reality of the filmed world and mocks our cinematic gullibility, our readiness to surrender to the illusion of human love. A more complex sort of "intervention" in the filmed narrative occurs in Godard's film *La Chinoise,* where the director's aim is to resolve the problem of his cinematic sincerity *within* the structure of a medium peculiarly effective at seducing the spectator with its illusion.

dom has another writer been able to do what Jane Austen did so gracefully, condensing a vision of the human condition and making it vividly present simply by means of a choice of tense.

5. Consider Part III, Chapter Two, of Virginia Woolf's *To the Lighthouse:*

> "What beautiful boots!" she exclaimed. She was ashamed of herself. To praise his boots when he asked her to solace his soul; when he had shown her his bleeding hands, his lacerated heart, and asked her to pity them, then to say, cheerfully, "Ah, but what beautiful boots you wear!" deserved, she knew, and she looked up expecting to get it, in one of his sudden roars of ill-temper, complete annihilation.

This passage illustrates how phrasing and punctuation can create, by themselves, a reading tempo that makes the movement of the reader's *real* consciousness correspond, point for point, to the interior movement of the character's *represented* consciousness. After we read the word "deserved," the syntax suddenly ceases to have a rhythmically cumulative, unifying force: it begins to decompose the reading consciousness that is coming into being; it suddenly brakes the reading momentum and introduces a rhythmic tension, an as yet inexplicable hesitancy, which of course exactly duplicates, in the reality of the reading experience, the tempo of Lily's own (for the reader, fictional) expectancy and the progression of her own (fictional) realization and which reaches its powerful resolution, finally (and only after the teasing indeterminacy of the pronoun in the phrase "expecting to get it"), in the rhythmically abrupt words "complete annihilation." The terror of these final words is at least in part a consequence of the way in which the *objective* syntax not only isolates them from the previous words but indeed so *accommodates* itself to the *subjective* experience of reading, an experience clearly determined by its own immanent temporality, that we are carried toward them in a dramatically modulated movement. By breaking up the forward reading momentum, by pulling the reader into traps of short phrasing (I count at least five: "she knew," "and she looked up," "expecting to get it," "in one of his sudden roars," and "of ill-temper"), and by creating a rhythmic and acoustic break after "ill-temper," the syntax allows the two words, "complete annihilation," to explode with an unexpected, devastating sense.

6. In Alain Robbe-Grillet's short novel *In the Labyrinth,* there is a phenomenologically interesting confusion of the boundaries that give conventional dimensions to the world being repre-

sented. At a certain point in the time of the story, it seems that the narrator's gaze halts and lingers over an old print ("The Defeat of Reichenfels") that is hanging on the wall. And he meticulously describes the scene that is represented in the picture. (A representation within a representation: the world of the picture is a world both inside and outside the dimensions of the primary world of the novel itself.) [6] "The picture, in its varnished wood frame, represents a tavern scene. It is a nineteenth-century etching, or a good reproduction of one. A large number of people fill the room, a crowd of drinkers sitting or standing, and, on the far left, the bartender standing on a slightly raised platform behind his bar." But this description continues for several pages, and in such a way that the details of the picture (the scene and the characters represented therein) somehow spill over and magically blend themselves into the represented world itself—into the world which *contains* the picture, but contains it as something belonging, as it were, to an ontologically discrete, ontologically discontinuous, dimension.

Where does the world of the *picture* end and the *story world* (likewise a represented, merely fictional world) that contains this picture begin? To the degree that this ontological boundary is punctured or destroyed, to the degree that the two strata—the story representation and the representation within the representation—are finally conflated, the reader's habitual skill in orienting himself as regards the distinction between a literary quasi-reality and a total literary fiction, or illusion, will be decisively frustrated and, in truth, irreparably shattered. The circularity of the narrative development, moreover, which allows the author to insert the details of the picture at points where we hardly expect them and where, in fact, we are easily tricked into taking them as details of the fictional world itself, naturally contributes to the various disorientations of the reader.[7]

6. Cf. Edmund Husserl's evocation of the Dresden Gallery in *Ideas I*, chap. 10, § 100.

7. The Chinese-box narrative structure of Jean Renoir's *Le Carrosse d'or*—a film of a play within the theater of *commedia dell'arte*—induces a similar disorientation and suggests, of course, that we, who think ourselves to be the absolute spectators, may in fact be the actors on some spectator's stage. In Richard Strauss's opera *Ariadne auf Naxos*, the plight of Ariadne exists as a serious opera constructed by, and thus within, an *opera buffa*. And, as in the case of Renoir's film, the serious opera of Ariadne, which exists at first in a rather precarious isolation and independence from the rival space of the comedy that produced it, eventually compels the audience to invest it with a quasi-reality much greater than the quasi-reality of the comedians. The closing of the curtains, how-

7. In his novel *Ada*, Nabokov has skillfully manipulated the writer's options in syntactic and semantic construction in order to explore the possibilities for flattening out and compressing, or else grossly inflating, the conventional *dimensions* of representation in the literary work. Here are three examples.

i) After we have read and thus moved through a lengthy narrative that has situated us in the fictional *present* of the characters, Ada and Van Veen, Nabokov suddenly jolts us out of our fictional complacency, our willing submission to the "as if" conventions of fiction-reading, so that we find ourselves obliged to contemplate the vertiginous possibility that what we have just read is nothing but a purely fictitious invention, or perhaps at least a partly invented and partly hypothetical autobiographical reconstruction, accomplished by the fictional characters themselves. Thus, we read:

> Van could not help feeling esthetically moved by the velvet background he was always able to distinguish as a comforting, omnipresent summer sky through the black foliage of the family tree. In later years he had never been able to reread Proust (as he had never been able to enjoy again the perfumed gum of Turkish paste) without a roll-wave of surfeit and a rasp of gravelly heartburn; yet his favorite purple passage remained the one concerning the name "Guermantes," with whose hue his adjacent ultramarine merged in the prism of his mind, pleasantly teasing Van's artistic vanity.

But then we read: "Hue or who? Awkward. Reword! (marginal note in Ada Veen's late hand)."—So what happened may be *redescribed*. ("Reword!" says Ada.) Can we be so sure that such redescribing does not alter the reality? Is there a reality in fiction which is independent of the depiction? Does this not seem in fact quite unlikely, when the "reality" in question is, or may be, nothing more substantial than a construction out of words, a tapestry of literary (sentential) descriptions? (A case where lan-

---

ever, and the bows of all the singers together, remind us that *both* worlds are but aesthetically posited illusions. (How willing we are to accept the artist's magic!) From a phenomenological standpoint, the fundamental point of these cases is that the relationship between the play (opera) and the play (opera) within the play (opera) is *not at all* an objective, or external, one (like the relationship of proximity between, say, my desk and my chair) but is, rather, a dramatically internal relationship of reciprocal modification. So any account of these Chinese-box structures must ultimately refer back to aesthetic consciousness—to their source in the corresponding modalizations of aesthetic quasi-belief and the modulations of aesthetic "distance."

guage is accusing itself: in the very act of founding a world, it destroys it.)

ii) Or consider the odd meshing of two ontologically distinct fictional depths in the following passage from *Ada:*

> Presently the vegetation assumed a more southern aspect as the lane skirted Ardis Park. At the next turning, the romantic mansion appeared on the gentle eminence of old novels. It was a splendid country house, three stories high, built of pale brick and purplish stone.

When we first read the word "turning," we naturally take it in its comfortable literal sense, and we submit to the fictional pretense. But we are forced at once to *return* to that word, forced to cancel our quasi-believing modality of consciousness, when we move on to read the word "romantic" (which shelters the French word for "novel") and then reach the end of the sentence, where the author explicitly mentions *old novels.* And is the splendid house "really" three stories high, or is this just another fabrication of the story—a *tall* tale? Is there even a world in this fiction? Perhaps we are simply reading a string of words, incestuously double-crossing, "purplish": words become ambiguous in such a way that, the more the two meanings pull apart, the more they stick, and now the one, now the other sense violates and betrays its partner. (A literary possibility: seeing the world as word.)

iii) Consider this sentence from *Ada:*

> She looked back before unlocking her (always locked) door.

Nabokov, here, is toying with the conventions of stratification that regulate the reader's consciousness of the distinction between fiction and life. He is, thus, inviting the reader to experience in an explicit, or heightened, manner the modalization of his own consciousness: to experience, so to speak, a playful shift of gears as the various aspects of sense and representation come into being. Why is it the case that the words "always locked" have been, in actual fact, locked within the printer's materially real parenthetical marks? So, in a very, very odd way, the properties of the material stratum, which are normally altogether *outside* the represented world, have here trespassed, broken into this world; and conversely, a state of affairs that seemed to belong entirely to the world of fiction has been fitted with an intentional reference that pierces the necessary wall separating fiction and life and puts it in contact with the materially real world of its readership.

8. The opening of Max Beerbohm's novel *Zuleika Dobson* demonstrates exceptionally well, I think, how a certain linear narrative progression can compose a very specific imaginary world, unfolding the schematic aspects of this world in a reading time which is arched in suspense. The suspense derives from the fact that, on the objective side (the side of the work itself), the order and "space" of the syntax and the order and "space" of the semantic units so perfectly accommodate the possibilities, phenomenologically inherent in the temporalized process of reading, for hastening and retarding the *pace* of consciousness, concentrating and expanding the *focus* of consciousness, and advancing and deflecting the natural *direction* of consciousness. Notice how very quickly, and how with such remarkably descriptive economy, the author not only positions us within the present space and time of his imaginary world but indeed inserts us, at once, into the vital *drama* of this world, with its receding margins of a wonderful past, its tense, carefully paced expansion in the direction of an event still distant but itself seeming to be coming toward us, as if the approaching train were carrying with it the limits of this world, the periphery, at least, of time itself.

That old bell, presage of a train, had just sounded through Oxford station; and the undergraduates who were waiting there, gay figures in tweed or flannel, moved to the margin of the platform and gazed idly up the line. Young and careless, in the glow of the afternoon sunshine, they struck a sharp note of incongruity with the worn boards they stood on, with the fading signals and grey eternal walls of that antique station, which, familiar to them and insignificant, does yet whisper to the tourist the last enchantments of the Middle Age.

At the door of the first-class waiting room, aloof and venerable, stood the Warden of Judas. An ebon pillar of tradition seemed he, in his garb of old-fashioned cleric. Aloft, between the wide brim of his silk hat and the white extent of his shirt-front, appeared those eyes which hawks, that nose which eagles, had often envied. He supported his years on an ebon stick. He alone was worthy of the background.

Came a whistle from the distance. The breast of the engine was descried, and a long train curving after it, under a flight of smoke. It grew and grew. Louder and louder, its noise foreran it. It became a furious, enormous monster, and, with an instinct for safety, all men receded from the platform's margin. (Yet came there with it, unknown to them, a danger far more terrible than itself.) Into the station it came blustering, with cloud and clangour. Ere it had yet stopped, the door of one carriage flew open, and from it, in a white travelling-dress, in a toque a-twinkle with fine diamonds, a lithe and radiant creature slipped nimbly down to the platform.

A cynosure indeed! A hundred eyes were fixed on her, and half as many hearts lost to her. The Warden of Judas himself had mounted on his nose a pair of black-rimmed glasses. Him espying, the nymph darted in his direction. The throng made way for her. She was at his side.

"Grandpapa!" she cried, and kissed the old man on either cheek. (Not a youth there but would have bartered fifty years of his future for that salute.)

"My dear Zuleika," he said, "welcome to Oxford."

Notice how the author gives you at once the advance signal of the approaching train; how he inserts you in a projective time-consciousness that maps a somewhat determinate region of space *outside* the immediate situation described. But notice that he does this only to keep you *waiting* thereafter: just as the undergraduates must *wait* for Zuleika's presence, though she *is* a known quantity, so must *we* wait to learn for whom or for what these eager young men are waiting. And these two worlds of waiting—ours, the real world of reading, and the undergraduates', which is the imaginary world of the novel—have been deftly, and most dramatically, paralleled. Notice, too, how the very phrasing of the third paragraph imposes on your reading a sensuously iconic equivalent of the rhythm of the coming train. Another correspondence between the world of art and the world of life: a correspondence that is, by the way, no less an instance of life imitating art than it is an instance of art miming life, and one that is, in any event, a dramatically devised confusion of the real and the illusory. And notice, finally, how frequently the author is trying to modify your orientation to (and within) the fictional world—transporting you forward or backward in time, and then abruptly framing you in the fictional present; putting you, first, in a fictional "here" and then replacing you, without apparent loss of continuity, at some distant and discontinuous "there"; showing you the *one* world now in this, and now in that, discrepant aspect. (It certainly would be quite impossible, despite the painterly details that suggest the contrary, to paint, or sketch, this zany Beerbohmian world. The painterly descriptions do yield an abundance of information; but precisely this fact is the source of the medium's resistance. In truth, not even the magic of cinematic art could duplicate the temporal darts and spatial bends and folds or the shades and depths of atmosphere which Beerbohm's prose style invents *ex nihilo* simply by means of an unusual or quaint phrasing, some word that modalizes consciousness, or a clever ironic fitting, maybe, of noematic aspects).

The literary work, after all, is the medium, the point of reference, of a very *special* production; the imaginary worlds it makes possible simply by *making* them could exist, as such, in no other medium of art. And it is the peculiar texture of such worlds—their coordinate aspects, the way they are put together —that the phenomenological approach can discover with a delicacy no other approach could ever match. Such, then, is the use of phenomenology for literary criticism. Perhaps the illustrations I have discussed assist you in seeing that this is so.[8]

Evanston, Illinois
November, 1972

8. I wish, here, to thank Hubert Dreyfus and Dale Harris, to whom I am especially indebted for some valuable criticisms and suggestions. Mr. Daryl Hine read a late draft of this essay, and to him, likewise, I am grateful.

Translator's Introduction

Das literarische Kunstwerk is a central achievement in Roman Ingarden's philosophical corpus and an essential work in phenomenological aesthetics and modern literary theory. Yet its English translation appears more than forty years after the first German publication (in 1931), after two additional German editions (1960 and 1965) and an amended Polish translation (1960), and after numerous discussions and polemics. This belatedness is a function of several factors: the decline in fashion of phenomenology (which Ingarden, for one, welcomed as being for the good of phenomenology),[1] the "inaccessibility" of much of Ingarden's Polish writings (despite the fact that an important part has been translated into German),[2] and, perhaps not least of all, the reputation for difficulty and "abstruseness" which his critics afforded him—more frequently than not in lieu of adequate analysis. This reputation does have a core of validity, however. *The Literary Work of Art* is indeed a rigorous and detailed study, defined variously by the author as dealing with "the borderlines of ontology, logic, and theory of literature" or with "ontology, theory of language, and philosophy of literature."[3] Its

---

1. Roman Ingarden, *Spór o istnienia świata* (The Controversy over the Existence of the World), 2 vols. (Warsaw, 1960), I, 60n; German translation: *Der Streit um die Existenz der Welt*, 3 vols. (Tübingen, 1964–65).

2. See *Untersuchungen zur Ontologie der Kunst* (Tübingen, 1962), with regard to his aesthetic analyses; English translation, *Investigations into the Ontology of Art*, forthcoming from Northwestern University Press. See also the Bibliography in this volume.

3. *Das literarische Kunstwerk: Eine Untersuchung aus dem Grenzgebiet der Ontologie, Logik und Literaturwissenschaft* (Halle [Salle], 1931); *O dziele literackim: Badania z pogranicza ontologii, teorii języka i*

unprecedented interdisciplinary concentration on a subject that is intentionally narrowly conceived—not literature, but the literary work as such, its structure and mode of existence—evoked a predictable reaction, one that revealed a certain uneasiness at the range of "points of view" [4] but, far more, an inability to grasp the argument in its entirety. In literary criticism in particular it manifested itself, with few exceptions, as a tendency to simplify and fragment Ingarden's basic theses. This fact, and what Ingarden saw as an openly hostile critical attitude in Poland,[5] caused him to write a number of "addenda"—amplifications, emendations, even self-criticism—the most notable of which was *O poznawaniu dzieła literackiego* (1937) (subsequently published in a substantially revised and enlarged form as *Vom Erkennen des literarischen Kunstwerks,* now translated as *The Cognition of the Literary Work of Art*).[6] These amplifications are an integral part, as Ingarden frequently notes, of the total philosophical argument initiated in *The Literary Work of Art.* Ingarden's phenomenological aesthetic is thus based on an *oeuvre* that has this work as its core and touchstone but is itself contained within the philosopher's broader concerns of formal ontology, cognitive theory, and logic. An adequate approach to *The Literary Work of Art,* therefore, requires a delineation of both the synchronic and diachronic, the philosophical and historical, dimensions of its context.

The Place of *The Literary Work of Art* in Ingarden's Philosophical Writings and Its Goals

IN THE PENULTIMATE and crucial chapter of this book, "The Ontic Position of a Literary Work" (Chap. 14), where,

---

filozofii literatury (trans. from German by Maria Turowicz) (Warsaw, 1960).

4. Cf. Charles Lalo: "Toutefois, le mélange de points de vue si différents reste quelque peu disparate. Logique, ontologie et science de la littérature ne se fusionnent pas aisément dans leur état actuel" (*Revue philosophique,* LVI, no. 9/10 (1931), 308.

5. See *O dziele literackim,* p. 15. Henryk Markiewicz questions the correctness of this opinion; see his "Twórczość Romana Ingardena a rozwój badań literackich" (Roman Ingarden's Work and the Development of Literary Investigations), *Fenomenologia Romana Ingardena* (Warsaw, 1972), p. 310.

6. Roman Ingarden, *O poznawaniu dzieła literackiego* (Lvov, 1937), and *Vom Erkennen des literarischen Kunstwerks* (Tübingen, 1968); Eng-

having anatomized the structure of the literary work in its utmost ramifications, he reconstructs the whole work in its intersubjective identity and ontically heteronomous mode of existence, Ingarden makes a most revealing statement. "The dangers [of psychologism] we are contending with here," he says, "have an incomparably greater significance than the relatively unimportant matter of literary theory." [7] This, of course, is already stated in the first Preface to *The Literary Work of Art*, but a full explanation is presented only in a later book, which is Ingarden's culminating philosophical work—*Spór o istnienie świata* (The Controversy over the Existence of the World). [8] In the Preface to this work, Ingarden briefly summarizes the course of his philosophical development, beginning with his decision in 1918 not to accept Husserl's idealism, a decision expressed in a long letter to his teacher setting forth his argument against the transcendental idealism of *Ideen zu einer reinen Phänomenologie*. [9] At first it appeared that to prove the existence of the real world independently of pure consciousness one need only correct and extend Husserl's analyses of sensory perception. [10] Around 1921 came the realization that subjectively oriented analyses do not suffice, that what is needed is a clarification of the form and the mode of existence of the world in question, in particular "the meaning of the various 'categories,' that is, the basic structures of real objects which Kant considered to be subjective forms of the intellect, without, however, analyzing them more closely." [11] Ingarden's subsequent efforts were directed at analyses of basic

---

lish translation (of the expanded German edition), *The Cognition of the Literary Work of Art*, by Ruth Ann Crowley and Kenneth R. Olson (Evanston, Ill.: Northwestern University Press, 1973).

7. § 65, p. 359.

8. With regard to the treatment of problems subsumed by *The Literary Work of Art*, see *Spór*, §§ 9–15, dealing with the concept and the modes of existence, and §§ 44–46, which deal with the purely intentional object.

9. The original of this letter, the precise date of which is not given, was destroyed, along with the rest of Husserl's correspondence, in an Allied bombing raid on Antwerp. Ingarden published it in Polish translation on the basis of an incomplete rough draft (the last section is missing) in his *Z badań nad filozofią współczesną* (Investigations in Contemporary Philosophy) (Warsaw, 1963), pp. 453–72. It constitutes one of the six parts of a treatise on the philosophy of Edmund Husserl contained in this volume. The section on Husserl's transcendental idealism was first published as "Über den transzendentalen Idealismus bei E. Husserl" in *Husserl et la pensée moderne: Actes du deuxième Colloque International de Phénoménologie, Krefeld, 1–3 Novembre 1956* (The Hague, 1959), pp. 190–204.

10. *Spór*, p. 5.

11. *Ibid.*, p. 6.

categorical structures, among them the question of the identity of individual objects. These, too, subsumed the more fundamental issues of ontology and cognitive theory which were broached in his habilitational dissertation, *Pytania esencyalne* (written in 1923; published in German as *Essentiale Fragen* in 1925); a separate path toward resolving the controversy between realism and idealism was indicated by the habilitational lecture "Stanowisko teorii poznania w systemie nauk filozoficznych" (The Place of Cognitive Theory in the System of Philosophical Sciences) in 1925 and was charted by the 1929 treatise *Bemerkungen zum Problem Idealismus-Realismus*.[12] And here we come to a key moment in Ingarden's development, and now a no longer unexpected formulation:

> My book *The Literary Work of Art*, which appears to be devoted to the philosophical bases of a theory of the literary work, was in effect a first step in the direction of contrasting real and intentional objects (in the Husserlian sense) on the basis of the fundamental difference in their formal structure.[13]

Not only is *The Literary Work of Art* seen as a prelude to the work on idealism-realism; its sequel, *The Cognition of the Literary Work of Art*, and other studies in aesthetics are indeed viewed as diversions or interruptions in the movement toward that goal.[14]

This historical reconstruction and the apparent subordination of the aesthetic studies should be seen more as an expression of a philosophical hierarchy than as an intrinsic valuation. These studies, the product of a thirty-year period that begins with the first publication of *Das literarische Kunstwerk*, are a most significant part of Ingarden's total philosophical contribution, and, for his importance as a phenomenologist, they are the major part. They, and especially *The Literary Work of Art*, which ushers in and becomes the model for Ingarden's aesthetic, have for him a prime value and, as later discussions and polemics

12. *Ibid.*

13. *Ibid.* "The ultimate goal" as Ingarden says at another point, "was a demonstration of the *real* existence of the world given to us in experience, and thus *The Literary Work of Art* was a first step toward a *realistic* resolution of 'the controversy over the existence of the world'" (*Studia,* I, 33n).

14. "Unfortunately, the necessity of writing my book *The Cognition of the Literary Work of Art* and then various studies in aesthetics prevented me, until the beginning of the war, from continuing the work I had begun. However, I was continually thinking of it" (*Spór,* p. 7).

show, are jealously defended. The essential function, therefore, of this autobiobibliographic account is to remind us of the philosophical center of gravity, the "center of orientation," of his investigations.

The Literary Work of Art is set in another framework, however—one which reveals another side of Ingarden's intellectual activity and thus qualifies the strongly deterministic conception expressed above. It results from Ingarden's actual involvement with literary theory as lecturer in German at Lvov University in the years 1940–41 [15] and the projected major work, *Poetyka* (Poetics), which, while never published *in toto*, was prepared and delivered in these lectures. [16]

In the first, published, part of this work, *O poetyce* (On Poetics) [17] Ingarden distinguishes, according to the aspect under which a work is studied and the mode of its cognition, the following subdivisions in all knowledge about literature: (*a*) philosophy of literature, (*b*) theory of literature, (*c*) literary scholarship, and (*d*) literary criticism. Poetics is the theory of artistic literature. [18] Philosophy of literature—which is easily distinguished from literary scholarship (which characteristically deals with facts and individual works or with general properties that are still based on actually existing works) and from literary criticism (which deals with the aesthetic concretization of literary works, with artistic and aesthetic valuation of a given work)—can be essentially narrowed to the ontology of the literary work. (Its other constituent disciplines, e.g., the theory of the cognition of the literary work, literary aesthetics, the philosophy of literary creativity, the sociology of literature, deal only partially with lit-

15. See p. 178, below. It is interesting to find that the literary work was already a factor in Ingarden's thinking in 1918. He mentions that his questioning of idealism (specifically, the idealistic conception of word meanings) was crystallized in the process of writing a dialogue, which remained unpublished, on the literary work; see p. 97n, below.

16. Cf. *Studia*, I, 325–34.

17. See *ibid.*, I, 271–325. Parts 2–4 of *Poetyka* (dealing with the basis of a general theory of a work of art, an analysis of the strata of a literary work, and the temporal and compositional extension of the work) are organized on the basis of *The Literary Work of Art*, though they elaborate on it significantly. The remaining parts, on form and content, on value, style, literature and man, etc., draw on the various "continuations" of this work; see *ibid.*, Vol. II.

18. *Ibid.*, I, 273. Ingarden notes that this designation and role for poetics was a direct outgrowth of the 1940 lectures on literary theory. At the time of his writing of *O poznawaniu dzieła literackiego* (1936) he did not distinguish it as a separate discipline of literary study and was inclined to believe that it was subsumed by a "typology" of literature.

erary works themselves. These disciplines are not the philosophical correlate of literary scholarship.) [19] Such an ontology, which deals not with discrete literary works but with "the content of the general ideas" of a literary work, is the goal of *The Literary Work of Art*. Its intention is

> to ask what in particular belongs to this idea, how a given individual object must be constructed, and what its general properties must be for it to be something which is a literary work or a literary work of art. Furthermore, it must ask what are the necessary and what the merely possible connections between elements and moments of *any* literary work or of *any* work of a certain kind; what are the possible types and variants of literary works that are allowed by the general basic structure of the work.[20]

As such an ontology, *The Literary Work of Art* is a realization of the *a priori* [21] "pure poetics" proposed by Friedrich Schlegel and, more recently, by Zygmunt Łempicki.[22] As the outline of Ingarden's projected *Poetics* shows,[23] the arguments of *The Literary Work of Art* serve as the basis for a broadly conceived "theory of artistic literature." The "basically modest" goal of providing an "essential anatomy" [24] thus contains, by its very nature, a program for defining the basic tools and concepts for wide-ranging analyses.

These analyses, aimed beyond the realm of literary theory, were meant as a foundation for a general phenomenological aesthetics. Significantly, the first planned edition of *Das literarische Kunstwerk* contained as its last section three treatises on other art forms—"The Structure of a Painting," "The Architectural Work," and "The Musical Work"; but because of technical diffi-

19. *Studia*, I, 275.
20. *Ibid.*, p. 276.
21. Ingarden is aware of the immediate connotation of this term and is thus at pains to contrast this meaning of *a priori* with the Kantian. "I am convinced," he continues, "that Kant's entire theory of categories and *a priori* forms of intuition is not only false but caught in a circle of contradictions. Here we are only dealing with a *different* form of direct cognition, different from sensory or internal experience—a form of cognition, however, which performs, with regard to deduced assertions, a role analogous to that which experience performs for assertions attained with the aid of incomplete induction" (*ibid.*, I, 276n).
22. *Ibid.*, I, 288–89. See also Zygmunt Łempicki's "W sprawie uzasadnienia poetyki czystej" (Concerning the Justification of a Pure Poetics) in his *Studia z teorii literatury* (Studies in the Theory of Literature) (Warsaw, 1966), pp. 121–36.
23. *Studia*, I, 325–34.
24. See p. 7, below.

culties and the likelihood of unmanageable proportions, these were not included. Later they were considerably expanded and published; [25] but the delay cost Ingarden the priority of his conclusions (specifically *vis-à-vis* Nicolai Hartmann's *Das Problem des geistigen Seins* [1932]), and it impeded demonstration of the full implications of his theory. In a retrospective paper "On Phenomenological Aesthetics," [26] while again stressing his methodological direction, Ingarden explicitly notes the wider dimension of *The Literary Work of Art*:

> When, in 1927, I began writing my first book in this field, it was clear to me that one cannot conduct investigations in aesthetics in an empirico-generalizing manner but must conduct an eidetic analysis of the general idea of a literary work (or work of art in general). The then current contraposition of the two directions of investigation—on the one hand, general analyses of the work of art and, on the other, separate analyses of the aesthetic experience, either as the creative experience of the author or as the receptive experience of the reader or observer, also seemed false to me.[27]

This traditional dichotomy of "subjective" and "objective" focus in aesthetic analyses was resolved by contrasting the work, the purely intentional object, as a schematic formation, with its concretizations.

Ingarden admits that, as seen by the very absence of the word in the subtitle, aesthetics as an analysis of the experiences of perception and valuation was secondary to the purely "objectivist" approach and to the primary issue of idealism-realism.[28] The writing of *The Literary Work of Art*, however, made the problem of the experiencing of the work a central concern, and this experiencing was subsequently analyzed in considerable detail.

The Historical Context: Precursors and "Models" for *The Literary Work of Art*

INGARDEN IS SCRUPULOUS to point out what continuity or specific parallels exist between his conceptions and those of

25. See *Studia*, Vol. II, and *Untersuchungen zur Ontologie der Kunst*.
26. Delivered at the Institute of Aesthetics at the University of Amsterdam on March 17, 1969; Polish redaction in *Studia*, III, 18–41.
27. *Ibid.*, III, 23.
28. *Ibid.*

his predecessors; however, he has little recourse to existing models, because his task is rather to draw distinctions and to indicate deficiencies in previous approaches. This applies equally to Husserl, who is by far the major formative influence. Indeed, a large portion of the Preface to the First Edition treats the relation of Ingarden's work to Husserl, in particular to the almost simultaneously published *Formal and Transcendental Logic* (1930). While expressing his still to be elaborated objection to Husserl's transcendental idealism, Ingarden outlines the main points of correspondence: (1) the idea of a subjective sentence-forming operation and the distinction between a pure proposition and a judgment, (2) the distinction between material and formal content of the nominal word meaning and the opposition of the full meaning of an isolated word and the syntactic elements which its meaning assumes in a sentence, and (3) the analysis of the constitution of a purely intentional objectivity in a manifold of connected sentences. As a final element, Ingarden mentions (4) various problems and assertions only indicated in passing by Husserl but developed at length in his own analysis—particularly, the mode of existence of objectivities represented in a literary work.[29] The point of departure, and an indicator of Ingarden's independent philosophical course, is in fact the "painful question" posed by Husserl of how ideal objects or identities can assume spatiotemporal existence in the cultural—and therefore real—world.[30] But while Ingarden concludes that the literary work, an intentional [31] ontically heteronomous object, belongs neither to the realm of idealities nor to the real world, the ideal concepts which (while under Husserl's influence at the time of writing) [32] he posits as one of the ontic foundations of the literary work and a source of its intersubjectivity (§§ 66 and 67) will themselves become a difficult and painful question (see p. lix, below).

In the area of specific formulations, Ingarden discusses in a long footnote in § 8 (pp. 31–32) two major precursors of his stratum concept—Juliusz Kleiner and Waldemar Conrad. Their theories, however, serve only as general analogues: Kleiner's model is burdened by strong psychologistic tendencies—the work itself is not divorced from the "psychic resonance" it evokes in

29. See p. lxxv, below.
30. See *ibid.*
31. Ingarden is working here, as he freely admits, in the tradition of Husserl, Pfänder, Brentano, and Twardowski.
32. Cf. *O dziele literackim*, p. 443.

the reader—while Conrad's provides but few "sides" of the literary work and, moreover, is unduly influenced by Husserl's *Logical Investigations* in its treatment of the "aesthetic object" as an ideal object.[33]

In a sense, the footnotes to Parts I and II function as a critical "side text," in which, while acknowledging specific borrowings (e.g., the idea of "orientational space" from Husserl) [34] and indicating further ramifications, Ingarden continually comments and not infrequently polemicizes on basic concepts: e.g., with H. Conrad-Martius on ontic autonomy and heteronomy in particular application to poetic fictions,[35] with other phenomenologists (Husserl, Pfänder) on states of affairs,[36] and so on.

The question of precursors is elaborated in the treatise "Z dziejow teorii dzieła literackiego" (Moments in the History of the Theory of the Literary Work), in which Ingarden maintains "that the many-layered conception of the structure of the literary work of art—though never previously developed—may still refer back to certain embryonic theories which appear in the two most outstanding treatises in the history of European poetics, namely, Aristotle's *Poetics* and Lessing's *Laokoon*." [37] Ingarden argues that Lessing's theoretical insights into the structure of the literary work, though to some extent inevitably dated, are more valid than various late-nineteenth-century conceptions. His achievements rest primarily on his search for a *general* structure of the literary work as such, free from psychologistic identification with psychic facts in the mind of author or reader, and his analysis of the relationship between the work of art and the perceiver, an analysis that attempts to determine the specific values that produce an aesthetic experience. Second, Lessing analyzes works of art under the twofold aspect of structural and aesthetically valuable elements. Despite normative tendencies, he seeks a theoretical conception of the structure of the work and distinguishes between works of literary art (poetry) and other written works (i.e., histories) and examines this difference in terms of the higher categories of beauty and ugliness rather than truth or falsity. Finally, he effects an "examination of concrete artistic

33. See also "On Phenomenological Aesthetics," *Studia*, III, 20.
34. See p. 223*n*, below.
35. See pp. 122*n*, 124*n*, below.
36. See p. 129*n*, below.
37. "Uwagi na marginesie *Poetyki* Arystotelesa" and "Lessinga *Laokoon*," *Studia*, I, 337–91; English translation of the former by Helen R. Michejda, "A Marginal Commentary on Aristotle's *Poetics*," *Journal of Aesthetics and Art Criticism*, XX, nos. 2 and 3 (1961–62), 163–73, 273–85.

facts and not generalized thoughts on art, that is, an examination not in terms of *chaotic empiricism* but through a selection of facts that pertain to the problems of art theory and to their possible solutions." [38] When reinterpreted in terms of the four strata established by Ingarden, Lessing distinguishes—though without theoretical grounding—(a) a stratum of represented objects, (b) a stratum of aspects (which, of course, are not conceptualized, the analogue being "*materielles Bild*" or "*poetisches Bild*") and (c) a stratum of word sounds. Meaning units, which for Ingarden form the basic constituent stratum, are ignored in their structural and aesthetic role and are seen merely as the means for representing objects. [39]

Ingarden's discussion of Aristotle's *Poetics* is considerably longer and more empathetic. One of its significant features is that, in prefacing his commentary, Ingarden takes the opportunity to contrast and compare four contemporary theories of the literary work (the first originating in Russia, the latter three in Poland, but all closely influenced by, and influencing, general theoretical developments): (1) the Formalist (which will be discussed at greater length below); (2) the Objectivist (in which the work is a complex of "representations" i.e., represented objects, and language is not an essential part of the work; proposed by E. Kucharski); (3) the conception of the work as a separate sphere of reality (containing four "spheres": [a] the linguistic material, [b] the organization of ideas, [c] the content or the represented objects as such, and [d] the creative power of the author; proposed by Juliusz Kleiner); and (4) Ingarden's own conception of the two-dimensional and stratified work. The basic questions raised by this comparison are both structural and ontological: (1) How many strata does a work have? (2) Is the literary work many-phased and thus similar to musical works and to films? (3) What is the "material" (qualitative) nature of the work, and what is its mode of existence? Is it something psychic, as the German psychologists of the end of the nineteenth century, as well as such theorists as Kleiner and Kucharski, have claimed? Is it something physical, as the "physicalists" among the Vienna neopositivists have claimed? Is it an ideal entity, as W. Conrad maintains (basing himself on Husserl's *Logical Investigations*)? Or, finally, is it, as Ingarden argues, indeed a separate "sphere of reality" which, more specifically, exists as a

38. *Studia*, I, 381 (italics added).
39. *Ibid.*, p. 391.

purely intentional object with a particular threefold ontic foundation? [40] The final question synthesizes the two categories, as it asks (4) whether—and if so, how—a literary work of art—a poetic work—differs essentially from other written works—scientific, political, propagandistic, etc. This question subsumes the following major issues: (*a*) What is the basic character of declarative sentences in a literary work of art? (*b*) What are the functions of the literary work of art with respect to the reader and the author? Is it meant to please or instruct, edify morally, raise class or national consciousness? (*c*) What is the relationship of the poetic work and, specifically, the world represented in it to "reality"? (*d*) What is the relationship of the literary work to its author? This last involves questions of "confession" and "sincerity" as well as the "expressiveness" of the author's personality, etc.[41] These are all issues that are treated at length in Ingarden's writings: the structure and ontology of the work in *The Literary Work of Art*, the other questions, as indicated by their titles, in such works as *The Cognition of the Literary Work of Art*, "The Various Meanings of the 'Truthfulness' of a Work of Art," "On So-called Truth in Literature," "The Aesthetic Experience," etc.[42]

Given these introductory formulations, it is not surprising that Ingarden's discussion of Aristotle's *Poetics* is conducted *sub specie* of the problems posed and that the moments of correspondence are viewed as a historical substantiation of Ingarden's positions. This implicit determinism, however, in no way detracts from the accuracy of Ingarden's observations. In brief, the salient precursive features of Aristotle's *Poetics*, as Ingarden sees them, are his focus on the literary work of art as such, which enables him to first formulate a general theory of the work and only then turn to its artistic function and its effect on the perceiver; his recognition, despite his lack of any clear notion of a stratified structure or of the resultant polyphony of the literary work, of such important structural features as the "longitudinal," sequential dimension of the work (prologue, parodos, choral passages, episodes, exodos) and the distinction of such proto-stratum concepts as *mythos, ethos,* and *dianoia* (all of which correspond to the work's "represented objects"), *lexis* (being both the sound and meaning of what is said), and, occurring only in

40. *Ibid.*, pp. 337–40. For a discussion of the ontic foundation, see below.
41. *Ibid.*, pp. 340–41.
42. Cf. *ibid.*, Vols. I, II, and III.

tragedy and not the epic, *opseōs kosmos* (which is not expressly limited to visual aspects and which can be taken to correspond to the whole stratum of aspects).[43] Ingarden places particular emphasis on Aristotle's distinction between the poet and the historian (i.e., on what he defines as the quasi-judgmental nature of poetic statement) and, quite understandably, on Aristotle's concept of mimesis, which, Ingarden argues, is not conceived as naturalistic imitation of extra-artistic reality but as "greater effectiveness," as a "relationship between parts of the represented world itself." "It seems likely, therefore," he continues, "that Aristotle had nothing other in mind than what in my book *The Literary Work of Art* [§ 52] I called the 'objective consistency' within the framework of the world represented in the work."[44]

The Argument of *The Literary Work of Art*

THE CENTRAL METHODOLOGICAL PREMISE of Ingarden's analysis draws as much on Aristotle as on Husserl: his task, like that of the natural scientist, is to focus on what is to be described, not on what has been said about it. Because there has been greater concern for erudition or psychology than for eidetic analysis, the literary work as such is still a mystery; an adequate literary theory, which would analyze the structure, the essential nature, and the interrelation of the parts of a work, its mode of existence and its relation to author and reader, has not been produced—nor has the problem even been correctly stated. As a first step in that direction, Ingarden demonstrates, after a provisional selection of examples which encompass works (of all genres) generally accepted as literature, as well as works generally considered worthless (§ 2), that the dichotomy of real and ideal for all objects is untenable and that, if this either/or were to be maintained, the very existence of literary works would have to be questioned (§ 3). At the same time, two complementary and, as Ingarden maintains, equally fallacious theories must be recognized and rejected. They are physicalism, a form of neopositivism, and psychologism. The former embodies the idea that the literary work is nothing more than a manifold of graphic signs (or sounds, if the work is read or presented aloud); the latter (either as a concomitant of neopositivism or independ-

43. Cf. *ibid.*, I, 344–51.
44. *Ibid.*, p. 372.

ently, as in the prevalent late-nineteenth and early-twentieth-century literary theories) holds that the literary work is identical with the psychic experiences of author or reader (§§ 4–7). The argument against these initial errors leads to Ingarden's first and very basic ontological conclusion:

> I. The literary work is neither a physical nor a psychic nor a psychophysical entity but a "purely intentional object" which has the source of its existence in the author's creative acts but at the same time has a certain physical ontic foundation. Thanks, above all, to its meaning stratum, it is an intersubjective intentional object.[45]

This, in turn, leads to the following major premise, which stems from the very approach that an analysis of the literary work demands, i.e., an approach that tries to establish the *essence* [46] of the literary work of art and must thus steer a course between an aesthetic stance (which by necessity focuses on individual artistic objects) [47] and the purely intellectual one (which would miss precisely what is essential for the work of art):

> II. Literary works have a basic structure which is "common" to all of them; "they are not individualities which cannot be conceived as examples of a certain determinate class. This is an assumption without which no theory of art or

45. *Ibid.*, p. 9. See *The Cognition of the Literary Work of Art,* § 4, for Ingarden's résumé of the major conclusions of *The Literary Work of Art.* With regard to the "existence" of intentional objects, as opposed to real objects, see *Spór o istnienia świata,* Chap. 4.

46. The concept of essence is clearly fundamental to Ingarden's theories. His apologia on the subject, in a note to *O poetyce,* is worth quoting in full: "Among positivistically and, in particular, neopositivistically oriented researchers there is a tendency to ridicule that direction of research which attempts to discover the essence of an object or its essential features. The reason for this is that by 'the essence of an object' the positivists, *presumptively,* understand something that is totally *unknowable* in general and for man in particular. Positivists are *de facto* negativists; as regards the theory of cognition and the theory of science, they are skeptics. In this, moreover, they do not attempt either to clarify or make precise the concepts they oppose. One of these unclarified concepts that is only caricatured by them is that of the essence of an object. It is indeed a difficult and polysemic concept. At another point I have tried to show that, after distinguishing many historically tangled meanings, one can draw out an understanding of what is essential in an object that keeps it fully within the bounds that are accessible to our cognition" (*Studia,* I, 283).

47. Cf. Ingarden's reply to René Wellek in his Preface to the Third German Edition (below, p. lxxxi).

aesthetics is possible."[48] Furthermore, this general structure, though now no longer containing fully determinate aesthetic qualities and having instead only loci which in given instances are filled out by specific kinds of values, is still a determinate structure pertaining to, and only to, works of art.[49]

Given these two premises, Ingarden proceeds to describe the literary work. It is, as noted above, a two-dimensional formation, with one dimension consisting of (at least) four "cross-sectional" strata and the other, the "longitudinal" one, consisting of the sequence of phases in the work.[50] The basic assertions, dealing with the stratified structure and temporal extension of the literary work, the quasi-judgmental nature of its sentences, its "spots of indeterminacy," and the all-important distinction between the literary work itself and its concretizations are summarized in § 4 of *The Cognition of the Literary Work of Art.*

As a purely intentional formation, "transcendent to all conscious experiences, those of the author as well as those of the reader,"[51] the literary work has a threefold ontic basis: (a) the creative conscious acts, that is, the subjective intentional operations, (b) the real fixed, concrete material, the "letters" of the

48. See *Formy obcowania z dziełem literackim* (Forms of Communing with the Literary Work) in Roman Ingarden, *Szkice z filozofii literatury* (Essays in the Philosophy of Literature) (Lodz, 1947), p. 186. Here, and in his definition of poetics (see § 2 of *O poetyce* in *Studia*, I, 281–90), Ingarden rejects the thinking of Bergson and Croce, who argue that since poetics deals with objects that are individual, unique, and discrete, poetics as a general theory is impossible.

49. *Szkice z filozofii literatury*, p. 186.

50. This second dimension, though explicitly discussed in *The Literary Work of Art*, was frequently ignored in paraphrases of, or comments on, Ingarden's work; of the few that there are in English, see, for example, René Wellek and Austin Warren, *Theory of Literature* (New York, 1949); Krystyna Pomorska, *Russian Formalist Theory and Its Poetic Ambiance* (The Hague, 1968), p. 21; Ewa M. Thompson, *Russian Formalism and Anglo-American New Criticism* (The Hague, 1971), pp. 111–14. Ingarden attempted to prevent precisely these misinterpretations in an essay that was originally written as an introductory section to his projected *Poetyka*, "Dwuwymiarowa budowa dzieła sztuki literackiej" (The Two-Dimensional Structure of the Literary Work of Art) (published in *Szkice z filozofii literatury*, I, 15–32); in subsequent summations of the structure of the work, he always began with this basic feature. The first formulation of the concept of two-dimensionality was, as Ingarden sees it, in Herder's *Kritische Wälder*, in his polemic with Lessing (*Szkice*, p. 17). N.B.: the terms "dimension" and "structure" are not metaphors from geometry or architecture. Rather, this usage, as in geometry or architecture, is a specific application of a much broader concept (*Szkice*, p. 16).

51. Cf. *The Cognition of the Literary Work of Art*, § 4, p. 12.

text (or sounds of a recording or recitation), *and* (*c*) ideal concepts, essences, and ideas (§§ 66–67). In light of his later commitment to realism, the notion of ideal concepts becomes a major problem for Ingarden, and, in the Preface to the Polish edition, he warns that he now questions their existence. Yet he finds no other basis for the objective identity of the meaning of a sentence which could replace ideal concepts without itself evoking serious doubts.[52] It is for this reason that, at the end of § 66, Ingarden suggests that they be accepted as a hypothesis, but one that is indispensable for overcoming "the danger of subjectivizing the literary work or reducing that work to a manifold of concretizations."

Ingarden's major conclusions are distilled and synthesized in the brief final chapter (Chap. 15, § 68), which deals with the literary work of art as an aesthetic object. It is the polyphonic harmony of aesthetic value qualities—arising from the content and the interrelation of the various strata—that makes the literary work a work of art. In itself, that is, apart from its concretizations, the literary work is a schematic formation existing in a characteristic state of potentiality; its aesthetically valuable and metaphysical qualities are not fully developed but are merely "held in readiness." "Only when the literary work of art attains *adequate* expression in a concretization is there—in an ideal case—*a full establishment, an intuitive exhibition, of all of these qualities.* . . . It follows, therefore, that the literary work of art constitutes an *aesthetic* object *only when it is expressed in a concretization.*"[53] This crucial distinction validates, on the one hand, the initial methodological decision to provide an analysis of the general structure of a literary work, and, on the other, it establishes a continuum, a philosophically rigorous transition to other basic aspects of aesthetic and literary theory: problems of cognition, aesthetic perception, value, and valuation. The charge, variously raised, that "there is no structure outside norms and values"[54] or that Ingarden does not reconcile the schematic structure of the work with the work *qua* aesthetic object is thus anticipated and answered in *The Literary Work of Art* itself.

Along with the major theoretical conclusions, highlighted by Ingarden himself, there are also a number of arguments which serve as valuable insights into particular aspects of aesthetics

52. See the Preface to *O dziele literackim*, p. 14, and § 66, below.
53. See p. 372, below.
54. René Wellek and Austin Warren, *Theory of Literature*, p. 156; also see, below, the Preface to the Third German Edition.

and literary theory. They draw their primary value from the integrated theoretical context in which they appear. This is true, for example, of the concept of ambiguity (or "plurisignation"), the essential feature of poetic language for Russian Formalism (and its continuation in Prague Structuralism) as well as for Anglo-American New Criticism.[55] But while the critics of these contemporary schools spoke in metaphor ("The aim of poetry is to make perceptible the texture of the word in all its aspects"),[56] Ingarden attempts to locate the irreducible source of ambiguity. This resides less basically in the indeterminacy that characterizes the time and space of the represented world than in the nature of the purely intentional correlate and, ultimately, in the difference between intentional and ontically autonomous objectivities. For Ingarden, too, ambiguity, or, specifically, the "opalescent" purely intentional sentence correlate, is essential for the literary work (see § 22, p. 144), but here its role is placed in a holistic perspective.

A centrally important theoretical issue that Ingarden touches on is that of distance. In keeping with the "objective" focus of his study, he does not examine it as either psychic or aesthetic distance, that is, along the line of analysis initiated by Edward Bullough and later expressed in the aesthetic theories of T. S. Eliot (his idea of "pure contemplation") and Ortega y Gasset (his purposefully radical doctrine of the "dehumanization of art"),[57] but rather as a structural feature of quasi-judgments and the quasi-reality of the represented world. (In phenomenological theory, a close analogue of "distancing" is the epochē.) [58] For Ingarden, as for the above critics, the test case and most inter-

---

55. Cf. Victor Erlich, *Russian Formalism,* 3d ed. (The Hague, 1969), p. 185. A massive, though highly psychologistic, study of ambiguity is William Empson's *Seven Types of Ambiguity* (London, 1930).

The term "plurisignation" ("plurisignate") was introduced by Philip Wheelwright as being more positive in its suggestion of richness of meaning than "ambiguity"; see his "Semantics of Poetry," *Kenyon Review,* II (1940), 263–83 and *The Burning Fountain* (Bloomington, Ind., 1954), p. 61.

56. Boris Ejxenbaum, *Lermontov* (Leningrad, 1924), p. 35, cited in Victor Erlich, *Russian Formalism,* p. 185.

57. See Edward Bullough, "Psychical Distance as a Factor in Art and an Aesthetic Principle," *British Journal of Psychology,* V, no. 2 (1912), 87–118; T. S. Eliot, *The Sacred Wood* (London, 1920); and José Ortega y Gasset, *The Dehumanization of Art* (Princeton, 1948). For all three the concept is strongly psychologized and, for Bullough and Ortega, sociologized as well.

58. Edmund Husserl, *The Paris Lectures,* translated, with an Introduction, by Peter Koestenbaum (The Hague, 1964), p. xx.

esting proving ground is drama,[59] but he also sees distancing as manifested by various cues in the literary work: not only quotation marks, signaling narrative shift, but also subtitles (e.g., "historical novel," "a drama," etc.) [60] or the very titles themselves. They correspond to the physical cues in other arts, e.g., a frame, a stage. In each case they provide a carrier for distance as an aesthetic principle—a conscious, intersubjective bracketing of experience.

Particularly provocative are Ingarden's reflections on the borderline cases of the literary work: theater, film, even pantomime. The perspicacity of his view of the basic (shared and unshared) structures of the various arts is attested by the attention that the problems he posed (for example, the transposition from one art into another: the filmed novel, the heroic epic in comic strip) now command in general semiotic theory. In the area of literary theory, one of the more interesting of his analyses of borderline cases is presented in a later paper on the theoretical problems posed by nonsense verse.[61] The tools and concepts of this analysis are drawn entirely from *The Literary Work of Art.*

Yet this book at no time aspires to a critical praxis. In its unequivocal definition of the structure and the mode of existence of the literary work, however, it necessarily provides a corrective for various stated or implicit critical assumptions. In its discussion of, for example, literary type, or of the "idea" or "truth" or "reality" of a literary work, it consistently reasserts the unique nature of the literary work and rejects all determinist and extrinsic matrices.

The Influence and Extension of *The Literary Work of Art*

THE IMPACT of Ingarden's work and the response to it was long confined largely to Poland and Germany. In his native country it was noticed, and its basic theses were accepted, by the prominent critics and theorists of literature, such as Juliusz Kleiner, Zygmunt Łempicki, and Manfred Kridl, but it was not

59. Se the Appendix, "The Functions of Language in the Theater," and p. 294n, below.
60. See *O dziele literackim*, p. 19n.
61. See "Graniczny wypadek dzieła literackiego" (A Borderline Case of the Literary Work), *Szkice z filozofii literatury*, I, 87–94; also included in *Studia*, III, 177–83.

extended in further studies; the only serious attempt at a critique (in Ingarden's estimation) came from Wacław Borowy.[62] Before the war, Ingarden's theories were utilized and discussed by such philosophers and critics as L. Blaustein, M. Des Loges, M. Giergielewicz, and, subsequently, attempts at extending his ideas were made by S. Skwarczynska (in her program of a phenomenological theory of literature), K. Wyka, and a number of younger investigators.[63] The major influence was in Germany, where the first recourse to Ingarden's insights was by Nicolai Hartmann, who, in his *Das Problem des geistigen Seins* (1932), applied the stratum concept of the literary work to other art forms without, as Ingarden observes, acknowledging the source.[64] As Ingarden sees it, his theories were subsequently applied to analyses of specific works by Lucie Elbracht-Hülseweh (*Jacob Bidermanns "Belisarius,"* 1935) and Franz Stanzel (*Die typischen Erzählungssituationen im Roman*, 1955); and his basic ideas, though without any overt dependence, were elaborated by Emil Staiger in his *Grundbegriffe der Poetik* (1946).[65] Wolfgang Kayser (*Das sprachliche Kunstwerk*, 1948), on the other hand, speaks of the influence of Ingarden and Günther Müller ("Über die Seinsweise von Dichtung," 1939) (whose work also draws on Ingarden—though Ingarden himself is not persuaded of its coherence).[66] Mikel Dufrenne's *Phénoménologie de l'expérience esthétique* (1953) is another work which relies heavily on Ingarden's conception of the general structure and the particular properties of the literary work; but, Ingarden, while fully approving the immediate phenomenological contact with the work that is achieved in Dufrenne's analyses in the first volume, is disappointed with the analysis of aesthetic experience, with its reliance on Kant's *Kritik der Urteilskraft*, that is presented in the second volume.[67]

A crucial but problematic continuation of Ingarden's theories is contained in René Wellek's and Austin Warren's *Theory*

62. *O dziele literackim*, p. 15. See Wacław Borowy, "Szkoła krytyków" (A School of Critics), *Przegląd Współczesny*, XVI, no. 2 (1937), 35–41.
63. See Henryk Markiewicz, "Roman Ingarden a rozwój badań literackich," pp. 311–12.
64. See, for example, *Studia*, I, v, or *O dziele literackim*, p. 17.
65. See *O dziele literackim*, p. 16, and Henryk Markiewicz, "Roman Ingarden," p. 311.
66. *O dziele literackim*, p. 18. Cf. Wolfgang Kayser, *Das sprachliche Kunstwerk* (Bern, 1948), and Günther Müller, "Über die Seinsweise von Dichtung," *Deutsche Vierteljahrschrift für Literaturwissenschaft und Geistesgeschichte*, XVII, no. 2 (1939), 137–52.
67. See *O dziele literackim*, p. 17.

of Literature, the central chapter of which, "The Mode of Existence of a Literary Work of Art," was written by René Wellek.[68] The importance of this work is indisputable, both for Anglo-American literary criticism [69] and, given its many translations, for literary theory and literary studies in general. Given the relative paucity of early critical reaction to Ingarden, it undoubtedly was instrumental in extending the range and maintaining the currency of his ideas. Yet Ingarden's reaction to it was more than ambivalent. He questions both the degree of acknowledgment of theoretical influences (which are particularly evident in Wellek's treatment of the ontological status of the work—its ontically heteronomous nature—as well as in his rejection of psychologism and physicalism) and their loose modification.[70] The major methodological and conceptual charge that Wellek raises against Ingarden and against phenomenologists in general, i.e., that they ignore or underrate the aesthetic dimension, that, in brief, "there is no structure outside norms and values," had been submitted ten years earlier by R. Odebrecht in *Ästhetik der Gegenwart* [71] and was answered by Ingarden in the second edition (see pp. 8–9, below) and in the Preface to the Third Edition. Additional proof of Ingarden's clear awareness of the importance of the problem of value and valuation is furnished by the papers included in Volume III of his *Studia z estetyki* in the sections on "Aesthetic Experience" and "The Work of Art and Its Value." [72] Like the original "appendices" to *The Literary Work of Art*, they are an integral continuation of its argument.

In addition to the polemics with Wellek and with Käte

---

68. It is based on Wellek's earlier essay "The Mode of Existence of a Literary Work of Art," *Sewanee Review*, VII (1942), 735–54.

69. Victor Hamm's suggestion, however, that Ingarden's conception of the literary work actually "animates," through the intermediacy of Wellek and Warren's *Theory of Literature*, such critics as Cleanth Brooks, Richard Blackmur, Northrop Frye, and Elizabeth Sewell seems to be quite tenuous. See his summary translation and paraphrase "The Ontology of the Literary Work of Art: Roman Ingarden's *Das literarische Kunstwerk*," *The Critical Matrix* (Washington, D.C.: Georgetown University, 1961), p. 171.

70. See, below, the Preface to the Third German Edition and, especially, "Werte, Normen und Strukturen nach René Wellek," *Deutsche Vierteljahrschrift für Literaturwissenschaft und Geistesgeschichte*, XL (1966), 43–55.

71. Rudolf Odebrecht, *Ästhetik der Gegenwart* (Berlin, 1932), pp. 23–24. The first to express doubts on this matter was P. Leon in his review of *Das literarische Kunstwerk* in *Mind*, XLI, no. 161 (1932), 97–105.

72. Cf. *Studia*, Vol. III.

Hamburger, which are included in this book (see § 25a, below), there have been a number of others, and these, along with the above-mentioned addenda, have significantly sharpened Ingarden's original ideas.[73] Since most of them are in Polish and are thus not readily accessible, this facet of Ingarden's work has been unduly eclipsed. Two of the more important dialogues, those with Manfred Kridl, the foremost Polish Formalist, and Henryk Markiewicz, a leading Marxist (and to some extent Formalist) literary historian and theorist, are included in Volume III of Ingarden's *Studia z estetyki*.

Perhaps the most instructive confrontation—instructive for an understanding of both Ingarden's theory and literary theory in general—is the one between *The Literary Work of Art* (and its elaborations) and the doctrines of Russian and, to a lesser extent, Polish Formalism. It is a relationship that has been noticed, though never really examined, in several recent studies on Russian Formalism.[74] The differences between them have perhaps been blunted by what they have in common: their shared Husserlian influence (which, to be sure, was rather more derivative and indirect for the Formalists), their resultant anti-psychologism, their conscious and determined focus on the literary work itself, to the exclusion of such extrinsic factors as biography, history, sociology, etc., their common major premise that a work of literature is, above all, a fiction and in this is essentially different from nonliterary works (this being the pretheoretical distinction of *Dichtung und Wahrheit* that motivates the decision to study the poet's works, not his biography), and, finally, their consequent concern with the "structure" (however broadly it may be formulated by some) of literary works.

To Ingarden, however, what is significant in the relationship are the differences; in terms of his theory, the putative points of contact merely conceal far-reaching disagreements. The reason is that, basically, the parallels we have listed can be reduced

73. See the Bibliography in this volume and the "Discussions" in *Studia*, Vol. III. In the field of logical criticism one should also note Jerzy Pelc's critique, "O istnieniu i strukturze dzieła literackiego" (Concerning the Existence and the Structure of the Literary Work), *Studia Filozoficzne*, No. 3(6) (1958), written from a position of Kotarbinski's reism, and its rebuttal by Danuta Gierulanka and Andrzej Półtawski, *Studia Filozoficzne*, No. 5(8) (1958).

74. Erlich, *Russian Formalism*, Pomorska, *Russian Formalist Theory and Its Poetic Ambiance*, and Thompson, *Russian Formalism and Anglo-American New Criticism*.

to the two central questions that are the axis of his work: the ontology and the peculiar structure of a literary work. Ingarden dismisses the idea of the literary work's fictionality as a dated insight, as old as Aristotle or Lessing, and one that begs the very analysis his work attempts to provide. Yet for the Formalists there is virtually no investigation of the literary work's ontology beyond this assertion.

The issue thus hinges on the diverging conceptions of the structure of a literary work or, to invoke a basic Formalist concept, its "literariness." Ingarden summarizes the Formalist conception as follows: "It conceives the literary work as a linguistic formation (a highly organized linguistic expression) containing a phonetic and semantic side. It does not, however, elucidate in any detail what these two sides are. It attempts to reduce and to narrow specific analysis of literary works to stylistic studies." [75] And, at another point: "It is said that it [the literary work] is artistically organized language. According to this view, the literary work contains *nothing other* than certain 'expressions' provided with meaning, that is, phonetic sounds, words, expressions, sentences, and complexes of sentences that mean something." [76] This, then, is the essential difference: Formalist theory (specifically, of the "Opojaz" group) does not admit the existence of the two nonlinguistic strata of the literary work (the stratum of represented objects and that of schematized aspects). For them the literary work is solely a verbal *product*, and an adequate theory of the literary work is thus a theory of poetic language. [77] For Ingarden, who is determined to present a theory of the literary work that provides for its entire complexity, such a definition is unacceptable. His answer again reminds us of the philosophical context of his theory. "In these [Formalist and linguistic] conceptions of the literary work even 'represented objects,'" he charges, "are to be removed and replaced by 'higher meaning units'":

75. *Studia*, I, 337.
76. *Ibid.*, p. 294.
77. As Pomorska puts it, "there is no such category as a '[re]presented world' in their theory. Their concept of a literary work is entirely oriented toward its *connotative character,* and therefore there is no need for the fictitious world ('para-universe') which has to do with the problem of denotation" (*Russian Formalist Theory,* p. 21; see also pp. 21–23). See also Erlich, *Russian Formalism,* pp. 171–91: "[in view of] the Formalist tenet that literature is essentially a linguistic or semiotic phenomenon—an 'unfolding of the verbal material' . . . the poet's job was defined as manipulation of language rather than as representation of reality" (p. 190).

Everything so as not to admit the appearance in the work of something different from language. None of us wants to accept such [represented] objects as certain intentional entities, since it is thought that this opens the road to idealism. Meanwhile, the precise reason why I concerned myself with these purely intentional, unreal objects was to find a way to oppose Husserl's transcendental idealism. I understand that one can take the position that one should not accept the existence of anything other than material things or psychic facts. In that case, however, I request that those who hold this view cease dealing with literary works or any other linguistic formation; for among neither material things nor psychic facts is there anything that would be a work or linguistic formation of this sort.[78]

Such a positivist, self-avowedly "scientific" rejection merely impoverishes man's cultural heritage. There is yet another, eminently phenomenological, argument for the existence of these strata, however: the intuitive immediacy of experience. Ingarden develops this argument with specific reference to the sound stratum and to the charge, raised by Markiewicz, that he (Ingarden) unjustifiably includes other nonphonic features in his phonetic stratum; but the general and more important application of his argument is to the stratum concept as such, to the question of how the strata are delineated:

Professor Markiewicz considers that one should, so to speak, prepare at the outset a definition of a given stratum, e.g., say that certain sounds are the phonetic stratum and only then determine what belongs to this stratum or what should be excluded from it. This is a most unphenomenological way of putting the matter. One should begin with the very object of investigation; one should attain its immediate experience manifesting itself in the phenomena and only then fit one's concepts—among other things, the concept of a "stratum" of a literary work—to the data that have been obtained. Otherwise, what we shall attain will be a certain construct, one that is frequently removed from reality, and not a faithful reproduction in the linguistic or conceptual material of what is given to us in experience and with which we concretely commune, both cognitively and emotionally. In particular, anyone who in reading my book attempts to find a verification of it by referring to immediate experience, which is achieved by contact with appropriately selected examples, will, I believe, agree that the concepts of the individual strata of a literary work are not

78. *Studia*, III, 421–22.

only unequivocal but are in accordance with the facts, that is, with what appears *in concreto* in the individual strata in the works themselves, regardless of previously constructed concepts of this or another sort—which is what I myself have personally attempted to avoid.[79]

Clearly, the brunt of Ingarden's attack on the Formalists is directed at their fundamental—the linguistic, theoretical—underpinning, as it is formulated, for example, in B. Tomasevskij's *Teorija literatury (Poètika)* (Theory of Literature [Poetics]), which Ingarden specifically mentions,[80] or the various programmatic works of Roman Jakobson. Thus, the longest and most polemical part of the chapter "Nauki pomocznice poetyki" (The Auxiliary Sciences of Poetics) in his *O poetyce* (On Poetics),[81] one that is continually related to the argument of *The Literary Work of Art,* is devoted to an analysis of the relationship of linguistics to poetics and to a sharp rebuttal of the claim that poetics is merely a part or subdivision of linguistics.[82] Ingarden does not deny common ground for these disciplines but sees them essentially as intersecting, not congruent or concentric, phenomena. On the one hand, this is because the literary work of art is composed of parts—complexes of sentences, chapters, and, as we have already seen, represented objects and their vicissitudes—which themselves are not elements of language. The largest unit that linguistics, as syntactics, deals with is the sentence. It does not come to grips, therefore, with the compositional principle of the literary work, a principle which stems from the artistic will of the creator and is not of a linguistic nature.[83] The major distinction between them, however, is that poetics, as opposed to linguistics, treats literary works of art in terms of artistic categories, which they share with other works of art and which can be perceived and clarified through a general

79. *Ibid.,* p. 423.
80. *Ibid.,* I, 294.
81. *Ibid.,* pp. 294–313.
82. Set forth most aggressively by Roman Jakobson; see his "Concluding Statement: Linguistics and Poetics" in *Style in Language,* ed. Thomas A. Sebeok (Cambridge, Mass., 1966), pp. 350–77. Curiously, though Jakobson proceeds to discuss the arguments against this claim, he does so without reference to Ingarden, who first formulated them. A rebuttal to Jakobson, from a position of Ingarden's *The Literary Work of Art,* is presented by René Wellek; see *Style in Language,* pp. 410–11. See also Ingarden's lead paper, "Poëtik und Sprachwissenschaft," in *Poetics, Poetyka, Poètika* (Warsaw, 1960), pp. 3–9.
83. See *Studia,* I, 309.

theory of art. In the praxis of stylistic analysis this delimitation of *Forschungsgebiete* is even more critical.[84]

Ingarden also challenges the Formalist (and what was subsequently the Prague Structuralist) rejection of the concepts of "form" and "content" in the literary work.[85] He does so not to reinstate an old and, as he observes, a totally vague dichotomy but rather to analyze, again on the basis of *The Literary Work of Art*, all the possible meanings and usages of this relationship—with particular reference to the examination and evaluation of specific works. In the course of this discussion, such issues of central concern for the Formalists as composition, fable and plot, action and character, motivation, etc. are placed in the context of the work's total structure and mode of existence. This is done without recourse to the Formalists' technical but structurally and philosophically unintegrated concept of the "device."[86] Still, there are distinct parallels, where a number of these devices, e.g., organization of narrative time (*zaderžanie*) or perspective (*ostranienie*)[87] correspond directly to elements of Ingarden's stratum of aspects (and indeed inhere in the specific "reality," the quasi-time and quasi-space of the represented world). Potentially, there are as many devices as there are schematized aspects, and the latter themselves reflect, as Ingarden points out, the style of a particular school or era (e.g., Impressionism, Futurism, etc.). Focusing on these devices (aspects) without reference to the total structure necessarily impoverishes the work. (It is interesting to note that for Ingar-

84. In this regard see Michael Riffaterre's critique of the analysis by Roman Jakobson and Claude Lévi-Strauss of Baudelaire's *Les Chats* (Roman Jakobson and Claude Lévi-Strauss, "*Les Chats* de Charles Baudelaire," *L'Homme*, II [1962], 5–21), in which he challenges this blurring of poetic and linguistic criteria (or "actualizations"): "The two critics obviously assume that the definition of categories used to collect data is also valid to explain their function in the poetic structure—that linguistic oppositions, for example, automatically entail stylistic differences" (*Structuralism*, ed. Jacques Ehrmann [New York, 1970], p. 198).

85. See "Sprawa formy i treści w dziele literackim" (The Question of the Form and Content in the Literary Work), *Życie Literackie*, IV, no. 5 (1937); published subsequently, in expanded form, as "O formie i treści dzieła sztuki literackiej" (Concerning the Form and Content of the Literary Work of Art), *Studia*, II, 357–494.

86. See V. Šklovskij's programmatic "Isskustvo kak priëm" (Art as a Device) in *Poètika* (Petrograd, 1919).

87. See V. Šklovskij, *O teorii prozy* (The Theory of Prose) (Moscow, 1929). *Ostranienie*, "making-it-strange," like the concept of "disautomatization," can be more far-reaching than a device, however; and as an artistic principle it approaches the problem of aesthetic distance, discussed above.

den the currently canonized Soviet doctrine of *obraznost'*, of literature as essentially [poetic] image,[88] which, at its most cogent, harks back to O. Potebnja [against whom the Formalists so strongly objected] and to Lessing [*poetisches Bild*] is, given a modicum of precision, fully reconcilable with the concept of schematized aspects.) [89]

A crucial difference between Ingarden and the Russian Formalists stems from the focus of their respective investigations: whereas Ingarden offers a theory of the literary work, their concern is ultimately with a theory of literature. This difference is centered on the issue of the literary context. To the Formalists, the work qua literary work can be perceived only against a background of other works; the "form" of a work, as Šklovskij put it, is perceivable only as a "deviation" from a "canon." [90] (An extension of this basic idea of a literary context is also suggested by Eliot's notion that "the whole of the literature of Europe from Homer . . . has a simultaneous existence and composes a simultaneous order.") [91] Though this is not ignored by Ingarden and is, in fact, analyzed in terms of the various strata (e.g., "live" and "dead" words, new or clichéd aspects, etc.), the "dynamic," or evolutionist, or simply historical focus of the Formalists (and subsequently the structuralist concept of "system") may indeed appear to be a more effective approach to a theory of literature as such. In essence, however, it is an example of the synthetic analyses that Ingarden foresaw as building on his fundamental investigations.

Along with a shared understanding of the separate reality of the literary work, a reality which for the Formalists rests on the conventionality of art and for Ingarden on the *sic iubeo* that is in all quasi-judgments and thus at the basis of all literature, there is perhaps a final, phenomenologically based similarity. Like the Formalists, who saw the prime goal of their critical and theoretical efforts in the creation of working hypotheses and in a "formal method" rather than a static doctrine, Ingarden, too, is opposed to viewing his aesthetic theories as a fixed and rigid

88. See, for example, L. I. Timofeev's authoritatively popularizing *Osnovy teorii literatury* (Foundations of the Theory of Literature) (Moscow, 1966), pp. 17–83.

89. *Studia*, III, 420–21.

90. V. Šklovskij, *O teorii prozy*, p. 31. See also Jurij Striedter, Introduction to *Texte der Russichen Formalisten*, 2 vols. (Munich, 1969), I, xxx.

91. T. S. Eliot, "Tradition and the Individual Talent," *The Sacred Wood*, p. 44.

"system." His achievement is above all a phenomenological method which continually requires verification and new investigations but which, therefore, promises an immediate, accurate, and coherent understanding of the object.

THIS TRANSLATION is based on the third, 1965, edition of *Das literarische Kunstwerk*. Except for the revision of § 26, the text is substantially the same as in the first edition: the polemical § 25a and the Appendix are the major additions. All other elaborations or emendations of Ingarden's earlier positions are incorporated into the footnotes. The Polish edition was helpful for elucidating occasional elliptical constructions; any recourse to it is indicated in the translator's notes.

I wish to thank Professors Donald Fanger, Craig LaDrière, and Omeljan Pritsak for their helpful comments on a late draft of this introduction. I am especially grateful to Professor Wiktor Weintraub for his initial encouragement to undertake this translation and for his generous advice throughout. I am most indebted to my wife, Oksana, for her unstinting support and good cheer.

Harvard University   GEORGE G. GRABOWICZ
December, 1972

Preface to the
First German Edition

THE MAIN SUBJECT of the investigations presented here is the basic structure and the mode of existence of the literary work, and in particular of the literary work of art. Their primary purpose is to indicate its peculiar construction and to free the concept of the work from the various kinds of blurring that in the studies to date stem, on the one hand, from the still strong psychologistic tendencies and, on the other, from considerations of a general theory of art and art works. I will deal with the former at greater length in Part I of this book, so it will suffice for me merely to mention it here. Concerning the latter, however, one has wavered, since the time of Lessing, between two opposite conceptions. Either one brought the literary work, and in particular the literary work of art, into too close a relationship with the "visual arts" (above all with painting), or one sought—following Lessing's first impulse—(as, for instance, T. A. Meyer did) to lay too much stress on the purely linguistic element of the literary work and hence deny the intuitive elements of the literary work of art.[1] In my opinion these two extremes arose from the fact that the literary work was always considered to be a formation having one stratum, whereas in fact it consists of a number of heterogeneous strata; in consequence, one always considered some—and, according to the various theories, always different—elements of the work as the only constitutive ones. Since my study attempts to bring out the

1. For a history of this problem see, among others, Jonas Cohn, *Zeitschrift für Ästhetik und allgemeine Kunstwissenschaft*, II, no. 3 (1907); in addition, see R. Lehmann, *Deutsche Poetik* (Munich, 1908), § 8.

many-layered structure, and consequently the attendant polyphony, as that which is essential for the literary work and thus
to take into consideration all the elements appearing in it, my
position occupies a middle ground between the two conflicting
camps. To avoid undue expansion of my already sizable book
and to enable the reader to take a pure attitude toward the
object of investigation, I have dispensed with providing extensive connections to existing theories. Usually this has the effect of
making the reader attune himself primarily to already existing
conceptual schemata, with the result that the pure observation
of situations that are really at hand is substantially impeded.

Although the main subject of my investigations is the literary work, or the literary work of art, the ultimate motives for
my work on this subject are of a general philosophical nature,
and they far transcend this particular subject. They are closely
connected to the problem of idealism-realism, with which I
have been concerning myself for many years. As I have attempted to show in my "Bemerkungen zum Problem Idealismus-
Realismus," [2] the conflict between so-called realism and idealism
conceals different groups of very involved problems, which
must be distinguished, individually highlighted, and worked out
before one can approach the main metaphysical problem. In
consequence, there are various ways in which one must prepare
oneself for this main subject. One of these is tied in with the
attempt of Husserl's so-called transcendental idealism to conceive the real world and its elements as purely intentional
objectivities which have their ontic and determining basis in the
depths of the pure consciousness that constitutes them. In
order to take a stance toward this theory, developed by Husserl
with the utmost refinement and in consideration of situations
that are most important and difficult to apprehend, it is necessary, among other things, to indicate the essential structure and
mode of existence of the purely intentional object so that subsequently one may see whether real objectivities can, according
to their own nature, have the same structure and mode of
existence. To this end I have sought an object whose pure
intentionality was beyond any doubt and on the basis of which
one could study the essential structures and the mode of existence of the purely intentional object without being subject to

2. See *Festschrift, Edmund Husserl zum 70. Geburtstag gewidmet,
Jahrbuch für Philosophie und phänomenologische Forschung, Ergänzungsband* (Halle, 1929), pp. 159–90.

suggestions stemming from considerations of real objectivities. The literary work seemed to me an object of investigation particularly suitable for this purpose. As I concerned myself with it in greater detail, however, specific problems of literary theory opened up to me, and their treatment, in conjunction with the basic goals mentioned above, produced the present book. Since, in the conception of this book, I was guided by such disparate motives, various matters had to be treated more precisely than would be necessary for a book dealing merely with the philosophical bases of a theory of the literary work. On the other hand, the very diversity of formations belonging to the structure of the literary work gave birth to a series of observations which, while being indispensable for this particular problem, are at the same time important for various philosophical disciplines. Thus, the investigations in Chapter 5 are a contribution to logic and to new directions in it; the observations on states of affairs and on the objectivities represented in the literary work seek to develop certain formal ontological problems, while the investigations concerning the mode of existence of represented objects are of significance for general existential ontology. So as not to imperil the unity of the book, I have avoided speaking of the very important consequences that arise from these findings, not only for the problem of "idealism-realism" but for other philosophical problems.

The present book was written in the winter of 1927–28 during a sabbatical leave. The preparation of other pressing publications and difficult working conditions caused the final preparation of the text and the appearance of the book to be delayed by two years. The result of this was that some of the findings of my investigation were published in the meantime in works of other authors. This applies to some of the conclusions of Chapter 5 of this book and to Edmund Husserl's *Formal and Transcendental Logic* (1929). The close relationship between some of my analyses and the conclusions of my esteemed teacher gave me particular pleasure in the reading of his new work. At the same time, however, a comparison of the two texts showed that, along with the points of agreement, there were also far-reaching differences, and this, perhaps, in some of the points most important for me. It was impossible for me to take note of this work simply by a supplementary inclusion of a series of quotations. I allowed the text of my book to be printed without change, and I wish only to indicate the points of relationship and difference in the hope that it will later be possible for me to devote a special publication to the new and significant work of my teacher.

My findings agree with Husserl's view, expressed in his *Formal and Transcendental Logic,* that word meanings, sentences, and higher units of meaning are formations which arise from subjective conscious operations. Thus they are not ideal objectivities in the sense in which Husserl himself determined them in his *Logical Investigations.* But while Husserl keeps the term "ideal" in most instances in his *Logic* and only at times adds the word "unreal" [*irreal*] in parentheses, I have totally abandoned this term and seek sharply to counterpose these formations to ideal objectivities in the strict sense. This is the first essential difference: all objectivities which he previously held to be ideal—in the old sense—Husserl now considers to be intentional formations of a particular kind, and in this way he arrives at a universal extension of transcendental idealism; whereas I today still maintain the strict ideality of various ideal objectivities (ideal concepts, ideal individual objects, ideas and essences) and indeed see in ideal concepts an ontic foundation of word meanings that enables them to have intersubjective identity and an ontically autonomous mode of existence. At the same time, for Husserl the new conception of logical formations springs primarily from *phenomenological* investigations and general transcendental-idealistic motives, whereas my observations are ontologically oriented and seek to show, in the logical formations themselves, a series of states of affairs which make ideal existence in the strict sense impossible for them and which simultaneously indicate their ontic origin in subjective operations. Only subsequently do I attempt to give some pertinent phenomenological outlines. In doing so, I refrain, in my book, from any judgment regarding the transcendental-idealistic point of view and, in particular, the idealistic conception of the real world. My book, however, does contain a series of specific findings which—if they are true—speak against this conception. This refers, for instance, to the peculiar dual structure of purely intentional objectivities, to the spots of indeterminacy appearing in their content, and to their ontic autonomy.

As regards the details involved in the relationship to Husserl's *Logic,* it will suffice to point out that the following arguments of mine are related to corresponding assertions of Husserl: (1) the conception of a subjective sentence-building operation and the distinction between a pure proposition and a judgment; (2)

the distinction between the material and the formal content of the nominal word meaning and the counterposition of the full meaning of an isolated word to the syntactic elements which its meaning assumes in the sentence; (3) the analysis of the constitution of a purely intentional objectivity in a manifold of connected sentences. Finally, there are a number of instances where Husserl indicates assertions or problems only in passing, since he cannot deal with them at greater length, while for my purposes I analyze them extensively. This refers, for example, to my reflection on the mode of existence of objectivities represented in a literary work, where Husserl only notes twice that "even fictions have their mode of being." [3] Subsequently, Husserl poses the "painful question" of

> how subjectivity can in itself bring forth, purely from sources appertaining to its own spontaneity, formations that can be rightly accounted as ideal *Objects* in an ideal "world."—And then (on a higher level) the question of how these idealities can take on spatio-temporally restricted *existence,* in the cultural world (which must surely be considered as real, as included in the spatio-temporal universe), real existence, in the form of historical temporality, as theories and sciences. [4]

These "painful questions," particularly the second, were the point of departure for my consideration of the literary work. It produced the conclusion that formations of this sort should be excluded, not only from the realm of idealities in the strict sense, but from the real world as well. Whether I have succeeded in justifying this is something the reader may decide on the basis of my book.

These comments are designed to facilitate the reader's orientation in the connections between my book and Husserl's *Formal and Transcendental Logic.* If, in making them, I have had to indicate some differences with the viewpoints of my esteemed teacher, I am not forgetful of how much I am beholden to him. Today, after twelve years of independent work, I know better than ever how much Edmund Husserl surpasses us all in his deep insight and command of vast horizons. If we succeed in discovering something which he previously has not noticed, we owe it primarily to the fact that Husserl's tireless research has made our task that much easier.

3. *Formale und transzendentale Logik* (Halle, 1929), pp. 149 and 226; English translation by Dorion Cairns, *Formal and Transcendental Logic* (The Hague: Nijhoff, 1969), pp. 166 and 256.
4. *Ibid.,* pp. 230–31; English translation, pp. 260–61.

In conclusion, I would like to express my deepest and warmest gratitude to those who helped me in the writing of this book. Above all, Professors Juliusz Kleiner and Zygmunt Łempicki supported me with valuable advice and criticism. I have discussed several chapters with Dr. W. Auerbach (who also helped me in reading the proofs) and with Dr. M. Kokoszyńska, and I am grateful to them for their accurate observations. Dr. Edith Stein was gracious in taking on the great task of editing the text.

I would like to express special thanks to Max Niemeyer, who, despite the general crisis, decided to publish my book and to provide it with the best possible appearance.

Lvov   THE AUTHOR
October, 1930

Preface to the
Second German Edition

IT IS MORE THAN THIRTY YEARS since I wrote this book. Much has changed in the world in that time. In deciding to publish this book in a new edition, I am motivated, not only by the circumstance that for many years it has been out of print and seldom to be found even in the libraries, but also by the fact that, despite violent changes in the cultural atmosphere, it has stayed alive and indeed is more noticed in recent years than when it appeared. Then, in 1930, it was a risky venture to pursue the ontology of the literary work of art and to discuss both purely structural and existential-ontological problems and, in doing so, to treat the literary work in light of the problem of idealism-realism. But it is precisely in this respect that the situation has changed essentially in the past thirty years. In the course of this time, these or analogous problems have been taken up from various sides and from various points of view and treated in a spirit very close to mine. Interest in questions of this sort has increased visibly, not only in Germany but in other countries as well. Whether this occurred under the influence of my book or quite independently of it is not of essential importance here. One also became conscious of the fact that ontological problems relating to the literary work are by no means merely a relatively isolated concern of literary criticism but rather are closely connected to various fundamentally important questions of philosophy. This was the position argued by this book. Today it is no longer as solitary in the scholarly world as it was at the beginning of its existence.

At the same time, it seems to me that the analyses and prospects on further problems given in it have by no means been utilized to a sufficient degree, nor have they been superseded by findings in other books and treatises to the extent that they no longer have meaning today. On the contrary, I believe that its findings go further than anything attempted by others in this field. I also hope that the situation in investigations of this sort has become more auspicious for this book and that today its views are perhaps more accessible to the reader than they could be at the beginning of the thirties. I present this book to the reading public in the hope that it can be of continuing benefit.

I have left it essentially unchanged. Only in some places have I sought to adapt the earlier formulations somewhat more precisely to the given facts. Here and there I have completed an argument by a further observation. I am quite conscious of the fact that for literary critics this book would be much more accessible and plastic if I have devoted a series of concrete analyses to individual works of art. But I had to abandon this from the first, since the book would have become unmanageable. I have refrained, moreover, from analyzing works of art written in a language foreign to me, since false interpretations could very easily arise in this way. Thus, this time as well, I have dispensed with an analysis of individual works of art. However, I have introduced in a number of places new bibliographical data and have quoted other points of view which to my mind seem to confirm my point of view in various individual questions. Of particular value for me were corroborations by authors who obviously did not know my book. Occasionally I have answered objections which in the course of time have been raised against me. Unfortunately, the newest critical literature is only partially taken into account, since only a small part of it was available to me.

In conclusion, I would like to extend my best thanks to my

loyal publisher, Dr. Hermann Niemeyer, for again deciding to publish my book.

Cracow, 1959   THE AUTHOR

Preface to the Third German Edition

THE NEW EDITION of this book appears at a time when its original "Appendix," now *Untersuchungen zur Ontologie der Kunst*, has already been made accessible to the German reader. Only now will it become evident that the study devoted to the literary work of art has from the beginning constituted only a part of a much broader set of problems and has had a far-reaching theoretical objective. Apart from the connection with the problem of idealism-realism, which, after the publication of my book *Der Streit um die Existenz der Welt*, may perhaps be distinctly seen, it is now clear that from the outset I wished to create, through a fundamental analysis of the structure and the mode of existence of works in the various arts, a concrete basis for phenomenological aesthetics as they existed up to then. Connected with this was the methodological requirement that literary study and art study in general should concentrate in their analyses on the work of art itself [1] and that all other problems pertaining to it should first be treated on this basis.[2] Indeed, the two books mentioned above constitute only a part, although the major part, of my writings that have appeared in Polish. However, I hope to make available to my German readers at least my book *The Cognition of the Literary Work of Art* and a selection of my papers. Only then will the contours of a phenomenologically treated aesthetic, as I understand it, begin to appear.

1. This is what René Wellek later called "the intrinsic study of literature." (Cf. René Wellek and Austin Warren, *Theory of Literature* [New York: Harcourt, Brace, 1949; 2d ed., 1956].)
2. At that time, in 1931, I was attacked from all sides for this—at least in Poland. I would be happy if today this requirement were to be considered trivial.

Originally I had the intention of dealing critically in the new edition with several theories that have appeared in recent years. But since this edition appears in photomechanical reprint, I had to abandon that and will only make some observations on René Wellek's and Austin Warren's *Theory of Literature,* with specific reference to those places where René Wellek expressly mentions my book.[3]

There are only two places (pp. 151 and 156) where my name is mentioned in the text of *Theory of Literature.*[4] In the first of these, my stratum conception of the literary work of art is reported on; basically, the strata are merely enumerated. It is noted, however, that I had distinguished *five* strata, and, among others, the stratum of metaphysical qualities. This is a mistake. I have indeed examined metaphysical qualities, but I have never considered them to be one of the strata of the literary work. It would have been absolutely false if I had done so. They appear only with relative infrequency in certain events and life-situations in the represented world. If they were to constitute a stratum of the work, they would have to belong to the basic structure of the literary work of art and as such appear in all such works. This is not at all the case, as Wellek, moreover, notes. Nonetheless, their role in the work of art is very significant. They are closely connected with the aesthetic value of the same, and they were treated by me precisely on this basis.[5] They may be made to appear in works of other arts, primarily music, but also in painting, architecture, and so on; and in this they may frequently belong to the "idea" of the work as I have conceived it. Thus their presence is in no way tied to the literary aspect of the work. If one were to consider them a stratum of the literary work of art, one would have to overlook the "anatomical" characteristic and the structural role of the strata in the literary work of art and in the work of art in general.

René Wellek presents my stratum concept under a (to me)

3. *Theory of Literature* first appeared in English in 1942, at a time when Poland, occupied by foreign troops, was for many years cut off from the scholarly life of the world. My book was then practically out of print and was hardly obtainable in the United States. The German translation of *Theory of Literature* appeared in 1959, but I came to know it only several years after the publication of the second edition of my book.

4. The title of my book is mentioned several times in the notes and in the bibliography, but a reader unacquainted with it cannot gather from that the degree to which René Wellek's book relies on my arguments.

5. This is already an indication of the fact that the charge raised by Wellek, which I discuss below, is unfounded.

alien and misleading aspect of "norm" and "norm system." [6] In addition, the second structural feature of the literary work of art—the sequence of parts—is quite disregarded by him. This represents a fundamental deformation of both the structure of the literary work and my conception. The disregard for the order of the sequence of parts of a literary work makes it impossible for Wellek to treat important problems of literary *art*.

Wellek reproaches me with the following:

> We have not discussed the question of artistic values. But the preceding examination should have shown that there is no structure outside norms and values.[7] We cannot comprehend and analyse any work of art without reference to values. The very fact that I recognize a certain structure as a "work of art" implies a judgment of value. The error of pure phenomenology is in the assumption that such a dissociation [!—R. I.] is possible, that values are superimposed on structure, "inhere" on or in structures. This error of analysis vitiates the penetrating book of Roman Ingarden, who tries to analyse the work of art without reference to values.[8] The root of the matter lies, of course, in the phenomenologist's assumption of an eternal, non-temporal order of essences to which the empirical individualizations are added only later [!—R. I.].[9]

To this one must answer:

1. I am totally unaware, and I personally find it quite strange, that "pure phenomenologists" make the "assumption" that "values are *superimposed* on structure, 'inhere' on or in structures." For Wellek the word "structure" has, in fact, so many meanings [10] that this sentence is hardly understandable. Whatever the words "value" and "structure" are meant to signify, the verb "superimpose" suggests that the underlying element should be "value" and that what is constructed on top of it is "structure."

6. I will deal with this at another time. [Cf. "Werte, Normen und Strukturen nach René Wellek," *Deutsche Vierteljahrsschrift für Literaturwissenschaft und Geistesgeschichte*, XL (1966), 43–55.—Trans.]

7. If the statement refers to the preceding part of Chapter 12 of *Theory of Literature*, then this examination does not at all deal with the relation among norms, values, and structures. Basically, it refers to *my* observations on the nature and mode of existence of literary works of art—without mentioning my name in the text. Only on pp. 151–52 (3d ed.) does there follow a résumé of my stratum conception.

8. This dictum of Wellek's has frequently been repeated by other authors without verification of the facts. It is for this reason that I return to it here.

9. *Theory of Literature*, p. 156.

10. I will point this out elsewhere. [Cf. "Werte, Normen und Strukturen."—Trans.]

This is exactly the opposite of what I would maintain. In other words, structures (and indeed not all, but quite particular structures) are the underlying, founding element, and what is founded are the values.

2. Max Scheler has in fact spoken of values as ideal objects or essences, but he distinguished them from "positive values" [*Güte*], which are individual and particularly real and whose value elements are likewise individual. But no phenomenologist would maintain that "empirical individualizations" should be "added only later" to these "essences."

3. It is two different things—something which René Wellek does not bear in mind—to analyze a single work of art, for example Goethe's *Faust,* and to construct a general philosophical theory of the literary work of art. In the first instance, it would be a mistake to consider a given individual work of art entirely "without reference," as Wellek puts it, to its artistic or aesthetic value, although there must be phases of investigation where elements of the work of art which are neutral as to value are considered without attention being paid at that instant to the value itself. In the second instance, however, where the examination is performed on the basis of an analysis of the content of a *general* idea of the work of art, one must make quite sure that works of art have artistic or aesthetic value to begin with, or that they embody value, while the *specific* value that a work of art has and can have in a given instance must here be left outside the scope of our interest, since, in the context of a general idea of the work of art, this particular value is, after all, a variable. Only single instances of this variable can appear in individual works of art. It is quite impossible to proceed otherwise. And despite the objection he makes, René Wellek does the same thing himself. He says quite expressly, and indeed fully in accordance with *my* sense and my *model:*

> This conception of literature is descriptive, not evaluative. No wrong is done to a great and influential work by relegating it to rhetoric, to philosophy, to political pamphleteering, all of which may pose problems of aesthetic analysis, of stylistics and composition, similar or identical to those presented by literature, but where the central quality of fictionality will be absent. This conception will thus include in it all kinds of fiction, even the worst novel, the worst poem, the worst drama. Classification as art should be distinguished from evaluation.[11]

11. *Theory of Literature,* p. 26.

This is precisely, entirely, *my* opinion. One must also note that, according to Wellek, literature is distinguished from other works not by its value but, to use his term, its "fictionality." This is again entirely *my* opinion. In this vague formulation, moreover, it is old history. In Germany it goes back at least to the time of Lessing. Thus I sought to take an essential step forward in this question by trying to determine somewhat more closely this "fictionality," at the same time indicating the quasi-judgments which are the means for bringing out this "fictionality."

4. Finally, I have never attempted "to analyse the work of art without reference to value," nor have I required this. Word for word, I said (pp. 21–22):

> Finally, we shall put aside for the moment [!] all general questions dealing with the *nature of the value* of a work of art, and in particular of a literary work of art. Indeed, we shall find that the latter has values and flaws that constitute a *peculiarly qualified* total value of the whole. . . . However, the question of what constitutes the nature of this value must remain beyond the scope of our study, since an answer to it *assumes,* on the one hand, a *solution to the problem of value* in general and, on the other, an understanding of the structure of the literary work. For this very reason our consideration of the literary work will disregard altogether the issue of whether the works we are dealing with have positive values or are worthless.

In other words, this is to say that I will consider the works that have positive value *as well as* "worthless" works, i.e., those with negative value. The only possibly misleading word is "worthless." Since it is used in contrast to "positive value," however, it should not in fact be misunderstood. Only the consideration of all works of art, those having both positive and negative value, can make it clear for us why some works "have value," that is, aesthetic or artistic value, while others, as René Wellek himself says, are "bad." And what did I really do in my book? I, in fact, did not examine the general essence of value. Instead, I looked, in the literary work of art and also in the order of sequence of parts of the work, for places where values (more specifically, artistic or aesthetic value qualities) can appear. I also indicated many such places. At the same time, I sought to bring to attention the specific element in the artistic or aesthetic value of the literary work of art, and I have characterized this value to the effect that it exists in a *polyphonic harmony of value qualities.* This may, of course, be false or still quite unsatisfactory. But it is not an indication that I have attempted to analyze literary works of art "without reference to value."

5. I cannot deal here with the meaning and the validity of the sentence which Wellek puts as the basis of his position: "But the preceding examination should have shown that there is no structure outside norms and values." Clarification of the meaning of this sentence, as well as a consideration of its bases, can be made only in a wider study, for which this is not the place. I shall do it at another time.

Cracow   THE AUTHOR
September, 1965

PART I

Preliminary Questions

§1. *Introduction*

WE STAND before a remarkable fact. Almost daily we deal with literary works.[1] We read them; we are moved and enthralled by some, while others do not appeal to us; we evaluate them and pronounce various opinions on them; we discuss them; we write essays on individual works and take an interest in their fates. Their existence seems to us as natural as the air we breathe. Thus it would appear that we know the objects of our concern universally and exhaustively. And yet, were someone to ask us what a literary work actually is, we should have to admit with some surprise that we cannot find an accurate and satisfactory answer to this question. Our knowledge about the essence of a literary work is, in fact, not only inadequate but very vague and uncertain. It might be surmised that this holds true only for the laymen among us, who merely associate with literary works and have no theoretical knowledge of them. That is not the case, however. If we turn to the historians or critics of literature or even to those who work in the realm of literary theory, we will not obtain an essentially better answer to this question. The various opinions we are offered are frequently contradictory and basically do not constitute tenable results of investigations actually directed at the essence of the literary work. They rather express the so-called philosophical convictions of the given author, i.e., usually nothing but the uncritical biases of a vanished epoch, established by habit and upbringing. The question of the essence of the literary work is not clearly stated even in outstanding works in the field of literary theory; they treat the problem as if it were an issue that is generally known and altogether insignificant.[2] Even if such a question appears here and there, it is entangled from the very outset in various

1. We are using the expression "the literary work" to denote any work of so-called belles-lettres regardless of whether it is a genuine work of art or a worthless work. Only where we are trying to develop those aspects of the literary work that are constitutive for the literary work of art do we use the latter expression.

2. This refers, of course, to the situation in force in 1927, when this was written. Much has changed since that time.

problems and assumptions with which it has little in common and which make adequate answers impossible. And while the central question is not posed at the outset, one zealously occupies oneself with various special problems which—though interesting in themselves—do not allow a complete solution as long as one is quite unclear about the essence of the literary work. It is to this central question that we wish to devote the following inquiry.

The goal we have set for ourselves is basically a modest one. For the present we would like to provide only an "essential anatomy" of the literary work; its main conclusions will only then open the way to an aesthetic consideration of the work. The special problems of aesthetics and literary theory which today are investigated from various aspects will remain outside the scope of our considerations and will have to be attacked later, in the light of our conclusions. But, in our opinion, even their correct formulation is dependent on the conclusions presented here.

Although we arrive at different basic assertions, we naturally do not want to disparage the significance that the results of other investigators have for the development of literary knowledge. Nevertheless, some questions cannot be resolved if a correct course is not adopted. We require a starting position toward the literary work that is fundamentally different from the still-dominant psychological and psychologistic tendencies. This new attitude will of itself lead to a refining and modification of hitherto prominent views. So long as we do not assume toward the object of investigation a phenomenological attitude that is purely receptive and directed at the essence of the thing, we are always inclined to overlook the specific and reduce it to something we already know. Such is also the case with considerations of the literary work. They are almost exclusively psychological or psychologistically colored. Even in those works which would gladly break with psychologism, e.g., von Dohrn's interesting book *Die künstlerische Darstellung als Problem der Ästhetik* or Zygmunt Łempicki's Polish work *W sprawie uzasadnienia poetyki czystej*,[3] there is still a very strong tendency to reduce the

3. "W sprawie uzasadnienia poetyki czystej" (Concerning the Justification of Pure Poetics) appeared in the *Festschrift* for K. Twardowski (Lvov, 1922). An essential step in the liberation from psychologism were some of Łempicki's conclusions in his review of O. Walzel's *Gehalt und Gestalt* that appeared in the *Zeitschrift für Philologie*, Vol. X. The first effort, as far as I know, at examining the literary work purely in and of itself, attempted by W. Conrad in his treatise "Der ästhetische Gegen-

literary work to certain psychic facts and relations and to identify it with them. Indeed, for many outstanding investigators it seems so self-evident that a literary work is a psychic thing that they will never agree to any other possibility. We, on the contrary, believe that it can be demonstrated that the literary work is an object with an altogether peculiar structure, one which is also interesting to us for the other reasons already indicated in this introduction.

---

stand," *Zeitschrift für Ästhetik und allgemeine Kunstwissenschaft,* III, nos. 1 and 3 (1908), 71–118, 469–511; IV, no. 3 (1909), 400–455, unfortunately produced no effect. But Conrad goes too far and sees the literary work as an ideal object, which, as we wish to show, is untenable.

1 / Initial Problems

§ 2. *Provisional delimitation of the range of examples*

To BEGIN WITH, we shall provisionally determine the range of objects we wish to investigate by means of a series of examples. We do this "provisionally"—that is, from the outset we are always ready to change such a definition of the range of objects if in the course of the investigation this appears to be necessary. In this way the investigation will be given a certain direction, though it can be modified at any time. A final definition of the range of literary works presupposes grasping and conceptually defining their essence. This will be possible only at the end of this study.

If we were to choose our examples according to the everyday (though unclarified and perhaps totally false) concept of the "literary work," we could enumerate works from all the possible "literary genres." For the time being, therefore, Homer's *Iliad* as well as Dante's *Divine Comedy*, any one of Schiller's dramas as well as any novel (e.g., Thomas Mann's *The Magic Mountain*), and finally any short story or lyric poem will pass as a literary work. We do not, however, want to consider only works of high literary or cultural value as literary works. That would be a complete mistake. At this point we still do not know what distinguishes a work that has value from a work that is worthless, nor do we know what it means when a work has value—in particular, *literary* value. It is not at all obvious, moreover, why there should be no "bad," no worthless, literary works. It is our

[7]

intent to demonstrate a basic structure that is common to all literary works, regardless of what value they may have. Thus we must also choose as examples for our investigation works and productions which, according to general opinion, are considered worthless, e.g., the serialized crime novel or a schoolboy's banal love poem.[1]

1. R. Odebrecht had in mind this methodological proposal and, in general, the basic tenets of the investigations performed in this book when he wrote, in his Ästhetik der Gegenwart [Philosophische Forschungsberichte, Vol. XV] (Berlin, 1932), pp. 25 ff.: "While evaluating, we can turn to a 'thing' without having the value itself be an object (Husserl). This requires first a peculiar 'objectifying' movement toward it. This is overlooked by all the phenomenologists, who, in their exaggerated fear of psychologism, exclude the aesthetic experience and concern themselves with the neutral value 'carrier,' as if the value were attached to it (which is what Rickert's school assumes) and could be detached from it at will. Roman Ingarden's work on the literary work of art is also not free of this basic error. The incisive investigations of the many-layered structure of the literary work, the characterization of the four different strata (phonetic formations, units of meaning, represented objectivities, schematized aspects) are, aesthetically speaking, suspended in air. One cannot deal with the work first as something simply representable and subsequently as something valuable, since one is then dealing with two different 'objects.' With an object that is thought of as a work of art, one must from the very beginning have the twofold intentio in mind."

To this one must say the following: neither Husserl (whom Odebrecht expressly mentions) nor I have overlooked the possibility of the two attitudes toward the aesthetically valuable object and the difference between them. Indeed, taking the matter more precisely, it is a question here—as I hope to have shown in my work The Cognition of the Literary Work, which appeared in Polish in 1937—of a number of different, frequently interwoven, attitudes toward the literary work. And certainly it is not—as Odebrecht correctly notes—merely a question of apprehending the work first without an "attached" value and subsequently with this value. According to the attitude, there occurs an altogether differently constructed, and in many features a differently formed, concretization of the given work (concerning which we cannot yet speak at this point; see below, Chap. 13). But this does not preclude us from apprehending in a purely cognitive manner the work itself precisely as the ultimate basis upon which all the potentialities of the concretizations constituting themselves in aesthetic and nonaesthetic attitudes rest. Naturally, this is done with reference to the various modes in which it shows itself to us in the various phases of aesthetic experience. In my book on the cognition of the literary work, I have provided, among other things, an extensive analysis of the aesthetic experience. I gave a short résumé of this at the Second International Congress of Aesthetics and General Theory of Art in Paris, 1937. Moreover: in an individual case, this purely cognitive apprehension of the work must be required if we are to have any understanding at all of how one can attain different concretizations of one and the same work. This is required even more for a general analysis of the nature of a literary work (and also the literary work of art), and this is exactly what our work attempts to realize. That this is not an "error," as Odebrecht thinks, is already seen from the fact that the literary work inheres, so to speak, as a skeleton in every adequately constituted con-

Along with the examples we have mentioned, there are others which we should not ignore, even though we may doubt whether they have anything to do with "literary works." These are, for example, "scientific works," clearly distinguishable from the works of so-called belles-lettres that will be the object of our study, and yet frequently spoken of as having greater or lesser literary value or as being devoid of it; the implication is that, generally speaking, it is possible to compare them with belles-lettres or that, in the final analysis, they are essentially the same. Newspaper articles also belong here, whether they treat important problems or events or are nothing but police communiqués. Next, there are the diaries, autobiographies, memoirs, etc. Other types of questionable examples are provided by cinematic works (comedies, dramas, and so on), pantomimes, and also staged theatrical works.

Let us now turn to the first series of examples and use them to discover the basic structure of the literary work. We will begin with a discussion of some preliminary questions, which, as will later become apparent, are the central problems.

§ 3. *The problem of the mode of existence of the literary work*

THE FIRST DIFFICULTY we meet is posed by the question: among what kind of objects is the literary work to be included—the real or the ideal?

The division of all objects into the real and the ideal seems to be a division that is most general and, simultaneously, most complete. One may thus believe that solving this problem will produce something conclusive about the literary work. The solution is not that easy, however. The reason for this is twofold: first of all, despite some significant attempts, the definition of ideal as well as real objects with respect to their mode of

---

cretization, which only clothes this skeleton with various features and particulars as with a living body. The work is, as it were, visible through this clothing but distinguishable from it—this clothing, which, among other things, contains aesthetically valuable qualities and depicts the aesthetic value founded in them. It is only when this skeleton is both contained and visible in the concretization that the identity of the work is demonstrably assured in all its changes during its life in the course of history.

existence has not been made conclusively; second, it is not immediately clear what a literary work actually is. Though we must be satisfied for the moment with insufficiently clarified concepts of real and ideal objects, the unsuccessful attempts to decide whether the literary work is an ideal or a real object will show us most convincingly how unclear and inadequate our knowledge of the literary work is.

We are speaking here of real and ideal objects only as of something which in itself is ontically autonomous and at the same time ontically independent of any cognitive act directed at it.[2] If someone were unwilling to agree to the ontic autonomy of ideal objects,[3] he would still have to distinguish them from real objects if only because the latter originate at some point in time, exist for a certain time, possibly change in the course of their existence, and finally cease to exist.[4] None of this can be said of ideal objects.

In connection with their timelessness, ideal objects are not subject to change, though it is thus far not clear what the basis of their immutability is. Real objects, on the contrary, undoubtedly can change—precisely as we have claimed—and actually do change, although it is again questionable whether they must always essentially change.

Assuming this, let us ask whether a determinate literary work, e.g., Goethe's *Faust,* is a real or an ideal object. We will immediately become convinced that we do not know how to resolve this "either/or," since there are various convincing arguments for each of these mutually exclusive possibilities. Goethe's *Faust* came into being at a determinate point in time; we can also provide with relatively great accuracy the period of its formation. We are all agreed that *Faust* has existed from the moment of its formation, though we do not fully understand

2. H. Conrad-Martius also stresses the "existential autonomy" of ideal objectivities; she seems to understand by that, however, only what we mean by "ontic independence." See her "Realontologie," p. 6: "There can no longer be any doubt that there is a 'number three' in an absolutely timeless untouchableness and therefore in absolute existential autonomy" (*Jahrbuch für Philosophie und phänomenologische Forschung,* VI [1923], 164).

3. For the sake of brevity, I am here using the expression "ideal object" in a broader sense than in my "Essentiale Fragen," *Jahrbuch für Philosophie und phänomenologische Forschung,* VII (1925) 125–304. There I made distinctions between ideal *objects,* ideas, and ideal qualities. The term used here denotes all three types of idealities.

4. I am speaking here only of objects of our direct experience and leave aside the possibility of an eternal real object, as well as the question of its relationship to time.

what it really means to speak of its existence. It is perhaps with less assurance that we would agree that from the time of its formation Goethe's masterpiece has been subject to changes of one type or another and that there will come a time when it will cease to exist. No one, however, will dispute the fact that it is possible to change a literary work in the event that the author himself, or the publisher of a new edition, sees fit to delete this or that passage and introduce another. In spite of this, the literary work can remain "the same"—provided the changes are not too far-reaching. Hence, on the basis of these assertions one must consider the literary work a real object. At the same time, who would want to deny that this same *Faust* is an ideal object? For, in fact, what else is it but a determinately ordered manifold of sentences? Yet a sentence is nothing real; as is frequently observed, it is supposed to be a specific ideal sense [*Sinn*] constructed out of a manifold of ideal meanings [*Bedeutungen*] which, taken together, constitute a whole, *sui generis*. If the literary work were to be an ideal object, however, it would be inconceivable for it to come into being at a given time and change in the course of its existence, as is actually the case.[5] In this respect the literary work differs radically from such ideal objectivities as, for example, a given triangle, the number five, the idea of a parallelogram, or, finally, the essence "redness." Thus both of the contrasted solutions of the problem seem to be untenable.

Is it possible that we have arrived at this pass only because we have falsely and unknowingly considered as a part, or a characteristic, of the literary work something which is in fact foreign to it? If a correction could be made, we could perhaps find a solution. And since the temporal origin of the literary work seems to be beyond any doubt, it may be reasonable to discard the view that ideal sentences constitute a part of the literary work and simply consider the literary work to be a real object. Stricter reflection, however, will show new difficulties, especially when, in concert with the psychologists, one denies

5. W. Conrad, who considers the literary work an ideal object, is not at all conscious of this difficulty. See "Der ästhetische Gegenstand," *Zeitschrift für Ästhetik und allgemeine Kunstwissenschaft*, Vols. III (1908) and IV (1909). Similarly, H. Conrad-Martius also seems to consider at least some literary works (or perhaps simply some literary characters) as ideal objects. See her "Realontologie," p. 163. On the other hand, one can think of de Saussure's well-known distinction between *langue* and *parole*, provided the concept of *langue* is defined sharply enough.

the existence of ideal concepts [6] and, in conjunction with this, claims that the latter also do not help the reader with the comprehension of the literary work. Let us be more specific.

§ 4. *Psychologistic conceptions and the problem of the identity of the literary work*

WHAT REMAINS of the literary work if one accepts both of the above assumptions? At first glance, nothing but a manifold of written (printed) characters (or, with a work read aloud, "word sounds"); closer examination will reveal not *one* but as many manifolds as there are copies of the given work. The elements and arrangements of the individual manifolds may be very similar to one another. If, however, nothing but this similarity were to unite the various copies of "one and the same" work (e.g., a novel), there would be no sufficient basis for regarding them as "copies" of this *one* novel. Therefore, one could not speak of "one and the same" literary work (e.g., *The Magic Mountain*) but would have to accept as many works as there are copies.

One could perhaps attempt to overcome this difficulty by claiming that these printed characters serve only as a means for communicating with or knowing the literary work itself; the latter would thus be nothing else but what the author had *experienced* during its creation.[7]

6. The second assumption is independent of the first. One can thus take the position that there are indeed ideal meaning units ("concepts") but that they are not part of the literary work. We shall later consider this possibility more thoroughly.

7. The view that the literary work is identical with the experiences of its author was frequently advocated during the heyday of psychologism (see, for example, R. M. Werner, *Lyrik und die Lyriker* [Hamburg and Leipzig, 1890]). However, we also find it in treatises that appeared much later. For instance, we read in Pierre Audiat's *La Biographie de l'oeuvre littéraire: Esquisse d'une méthode critique* (Paris, 1924): "The work is in its essence an act of our mental life; it is the drive of our entire past toward an uncertain future" (p. 40). "It represents a certain period in the writer's life, a period that one can measure with the precision of a watch; . . . To be realized, the work must endure; and, since it endures, it must necessarily change" (p. 39). In Polish literary criticism we also find characteristic examples of this conception of the literary work. In his treatise "O metodę estetycznego rozbioru dzieł literackich" (Toward a Method of Aesthetic Analysis of Literary Works), *Pamiętnik Literacki* (Lvov, 1923), E. Kucharski denies that language constitutes the material of the literary work and claims that this material can be found only in

If this view were correct, then in terms of the previous assumptions it would be impossible either to have direct intercourse with the work or to know it.[8] Can a manifold of meaningless[9] colored spots (or sounds)—since it is exclusively with them that one would have direct contact—enable us to comprehend someone else's experiences? No one would agree with this. One could answer by saying that, while the characters are in fact meaningless, in the sense that "ideal meaning" is a scientific

"living, continuously operative and active human consciousness" and, in particular, in "ideas" [*przedstawienia*]. The work does have a second existence, so to speak, in the reader's experiences; but the essential, original work inheres in the author's consciousness, as it were, and consists of "ideas." "Thus the content of poetry is that which lived in the poet at the moment of creation and which ought to live again in us in the perception of the work" (p. 15) (the reconstructed "content"). "The concept of literary character comprises all the ideas Mickiewicz had about the created character at the given moment in the poem" (p. 26). (At this point Kucharski is speaking of a given poem by Mickiewicz. The "character" should constitute an element of artistic form.) Likewise, the greatest Słowacki scholar in Poland, Juliusz Kleiner, speaks of "the work in the creator's mind," to which he contrasts "the work in the reader's mind." See his *Analiza dzieła* (The Analysis of the Work) (1914), *Charakter i przedmiot badań literackich* (The Character and Object of Literary Study) (1913), and *Treść i forma w poezji* (Content and Form in Poetry) (1923), three treatises that later appeared in the omnibus volume *Studia z zakresu literatury i filozofii* (Studies in Literature and Philosophy) (Warsaw, 1925). To be sure, Kleiner's final determination of the literary work as an object of literary study is somewhat different from what it is here; and, along with the various interesting observations that we may find in his works, we see that Kleiner, although he foresaw some of the difficulties connected with the psychologistic conception, never really managed to free himself from it. For we do find him saying: "The whole with which the investigation deals is not an individual object that is really given but the richest possible psychic whole that the contents of the text can evoke in any appropriately sensitive perceiving individual." Here the "contents of the text" means "all the *psychic elements* contained in it" and thus both the "content" as well as the "form" (italics mine). The whole determined in this manner is an ideal which ought to be the object of literary criticism. If one has to reach for it, however, it is only because the "essential" literary work which inheres "in the mind of the author" is not directly accessible to investigation. The study of this ideal should serve the purpose of reaching, in this roundabout way, the work in the mind of the author and clarifying it. Thus Kleiner's conception must also be included among the psychologistic ones.

8. Kleiner himself admits this, even though in his reflections he does not exclude ideal meanings from the literary work. But the "contents of the text" mean for him "all the psychic elements contained in it"; thus, according to Kleiner, meanings are either conceived as "psychic elements" or they do not belong to the contents of the text. We have to decide for the former, since at another point we read: "What is contained in a text is not only a system of meanings; it is a system of various stimuli" (*Studia*, p. 153).

9. They would have to be meaningless if their meaning were to be considered as nonexistent.

fiction, they are not simply colored spots. Thanks to habit or convention, they always "tie in" with our corresponding ideas, in which we imagine what the characters denote, i.e., in our case, the experiences of the author. In the process, we experience still other "psychic states" produced by these ideas.

This whole argument does not change our contention in any way. The reason is that everything that would be directly accessible to us—except for the perceived characters—would be only *our* ideas, thoughts, or, possibly, emotional states. No one would want to identify the concrete psychic contents experienced by us during the reading with the already long-gone experiences of the author. Thus, the work is either not directly comprehensible, or else it is identical with our experiences. Whatever the case, the attempt to identify the literary work with a manifold of the author's psychic experiences is quite absurd. The author's experiences cease to exist the moment the work created by him comes into existence.[10] There is likewise absolutely no means by which one could fix these experiences—by their very nature transitory—so that they could continue to exist after they had been experienced. Apart from that, it would be entirely incomprehensible why we should not be inclined to include in Reymont's novel *The Peasants* his experiences of a toothache he might have had in the course of writing it, while, at the same time, we feel justified in considering as part of the novel the desires of a character, Jagusia Boryna, which the author himself certainly did not, and could not, experience.

Yet if we exclude the experiences of the author from the work he creates, then, according to these assumptions, all that remains of the work are the individual printed characters on paper. We would then have to accept the already indicated consequence that, for example, there is not one, single *Divine Comedy* but any number of *Divine Comedies* of Dante and that the number varies according to the number of copies extant at a given time. Moreover, most of the opinions concerning the literary work that until now have been considered correct would have to be quite false, even senseless, while other, entirely absurd statements, e.g., that individual literary works differ ac-

---

10. A few weeks after making this observation in my university lectures in the summer semester of 1927, I found a similar assertion in Vol. II of Władysław Witwicki's *Psychologia* (Lvov, 1930). Unfortunately, in his subsequent observations regarding the literary work, Witwicki does not draw the necessary conclusions. The very fact that he deals with the literary work in a textbook on psychology is sufficiently revealing.

cording to chemical composition, or that they are influenced by sunlight, would have to be true.

But the view that the literary work is nothing but a manifold of experiences felt by the reader during the reading is also altogether false and its consequences absurd. For there would then have to be very many different *Hamlets*. The degree to which they would have to differ is best shown by the fact that differences in the experiences of individual readers stem not only from the purely accidental but from deep, underlying reasons, such as a given reader's cultural level, the type of individuality he has, the general cultural atmosphere of the time and its religious views, system of values, and so on. To the extent that this is possible, every new reading would produce an entirely new work.[11] In addition, one would again have to hold as true various false assertions. Thus, e.g., Thomas Mann's *The Magic Mountain* could not exist as a uniform whole, since it is quite likely that there is no person who could read this novel in one sitting, without a pause. Hence, only individual, disconnected "pieces" of the work would remain, and it would be hard to understand why they should be parts of one and the same work. Conversely, various opinions on particular literary works of art would have to be false or preposterous. For example, what would it mean to say that the *Iliad* is written "in hexameter"? Can any experience or psychic state be "written in hexameter" or have the form of a sonnet? These are absurdities, and we mention them only to show what consequences one must arrive at if, for once, one takes the psychologistic conception of the literary work seriously and is not satisfied with vague generalities.[12] It may indeed be questioned whether there are, at all, literary works that exist for themselves or whether they are, in any sense, "mere fictions"; one may not, however, foist upon the literary work various objects which are altogether foreign to it and which we never have in mind when we speak of individual literary works and make judgments about them. When applied to a particular work, these

11. Kleiner also sees this consequence (see *Studia*, p. 151), and it leads him, among other things, to the above determination of the literary work.

12. Herder already saw this correctly in *Kalligone* (*Werke*, Vol. XXII [Leipzig, 1800]): "What is symbolic in sounds or even in letters is, in the case of a language known to us, beyond our soul. This soul creates and forms out of words its own world, ideas, images, and essential forms, which are, however, totally foreign to the words." If we are to understand the correctness and importance of this assertion, however, we must construct a positive theory of the essence and mode of existence of meaning units.

judgments (comprising the psychologistic conception of the literary work) turn out to be simply absurd.

If we wish to avoid this absurdity and adhere to our assertion that each literary work is something that in itself is one and identical,[13] it appears that we must consider the stratum of meaningful words and sentences a component part of the literary work. If the latter are ideal objectivities, however, the problem of the mode of existence of the literary work returns in all its acuteness. Yet a possible way out does open up; we do not wish to leave it unnoticed, if only because it can be used to challenge the line of argument presented above.

§ 5. *The literary work as an "imaginational object"*

THE POSSIBLE OBJECTION is the following: the difficulties described in the preceding sections stem solely from a false interpretation of that point of view which sees the literary work of art as a manifold [of psychic facts] experienced by the author during the creation of the work. The concern, in effect, is not at all with the stream of experiences, i.e., with the *experiencing* of something, but with what these subjective experiences *refer to,* that is, with the *objects* of the author's thoughts and ideas. These objects—i.e., certain persons and things whose fates are portrayed in the work—constitute what is essential in the structure of the literary work. It is these objects that radically differentiate any two literary works, and without them any such work would be impossible. They are at the same time entirely different from the printed characters and the word sounds and also from the sentences themselves—however these may be understood. On the other hand, they are not something ideal but are, as one may put it, forms of the author's free fancy, his pure

---

13. Since we are laying so much stress on the identity of the literary work, we feel ourselves to be entirely in accord with M. Scheler when he says: "A work of spiritual culture can simultaneously be apprehended by any number of people and felt and enjoyed in its value." See "Der Formalismus in der Ethik und materiale Wertethik," *Jahrbuch für Philosophie und phänomenologische Forschung,* I (1913), 496. [English translation by Manfred S. Frings and Roger L. Funk, *Formalism in Ethics and Non-Formal Ethics of Value: A New Attempt toward the Foundation of an Ethical Personalism* (Evanston, Ill.: Northwestern University Press, 1973).]

"imaginational objects," which are entirely dependent on his will and *eo ipso* not to be separated from the subjective experiences creating them. As such they must be considered to be something psychic. It would thus be quite understandable how a literary work—subject as it is to the author's *sic iubeo*—could originate in time, undergo changes of one kind or another, and disappear. As opposed to the variety of individual "copies" or "readings," the unity and the uniqueness of the literary work would be assured by virtue of the identity of these "imaginational objects." Thus, in order to secure uniqueness and identity for the literary work, one would not have to reach for such questionable hypotheses about the ideality of sentence meanings.

Nevertheless, even this conception—at least in the formulation just given, and with its attendant assumptions—is untenable. It ignores, above all, the main difficulty, which appears as a result of the exclusion of ideal meaning units from the structure of the literary work and the denial of their existence. It is undoubtedly true that the objects represented in the literary work constitute an important and indispensable element of the work. As soon as we limit them to "imaginational objects," however (and this, after all, is still quite ambiguous), in the sense that they are components of the psychic life of the author, and if simultaneously we are obliged to detach them in some way from this concrete life, there arises a problem that is insoluble, given the stated assumptions: how is it possible to reach these "imaginational objects" as identical entities and to guarantee their identity? For it is not as if the represented objects founded the identity of the work; on the contrary, these very objects must be founded in its identity. According to the assumptions of the viewpoint we are examining, there are indeed only two basic domains of existing objects: physical-material things and psychic individuals, together with their experiences and states of mind. Objects represented in the literary work cannot be included in either of these two spheres of existence: they do not belong in the psychic sphere since—though they are only called "imaginational objects" or "objects of phantasy"—they are at the same time contrasted with subjective experiences and are thereby in fact removed from the sphere of psychic objects.[14] This removal would be indispensable if, as identical units, they, in contrast to

14. If one were to submerge onself in the sphere of experiences, then the literary work would have to be identical with a manifold of experiences of author (or reader), and one would again return to the untenable situation discussed above.

the manifold of individual psychic experiences, were to found the identity of the literary work. Nor can they [the objects] be included among physical objects, since they are supposed to be "merely imagined objects," basically a nothing. Indeed, one could claim, on the basis of superficial reflection, that, in the case of "historical" dramas, novels, and the like, represented objects are identical with the persons, things, and their fates that once really existed. On closer inspection, however, this identity cannot be demonstrated, nor can the argument be applied to all literary works. The reason is that there are many works which represent wholly fictional objects and are not "historical" in any sense. What speaks most convincingly against this alleged identity is the fact that one can justifiably compare objects so represented (e.g., Julius Caesar in Shakespeare's play) with corresponding real objects and demonstrate material differences between them. Yet if every represented object (whether "historical" or not) differs radically from every real one, and if it is dependent in its being and essence only on the appertaining manifolds of experience of the author, then according to these assumptions it would not only be impossible to find a place, so to speak, where they would be independent, but at the same time their own identity and uniqueness would require founding. Since they are to be conceived within subjective experiences and, as it were, carried by them, and since, according to these assumptions, there is no approach other than through the author's subjective experiences, their identity must be based solely on these experiences. These experiences are individual units, however, differing qualitatively among each other, and therefore everything constituting a part of any one of them, or drawing the source [of its existence] solely from them, must be as individual as the experience itself and must differ from everything that has its source in other experiences or is a component of them. Thus it would not only be impossible for the reader to grasp the "imaginational objectivity" conceived by the author, but it would also be impossible for the author repeatedly to imagine the same object. How could one then, according to these assumptions, still speak, e.g., of one and the same Julius Caesar as a character represented in a Shakespearean drama?

Thus, this attempt to save the unity and identity of the literary work also fails. There remains only one way out of this difficult situation, namely, to admit the existence of *ideal* meaning units and yet not incorporate them into the literary work—so as to avoid the difficulties presented above—but invoke their aid only for the purpose of securing the identity and unity of the literary work. How this idea is to be implemented will be seen in the course of our investigation. If this attempt were also to fail, however, and if at the same time it became apparent that one can assume only two spheres of objects—those of real and ideal objects—then the problem of the literary work's mode of existence and its identity would not admit a positive solution, and one would have to deny the existence of the literary work altogether.

The present deliberations not only cast light upon the difficulties with which a tenable literary theory has to contend; they likewise demonstrate how unclear and uncertain our knowledge is concerning the essence of the literary work. We do not know which elements are to be included in it. The meaning units of sentences? Or the represented objects? Or perhaps some elements not yet touched upon? Or, finally, a manifold of these? We are also altogether unclear up to this moment as to the specific properties of the elements that may eventually be considered. And if a number of them were to partake in the structure of the literary work, the manner in which they combine into *one* literary work is also not understood at this time. But the mode of its existence and the basis of its identity are also dependent on the essential structure of the literary work. If the problems discussed above are to be resolved, it is necessary, for the time being, that they be put aside while we turn our attention directly to, and fundamentally analyze the structure of, the literary work as it stands before us in a series of concrete examples. We will thus be able to move from these vague generalizations, with which, for the present, we have had to content ourselves, to concrete situations. To this end, everything that impedes our view must be removed at the outset. In particular, we must determine what undoubtedly does *not* belong to the literary work, regardless of what the literary work, itself, is. In this respect the results of the discussion thus far can be essentially helpful.

2 / Elimination of Factors Extraneous to the Structure of the Literary Work

§ 6. *Closer delimitation of the topic*

FIRST OF ALL, we shall limit the scope of objects of our study and rule out all questions that can be broached successfully only after the essential nature of the literary work has been apprehended.

Here we shall deal exclusively with the finished literary work. We shall consider a literary work "finished" when all the sentences and individual words that appear in it have been unequivocally determined and fixed in their meaning, their word sounds, and their over-all pattern. On the other hand, the work's completeness will not be essentially affected for us by whether it is actually written down or whether it is expressed orally, provided that, in the event of repeated recitation, it shall occur without essential changes.[1] We thus place the formation phase of the literary work itself, as well as all questions dealing with artistic creation, beyond the scope of our consideration. We do this, not out of any unfounded arbitrariness, but because we see the perennial confusion of two fields of investigation: that of the ontology of the literary work and that of the psychology of artistic or literary creativity. This is a source of innumerable misconstructions of the problem, as well as a source of artificial problems, and consequently we wish to avoid it. Only where the structure of the literary work itself refers to acts of consciousness and manifolds of acts are we obliged to concern ourselves with

1. Naturally, we will be able to show only much later which changes are "essential" and which are not.

[20]

them, and then only to the extent that this is necessary for elucidating the essence of the work. Even then, however, an analysis of these acts of consciousness will differ from a psychology of artistic creativity, and these acts of consciousness should not be confused with the literary work itself.

Furthermore, all questions dealing with the cognition of the literary work, its particular modes and limits, shall remain beyond the pale of our study. Hence such questions as: In which acts of consciousness is cognition of a literary work of art attained? Which conditions must be met by the subject if the literary work is to be perceived as one and the same by many perceiving subjects? Which criteria allow us to differentiate the "objective" cognition of a literary work from false subjective opinions? Is there ultimately an objective cognition of the literary work? And so on. These are all questions dealing with the *possibility* of a "science of literature." As far as we know, these problems have hardly been fully acknowledged, let alone correctly formulated. Yet we cannot approach them so long as there reigns such chaos and conflict of opinions as is currently the case.[2]

We do not intend, moreover, to deal in detail with the various attitudes that the reader may possibly take toward the literary work. We will have to fall back on the subjective attitude in which objects of this sort are directly given only when it is indispensable for understanding the literary work, for elucidating it as an aesthetic object.

Finally, we shall put aside all general questions dealing with the nature of the *value* of a work of art, and in particular of a literary work of art. Indeed, we shall find that the latter has values and flaws that constitute a peculiarly qualified total value of the whole literary work of art. However, the question of what constitutes the nature of this value must remain beyond the scope of our study, since an answer to it assumes, on the one hand, a solution to the problem of value in general[3] and, on the

2. My book, *O poznawaniu dzieła literackiego* (The Cognition of the Literary Work), which first appeared in Polish (Lvov, 1937), is devoted to this problem. [English translation of the German edition by Ruth Ann Crowley and Kenneth R. Olson, *The Cognition of the Literary Work of Art* (Evanston, Ill.: Northwestern University Press, 1973).]

3. Despite some significant contributions in the past twenty years, especially those of Max Scheler, devoted to the solution of the problem of value, I do not believe that one can consider them complete and irreproachable. Investigations dealing with the individual spheres of value (e.g., ethical, aesthetic, and so on) are in an even less satisfactory state. See, e.g., C. Lalo, *L'Art et la morale* (Paris, 1925).

other, an understanding of the structure of the literary work. For this very reason, our consideration of the literary work will disregard altogether the issue of whether the works we are dealing with have positive value or are worthless.

§ 7. *What does not belong to the literary work?*

THE ARGUMENTS thus far permit us to assume what, in our opinion, is to be excluded from the structure of the literary work as an element that is by its very nature foreign to it. Let us make this explicit.

1. First of all, the author, with all his vicissitudes, experiences, and psychic states, remains completely outside the literary work. In particular, however, the experiences of the author during the creation of the work do not constitute any part of the created work. It may happen—and one should not dispute this—that there are various close relations between the work and the psychic life and individuality of the author. The genesis of the literary work in particular may be conditioned by the author's determinate experiences, and it may be that the whole structure of the work and its individual qualities are functionally dependent on the psychic qualities of the author, his talent, and the type of his "world of ideas" and his feelings, and that the work thus carries the more or less pronounced traces of his total personality and in this way "expresses" it. But all these facts in no way change the primary and yet frequently unappreciated fact that the author and his work constitute two heterogeneous objects which, already on the basis of their radical heterogeneity, must be fully differentiated. Only the establishment of this fact will allow us to expose correctly the manifold relations and dependencies existing between them.

Among the investigators who have concerned themselves with the essential nature of the work, it would indeed be hard to find one who consciously and expressly would wish to claim the contrary.[4] In fact, however, the distinction between the two objects has never been clearly made, and the results are the varied and basically absurd confusions that we have indicated above. It is these absurdities that first compelled us to the assertions ex-

4. That this, too, is possible is seen, for instance, in the already cited book of Pierre Audiat, *La Biographie de l'oeuvre littéraire: Esquisse d'une méthode critique* (Paris, 1924).

pressed; the subsequent course of our analyses will substantiate these positions. We should not assume, on the other hand, that the literary work of art is *eo ipso* an ontically autonomous object. The rainbow, too, is not part of a perceiving person (and vice versa), and yet one cannot ascribe any ontic autonomy to it. Only our subsequent investigations will show how this question is to be answered in the case of a literary work. But if it is to be answered at all, in whatever manner, the distinction can be attained only on the basis of an insight into the essential structure of the literary work and not on the basis of inherited opinions and theories which allow its essential nature to remain in complete darkness.

2. Likewise, the attributes, experiences, or psychic states of the reader do not belong to the structure of the work. This assertion seems manifestly banal, and yet the suggestions of positivistic psychologism are still alive among literary scholars, art theorists, and aestheticians.[5] To convince ourselves of the correctness of this, we need only take a random look to find the ever recurring talk about "ideas," "sensations," and "feelings" whenever works of art or literary works are at issue. Psychologistic tendencies are most evident when the issue is one of beauty or, in general, the artistic value of a work. In this case the general tendency to reduce all value to something subjective is strengthened all the more, on the one hand by the particular attitude one assumes while reading a literary work of art, on the other hand by a consideration of the subjective conditions that must be met if a value is—to use a Heideggerian term—only "revealed" for the conscious subject but is not meant to be objectively apprehended by him.

Instead of entering into living spiritual intercourse with the work of art (and in particular with the literary work), instead of

5. This "still" applied to the situation before 1930. However, it appears to me that the situation is not essentially different in 1960, if we are dealing with the nonphenomenologically oriented investigators. One only needs to look into André Lurçat's book *Formes, compositions et lois d'harmonie: Eléments d'une science de l'esthétique architecturale* (Paris, 1929) to establish that all aesthetically valuable elements of the work of art are considered to be "impressions" of the perceiver. Positivistic tendencies and the resulting psychologistic reinterpretation of all qualitatively determinate objectivities have been essentially strengthened since 1930, due primarily to the propagation of Vienna positivism. The culmination of this tendency came in the thirties; but even now, especially in Anglo-Saxon countries, positivistic tendencies are all too strong, and among wide, philosophically unsophisticated circles they pass for the only "scientific" standpoint.

submitting to it in direct perception (which is not at all to be identified with theoretical objective apprehension!), instead of enjoying it in characteristic self-forgetfulness and simply evaluating it in this enjoyment without objectifying value,[6] the reader often uses the literary work of art as an external stimulus for evoking, within himself, feelings and other psychic states he considers valuable, and he allows the work of art to come into view only to the extent that it is indispensable for the performance of this service. He gives himself over to his experiences, he luxuriates in them; and the deeper, stronger, and richer his own states of mind (above all, the feelings that are released and yet at the same time only phantasied), the more they allow him to "forget" everything else (including the work of art and its inherent value), the higher is the value he is inclined to place on the given work of art. But in fact he does not value the work for its inherent value since, due to his attitude, this is not at all perceived but rather is concealed by the profusion of his subjective feelings. He considers it "valuable" only because it is a means of evoking pleasurable experiences.[7]

This attitude toward the work of art—especially the musical work—is encountered very frequently. Small wonder, then, that what is essential and valuable in the literary work of art is considered to be what develops in the reader under the influence of the reading. For such a reader, what is truly valuable lies in the particular qualities and in the profusion of feelings released by the poetry, while the value of the work of art itself is never made apparent. Thus the subjectivistic conception of artistic value is a result of defective standards in communing with the work of art.

It is true that the psychologistic subjectivization of aesthetic values, as we have already mentioned, is encouraged by a factor whose factual existence, in conjunction with a generally held, but at the very least doubtful, epistemological conviction, compels this subjectification. For it is indubitable that aesthetic and other values are given to us only when a determinate attitude—in our case, an aesthetic one—is assumed by the conscious subject. In contrast to the strong emotion of the unsophisticated reader, the aesthetic attitude certainly shows a certain contem-

6. See E. Husserl, *Ideen zu einer reinen Phänomenologie* (Halle, 1913), pp. 66 ff. [English translation by W. R. Boyce Gibson, *Ideas: General Introduction to Pure Phenomenology* (New York: Macmillan, 1931).]

7. See M. Geiger's very noteworthy arguments in "Vom Dilettantismus im künstlerischen Erleben," *Zugänge zur Ästhetik* (Leipzig, 1928).

plative inner peace, an immersion in the work itself, that does not permit us to concern ourselves with our own experiences. This contemplative calm, however, which can coexist quite well with the highest rapture, does not signify cold or, more exactly, altogether neutral, purely analytic behavior, to which all feeling is alien and which characterizes a purely theoretical and rational apprehension of the object. As a result of such an analytical stance the elements of the work which are value qualities do not achieve phenomenal visibility. Hence it is possible for the literary work of art to be directly given in various ways: once in an aesthetic attitude—in its value-quality elements—and again in a purely theoretical consideration, without the latter, and, finally, in a thematically objectified apprehension of the values constituted in the value-quality elements—as carriers of these aesthetic values. The above-mentioned epistemological bias intervenes here. It says that only that is "objective" which is *always* given as a property of an object for *every* knowing subject, with the total passivity of the latter and under any subjective (or objective) conditions. One thus considers the purely theoretical, rational, cognitive method as the one which, at least in principle, fulfills these conditions. In those instances in which the givenness of an objectivity requires special attitudes and operations on the part of the subject if it is to be realized at all, in which a change of attitude carries with it a change in the scope of what is given, this given is *eo ipso* considered "merely subjective" and "in reality" nonexistent. Without further deliberation, this "subjective" is then construed as something psychic, in the sense of being a component of psychic existence; and in this way one arrives at, among other things, a psychologistic theory of value.

It would take us too far to demonstrate in detail the fallacy of the above epistemological point of view. It should suffice if we point it out as a source of psychologistic subjectivization of value and thereby also indicate how the psychologists' seemingly self-evident argumentation conceals uncontrolled and, at the very least, questionable epistemological assumptions.

3. Finally, the whole sphere of *objects* and *states of affairs* which constitutes, as the case may be, the model of the objects and states of affairs "appearing" in the work must be excluded from the structure of the literary work of art. If, for example, the action of Sienkiewicz's *Quo Vadis* takes place "in Rome," Rome itself—the real capital of the Roman Empire—does not belong to the given work. In connection with this, the question of how we are to understand the expression that the action "takes place

in Rome" and how the real model is in a certain sense still visible, despite this exclusion from the literary work, is a special problem with which we will be able to deal only much later.

With the subject of our investigation narrowed in this manner and a series of objectivities excluded from the structure of the literary work, we can now turn to an analysis of the work itself.

PART II

The Structure
of the Literary Work

3 / The Basic Structure of the Literary Work

§ 8.   *The literary work as a stratified formation*

LET US FIRST OF ALL sketch the basic structure of the literary work and thus establish the main features of our conception of its essence.

The essential structure of the literary work inheres, in our opinion, in the fact that it is a formation constructed of several heterogeneous strata.[1] The individual strata differ from one another (1) by their characteristic material, from the peculiarity of which stem the particular qualities of each stratum, and (2) by the role which each stratum plays with respect to both the other strata and the structure of the whole work. Despite the diversity of the material of the individual strata, the literary work is not a loose bundle of fortuitously juxtaposed elements but an organic structure whose uniformity is grounded precisely in the unique character of the individual strata. There exists among them a distinct stratum, namely, the stratum of meaning units, which provides the structural framework for the whole work. By its very essence it requires all the other strata and determines them in such a way that they have their ontic basis in it and are dependent in their content on its qualities. As elements of the literary work they are thus inseparable from this central stratum.[2]

The diversity of the material and the roles (or functions) of

1. The meaning of the figurative expression "stratum" will become clearer in the course of our analyses.
2. This is not to say, however, that the stratum of meaning units plays the central role in the aesthetic apperception of the literary work of art.

the individual strata makes the whole work, not a monotonic formation, but one that by its nature has a polyphonic character.
That is to say, in consequence of the unique character of the individual strata, each of them is visible in its own way within the
whole and brings something particular into the over-all character
of the whole without impairing its phenomenal unity. In particular, each of these strata has its own set of properties which contribute to the constitution of specific aesthetic value qualities.
There thus arises a manifold of aesthetic value qualities in which
a polyphonic yet uniform value quality of the whole is constituted.

Usually one distinguishes various genres of literary works of
art. If we are to speak of "genres" at all, however, the possibility
of their various changes and modifications must come from the
essence of the literary work in general.[3] It would also have to be
shown that, although a certain number and selection of strata
are indispensable in each literary work, the essential structure of
these strata allows various and not always necessary roles for
each of them, as well as the appearance of new strata that are
not present in every literary work. Which, then, are the strata
that are necessary for every literary work if its internal unity and
basic character are to be preserved? They are—and we already
anticipate the final result of our investigation—the following:
(1) the stratum of *word sounds* and the *phonetic formations* of
higher order built on them; (2) the stratum of *meaning units* of
various orders; (3) the stratum of manifold schematized *aspects*
and aspect continua and series, and, finally, (4) the stratum of
represented objectivities and their vicissitudes. Subsequent analyses will show that this last stratum is, so to speak, "two-sided":
on the one hand, the "side" of the representing intentional sentence correlates (in particular the states of affairs), on the other,
the "side" of objects and their vicissitudes achieving representation in these sentence correlates. If, in spite of this, we speak of
one stratum, it is for important reasons, which we shall discuss
later. The questions of whether the stratum of "ideas" expressed
in a work must appear in every work and what the expression
"ideas" means here are mentioned for the present only as problems awaiting eventual solution.

In each of the strata, aesthetic value qualities are constituted

3. In the more precise terminology of my "Essentiale Fragen," *Jahrbuch für Philosophie und phänomenologische Forschung*, VII (1925),
125–304 (also Halle, 1925), this would read "from the content of the
general idea of the literary work."

which are characteristic of the respective stratum. In connection with this, the question may be raised whether it would not be necessary to distinguish yet another special stratum of the literary work, one which would, so to speak, "cut across" the above-mentioned strata and have the foundation of its constitution in them—a stratum of aesthetic value qualities and the polyphony that is constituted in them. This can be determined, however, only on the basis of an analysis of the individual strata. In consequence, the question of what the proper object of the aesthetic attitude is in the total structure of the literary work must also be deferred for later consideration.

The many-layered nature of the structure does not exhaust the peculiar essence of the literary work. It will still be necessary to discover what structural element causes every literary work to have a "beginning" and an "end" and allows it to "unfold" in the course of a reading in its specific length from beginning to end.

The establishment of the stratified polyphonic structure of the literary work is basically trivial. But trivial though it is, none of the authors known to me has seen clearly that in it lies the essential basic structure of the literary work.[4] In the practice of

---

4. Juliusz Kleiner distinguished on two different occasions between the various "strata" or "spheres" of the literary work: (1) in the treatise *Treść i forma w poezji* (Content and Form in Poetry) and (2) in the article *Charakter i przedmiot badań literackich* (The Character and the Object of Literary Study), both in *Studia z zakresu literatury i filozofii* (Studies in Literature and Philosophy) (Warsaw, 1925). In the first instance, the concern is not with the strata of the finished literary work but rather with individual phases of its formations, which, to be sure, also become apparent in the work itself. These individual "strata" are the following: (*a*) the state of strong psychic arousal which insists on "expression"; (*b*) any form, situation, or reflection which satisfies this yearning for expression and gives a fixed determinacy to these psychic contents; (*c*) a structuring of what is contained in (*b*), which gives a detailed plan and a concrete determinacy to the genre of the given work; and, finally, (*d*) an altogether distinctive system of ideas and a system of words equivalent to it.

Unfortunately, Kleiner does not tell us how these individual "strata" appear in the finished literary work. However interesting these arguments may be, they do not pertain to what we have in mind when we speak of the "strata" of the literary work. This follows from the fact that we distinguish these strata only in the finished literary work. It is also more than doubtful whether our strata correspond to the individual phases of formation of the literary work as distinguished by Kleiner.

In the second of the treatises mentioned, Kleiner deals with the finished work and believes that he can see in the "content of the text" a "separate sphere of human reality." In this sphere he distinguishes four more "spheres": "This separate reality contains four regions, four spheres: (1) the totality of the verbal material (individualization and organization of the material), (2) the cognitive grasp and recomposition

literary criticism, i.e., in the discussion of individual works, in the distinguishing of their various types, in the contrasting of various literary movements and schools, etc., the usual practice has been to contrast the individual elements of the literary work and in individual instances point out their properties. But it has never been noticed that what is involved are heterogeneous strata which are mutually conditioned and are joined together by

---

of the content, (3) the system of ideas [przedstawien] analogous to the 'reality of life' but isolated from it and imposed in a specific way upon the consciousness, and (4) spiritual strength and skill manifesting itself in creation and formation" (Charakter, p. 173). It is not clear from his later arguments whether these four spheres are elements of the text itself or phenomena of psychic resonance arising in the mind of the reader under the influence of the text being read. The explanation given above, that the content of the text contains "all psychic elements," also compounds the confusion. Finally, Kleiner believes that distinguishing the individual "spheres" is an altogether secondary matter (see Charakter, p. 280). The relation of our conception to Kleiner's will become clear only in the course of our investigation. For the moment we may simply note that only the first and third "spheres" of Kleiner's scheme could correspond to the various strata we have differentiated, provided, of course, that his analysis were clearly stated and freed from psychologistic concepts. But the juxtaposition of these "spheres" with spheres (2) and (4) shows that by "sphere" Kleiner understood something quite different from what we understand by "a stratum of the literary work."

As regards other authors, my conception is closest to that of W. Conrad, as set forth in his treatise "Der ästhetische Gegenstand," Zeitschrift für Ästhetik und allgemeine Kunstwissenschaft, Vols. III (1908) and IV (1909). Conrad also distinguishes four different "sides," as he calls them, of the literary work: the phonetic sign, the meaning, the intended object, and the expression (or expressed object). At another point in this treatise he gives in fact only three essential "moments" of the literary work: symbol, meaning, and object (p. 489). At any rate, he excludes from the literary work the stratum of aspects (which he there calls "Vorstellungsbilder"). Despite this kinship, our conception of the literary work differs from Conrad's on many points, especially as regards the results of specific analyses. It is impossible to comment here on all the individual points or to conduct a general discussion [on his theory]. I would like to point out only the following: (1) Conrad does not see that the polyphony of the heterogeneous strata is essential for the literary work. He was quite unaware of the existence of this polyphony. His distinguishing the various "sides" of the work, though correct in principle, does not go deep enough to place in a proper light the basic structure of the literary work, with its peculiar design and unity. (2) His conception of the "aesthetic object" as an ideal object is not tenable, as will be seen from the final findings of this present book. Conrad is here too much under the influence of Husserl's position in the Logical Investigations to grasp the peculiar mode of existence of the literary work. But he, too, feels that a difference does exist between a literary work and, for example, a mathematical objectivity, though his arguments regarding this question are still quite primitive. And no wonder. Without existential-ontological investigations, which were then barely possible, the problem of the mode of existence of the literary work cannot be attacked. Nevertheless, I consider Conrad's work an important beginning.

manifold connections; nor has anyone ever clearly distinguished them in their general structure and shown the connection between them which arises from this structure. Only a detailed analysis of both the individual strata and the kind of connection arising from them can disclose the peculiarity of the structure of the literary work. It can also provide the solid foundation for solving the special literary and literary-aesthetic problems with which until now one has contended in vain. For it is precisely as a result of the failure to consider the stratified nature of the literary work that one fails to attain clarity in the treatment of various problems. Thus, for example, the much-discussed problem of "form" and "content" (or *Gestalt* and *Gehalt*) [5] of the literary work cannot be put correctly at all without taking into account its stratified structure, since, prior to the differentiation, all the necessary terms are ambiguous and unstable. In particular, every attempt to solve the problem of the form of the literary work of art must fail as long as one constantly considers only one stratum and disregards the others, since in doing so one overlooks the fact that the form of the work arises from the formal elements of the individual strata and their concurrent action. In conjunction with this, the problem of what constitutes the "material" of the literary work of art cannot be solved without taking our findings into account. Even the problem of "literary genres," mentioned above, presupposes an understanding of the stratified structure of the literary work. Our first task, therefore, is to clarify this matter.

5. See O. Walzel, *Gehalt und Gestalt im Kunstwerk des Dichters* (Berlin, 1923), p. 192. For that matter, the words "form" and "content" are also inordinately ambiguous, which caused Walzel to use, along with the traditional expressions, the words "*Gehalt*" and "*Gestalt*." A detailed analysis of Walzel's works shows, however, that he is still subject to various ambiguities in the use of these terms. As I have shown in my book *Der Streit um die Existenz der Welt* (3 vols.; Tübingen, 1964–65) (which first appeared in Polish as *Spór o istnienia świata* [2 vols.; Cracow, 1947–48]), one can distinguish nine different, though usually confused, concepts of "form" or "content." In a special paper "Über 'Form' und 'Inhalt' im literarischen Kunstwerk," which appeared in the second volume of my *Studia z estetyki* (Studies in Aesthetics) (Warsaw, 1957–58), and in *Erlebnis, Kunstwerk und Wert: Vorträge zur Ästhetik 1937–67* (Tübingen, 1969), I have shown the tangled situations that result from the usage of these various concepts of form and content in the literary work of art.

4 / The Stratum of Linguistic Sound Formations

§ 9. *Single words and word sounds*

IT IS AN OLD PROBLEM whether language is an essential element of the literary work of art. It has frequently been answered, both positively and negatively. We should like to discuss this problem in the light of those examples which leave us no doubt that what we are dealing with are works of art. On the basis of these, we come to the conclusion that the stratum of language actually does belong to the structure of the literary work taken in this sense. In each of the examples we choose, we first come upon words, sentences, and clusters of sentences. But this simple and obviously purely factual assertion leaves open various questions which must be answered before we can determine its exact sense and importance. The first question is: in what sense of the term does "language" belong to the literary work? Second, is it—as some investigators hold [1]—perhaps indispensable, but still only a *means* which merely allows an approach to the literary work, or is it a much more essential constituent of the work itself, and in particular a constituent which plays an essential role in the work qua work of art? Let us consider these questions in turn.

"Language" may first of all signify a physiologically conditioned psychic function, either as speech with someone else or as

---

1. See, for example, E. Kucharski, "O metodę estetycznego rozbioru dzieł literackich" (Toward a Method of Aesthetic Analysis of Literary Works), *Pamiętnik Literacki* (Lvov, 1923).

so-called internal speech with oneself.[2] It is clear that "language" in this sense does not come under our consideration. But also "language" in the sense in which one speaks of "the English language" must be excluded here. The only issue of concern to us is that in every literary work there appear linguistic formations— words, sentences, sentence complexes. What are they? That is the first question.

In each of these formations one must distinguish two different sides or components: on the one hand, a determinate *phonic material*,[3] which is differentiated in manifold ways and variously ordered, and, on the other, the *meaning* that is "bound up" with it. These components appear in every linguistic formation, regardless of the function it performs, whether in verbal intercourse between psychic individuals or, for example, in a literary work. Thus, at the outset one must examine these two components in themselves and in their interrelation.

The simplest—if not the original—linguistic formation is the single word.[4] We find in it, on the one hand, the word sound and, on the other, its meaning. In particular, a given phonic material becomes a word sound only because it has a more or less determinate "meaning." It fulfills the function of carrying a meaning

2. The distinction between *Sprechen* and *Reden* that is made by H. Ammann (see *Die menschliche Rede*, 2 vols. [Lahr i.B., 1925–28], I, 38 ff.) does not come into play here.

3. The term "phonic material" [*Lautmaterial*] is indeed still ambiguous. See the analyses below.

4. Here we have primarily the "spoken" word in mind. However, there are also "written" and "printed" words. One can, therefore, speak of a "written" word in a twofold sense: (1) as of an individual real sign formation, arising, continuing, and ceasing to exist in time, which performs the particular function of a proxy for the spoken word. Both its individuality and its reality are irrelevant for this function. In connection with this, we speak of the written word in a second, intrinsic sense (2), by which we understand a certain vague type of Gestalt quality which is concretized in a real sign when the latter functions as a "word." Since the written word in the first sense does not belong to the literary work at all, and since it belongs in the second sense only when we are dealing with written (or printed) and visually read works, we will be obliged to deal with the written word in the second sense only later (see Chap. 14).

Conrad's claim that only the word sound and not the visual sign belongs to the essence of the word (see "Der ästhetische Gegenstand," *Zeitschrift für Ästhetik und allgemeine Kunstwissenschaft*, III [1908], 479) seems to be, at the very least, a dubious one. Conrad is correct, however, in that the word sound belongs primarily to the word. Otherwise, he does not differentiate the word sound, in the sense that we take it, from the concrete phonic material.

and eventually transmitting it in the intellectual exchange between conscious subjects. Even the demarcation of phonic material into a discrete tonal whole is disclosed through the exercise
of this function.[5] But, as we shall see, the concrete tonal whole,
or the concrete phonic material, is not the same thing as the
"word sound." As far as the constitution of the word sound is
concerned, the strictly identical[6] meaning bound to it by repeated usage also contributes essentially, but in a different way.

We are correct in saying that it is "the same" word (e.g.,
"house") which is spoken a number of times, for instance, in a
high and sharp tone, and again in a low and soft one. In saying
this, we also take into consideration the meaning that is identically intended in the two instances, but at the same time we believe we are apprehending the sameness of the word also with
respect to its word sound, which is one and the same even though
the concrete phonic material is not only individually new in each
case but also different in various respects (e.g., in intonation,
quality of timbre, strength of voice, etc.). The question arises as
to what this one and the same "word sound" really is and what
conditions the fact that it is given to us in the articulation of a
word. With regard to the first question, someone may venture the
opinion that the word sound is nothing but a certain selection
and ordering of parts chosen from the concrete phonic material,
which parts repeat themselves in many different phonic wholes
and thus give the appearance of reality to the various individual
phonic materials. As a corollary, one would have to admit that
during the apprehension of the phonic material a selection is in
force: some parts and features of the phonic material heard at a
particular time would be ignored as if they were totally nonexistent, while others would be especially noticed and selected;
they would come to the fore and, so to speak, take the place of
the total phonic material.[7]

We consider this view to be false. When we hear a certain
word, what we are prepared for is not certain specially selected
parts or features of the concrete phonic material, which we then

5. As far as I know, Henri Bergson, in his *Matière et mémoire* (Paris,
1896), was the first to point out this fact.
6. Despite this identity, certain changes can occur in the contents of
one and the same meaning; see below, § § 16 and 17.
7. A few months after the appearance of this book (in the beginning
of December, 1930) K. Bühler published a paper entitled "Phonetik und
Phonologie," *Travaux du Cercle linguistique de Prague* (1931), in which
he treats analogous problems. See also his "Axiomatik der Sprachwissenschaft," *Kantstudien*, Vol. XXXVIII, no. 1/2 (1933).

hear—features which are as concrete and individual as the material itself—but a typical phonic form [*Gestalt.*] This form shows itself to us only through the concrete phonic material. It is given to us on the basis of this material, and it continues in existence even though quite extensive differences frequently occur in the material. If we are truly prepared for *words,* the typical phonic form is in no way apprehended as that which sounds *hic et nunc.* This unchangeable phonic form,[8] made strictly identical by the repeated utterance of the word, is precisely what one calls "the same word sound" of a word. It is not a "selection" of properties or parts of the concrete phonic material, but it is built upon it, and it achieves its self-presentation by being concretized in it. At the same time, it cannot be identified with either this phonic material or its individual concretizations, because it is *one* and *the same,* while the phonic material carrying its concretizations is many and manifold. Nor can it be considered something real, for by its essence the real cannot appear as identically the same in many real individuals or real individual occurrences. On the other hand, it would naturally be an error to see an ideal ontically autonomous object in a word sound, in the sense of a phonic form, and to place it on the same level as, for instance, mathematical objects. One would have to agree, then, that we know word sounds by discovering them to be timeless, unchangeable entities and that we find them to be simply existing, as we find mathematical objects or pure essences. Nevertheless, a word sound is built only in the course of time, under the influence of various real and cultural conditions, and it undergoes, with changing time, numerous and varied alterations and modifications. It is not real; yet it is anchored in reality, and it is changeable according to changes in the latter. But its change is fundamentally different from change in the concrete phonic material, which originates at some point in time, exists, and then forever ceases to exist. Whereas the word may be uttered countless numbers of times, and the concrete phonic material may

8. In his review in the *Zeitschrift für Ästhetik und allgemeine Kunstwissenschaft,* XXV no. 4 (1931), 379–87, H. Spiegelberg assailed this identity by indicating certain theoretical dangers that seem to stem from it. In connection with this, it must be noted that the concern here is, so to speak, with a purely qualitative, not a "numerical" (taken in its individuality in the concretization), identity of this form. That it is then "concretized" and that it then appears in a different concrete phonic material—and to that extent is "multiplied," so to speak—is something that cannot be denied or, for that matter, doubted. It is a special case of the general problem of "participation," which in itself cannot concern us here.

always be new, the "word sound" remains the same. Only a radical change in the cultural atmosphere of an epoch or a change in the external circumstances under which a certain word is used can effect a change in the word sound.

It would take us too far to pursue this in detail. Of greater importance for us is the question of what causes the difference between a word sound and the concrete phonic material. It appears that the utilization of the phonic material as the carrier [9] of one—and indeed one and the same—meaning leads to the demarcation of the word sound as an identical phonic form distinct from the concrete phonic material. The meaning of a word requires an external frame in which it can be "expressed." The utilization of a specific meaning from a variety of different meanings standing in manifold relations to one another necessitates an unequivocal coordination between the meanings and their external expressions. It is understandable, therefore, if something is chosen for the "expression" of one and the same meaning which is as identical [unchangeable] as the meaning itself. But both the nature of the concrete material (acoustical, optical, etc.) which one can utilize for the formation of the "word sound" and, on the other hand, the number of instances— in principle, limitless—in which one and the same meaning can appear in different connections make it impossible for anything which functions as the external expression of one and the same meaning to be any kind of individual real object or real occurrence. It is therefore unavoidable for us to use in individual cases a concrete material which is not the same but merely similar and which, while not itself the "word sound," forms the "sensory" [*sinnliche*] basis for the concretization of one and the same typical form, which then functions as the "word sound." This word-sound form is bestowed (*octroyé*) on the concrete phonic material through the identical meaning and is thereby made apparent. It is also something which belongs to the meaning and "carries" it.

This conception is likewise supported by the fact that for words which have—as we incorrectly express it—"the same word sound" and different meanings, the word sound, strictly speaking, is usually not entirely identical but shows instead a discernible difference. If it carries a different meaning, it is usually not merely expressed in a slightly different manner, in terms of the

9. Which is, after all, not quite correct, since it is not the concrete phonic material but the word sound which is the carrier of a meaning.

purely phonetic, but it also carries specific differentiating characters which, though they are still characters of the word sound,
transcend the purely phonetic (or optical). These characters
which modify the form of the word sound are like special re-
flexes referring back from the meaning to the word sound.[10] On
the one hand, the difference in meaning produces a difference in
what is apparently "the same" word sound; so likewise, on the
other hand, the identity of the meaning leads to an identity of
the word sound and compels us to proceed from the concrete individual to the nonconcrete word-sound form which simply appears in what is concrete.[11]

It is, in general, difficult to say what belongs, in individual
instances, to the word sound, since the formation of the word
sound is dependent on many different circumstances. At any
rate, it would be a mistake to believe that only a certain arrangement of syllables comes into play, although in normal circumstances this is what undoubtedly plays the most important role.
As experience shows, the height of the tone in which individual
syllables are expressed (e.g., in German the high "ie" in *Liebe*)
can also belong to the word sound. Often a mere change of tone
in the course of maintaining the arrangement of syllables can
produce differentiation in the word sound and the meaning that

10. J. Stenzel's well-known example, "The Lord giveth and the Lord
taketh away" and "The lord forgot his umbrella," is relevant here. See
J. Stenzel, "Sinn, Bedeutung, Begriff, Definition," *Jahrbuch für Philosophie und phänomenologische Forschung*, I (1913), 160 ff. Stenzel also
gives good examples in his *Philosophie der Sprache* (Munich and Berlin,
1935), pp. 16–17.

11. For this reason it strikes me as incorrect to speak of the word
sound as the "sensory side" of language (a usage that appears from time
to time in E. Cassirer's *Philosophie der symbolischen Formen*, Vol. 1: *Die
Sprache* [Berlin, 1923]; English translation by Ralph Manheim, *The Philosophy of Symbolic Forms*, Vol. I: *Language* [New Haven: Yale University Press, 1953]), if by "sensory" one means the equivalent of "given
in simple external perception." A special apprehension must always
accompany the perceptional intention so that something like a word
sound can appear as an intentional correlate of this apprehension. Already in his *Logical Investigations* Edmund Husserl seemed to have the
difference between the concrete phonic material and the word sound in
mind when he stated: "The ideality of the relationship between expression and meaning is at once plain in regard to both its sides, inasmuch
as, when we ask for the meaning of an expression, e.g., 'quadratic remainder,' we are naturally not referring to the sound-pattern uttered here
and now, the vanishing noise that can never recur identically: we mean
the expression *in specie*" (*Logische Untersuchungen* [Halle, 1900], II, 42;
English translation by J. N. Findlay, *Logical Investigations* [New York:
Humanities Press, 1970], I, 284). One must only note that the word
sound is not a "species" in the Husserlian sense of that period, since it
is not an ideal, timeless object.

is bound to it.[12] Finally, various characters which by their very nature are no longer purely phonic phenomena (though they are based on the phonic) and depend directly on the content of the corresponding meanings can also belong to the word sound.

Our conception of the word sound is not contradicted by the fact that, in various sentences and sentence complexes, one and the same word can undergo secondary differentiation with respect to its word sound according to the position it occupies in a higher meaning unit and according to the function it has to perform. (Thus, for instance, we have emphases dictated by the meaning of the sentence.) This does not suggest that there are no "word sounds" in our understanding of the term and that, in consequence, one must always deal with a constantly changing phonic material. On the contrary, it makes us cognizant of the fact that one and the same word-sound form can unite under certain circumstances with secondary, but equally typical, Gestalt qualities and, as a result, be able to express further nuances of the meaning that is bound to the word sound. The closer analysis of the structure of meaning which we shall conduct later will also elucidate what roles are played by these changing phonic characters.[13]

To complete our refutation of this concept of the word sound, we must still add the following. It is not at all true that the properties of the concrete phonic material, changing as they do from instance to instance and having no influence on the concretization of the word sound, are not noticed or apprehended in the process of hearing. It is true that under normal circumstances they are of little interest; but when the primary tendency is to grasp the meaning, the word sound commands exclusive attention. The characteristics of the concrete phonic material, how-

12. See E. Cassirer, *The Philosophy of Symbolic Forms*, I, 194: "And particularly in the Sudanese languages, the most diverse shades of meaning are expressed by tonal variations, by a high, middle, or low tone, or by composite shadings, such as the low-high rising tone, or high-low falling tone. These variations serve as a basis both for etymological distinctions—i.e., the same syllable serves, according to its tone, to designate entirely different things or actions—and for spatial and quantitative distinctions, i.e., high-pitched words, for example, express long distances and rapidity, while low-pitched words express proximity and slowness, etc."

13. A special problem, one which we cannot develop at greater length, is posed by the question of how an identical word-sound form holds out in the transformations that the word undergoes in declension and conjugation. The fact that this is really the case is precisely an argument for our conception. A change in the sound of a word accompanies a corresponding change in its meaning.

ever, are always coperceived by us; and as soon as they deviate somewhat from the normal tone of speech, they are noticed and at times grasped with greater attentiveness.[14] The difference between the apprehension of the word sound and the apprehension of properties of the concrete phonic material corresponds to the difference between the functions of the already constituted word sound and the changing properties of the concrete phonic material in the living utilization of words as a means of reciprocal communication. The word sound in effect characterizes a given word for itself and defines its meaning in the sense that its apprehension by the listener directs the understanding to the corresponding meaning and leads to the execution of the meaning intention by the person understanding it. As a result—in the case of normal understanding—the main stream of attention of the person understanding the text is directed, through the understood meaning, to the object determined by it. On the other hand, the changing properties of the concrete phonic material do not contribute anything essential to this function of the word. For example, the fact that a given word is expressed in a low or a high tone does not change anything in its meaning, in its rational sense, provided the height of the tone is not part of the given word sound. Instead, these properties play an essential role in the function of manifestation [15] which the spoken word has in living intercourse. Along with this, they can have considerable influence on the formation of the over-all concrete psychic content which arises in the person addressed during his comprehension of speech, as well as influence on the behavior of the people conversing. One and the same word, spoken at one time in a sharp and unpleasant tone and at another time in a mild and mellow manner, expresses, for example, the rudeness or the kindness of the speaker. Moreover, in both instances it evokes entirely different emotional states in the person addressed and effects different behaviors (e.g., the "sharp" tone of command, the pleasant tone of invitation, etc.). Naturally, in both respects

14. In these cases we also see at its best the difference between the word sound and the concrete phonic material.

15. With regard to the "function of manifestation," see E. Husserl's *Logical Investigations*, Vol. II, First Investigation. Before Husserl, K. Twardowski had distinguished between the various functions of words (and, in particular, names); see *Zur Lehre vom Inhalt und Gegenstand der Vorstellung* (Vienna, 1894). In his *Sprachtheorie*, published in 1934, K. Bühler uses the term "expressive function" [*Ausdrucksfunktion*] for this function, a term which, for that matter, had already been used by Twardowski.

the pure word sound is also not without meaning, and for this reason we shall soon differentiate various types of words. Nonetheless, the primary and essential function of the word sound itself is to determine the meaning of the given word.

§ 10. *Various types of word sounds and their functions*

IF WE WERE TO CONSIDER words without regard to the various applications and functions which they find in the living intercourse of psychic individuals, laying stress solely upon the unequivocal coordination of word sounds and meanings in a terminological system, then the statement would be true that the bond between a determinate word sound and a determinate meaning is entirely accidental and arbitrary. Hence, in principle, every word sound could be bound to every meaning. This is also supported by, among other things, the fact that in various languages one and the same meaning is bound to more or less different word sounds. Nevertheless, within the framework of one and the same *living* language and in its manifold applications in various life-situations, some word sounds seem to be particularly qualified, so to speak, to carry very specific meanings and, in connection with this, to perform special language functions. This predisposition, naturally, is not based on the properties of the word sound that are purely phonic and removed from the life-context, nor is it based on the purely rational content of the word meaning. As is well known, words, and especially word sounds, have passed through a history of development which is closely connected with the total life of a human community. In such a history we can find the justifications and causes for the fact that —within the framework of one and the same living linguistic community—some words appear to be particularly qualified to carry a specific meaning and, as a consequence, not only seem to be "more understandable" but contain, hidden within them, various special possibilities of application.[16]

16. In connection with these considerations cf. M. Dessoir's *Ästhetik und allgemeine Kunstwissenschaft* (Stuttgart, 1906) p. 356: "The possibility, however, of hitting an object or property or state at all, in all their sensory constitutions, is currently explained by the fact that the original linguistic sound is supposed to be a phonic gesture and, subsequently, like other gestures, an externalization of the impression that is gained from the object." See also W. Wundt, *Völkerpsychologie* (Leipzig, 1900–

In view of this, we can distinguish various types of words—and, in particular, various types of word sounds—of which some have special importance for the structure of the literary work. To begin with a type that is least appropriate for the literary work of art, let us mention, first of all, the "lifeless," dead words whose most conspicuous form are the scientific *termini* of an artificially constructed scientific terminology. Their entire function is exhausted in having clear, unequivocal, specific meanings and transmitting them during exchange of information. The word sound is irrelevant for their function, and, in principle, it can be replaced by an *arbitrarily* different one. For this reason, therefore, it must be fixed in a known, closed, conventional system. Hence, it is characteristic that it is not individual word sounds which are established without rule; rather, it is always an entire system of terms that is formed on the basis of a unified principle. The ideal is then to form the words or "signs" in such a way that their external form will reflect the connections of the corresponding "concepts" (cf. Leibniz' idea of an *ars combinatoria*, the "concept language" of modern logistic, etc.). The goal that is pursued here reflects the tendency to free oneself as much as possible from an intuitive grasp of objects belonging to the terms and to replace it by a combinatorial use of terms. For a person who does not know the principle of formation of the terms and the corresponding nominal definitions, the terms are either wholly incomprehensible or at least are not understood in the sense in which they are used in the given science. But even in everyday colloquial speech there are numerous words which have sunk, so to speak, to the level of scientific terms: the lifeless, mindlessly repeated catchwords which are stripped of the

1909), Vol. I, pt. 2, p. 607. A few years after the appearance of my book, Julius Stenzel wrote the following in his *Philosophie der Sprache* (p. 11): "The necessary relationship between meaning and sign can indeed be assumed, but the content of the intended meaning can be freed as much as possible from everything that is 'accidental' in the designation. This succeeds most wherever the system of signs is freely established, in a mathematical language, to the extent that mathematical states of affairs can be 'constructed,' i.e., strictly delimited in their essence and freed of all things accidental. One can disregard here the difficulties that are caused on this ground as well by 'intuition,' by intuitive features, since it is through opposition that an entirely different situation is to be simply designated where there is no free symbolization but rather where expression is created independently of any arbitrariness regarding or accompanying what is intended, a case which is seen most clearly in natural language. A closer connection between meaning and expression becomes a standard type for all the higher possibilities of expression that are realized in poetic language and in other spheres of aesthetic expression in the creation of culture."

function of evoking in a speaker an intuitive relation to the corresponding objects.

To all such words one must contrast the "living" and, in particular, the "vibrant," "powerful" words which one uses most frequently in the direct intercourse of daily life. Among these there are, first of all, those words whose word sound can fulfill the function of the directly understandable "expression"—both in the sense of "manifestation" and in the sense of "expressing the intended meaning." The issue in question is not that the person to whom the words are directed knows, by means of a "bare rational act"—as Husserl would say—that the speaker has precisely these experiences. This can also be evoked by wholly lifeless words. What is at issue is that the special characters of the word sound—and in fact the "tone" in which they are spoken—"reveal" the concrete, the just-then-occurring experiences of the speaker in such a manner that they are graphically given to the listener without aid of inference or conjecture. The experiences or the psychic states of the speaker are "exhibited," so to speak.

Other types of "lively" words are distinguished by the fact that the characters which arise from the purely phonetic "Gestalt qualities" and move from the meaning onto the word sound reveal themselves more clearly in the word sound and color it, so to speak, with the quality that is characteristic of the designated object (for example, all "obscene" and "crude" words, etc.). Thus it is not so much the expressive function (the *"Kundgabe"*) which comes into the foreground but rather the actualization of the relationship of the perceiver of such a word to the object determined by the meaning of the word. They call forth in the listener lively, graphic images of the given object, and they can essentially facilitate its intuitive comprehension. With their use, manifold "aspects" of the given objects can be reactualized in an imaginational modification which allows us, as it were, to "see" the object.[17] One could say that one of the most essential functions of these words consists of their holding ready the "aspects" that belong to the object intended by them and in giving this object an intuitive fullness [*Fülle*].*

In this regard, it is the special characters of the word sound and not the corresponding meaning itself which plays the essential role. This is best shown by the fact that when it is necessary, for example, to say something delicately and least drastically, it

17. With respect to "aspects," see Chap. 8, below.
* [Cf. Husserl's *Logical Investigations*, Vol. II, Sixth Investigation.]

is possible to avoid the particular effect of an obscene word by substituting one with an identical meaning but with a more neutral word sound.

These differences between words which have their foundation in the type of their word sound play—as one can both demonstrate and expect—an important role in the structure of the literary work. For it is not only the particular character of the sound stratum of a given work that is dependent on the type of words used in it—and this, naturally, is also reflected in the overall character of the whole work—but also the manner in which the language stratum fulfills its role with respect to the other strata. We will have to return to this later.

Finally, the following must also be noted: the purely phonetic content of the word sound and, above all, the whole word sound can already contain qualities that are aesthetically relevant. Thus one often distinguishes, e.g., "beautiful" and "ugly" sounding words (or, more precisely, word sounds).[18] There are, in addition, "light" and "heavy" words, words which sound "funny" or "serious," "solemn" or "pathetic," and those which are "simple" and "straightforward." These are all differences and characteristics which find their expression in the word sounds themselves, though we cannot doubt that they are also closely connected to the corresponding meanings and are frequently attributed to the words by the manner of expression, by the "tone."

§ 11. *Phonetic formations of a higher order and their characters*

THE INDIVIDUAL WORD is only an element of language; its isolation [from the sentence] and its constitution as a whole in itself is probably a comparatively later occurrence. In a living language, as well as in literary works, it never, or almost never,

18. In particular, when one compares various languages in this respect, one sees that each contains different "beauties" in its word-sound material. The same can be observed when one compares different "pronunciations" of one and the same language (e.g., French). In this, one always postulates a certain manner of pronunciation as a "proper" or "ideal" one, in the conviction that it is particularly suited for expressing the beauties contained in the word-sound material of the given language. Naturally, in every language there are manifold changes in the word sounds of individual words, changes which express local color. But this does not contradict our conception of the word sound.

appears in isolation. Even where it seems to appear as something self-sufficient, it forms only an abbreviation that takes the place of a whole sentence or even a complex of sentences. The truly independent linguistic formation is not the individual word but the sentence.[19] Thus it is not simply an accumulation of words which leads to particular word groups which, for short, one calls a "sentence." On the contrary, the sentence, as a unit of meaning —and, with respect to the word, a formation of a totally new kind—contains an arrangement which ultimately allows us to distinguish words as its relatively dependent elements.[20] If the sentence, however, is a new kind of formation with respect to individual words, this is due solely to the particular structure of its meaning content. In other words: "word sounds" undoubtedly exist as uniform, typical forms; in that same sense, however, there are no "sentence sounds." To be sure, the unity of the meaning of the sentence, as well as the special qualities of its functions, also causes the word sounds of the words belonging to the sentence to be bound to one another [21] and, what is more, to produce a sentence melody characteristic of the sentence as a whole, a melody which still allow various modifications,[22] however. In spite of this, with respect to their purely phonetic side, sentences do not constitute a phonetic formation that is equiva-

19. The fact that a sentence, too, is only a relatively independent formation when it appears as part of a sentence complex will be shown subsequently. See § 23, below.

20. See, for example, already in W. Humboldt: "In reality speech does not consist of words prior to it; on the contrary, words emerge from the totality of speech" (*Über die Verschiedenheit des menschlichen Sprachbaues, Akademische Ausgabe*, VII, pt. I, 72; English translation by George C. Buck and Frithjof A. Raven, *Linguistic Variability and Intellectual Development* [Coral Gables: University of Miami Press, 1971]).

21. See below, p. 53.

22. Sentence melody has most recently been discussed by H. Ammann in *Die menschliche Rede*, Vol. II (Lahr i.B., 1928). The language melody which Stenzel had in mind (*"Sinn, Bedeutung"*) also belongs here. However, he certainly goes too far when he asserts that "Only by starting from language melody can one construct a theory of sentences; all that is required is that language melody be examined in direct relationship to the organized series of meanings" (p. 188). But one has to agree with Stenzel when subsequently, in *Philosophie der Sprache* (p. 17), he writes: "Thus the acoustic form of language is essential, not only in the individual articulated sound, but in the whole sentence which is formed by the uniform energy of meaning-bestowal. This energy—later I speak of a 'sentence-forming operation'—which from the beginning intends the whole of the sentence, is significant not only for the pathetic, emotional sphere; rather, its 'transparency' is grounded in the rhythmical 'organization' of every sentence. Whoever does not take in the whole [of a sentence] in a reading does not 'understand' the sentence in the concrete execution of meaning and is likewise not understood."

lent to word sounds, and in particular they do not constitute a phonetic *element* with which, as in the case of word sounds, one can operate and which one can apply toward the formation of different kinds of entities.[23] In everyday colloquial speech, some phrases are undoubtedly formed which, even with respect to the phonic side, seem to be uniform and which seem to be analogues of word sounds. Thus, for example, the greeting "Good morning" or "How do you do" sounds like one word. Strictly speaking, however, these are incompletely expressed, abbreviated sentences. The unity of their meaning lends an appearance of uniformity to the corresponding word manifold precisely because their sense, "compressed," so to speak, and condensed in the abbreviation, does not show the arrangement which appears in a fully developed sentence and which can accentuate the demarcation of individual word sounds. If the sentence is fully developed or expressed, however, the word sounds form a manifold composed of independent elements.

In spite of this, the succession of word sounds leads to the formation of certain phonic formations and sound phenomena or characters of a new type which could not be evoked by individual word sounds. On the other hand, as we have already mentioned, the uniformity and the peculiar structure of the sentence meaning is also not without influence on the manifold of corresponding word sounds. The observations of the preceding paragraphs must be supplemented in both of these directions.

If we were to begin with the first group of phonetic phenomena,[24] we would be struck first of all by the fact that the succession of word sounds produces certain secondary characters which build on these word sounds. It is true that, by appearing in a determinate manifold, individual word sounds do not change in the sense that a word sound can change into another, a different one, merely because a determinate word sound precedes it and another one follows it. Nevertheless, there sometimes appear in them perceptible relative characters, if one may so call them, which have their origin in the proximity of other word sounds. The source for this is, above all, the purely phonic moments of the word sounds; but the remaining moments can both produce the secondary modifications and appear as these modifications. If, for example, word sounds with a truly soft

23. Cf., on the other hand, the truly phonic entities which go beyond the unity of a word sound; these are discussed on p. 51, below.
24. With regard to the following, cf. Lipps, *Grundlegung der Ästhetik* (Leipzig, 1903), pp. 487–92.

sound are followed by a sharp and hard word sound, there is an accentuation of the sharpness of the latter in the guise of a distinct phenomenon of contrast. An analogous situation arises when, in a phrase consisting of "fine" words, there suddenly appears a word that is coarse, not only in its meaning but also in its word sound. It rings much more coarsely than it would if it were in less "fine" surroundings. There is, of course, a great variety of such "relative" characters.

Far more important than those discussed above are the phonetic phenomena, of a wholly different type with respect to the word sounds, which characterize whole manifolds of word sounds. Above all, rhythm and tempo belong here. If we confine ourselves to the kinds of rhythm that build on the phonic material,[25] then rhythm clearly rests on the recurrence of determinate sequences of accented and unaccented sounds. It is relatively independent not only of the absolute and the relative height of sound but of other qualities of the phonic material. One can produce "the same" rhythm with the help of the phonetic material but also with the sounds of this or that instrument, with drumbeats, or with other noises. Naturally, rhythm itself is not to be identified with such a sequence of accents. It is a specific Gestalt quality [26] that is constituted only in the recurrence of such sequences. Thus, there are two different basic types of rhythmic qualities: on the one hand, those which require for their constitution a *strictly regular* recurrence of always the *same* succession of accents, and, on the other hand, those for which this strict regularity is not unconditionally necessary. The latter in fact require a certain degree of variability in this respect as a condition of their appearance. We will call the first "regular" and the second "free" rhythm. Rhythmic qualities of the first kind are constituted only in verses that require a strict recurrence in the verse order, while free rhythm already comes into play in so-called free verse and is fully realized in various kinds of prose. A literary work obviously need not be written in all its parts in the same rhythm in order to be characterized generally as rhythmical. On the contrary, rhythmic

25. There is also a rhythm of visually or kinaesthetically projected movement, as well as rhythm phenomena in drawing and architecture and so on. Cf. O. Walzel, *Wechselseitige Erhellung der Künste* (Berlin, 1917), and the studies of Schmarsow, Pinder, Russack, *et al.*, which he cites. For us this question is of minor significance.
26. The fact that rhythm is a "form" [*Gestalt*] is also asserted by J. Stenzel in "Sinn, Bedeutung, Begriff, Definition," *Jahrbuch für Philosophie und phänomenologische Forschung*, I (1913), 175.

change contained within certain bounds produces rhythmic characters of a higher degree. The only provision is that such changes should not occur too frequently.

Strictly speaking, every literary text is provided with some rhythmic qualities. There are, however, degrees of distinctness and forcefulness to these qualities, especially in the case of "free" rhythms. If a certain rhythm is barely "forceful," striking, or conspicuous, or, on the contrary, if it is too complicated and "difficult," its particular quality does not reach the [reader's] consciousness. For this reason, one is inclined at times to deny its very presence. Yet one must make a distinction here between (1) a rhythm that is prescribed, so to speak, by a given set of word sounds and is immanent in it and (2) a rhythm that can be produced with greater or lesser artistry in a specific reading by a certain kind of performance and thus be imposed on the text in question. An imposed rhythm can deform an immanent one or can change or conceal it.[27] The unwarranted identification of these two different matters, the fact that in separate readings of the same text an imposed rhythm can show far-reaching differences, and, finally, the dependence of the reading on the arbitrariness of the reader can easily lead to the false conclusion that the language of the literary work is itself devoid of any rhythmic qualities. In fact, however, the selection and ordering of word sounds determines the rhythmic qualities of the text and places specific demands on the manner of performance. These demands may, of course, not be followed in individual cases; but when they are not, a falsifying reconstruction of the phonetic stratum of the given work results, and at times this may contradict the essence of this stratum to such a degree that the remaining strata cannot achieve expression at all in the given reading.

With respect to the rhythm of language which is evoked solely by the properties of its phonetic aspect, one must distinguish those rhythmic qualities which are produced by the meaning of the sentence. We shall deal with this matter presently.

The various rhythms and rhythmic characters introduce a new phonetic phenomenon, namely, *tempo*. By tempo we do not mean an arbitrarily effected and altered objective speed of performance in an individual reading but a determinate character

---

27. Whether this is possible in every given case is something that I cannot decide here.

of the phonetic side of language, its "quickness" or "slowness," its "lightness" or "lazy heaviness." This character is conditioned by the properties of the rhythm that is immanent in the text and is produced by a speed that is peculiar to and dictated by it. As we know from music, one and the same rhythm allows various objective speeds without thereby being changed into another rhythm. In spite of this, there are certain, if only vaguely determined, bounds within which the speed of the delivery can in fact be changed; overstepping these bounds seems "inappropriate," "unnatural" for the rhythm, since it introduces characters of tempo which seem to be in "disharmony," in "conflict," with the given rhythmic Gestalt quality.[28] For this reason and in this sense we may contend that a specific rhythm "predetermines" and requires objective speeds of sound succession. Nevertheless, in a particular reading, one may of course use speeds which introduce tempi that clash with the rhythmic quality in question. Yet this possibility does not, generally speaking, concern the literary work itself but rather its individual readings; and it occurs only when it is immaterial to us whether or not such a reading faithfully reflects the particular characters of the work itself. If it is a question of a true reflection of the properties of a work, the range of extant possibilities is essentially narrowed. On the other hand, a realization of disharmonious phenomena can be achieved by appropriate means in the work itself, as when the "stage directions" [29] of a "dramatic" work "inform" us that a character has to speak "very rapidly" or "very slowly" in order to produce a dissonant effect that belongs to the structure of the work.

The appearance of various tempo characters also depends on whether the words occurring in a sentence or a sentence complex have long or short (monosyllabic or polysyllabic) word sounds or word sounds which, according to their Gestalt quality, require long or short articulation. Finally, tempo is also connected to the meaning of the sentence and to its arrangement. Short sentences, for example, introduce faster tempi. On the other hand, a series of quickly changing "states of affairs" [30] which are determined by the sentence meaning reflects upon the phonetic side of language and modifies the tempo characters that are determined solely by the latter.

28. The dependence between tempo and rhythm can be shown most easily by examples from Greek metrics.
29. See below, § 30.6.
30. See below, § 22.

The presence of a "regular" rhythm leads to the constitution of phonetic units of a higher order, e.g., the "verse" and the "stanza." These units are dependent on word-sound material only insofar as sequence of word sounds determines rhythm. They are also not to be placed on the same level with the unity of a word sound. At the same time, they must be distinguished from the homogeneity of word sounds produced by units of meaning. Units of "verse" can exist, for example, even when meaning is entirely omitted, which is the case in individual readings arising from "senseless recitation"; in such cases the character of belonging-together of the respective words ceases to exist. Moreover, both types of unity can in principle intersect.

Another group of phonetic properties is formed by various "melodies" and melodic characters. They are conditioned or constituted above all by the occurrence in word sounds of a succession of vowels [31] with a specific pitch. It is natural, therefore, that in the constitution of a melodic character "rhyme" and "assonance" play an important role. Equally essential for them are the relative characters of individual word sounds which arise from their milieu, a factor we have already discussed. They initiate, as it were, the organization of distinct word sounds into formations of a higher order, and especially into various kinds of melodies. Every living language and, to a higher degree, every dialect has its characteristic melodic properties. One can say that even the speech of an individual person (where social and class differences play a significant role) possesses a special melodic stamp. This has obvious importance when the living language is utilized as the material for the formation of a literary work. In this respect individual works differ very strongly, since the melodic properties of the author's living language are usually quite tangible. It is also an aspect of the poet's art to master and apply in an artistic manner the various melodic properties of language, either for the purpose of the purely melodic beauty of the text or for the manifold purposes of representation that we shall discuss later.

Finally, we must mention a very special property of the phonic aspect of language, one which has its basis in a succession of determinate word sounds. At issue are characters which in themselves are no longer purely phonic but which have their basis in the purely phonic properties of the word-sound sequence

31. Cf., in this connection, the studies in empirical psychology, e.g., those of Gesa Révész; see also Dessoir, *Ästhetik und allgemeine Kunstwissenschaft,* p. 385.

and the formations arising in it (the kind of rhythm, tempo, melody, timbre of individual word sounds) and also achieve their appearance through them. These are the many and various "emotional" or "mood" qualities: "sad," "melancholy," "merry," "powerful," etc.[32] Their appearance can also be conditioned and influenced by the meaning that is bound to the word sound.[33] But, as is clearly shown in musical works, they can also be produced solely by the phonic material. For example, we frequently do not need to understand at all a poem read in a foreign language in order to apprehend clearly the characters here in question.

Again, the manner in which a poem, for example, is read can exert an influence on the appearance of these emotional qualities, since the concrete phonic material can be modified in this or that manner. Moreover, the mood in which a hearer finds himself favors or hinders the "coming to appearance" of these qualities. It would be a mistake, however, to think that the phonic aspect of the language of a literary work is entirely neutral and that the emotional qualities are arbitrarily "projected," as one may put it, solely by the reader or listener. The instances in which we can say with complete justification that a reading is "false" or in which, despite the subjective mood with which we begin to read or hear the given work, totally contrary emotional qualities obtrude upon us are, in my opinion, sufficient argument against this viewpoint. We feel the presence of the "emotional qualities" appearing in the phonic side of language most clearly precisely in those instances where there is a conflict between them and the emotional qualities that appear in other strata of the literary work.

If we turn now to the second group of phonetic phenomena, namely, those that are conditioned by the meaning of the sentence, we find, first of all, the already-mentioned secondary modifications of individual word sounds,[34] modifications which

---

32. Max Scheler speaks of such "emotional qualities" in his article "Zum Phänomen des Tragischen" [Vom Umsturz der Werte, 4th ed. rev., Gesammelte Werke, Vol. III (Bern, 1965]. He deals there with the "emotional qualities" that can appear, e.g., in a landscape. However, they also appear on the basis of various phonetic formations.

33. In his Völkerpsychologie, Vol. I, pt. 1, p. 326, W. Wundt writes: "Sound metaphor is what we call the relationship of a phonetic unit to its meaning, the meaning which enters our consciousness through the fact that the emotional tone of the sound is related to the emotion that is bound to the designated representation." This is not a formulation which we would accept today; but, taking the matter purely factually, Wundt has hit upon precisely what we have in mind here.

34. See above, p. 40.

arise from the fact that the words have various functions within the whole of the sentence. This is primarily a question of the *accentuation* (the stresses) of those words whose meaning is stressed in the sentence as a whole, and only secondarily of the tonal unity of a number of words and their separation from other word groups. These separations—which in the written language have their correlates in the various punctuation signs —show an entire manifold of different types of demarcation, depending on whether it is a demarcation of a whole sentence or only a part of a sentence. In general these demarcations are produced by pauses of varying lengths, as well as by the way in which the last word before the pause is articulated. In contrast, words belonging together are uttered, as far as possible, directly, without a break.[35] Naturally, we again have in mind, not the individual occurrences of the particular readings, but the typical phonetic phenomena which belong to the set of word sounds as such. The fact of their belonging to the phonic aspect of the literary work stems precisely from their being conditioned by the meaning of the sentence. One could say that they reflect in the phonetic material various properties of the meaning of the sentence, and their existence best shows how closely the two sides of language—phonic and semantic—are bound together.[36]

§ 12. *The range of phonetic formations that belong to the literary work*

IT IS NOW TIME to answer the question of what it is in the phonic aspect of language that forms a component of the literary work. The distinction we made between the concrete phonic material and the word sound already allows us to assume that one should eliminate the concrete phonic material from the literary work. And, in fact, it constitutes only the phonic basis for the word sounds' being concretized in individual readings and for the other phonetic phenomena to which we have referred in preceding sections. It may be questioned, however, whether the word sound in our sense can be considered a component of the literary work. Thus, to E. Kucharski it appears that the phonic aspect of language does not belong to the literary work

35. J. Stenzel has all of this in mind (though not only this) when he speaks of "language melody."
36. Here Stenzel is absolutely correct.

because, on the one hand, he does not at all recognize language as the material of the literary work, and, on the other hand, he expressly says that through the phonic aspect of language a factor is introduced which in principle is foreign to the essence of poetry, i.e., that of sensory perception.[37] We believe this position to be untenable. It is merely an attempt to extricate oneself from a situation that arises from Kucharski's false assumption that the essence of a literary work lies in experiences. We, on the contrary, believe it necessary to assert that word sounds cannot be eliminated from the structure of the literary work—at least in those works which belong to the first series of examples we proposed.[38] This, however, by no means proves that all literary works actually known to us contain a stratum of word sounds, since our question is directed at what belongs in essence, not in fact. Moreover, we cannot draw on this fact, since it has not yet been demonstrated whether cinematographic works, for example, should be counted among literary works. Only a positive demonstration of the functions performed by the phonic aspect of language in a literary work, as well as a demonstration of the indispensability of these functions, can effect a resolution. Before we proceed to that, however, it must be noted that we would rob the literary work of major, and at times indispensable, elements if, of the entire phonic aspect of language, we ascribed to it only word sounds. In fact, other typical phonic Gestalt qualities also belong to it. Among them are, above all, those which, concretized in the various ways of expressing words, perform the function of "expressing" the psychic states experienced at a given moment by the speaker. These Gestalt qualities

37. See E. Kucharski, "O metodę estetycznego rozbioru dzieł literackich," p. 35 (cf. n. 1, above). Moreover, Kucharski seems to take a position similar to that of Eduard von Hartmann in his *Philosophie des Schönen* (Leipzig, 1888), p. 715: ". . . the poetic effect as such is dependent only on the word meaning [*Wortsinn*], not on beautiful language or its beautiful delivery; when the effect is reinforced by the two latter factors, we are dealing with the addition of an extrapoetic effect to the poetic one, that is, with the compound effect of a work of art compounded from a number of arts." It is clear that Hartmann presupposes a concept of "poetic"—one which does not arise from a concrete analysis of poetic works. He is thus obliged to view these works as "compounded"—as if there were, or indeed could be, poetic works that are bereft of the phonetic stratum and to which another "art" (music?) must first be added so as to create "compound works of art." There are, of course, "compound" works of art, as, for example, lieder or the opera; but then the music enters in as a factor in a way that is entirely different from the function that the phonetic stratum can perform in a purely literary work.
38. See above, p. 7.

come into play in every work where speaking personae are represented,[39] as, for example, in every dramatic work. Thus, there are various Gestalt qualities of the tone in which one speaks: "plaintive" or "joyful," "lively" or "tired," "passionate" or "calm." On the other hand, there are Gestalt qualities of the tone in which one addresses others, e.g., a "sharp" or "gracious" tone, a tone in which one "talks down" to others, or "friendly," "surly," "loving," or "spiteful" tones in speaking to other people. Naturally, we have in mind the phonic Gestalt qualities themselves, but they are bound so closely to what they directly express that we can name them, so to speak, only *sub specie* of the expressed. These few examples may suffice to elucidate what we have in mind. Let us call them *manifestation* qualities, since the concealed psychic states of the speaker are manifested in them. If we were to eliminate them from the works [in which speaking personae appear], some of these works would be so strongly deformed that perhaps their most important elements could in no way be constituted. There can be works, or at least parts of works, however, where there are no manifestation qualities of this kind, as, for example, in "quiet," "objective" descriptions of surroundings or events.[40]

In addition to these manifestation qualities, the other phonetic phenomena mentioned in the preceding sections may also be present: rhythm, tempo, melody, units of a higher order conditioned by the rhythm or the meaning of the sentence, etc. All of them belong to the literary work, but always in the sense of particular typical Gestalt qualities and not as occurrences appearing only in the concrete phonic material. These phonetic formations need not appear in every literary work; they are present in a work when they are produced by the manifold and the pattern of word sounds conditioning them. They are only the aftereffects of these primary elements of the word-sound aspect of language.

Having established in this manner the range of all the phonetic formations and characters which in our opinion do or can belong to the literary work, we can now proceed to

39. On the concept of "representation," see below, § 29.
40. What means the poet has for including such manifestation qualities in the work and conveying them to the reader is, of course, a separate problem. For the task here is much more complicated than the mere establishment of a manifold of word sounds that are determined by means of written signs. Whatever the solution for this problem may be (and we shall deal with it later), it changes nothing in the fact established by us.

substantiate our position by demonstrating the functions which they perform in it.

§ 13. *The role of the phonetic stratum in the structure of the literary work*

THE PHONETIC FORMATIONS and characters discussed above play a significant role in the structure of the literary work in two different ways. First, they constitute, thanks to their manifold properties and characters, a particular element in the structure of the work; second, they perform their own functions in the unfolding, and also partly in the constituting, of the other strata.

In the first case, they enrich the whole of the work by a particularly formed material and by particular aesthetic value qualities which constitute, along with the value qualities stemming from the remaining strata of the work, the peculiar polyphony of the literary work of art to which we have already called attention. The fact that the phonetic formations and characters truly possess their "own voice" in this polyphony is best supported by the drastic change which the work undergoes when it is translated into a "foreign" language. However faithful one tries to make the translation, whatever pains one takes to keep the closest resemblance between phonetic qualities, one can never reach the stage where the translation would in this respect fully match the original, because the otherness of the individual word sounds inevitably carries with it other phonetic formations and characters. Moreover, the phonetic aspect of language is not irrelevant for its artistic value. Some of its properties and formations lead to the constitution of completely individual characters, which we usually name with such words as "beautiful," "ugly," "pretty," "nice," "strong," "powerful," etc.[41] These words, however, are not capable of reproducing the whole variety of differing aesthetically relevant characters. It may be true that in all cases where we speak, for example, of "beauty," we may

41. Whether, along with the founding through determinate manifolds of sound qualities, a certain attitude and conception are necessary on the part of the perceiving subject for the constitution of such characters is a special problem that cannot be solved here. If these various subjective conditions (which are still to be determined) are fulfilled, however, we find the above characters as something adhering to the sound formations.

discover a common element. Usually, however, we are not concerned with the common element but with the full concrete character that adheres to the individual work of art; and the word "beauty," therefore, is quite inadequate for describing it. There are not only various "beauties" but various types of them, which are differentiated according to their underlying qualities and manifolds of qualities. For example, there is not only the fact that a Romanesque church is "beautiful" in a specifically different sense than a Gothic cathedral, but also the fact that the "beauties" that are expressed by phonetic and, in particular, musical formations are, in accordance with their own essence, typically different from, e.g., an architectural work of art. Similarly, the various "characters of beauty" that are constituted on the basis of sound combinations and sequences in two different languages (e.g., German and French) are totally heterogeneous in the fullness of their content to those characters of beauty which can be shown by a tragic situation or by the impact of a form. This very heterogeneity has its basis in the heterogeneity of those qualities which found the characters that appear on the one hand as phonetic formations and on the other as something spiritual. If—as is frequently though not quite correctly done—we call the formations or the qualities which found the character of beauty the "material," then we may say that the fundamentally different basic types of characters of beauty are dependent on the properties of the "material" and are differentiated in accordance with them. The same applies to each one of the different aesthetically relevant characters represented by the words enumerated above.[42]

The appearance of an appropriately selected manifold of such characters in a single work leads to the constitution of aesthetically relevant characters of a higher order, to certain particular synthetic moments that, in the final end, constitute what is unique in a work of art: its own artistic value.

As we have stated, the literary work of art is a many-layered formation. Above all, this means that the "material" whose properties lead to the constitution of aesthetically relevant characters consists of several heterogeneous components or "strata."

42. With respect to the concept of the character of beauty or, in general, of value qualities and their specific modifications, see Max Scheler, "Der Formalismus in der Ethik und materiale Wertethik," Chap. I, § 1, "Güter und Werte" (*Jahrbuch für Philosophie und phänomenologische Forschung*, I [1913], 412 ff.; English translation by Manfred S. Frings and Roger L. Funk, *Formalism in Ethics and Non-Formal Ethics of Values* [Evanston, Ill.: Northwestern University Press, 1973]).

The material of each stratum leads to the constitution of its own aesthetic characters, which correspond to the nature of the material. Consequently, there occurs, or at least there may occur, a formation of synthetic aesthetic characters of a higher order, and indeed not only within each of these groups of characters peculiar to the individual strata; there may also be syntheses of a still higher order among moments of different groups. In other words, the stratification of the "material" produces in the literary work of art a remarkable *polyphony* of aesthetic characters of heterogeneous types, whereby the characters belonging to the various types are not alien to one another, as it were, but enter into various mutual relationships. As a result, totally new syntheses, harmonies, and disharmonies arise in the most varied modifications possible.[43] Each such synthetically constructed harmony contains elements which lead to synthetic formations in such a way that the elements do not disappear behind the synthetic moments but are in themselves tangible and visible behind them. The whole is precisely a *poly*phony.

The aesthetic value qualities which are constituted in the phonetic stratum take part in this polyphony and enrich it. At the same time, however, they lead to the creation of particular harmonies of synthetic aesthetic value characters which are possible only due to the presence of the phonetic stratum in the whole of the work. This fact gives us an important argument for the assertion that the phonetic stratum is not simply a means for revealing the literary work but belongs to it in such a way that its absence from the work must lead to far-reaching changes in it. The polyphony must then not only be the poorer, lacking a "voice," but it must also be thoroughly different, since other types of harmonies would then have to be constructed.

However, if the contribution of the phonetic stratum to the structure of the work is only an enrichment and modification of its polyphony, the elimination of this stratum would not yet make the existence of the literary work impossible. It is a different matter when its role in revealing the work, and in part

---

43. In particular, what is opened to us here are the problems of the connection between the properties and aesthetic characters of the phonetic stratum (among them meter, verse form, aesthetic characters of the verse melody, etc.) and the properties of the represented world as well as the aesthetically valuable moments that appear in it. We will subsequently go into these matters in greater detail. These connections were observed and analyzed relatively very early, e.g., by W. Schlegel (*Collected Works*, Vol. II), as Oskar Walzel correctly points out in his *Gehalt und Gestalt im Kunstwerk des Dichters* (Berlin, 1923), pp. 182 ff.

also in constituting the remaining strata, is taken into consideration.

These roles must be viewed from two different standpoints: first, from the purely ontological, with reference to what the phonetic stratum accomplishes for the existence of other strata; second, from the phenomenological standpoint, with reference to what function it performs for a psychic subject when the whole work is given and revealed.

In the first instance, the phonetic stratum, and in particular the manifold of word sounds, forms the external, fixed shell of the literary work, in which all the remaining strata find their external point of support or—if one will—their external expression. The constitutive foundation proper of the individual literary work certainly lies in the stratum of meaning units of a lower and higher order. But the meanings are *essentially* bound to the word sounds.[44] To be sure, this cannot be claimed of *determinate* word sounds, which are *in fact* bound to meanings, since in principle one and the same meaning can be bound to various word sounds, e.g., in different languages. But it is part of the idea of meaning that it be bound to *some* word sound (or to some word sign of a visual, acoustic, or tactile nature) and hence be *its* meaning. The meaning finds in it its external shell, its "expression," its external carrier. Without the "word sound" (in the now broadened sense of any Gestalt-quality factor) it could not exist at all. It is indeed true that the determinate word-sound material that a literary work has in a given language (German, French) is not essentially indispensable. But with the elimination of all the word-sound material, the stratum of meaning units would cease to exist; and, with it, the remaining strata of the work—at least in the form which is characteristic of them while they are in the literary work of art—would also disappear.[45]

Yet precisely because the phonetic stratum forms the external, indispensable shell for the stratum of meaning units and thereby also for the whole work, it plays an essential role in the apprehension of the work by a psychic subject. Even though the word sounds are only a "shell" and therefore something which, according to its material, is essentially different from everything else in the work (so that in the case of an inappropriate attitude

44. See Chap. 5.
45. One should not, however (as is almost commonly done), confuse the units of meaning with the ideal meaning of a concept. See Chap. 5, below.

on the part of the reader they can "conceal" or hide the rest of the work), it is they that precisely as carriers of meanings, can reveal the whole work. Hence the essential accomplishment of word sounds lies in the fact that they "determine" the attendant meanings as soon as the coordination of word sounds and meanings is established. This means that, when a determinate word sound is apprehended by a psychic subject, the apprehension leads directly to the execution of an intentional act in which the content of a determinate meaning is intended. Here, this meaning is not given as an object [of thought] but is rather set into a function; and, for its part, this setting-into-function brings about the fact that the corresponding objectivity which belongs to the word meaning or to the meaning of the sentence is intended, and thereby the subsequent strata of the literary work are revealed.

But besides their primary and intrinsic function of "determining" corresponding meanings, the word sounds or, more precisely, some of them, perform other functions in revealing the literary work. Above all, "living" word sounds cause the objectivity that belongs to its meaning to be not simply, blankly intended but also to be fully, graphically "imagined" in appropriate "aspects." The appearance of such living, powerful words also determines the selection of manifolds of aspects in which the represented objects are to appear.[46] But it is not only the manner in which these objects appear that is codetermined by the stratum of word sounds; in certain cases the constitution of some elements of the represented objectivities can also be achieved only through the utilization of certain phonetic means. Wherever a word not only exists in its meaning-determining function but also performs the "manifestation function" [Kundgabefunktion] (in the Husserlian sense), i.e., above all in so-called "dramatic" works, the word-sound material and, in particular, the various manifestation qualities of the tone in which the word is articulated play the irreplaceable role of "manifesting" the various psychic states of the represented personae. It is only on this path that the concrete physical life of these personae, which cannot be reduced to thoughts or to that which is thought, arrives at its constitution. If the corresponding word sounds were to be eliminated, so that the meaning units were, so to speak, naked (if this were at all possible), we would still know that the

46. See Chap. 8, below, and T. A. Meyer, *Das Stilgesetz der Poesie* (Leipzig, 1901), pp. 160 ff.

represented hero is thinking this or that, we could still find out, with the help of corresponding descriptions, various facts regarding his psychic constitution and his psychic transformations, but the inexpressible, that aspect of psychic life which cannot be described conceptually would, even though it is graphically demonstrated in the manifestation qualities, nevertheless remain indeterminate. Thus, the existence of the phonetic stratum in the literary work leads to an important supplementation of the stratum of represented objects, without which supplementation individual literary works would necessarily have to be essentially different. On this path, however, there may also occur an improvement in the already-mentioned function of word sounds, i.e., their "determining" of meaning units. The reason for this is that the cogivenness of the manifested psychic states makes precise, often only at the very moment they are spoken, the meaning of the sentences, whereby this meaning either attains full development or is modified in specific ways.[47] Thus, for example, a sentence articulated with the same manifold of word sounds attains in each case a different meaning if at one point—due to the phonic manifestation qualities—it appears to be uttered in a towering rage and at another point with absolute calm or sublime malice or spiteful irony.

The various phonetic Gestalt-quality formations and characters of a higher order which we have previously referred to also play an irreplaceable role, both in determining the meaning and in constituting the remaining strata of the work; above all, they coconstitute the irrational moments of the objectivities that are represented. Only later, however, will we be able to clarify with greater precision the meaning of this function.[48] For the present we can say briefly that the phonetic stratum is an essential constituent of the literary work; if it were eliminated, the whole work would cease to exist, since meaning units necessarily require a word-sound material. If it were formed differently than it actually is in a given work, that work would undergo sweeping changes. Finally, if it did not contain any special value-quality elements, the polyphony of the work would be poorer by a significant element. This first, external stratum is, therefore, not merely a means of access to the literary work, not a "factor essentially alien to poetry"; it is, on the contrary, an indispensable element in the structure of the literary work of art.

47. In this regard, see the interesting if still strongly psychologistically colored arguments in Meyer's *Das Stilgesetz*, p. 19n.
48. See below, §§ 47–50.

5 / The Stratum of Meaning Units

§ 14. *Preliminary note*

THE INVESTIGATIONS now following will set forth the manifold formations and functions which together constitute the second stratum of the literary work of art, namely, the stratum of meaning units. In particular, they will determine more closely all the factors of this stratum, the knowledge of which alone enables us to understand the role of the units of meaning in the literary work. At the same time, however, the general essence of the word meaning and the higher units of meaning must be made clear to the extent that this is necessary for answering the question of the ideality of the units of meaning. Since we cannot set forth here a comprehensive theory of the units of meaning, we shall understandably leave unanswered a number of pressing questions and only sketch an outline for others.

§ 15. *The elements of the word meaning*

WITHOUT AT ALL occupying ourselves for the present with the essence of the word meaning, we shall now distinguish the various elements that occur in a word meaning and determine the relationships among them.

If we juxtapose various word meanings, we are struck above all by the fact that not every word meaning is constructed in the same way. Thus we have, on the one hand, such words as "table," "redness," "black," and, on the other, words which were formerly called "syncategorematica" and were practically never investigated but which have gained an ever greater significance in recent logical literature, especially since the time of Husserl.[1] A. Pfänder called them "functioning concepts."[2] These are words such as "and," "or," "is," etc. Words of both groups have a meaning, but the structure is in each case altogether different. For lack of a better expression, we shall call the words that belong to the first group "names," and we shall call the meanings that belong to them "nominal word meanings";[3] and it is to this group that we shall first turn our attention.

a. The meaning of names

If, for the present, we call everything which is bound to a word sound, and which in conjunction with it forms a "word," a "meaning,"[4] then, provided it is isolated in itself and not taken as part of a sentence, the following different elements can be distinguished in the meaning of a name:

1. the intentional directional factor
2. the material content
3. the formal content
4. the moment of existential characterization, and sometimes also
5. the moment of existential position

Naturally, one should not think that the meaning of a name is a sum or a manifold of disconnected elements held together in some artificial manner. On the contrary, this meaning forms

1. Cf. Husserl, *Logical Investigations*, Vol. II, First Investigation and Fourth Investigation.

2. See A. Pfänder, "Logik," *Jahrbuch für Philosophie und phänomenologische Forschung*, Vol. IV (1921); also *Logik* (Halle, 1921). Whether the term "concept" is correct here will be seen later.

3. In his "Logik," Pfänder calls them "object concepts" [*Gegenstandsbegriffe*]. Since in our subsequent discussion we shall aim for a distinction between word meanings and "concepts," we shall avoid this term.

4. To prevent any misunderstanding, it must be specially stressed that neither the concrete psychic experiences and states of the speaker, which are at times manifested by the word sound, nor the aspects "held in readiness" by the word sound belong to the "meaning" of the word. Likewise, they are not "bound" to the word sound and do not belong to the unity of the word but, generally speaking, come into question only when the word is used in various functions in living speech. Cf. Husserl, *Logical Investigations*, Vol. II, First Investigation.

a unit of meaning in which internally connected and variously interdependent elements can be distinguished. This applies most particularly to the close connection between the material and the formal content of a name. It is precisely this internal connection that has almost caused us entirely to overlook the difference between the elements of the nominal word meaning that we have just distinguished.

If the name appears as part of a higher unit of meaning, and particularly as part of a sentence, there appears in its full meaning yet a sixth group of elements—the apophantic-syntactic ones. We shall deal with them later.

Ad 1. If we take, for example, such expressions as (*a*) "the center of the earth" and (*b*) "a table," we notice that both of them *refer* to an object; both *designate* an object, and *direct* themselves to an object. They do this, however, only because in its meaning each of them contains moments which decide, as it were, what kind of object is in question or how this object is constituted (i.e., "a table" or "the center of the earth"). Those moments of the word meaning which determine an object with respect to its qualitative condition we shall call the *material content* of the word meaning, whereas that moment wherein the word "refers" to this and no other object, or, in other cases, to this kind of object, we shall call the *intentional directional factor.*[5]

We notice at the outset that the intentional directional factor of the nominal expression can be quite heterogeneous. Thus, it can be single-rayed, as in the two examples given above, or it can also be multirayed, in either a determinate or indeterminate way. It is indeterminately multirayed in the word "people," and,

5. In his *Logical Investigations* Husserl distinguishes between "meaning" [*Bedeutung*] and "objective reference" [*gegenständlicher Beziehung*] (Vol. II, First Investigation, §§ 12 and 13). As I understand Husserl, he has in mind the same things that I here call the "material content" and the "intentional directional factor." Of course, not all of his examples agree with my distinction. According to Husserl, it is only the "meaning," in his sense of the term, which constitutes the essence of expression, but this is correct only to the extent that not every meaning has a directional factor. For nominal expressions, however, the intentional directional factor is essential. It would be appropriate to investigate more thoroughly the relationship between the nominal directional factor and the function of naming, which Twardowski, among others, contrasts to the functions of expressing and "meaning" (see K. Twardowski, *Zur Lehre vom Gegenstand und Inhalt der Vorstellungen* [Vienna, 1894] p. 11n). According to Twardowski, the function of meaning is based on the fact that the name evokes an imaginational experience in the hearer. This has nothing to do with "meaning" in my sense of the term.

conversely, it is determinately multirayed in the expression "my three sons" as well as in the dual form still retained in some languages.[6] On the other hand, the directional factor can be either constant and actual or variable and potential. The former appears in such expressions as "the center of the earth," "the capital of Poland," etc., and also in the expression "the triangle" (in the sense of a general idea), i.e., whenever the expression designates a real or ideal object (or idea) that is numerically totally determined. If we take the word "table," however, in the sense of "a table," its directional factor is potential and variable. The fact that it is only potential in this case, but that it can be actualized, can best be noticed when we apply the word "table," for example, to a determinate individual object and, in answer to the question "What is that?", reply "a table,"[7] whereby we do not mean "a table" as a member of the class "table," but where, instead, this individual object is apprehended and named for itself by means of a "schema."[8] The word "table," however, can be applied to various individual objects, and it is precisely in this that the variability of its directional factor is manifested.[9] Naturally, this factor is potential and variable only so long as the word is not applied to a totally determinate object. With application it becomes actualized and stabilized.

The intentional directional factor appears in every nominal

---

6. Pfänder distinguishes between "individual" and "plural" concepts. He does not, however, distinguish the intentional directional factor from the other meaning elements; thus, according to him, the basis of the difference between individual and plural concepts is not clear.

7. Husserl refers to this fact already in his *Logical Investigations*, even though he does not speak of the directional factor.

8. In this regard, see my arguments in *Essentiale Fragen* (Halle, 1925), p. 31*n*.

9. Connected with this is the question of how one is to determine the so-called common names or objective concepts. Since the time of Berkeley up to the present, the tradition has been developed that one defines the "common" concept as the one that designates more than *one* object. This has been asserted almost without exception by the logicians of our time, for example, in Poland, by T. Kotarbiński in his *Elementy teorii poznania, logiki formalnej i metodologii* (Elements of Cognitive Theory, Formal Logic, and Methodology) (Lvov, 1929). Pfänder correctly observes that only plural concepts designate more than one object. So-called common names, on the other hand, are generally not plural concepts and must be defined differently. That is, a name is "common" when it designates any one object (any one individual) from a class of objects unequivocally determined by the material content of the name. A name is "individual," however, when it designates an individual (center of the earth) or a group of individuals (the four brothers of King Casimir the Great) that are unequivocally determined by their material content. In the latter example it is both individual and plural.

word meaning, both noun and adjective; it is absent, on the other hand, in almost every purely functional word, such as, e.g., "and," "or," etc. Its nature—i.e., whether constant or variable, etc.—is dependent upon the material content of the nominal word meaning. The directional factor can be constant and actual *on the basis of the meaning itself* only where this content determines the intentional object with properties which—if they apply to an object at all—determine it fully and unequivocally as an individual. It is always variable and potential, however, if the material content of the word meaning determines the object ("table") through a moment ("tableness") which in fact belongs to the individual constitutive nature of the object but which it itself is not capable of constituting.[10] In this case, the material content cannot of itself compel, as it were, the actuality and constancy of the directional factor, and only a determinate utilization of the given word in a concrete case can lead to it. It is of special importance for the problem of the mode of existence of meaning units that a utilization can, and actually does, bring about such a change in the full meaning of a word. Subsequently, we shall indicate still other changes of this kind. The limits of variability of a variable directional factor are precisely what at one time was considered the "scope" of a "concept" and what was quite erroneously identified with the range of objects which come under that "concept."[11]

Ad 2. The material content, a term which we use because it determines the *qualitative* constitution of an object, is likewise primarily characteristic of names and does not appear in purely functional words.[12] Its operation consists of performing the determining function. It can perform it only because in its essence it is an intentional supposition.[13] It is part of the essence of an intentional objective supposition that by its execution something different from it—the "intentional object" as such—is "projected," is, in a figurative sense, "created." The function of the material content rests on the "determination" of this

---

10. It belongs to the "doubly dependent" moments of the immediate *morphē* of the object; see *Essentiale Fragen*, pp. 62 ff.

11. Assuming our distinctions, we can also provide definitions: a name is *common* when its directional factor is variable and potential; it is *individual* when its directional factor, on the basis of its own meaning, is constant and actual.

12. In Pfänder's sense; cf. "Logik," pp. 299 ff.

13. The source and nature of this intentionality is a separate problem, one which we shall take up later (§ 18, below).

object with respect to its qualitative constitution.[14] The material content, in other words, "attributes" determinate material features to the intentional object and "creates" it in conjunction with the formal content of the nominal word meaning. One can say that in each material content there is an element of *sic iubeo*, a "let it be such and such." The manner in which the purely intentional object of the nominal word meaning is qualitatively determined depends *exclusively* on the material content of the nominal word meaning.[15] Or, to view the same from another perspective: the purely intentional object, which in its essence belongs to the nominal word meaning, presents, with respect to its qualitative constitution, those moments—and only those—that are attributed to it in the material content of the meaning. The intentional directional factor of the name—if we view the given nominal expression purely in itself, i.e., before any possible reference to something existing really or ideally— indicates precisely the object that is determined by the material content [16] and throughout remains dependent in its direction on this content.

One should also notice the following: it is not necessary for the material content of the nominal word meaning to determine the intentional object exclusively through the lowest, no longer differentiable, moments. On the contrary, it is possible that, along with those intentional moments that do this, there also appear those which provide the object with generic moments of a higher order. It is also possible for the object to be intentionally determined only by generic moments even when the lowest differentiae are not at the same time expressly (explicitly) given. If, for example, we take the expression "a colored thing," its material content determines the intentional object only with regard to the fact that it is to be a thing and a colored thing; the color of the thing is in no way indicated by the meaning. But that it must have some color qualities inheres in the fact that

14. The expression "qualitative constitution" should be understood in a very broad sense, in which it comprehends all the determinations of the object which do not belong to the "form" of the object in the analytical-formal sense of formal ontology as it is understood by Husserl.

15. This sentence is not formulated quite correctly. A stricter formulation can be arrived at only by introducing a distinction between the intentional object and its content; here the sentence is valid only for the qualitative composition of this content. See §§ 20 and 21, below.

16. The formal content of the nominal expression also shares essentially in the intentional projection of this subject. See below, p. 69.

the thing is to be, precisely, a "colored" thing. Thus, on the one hand, a moment must be present in the material content of the given word meaning which determines the intentional object as being "colored" in general; and, on the other hand, a moment must be present which determines it as having "some" *determinate* color. The moments of the material content juxtaposed above differ essentially in the fact that while the first determines the object through a fixed, unequivocally determined constant, the second assigns an altogether peculiar indeterminacy, one which can be removed in a manner prescribed by the relevant constant moment ("colored") and transformed into determinacy only by an unequivocal, fixed, lowest quality-moment, e.g., a "red" of an entirely determinate hue. We shall call those moments of the material content whose example constitutes the first moment the "constant" moments of the content. Those belonging to the second type we shall call the "variables" of the material content. In doing so, we make special reference to the fact that such a moment does not merely assign indeterminacy to the intentional object but in addition allows (brings with it) a variability of possible individual moments which can remove the indeterminacy.[17]

A special problem, one which cannot be resolved here, is whether, in every nominal word meaning, along with the "constants," there must also appear the "variables" of the material content and whether the manner of appearance of the variables is the same as that of the constants. Whatever the case, it is important that variables can appear in the material content of a nominal word meaning. Only a recognition of their existence allows us to resolve various important logical problems, e.g., the problem of ordering various "concepts," as one usually calls them, according to the degree of their generality.[18] The failure to consider the "variables" has led, among other things, to a thoroughly false interpretation of the so-called content of a "concept." Namely, when one spoke of the "content of a concept," one had in mind solely the range of "constants" of the material content of a nominal word meaning and believed that one had thereby exhausted the full content of a concept. This led to

---

17. The variables, of course, need not always determine the lowest kinds of qualities, but they must determine the moments of the respective lowest kind, since it is the one that is determined by a corresponding constant.

18. Here it is a question of a relative generality, which should not be confused with the absolute generality we determined above (pp. 64 f.).

various far-reaching errors. In the process, the "content of a concept" was defined, quite nonsensically, as the range of "common features" of the objects subsumed by the concept.

Finally, it must be stressed that the variability of the intentional directional factor of a name is closely connected with the appearance of "variables" in its material content. In fact, the directional factor is always variable if, in this content, any "variable" is present which belongs to the determination of the individual constitutive nature of the object, provided that, at the same time, an individuating property is not determined in the material content through a special operation in compound names. This is always the case when an intentional object is conceived as if by a "schema," through a doubly dependent moment of its nature, so that the qualification of the variability of the directional factor that we gave above (pp. 65 f.) is equivalent to the one we have just now indicated. The question whether the material content of an *individual* name must, on the contrary, be composed of pure constants is one that has to be put aside for the moment.

Ad 3. If the nominal word meaning, however, were to contain nothing besides the material content and the intentional directional factor, together they still could not project an object, and especially an object of the type "individual thing." For it is part of the essence of every truly ideal, or merely intentional, object not only to have a determinate manifold of qualitative essence-determinants but also to manifest a characteristic *formal structure*. And this structure differs according to whether what we are dealing with is an ontically independent object (i.e., a "substance"), or, in particular, a "thing," or whether it is a quality, a state, etc. In nominal word meanings, as well, the objects under consideration are actually indicated as having this or that formal construction. Thus, along with the "material content," it is also necessary to admit a "formal content" in these meanings. Until now, this has almost never been done, and, consequently, nominal word meanings have been reduced solely to their material content; the reason for this lies in the particular manner in which the formal content appears in a full nominal word meaning. In this it differs radically from the material content. If, for example, we examine the compound word meaning "an equilateral triangle," we see its material content existing in a series of intentional moments connected together into one unit of meaning. These individual moments, which determine the individual features of the object, can still be discerned in the meaning as discrete, individual elements. In general, this is not true of the moments of the formal content. The formal structure of an object (e.g., of a triangle, a table) is, generally speaking, not intended in the nominal word meaning in the explicit way that its material determinants are intended. Nevertheless, the moments of a formal structure are also co-intended, and indeed in a functional manner. One can say that the nominal word meaning performs a *forming* function with respect to the object—which is qualitatively determined by the material content (though this *in itself* does not yet make it an "object")—by treating what is determined by the material content as a formally determined structured entity, e.g., as a "thing," a "property of something," a "process," a "state," etc. This treating something as a thing (or as a property of something) is what in a normal case constitutes the "formal content" of the nominal meaning. It is in fact possible for the formal content, which is usually present only in a functional way, to be made explicit, so that the corresponding feature of the formal structure of the given object would be explicitly intended in the same way as the material determinants themselves. (This is the case, for example, in the compound nominal word meaning "the redness determining the thing that is a table.") But this is an anomalous manner of appearance of the formal content of the nominal word meaning. Still, the possibility of such an "explication" best proves that the formal content is in fact present in nominal word meanings.

Ad 4 and 5. Finally, in the nominal word meaning there always appears a moment of existential characterization in a functional, and at times even in an explicit, manner. For example, in the meaning of the expression "the capital of Poland," the city in question is intended not simply as a "city," etc., but also as something which, according to its mode of existence, is real. Similarly, the object of the meaning "the equilateral triangle"—in the mathematical sense—is conceived as something existing ideally. This moment of existential *characterization*, however, must not be confused with the moment of existential *position*. Thus, the name "Hamlet," for example (in the sense of the character from the Shakespearean drama), intends an object that never really existed or will exist but one which, if it were to exist, would belong among objects to which the existential mode of "reality" applies. There is, therefore, a moment of existential characterization in the full meaning of this name; an existentially real position, however, is thoroughly lacking. The expression "the capital of Poland," on the other hand, can be utilized in such a way that the existentially real position also appears in the meaning, along with the moment of existential characterization. Its object will then be intended not only as something that is real according to its ontic mode but also as something really existing *in fact*. But the expression "Hamlet" can also be used in such a way that, along with the moment of existential characterization, the moment of a particular existential position is included, which then places the object not in factually existing space-time reality but in the *fictional* "reality" created by the sense contents of Shakespeare's drama. Particularly difficult issues are operant here, and they will be analyzed subsequently. For the present, our concern is to distinguish the two existential moments—the moment of existential characterization and that of existential position—and to emphasize that they are already present in simple nominal expressions, and not only in sentences or judgments.

The moments or groups of moments that I have distinguished in nominal word meanings are in various ways functionally dependent upon one another, and thus a difference in the material content, for example, can produce a corresponding difference in the formal content. Determinate, a priori laws prevail here, but we cannot investigate them more closely at this point.

As we will presently show, the differentiation of the various moments contained in a nominal word meaning does not yet suffice for its characterization as a *nominal* meaning. This differentiation, however, is indispensable for contrasting this characterization with other types of meaning units.

b. The difference between names and functional words

In order to approach the essence of nominal expressions more closely, let us contrast them for the present with so-called functional words.

At first glance, it seems quite easy to make a distinction between these two kinds of words since, first, nominal expressions are distinguished by the presence of a directional factor and a material content in their meaning, both of which are absent in functional words, and, second, since the latter perform various functions, while nominal expressions can perform no functions at all.

Nevertheless, this separation cannot be made that easily. In the first place, among purely functional words there are those whose function consists primarily of possessing an intentional directional factor in their meaning. These are the "indicating" functional words defined by Pfänder * that appear in various modifications, such as "this," "that," "here," etc. Whether this directional factor is variable or constant and what direction it indicates depends wholly upon the other—i.e., the nominal—word meanings with which it appears.[19] On the other hand, it is also not true that functional words do not possess any material content, or at least some analogue of it. In fact, all those functional words which Pfänder correctly observed as setting up a factual relationship between objects do have a material content. If, for example, we take the word "beside," its meaning by itself does not determine any object with respect to its qualitative properties; the meaning does not ascribe any attribute to the word, since it does not "project" any object at all. However, as soon as an object is projected by a nominal word meaning that is bound to the given functional word, as in the expression "the chair beside the table," the word "beside" characterizes the object of the corresponding name with respect to its position in space in comparison with another object. Thus, at least an analogue of the material content of a nominal word meaning is present here. Finally, it is also not true that nominal word meanings cannot perform any functions with respect to their objects. The formal content is usually already contained in them in a functional manner. The true functions of a nominal word meaning, however, become evident only when a nominal word meaning appears as part of a compound nominal meaning.[20] Let us take, for instance, the expression "the smooth red sphere" and observe the changes that occur in the word meanings "red" and "smooth," taken in isolation for the present, as they change into components of the given compound expression. In isolation, each of these words, along with its own material and formal content, also has its own directional factor, which indicates an object peculiar to it. The moment they become components of the compound expression, they perform entirely determinate func-

* [Cf. Pfänder, "Logik," p. 303.]

19. In this regard, see Husserl's considerations of "occasional" meanings (*Logical Investigations*, Vol. II, First Investigation).

20. Quite particular and indeed syntactic functions are performed by nominal word meanings when they are parts of a sentence. It must be stressed, however, that these functions are already possible in the case of compound nominal expressions which are not parts of a whole sentence.

tions with respect to their object. Above all, their directional factor becomes characteristically stabilized and actualized— either absolutely or only relatively;[21] in fact, it points to the very same object which the word "sphere" indicates. If the directional factor of the latter word is already stabilized,[22] the directional factor of the word "red" (or "smooth") is likewise stabilized and thereby also achieves its full actualization. If the directional factor of the noun is still variable, however, the result is a "convergence" of all three directional factors. This convergence depends on two different circumstances. First, there occurs a modification of the limits of variability of the directional factors of all the words appearing in the given expression, in that the limits of variability which are different at the outset are mutually narrowed, and the result is one limit of variability for the directional factor of the whole compound expression. In the second place, this mutual accommodation of the individual limits of variability is possible only because the factors in question *fuse* into one, so that the entire expression points to only one object, provided that the directional factor is single-rayed and stabilized. But this fusion of directional factors into a single one constitutes only the external expression, so to speak, of a much deeper unification of the three meaning formations into one meaning unit, a unification which for its part has its basis in the particular functions that are performed by adjectives appearing as epithets. If, e.g., the word "red" is taken in full isolation, it projects, by means of its material and formal content, an *object* that is qualitatively determined only by the property of "redness" but that remains indeterminate with respect to its nature, i.e., with respect to *what* it is.[23] The fully developed but thereby undoubtedly modified meaning of the word "red" may thus be indicated by the expression "a red something." In this sense, its meaning is dependent to the extent that it requires a completion

21. If these words are taken in isolation, their directional factor is variable and potential.

22. It must be noted that the definite article does not suffice for this. For this reason the definite article is particularly stressed in German [and English] if the given expression is to have a fully stabilized directional factor.

23. To that extent the word *rote* is different from the word *rot* when the latter appears, for example, in the sentence "*Die Kugel ist rot.*" Taken separately, the latter does not project any object of its own. Its meaning is dependent. It is made self-reliant by the *ist* and by the subject of the sentence. At that point it performs the function of determining the feature that is ascribed by the whole predicate to the object that is designated by the subject of the sentence.

which would determine the carrier of this object with respect to what it is. As soon as it is linked to the substantive "the sphere," however, it has no intentional object of its own; and it has none precisely because its performs a fully determinate function with respect to its own object. As an "adjective" attached to a substantive, it treats its own intentional object as if it were the one projected by the noun and determined, in accordance with its nature, as a "sphere." Thus the function of the epithet depends here on (1) the identification of its intentional object with that of the noun and, as a result of that, (2) the closer qualification of the latter through the moment of redness so that it undergoes an appropriate modification and now carries, as a correlate of the whole expression "the red, smooth sphere," these qualitative determinants which, in the isolated appearance of the given adjectives, were the qualitative determinants of their intentional objects.[24]

Our example thus shows that the nominal word meaning can perform determinate functions vis-à-vis the objectivities belonging to it. Consequently, the distinction between nominal and functional word meanings cannot be made from the standpoint of the performance or nonperformance of such functions, and thus, too, the essence of nominal word meanings remains not fully clarified. Indeed, the thought comes to mind that the distinction between these two types of meanings can be made on the basis of the difference between the functions they perform. Yet the great variety of functions that come under consideration and the concomitant complexity of their types and interrelationships would pose great difficulties for the solution of our problem. It seems much more to the point to see this distinction as conditioned above all by the particular quality of the formal content of the nominal word meaning. In effect, while the nominal word meanings determine ("project"), with the essential cooperation of the formal content, *primarily* an intentional *object* and perform various functions only on the already constituted object, "functional" words cannot, in themselves, intentionally project any object. They perform only various purely formally or also materially determining functions with respect to objectivi-

24. Pfänder was the first to point out ("Logik," pp. 306 ff.) that nominal word meanings ("object concepts," in his terminology) perform determinate functions with respect to their objects. But the functions I have indicated above are different from the ones Pfänder had in mind. In addition, I cannot agree with the particulars of his conception, but it would take us too far afield to go into this in detail. Later on I shall come back to what I consider to be correct in Pfänder's conception.

ties that are projected by other, and indeed usually by nominal, word meanings.[25] Thus it appears that the formal, object-forming content of nominal expressions is precisely what makes them nominal and that they may, therefore, justifiably be characterized, in agreement with Pfänder, as *"object* concepts." In the meantime, however, new difficulties emerge when one observes that (1) nominal expressions can differ considerably among themselves in their formal content (there may appear in them formal contents that project the formal structure of the thing, property, state, process, activity, relation, etc.) and (2) at least some of these formal contents can appear in word meanings that are radically different from nominal expressions, i.e., in purely *verbal* expressions. With reference to the first, it is very advantageous to contrast nominal expressions with verbal ones, and this will also be most useful for us in preparing for an apprehension of the essence of a sentence.

As a further point in the difference between nominal word meanings and functional words, one can indicate the fact that in the meaning of a name there are many heterogeneous elements to be distinguished, while such a plurality is lacking in the meaning of functional words, so that each of them performs but one function. Here again it is questionable whether this can be asserted quite generally, especially in view of the fact that there are some functional words which perform several functions at the same time (as, e.g., the "is" in a categorical sentence, which usually performs both an asserting and a predicating function). Nevertheless, it is true that it is always possible in such cases to distinguish between the individual functions and assign each of them to a different functional word. This is not possible with names. Thus, e.g., it is not possible to create nominal meanings that would contain only a material content without any formal content and without a directional factor. The full meaning of a name appears, therefore, to constitute an internally connected whole composed of heterogeneous but appropriately selected elements; nothing of the kind appears in functional words.

c. The meaning of the finite verb

Let us now analyze an isolated finite verb in any determinate form, for example: "writes," "stands," "(I) go," *"amatur,"* etc.

---

25. Therein lies the reason why the linking of purely "functional" words, e.g., "and" or "is," produces no meaning units.

Are the same heterogeneous elements that we indicated in nominal word meanings present in its full meaning?

First of all, we can doubtless speak of a "material content" in conjunction with finite verbs. If we take two verbs of exactly the same "grammatical form," e.g., "writes" and "goes," then—formally speaking—the "material content" is that in which the meanings of these words differ. Both words deal with an "activity," as one usually calls it; but it is different in each, and it is materially differently determined. In contrast to this, there is something identical in the words "goes," "went," "(we) will go," etc., despite the variability of the "grammatical form": they deal throughout with exactly the same kind of activity. To put it differently: the material content of a finite verb is that element of its full meaning which distinguishes what kind of activity is in question and in what way it is qualified. For the present, therefore, there appears to be no difference between the material content of a nominal word meaning and the material content of a finite verb. This seems to be substantiated by the fact that a comparison of the words "writes" and "the writing" leads us to seize on an identical element, i.e., the fact that in both cases exactly the same kind of activity is at issue. Is it possible that the difference between the two kinds of words lies simply in the fact that a different *formal* content appears in their respective meanings? Is not the formal content, however, that element in the meaning of a word that determines the formal structure of what is intended at the time? And does not that which is intended by the words "writes" and "the writing" have the *same* formal structure, i.e., that of an activity? It is true that the one is intended "substantively" and the other "verbally"; but, as far as the meaning of the two words is concerned, is this not an entirely irrelevant circumstance of a purely "grammatical" nature? Indeed, no one would consider that the use of "the writing" implies a thing simply because the word is a "substantive." Similarly, no one would think that an activity was involved if someone said, "The sky blues." [26] Despite the "purely grammatical" verbal "usage," the blue of the sky is intended as a property of the sky; thus, a formal content that is often found in nominal word meanings also appears in a "verb." Is there no essential

26. This example is a figure of speech that is, after all, seldom used in the living language. And whenever, in German, verbal expressions of this kind are used in the living language (*"Die Wiesen grünen"*), the meaning is also perceived as being verbal.

difference, therefore, between a nominal and a verbal word meaning? [27]

The answer to these questions must, nevertheless, be a negative one, even if some of the above assertions are true. These assertions arise from a superficial analysis of the two types of meanings. First of all, one must note that an intentional directional factor is contained in the nominal word meaning, whereas such a directional factor, which would refer to the activity that is qualified by the material content of the verb (e.g., "writes"), is entirely lacking in the finite verb.[28] However, the absence or presence of such a directional factor only makes more apparent the more fundamental difference between the two kinds of meanings. This difference inheres in the entirely different *type of intentionality*, in the *manner* in which the intentional correlates of the given meanings are intentionally created. If in this respect we contrast the words "the writing" and "writes" (i.e., words with exactly the same formal and material content), the difference becomes immediately obvious. In the first instance, a determinate activity (or, in the case of other nominal expressions, a "thing," a "property," a "state," etc.) is "projected" as something *completed* and *existing in its completion,* as something determined and limited in this or that manner and *immediately* grasped in its determinacy as a *whole* and, as such, also juxtaposed or contrasted to the word designating it (or to the ego utilizing the word and raising the intentions contained in it.) It is only in this

27. It is, of course, not my intention to cover up this difference, which is due to the appearance of analogous formal contents [in both categories of words]. Yet, in fact, there are investigators who deny the existence of this difference. A. Marty, for example, does not see any difference in the *meaning* of the two kinds of words and looks for it only in the "external and internal linguistic form" (see *Satz und Wort* [Reichenberg, 1925]). Moreover, by "meaning" Marty understands a psychic experience, that is, something that has nothing to do with meaning in our sense of the term.

28. It should be noted that here I am taking the finite verb in its purely verbal function and am examining it only as such. But it is possible to use the finite verb in the nominal function as well. Then the above statement is not valid. If, for example, in answer to the question, "What is he doing, anyhow?", I say "He writes [is writing]," I am only *naming* the activity that is already projected by the question and assumed to be existing, and I add an indeterminate something. At this point the finite verb "writes" has an expressed intentional directional factor pointing to the activity performed. We will soon see that even in purely verbal usage the finite verb has a directional factor, though an entirely different one.

confrontation [29] that the activity (or the respective object of the nominal meaning) becomes an immediate target of the intentional directional factor.[30]

Hence it is not the given contents of the formal and material content of a word meaning but rather the manner of the projection, of the creation, of the peculiar *type of intentionality* of these contents (which is reflected in the above-mentioned characters of the correlate) that distinguishes whether a meaning is "nominal." This manner, this type, may be characterized from another point of view as a static projection, through the formal content, of a "completed" formal schema (of whatever particular modification), which is again, so to speak, "statically filled" with qualitative moments through the material content. Naturally, when we speak of "filling" a schema, the image should not be understood as implying that there are qualitative moments that are free of any formal structure and and that there are formal schemata lacking any qualitative determination. The two are always indivisibly linked. Nevertheless, the metaphor of static filling, of assigning, is quite justified for characterizing the peculiar manner of nominal intentionality. This nominal manner of intentional determination is not the only one possible. Another one occurs precisely in the case of purely verbal expres-

29. Cf. the "distancing" which H. Conrad-Martius considers to be characteristic for the objective mode of givenness ("Zur Ontologie und Erscheinungslehre der realen Aussenwelt," *Jahrbuch für Philosophie und phänomenologische Forschung*, III [1916], 470).

30. Pfänder, who of course has only what he calls the "principal concepts" in mind—whereas we wish to determine all nominal word meanings and thus some of his "auxiliary concepts"—says ("Logik," p. 307*n*) that "the principal concepts are *not* characterized by the fact that they intend independent objects; indeed, in a principal concept the dependence of an intended object may be cointended. . . . Rather, what is common and decisive is the fact that the principal concepts *mentally* totally circumscribe and define the intended object, whether it is materially independent or dependent; they set it apart in and of itself; in short, they mentally complete it or substantify it." To this Pfänder adds: "If we call this form of independence a *logical* category, this logical category should be strictly distinguished from the material [*sachliche*] category of a 'thing'" ("Logik," p. 308. Pfänder is indeed correct when he makes this last distinction and stresses that objectivities of very different formal structures can be determined by nominal word meanings and that therefore—according to our distinctions and our terminology— it is not essential for nominal word meanings to have a determinate formal content which projects the structure of the thing. But the contrast of "independent" and "dependent" and then the assertion that something "materially" dependent is mentally completed does not suffice, in particular since it is not clear how, and by what means, one and the same objectivity can be conceived in such opposed categories.

sions. The nominal manner of determination, however, makes possible the existence of the intentional, directly indicating directional factor—which from now on we shall call the "nominal" one—and at the same time necessarily carries it along with it. The nominal word meaning is in fact an organically constructed unit in which all the elements not only rationally belong to one another and mutually condition one another but also "work" (if we may use the word) "in one sense." The total performance of all its elements functioning in this way is precisely what one may call the "objectification" of what is intended [by the meaning of the name], and it is characteristic of the naming function of nominal expressions. The "objectification," however—which Pfänder probably had in mind when he spoke of "substantification"—is neither connected with nor contradictory to the formal structure of the corresponding intentional objectivity, which is projected by the formal content. In the case of an activity, for example, it rests upon the fact that the activity is statically conceived in its "activity character" as a subject of particular features, as "something existing in its performance." It is not connected with the formal structure of the respective objectivity, since the same activity can also be projected in another manner, i.e., by means of the finite verb. And it is not contradictory to it since everything, to the extent that it is anything at all, i.e., to the extent that it is, is a "subject of features," regardless of whether it is an occurrence, activity, state, relation, or, finally, a substantial, universally delimited, ontically independent thing. It is only that it need not be apprehended in its "subject existence" [i.e., as a subject of features]. Through the particular type of their intentionality, nominal word meanings bring this "side" into focus, as it were, without changing anything in the particular formal structure that is projected by the given formal content.[31]

The situation is altogether different in the case of finite verbs. The meaning of the verb "writes," for example, does not lead to any conception of something as a subject of features. For that

31. In Volume II of my *Spór o istnienie świata* (The Controversy over the Existence of the World), 2 vols. (Warsaw, 1947–48) (published in German as *Der Streit um die Existenz der Welt*, 3 vols. [Tübingen, 1964–65]), I have shown that an activity or, more generally, a process or a relation has a remarkable two-sided structure: it is, on the one hand, a process of development of a growing totality of consecutive phases and, on the other, a structurally unique subject of properties which attains ever new properties in the course of the consecutive phases and is never fully constituted in the course of the process. The analysis of the difference between nominal and purely verbal meanings, provided here, agrees with this.

reason not only does it lack the directly indicating directional factor, but the material content of this meaning also qualitatively determines the activity in question in a manner that is totally different than in the case of a nominal material content. For if a subject of features is not projected, or if something is not posited under the aspect of a subject of features, then the qualification will also not be effected as a qualification of a subject of features. Yet a qualification takes place even in finite verbs, and here, too, we can speak, with full justification, of a "material content." The only proviso is that the manner of qualification be quite different. The only question is—how?

As we said, in the nominal expression "the writing," an activity is conceived as something existing in this or that manner. In the word "writes," however, this is not at all the case. Here the activity is dynamically developed, if we may so put it, as something occurring, as something happening, or, better still, as an occurrence, a happening, a consummation.[32] It is unfolded here in the character of pure happening, it is represented without being conceived as something, as a subject of features. This "unfolding in pure happening" is the essential function of the finite verb. This pure happening is naturally developed as something determinately qualified, and the fact that this occurs depends exclusively on the material content of the verb. But it is neither this qualification nor, even less so, the contents of the material content of the verb (which usually projects the formal structure of a happening, an "activity") that distinguish finite verbs from nominal word meanings, for both the qualification and the contents can appear in a nominal word meaning. It is instead the unique manner of development that distinguishes the material and formal content of finite verbs from those of nominal word meanings and precludes the existence of the nominal

32. We are struggling here with an unavoidable difficulty of verbal expression. For in analyzing the meaning of the finite verb and its intentional correlate, we have to call the reader's attention to what we have in mind, and this occurs necessarily through a *naming* reference. In doing so, however, we must make use of nominal word meanings and thus introduce the objectified mode of intentionality, which puts into the intentional correlate of a finite verb precisely what is not present in it in the simple usage of the verb and which must necessarily be removed if we are to have a faithful rendering of the situation that exists in a finite verb. Strictly speaking, this situation cannot be given by any nominal word meaning; it is only intuitively apprehendable, through a submergence in the meaning of the finite verb. For this reason, all our figures of speech are but technical means for facilitating this submergence for the reader, and they are not intended to be taken as "determinations" (in the strict sense) of the situation to be perceived.

intentional directional factor. Only this particular manner of development "in pure happening" enables us to understand that finite verbs can appear in various "temporal forms" and can at one point develop the "activity" in question as occurring "now" (or, more precisely, as a materially, determinately qualified now-occurrence) and at another point as a determinately qualified "something that has occurred in the past." [33] This kind of temporal development without further characterization is impossible in the case of nominal word meanings. We can, of course, speak of a "former occurrence" of an "actually existing state" as well as a "currently existing house," but this is possible only because a special moment appears in the material content of a compound nominal meaning through which the objectivity, which is projected throughout as nontemporal by the remaining elements of the material and formal content, can first be temporally determined in an expressly nominal manner. However, such an element does not appear in either the material or

33. Pfänder probably had this particular intentionality of "development" in temporal occurrence in mind when he expressed, with respect to the "action concepts" (in his sense of the term), the following difficult and, strictly speaking, untenable statements: "However, they differ essentially from the attributing concepts in that they mentally clothe the object, perceived as being dependent, in the form of a temporally extended activity. In this, they again make no claim that the object itself is an activity; they do not materially coordinate action with it" ("Logik," p. 311). I call these statements untenable because (1) the "action concepts" (finite verbs) do not "project" objects or subjects of features; this "aspect" of the developed "action" (the happening) remains concealed or, if one adheres strictly to the pure intentionality, undetermined; (2) neither the concepts, in Pfänder's sense, nor word meanings can, as such, "assert" anything. Pfänder is correct, however, when he says that the intentional correlates of the finite verb do not have to have the formal structure of activity (cf. "The sky blues."—Pfänder's example! [in which "blues" is a verb]) and that their formal structure is in no way dependent on the particular intentionality of development of the finite verb or affected by it. As to the manner of development, the statements found in H. Lotze's *Logik* are worthy of note: "In order to fully think the meaning of such verbs as we have used in our examples, we have to link a number of individual contents by the movement of our imagination, a movement which in its entire extension is indeed in time but which is independent of any time lapse in what it signifies or wishes to say. In a word, it is not an occurrence but a relationship among a number of points of reference which is the general meaning of the verbal form; this relationship can occur just as well among contents that are continuously extratemporal, being only in the world of what can be thought, as among contents that, pertaining to reality, are subject to temporal change" (H. Lotze, *Logik* [Leipzig, 1843], pp. 18 f.; English translation by Bernard Bosanquet, *Logic* [Oxford, 1884]). To be sure, one cannot speak of either a "movement of our imagination" or a relationship among a number of points of reference, yet this does seem to be a presentiment of what I have called, above, the "development" of an activity.

the formal content of the verbal meaning, and in spite of that the temporal element is introduced *eo ipso* by the particular mode of intentionality which in general is characteristic of finite verbs.[34] This temporal manner of representation, always somehow originally characterizing and occurrence-oriented, is, in other words, the peculiar function of the finite verb, a function, moreover, which distinguishes the manner of appearance and performance of the material and formal verbal contents from other units of meaning.

The difference between nominal and verbal word meanings will appear even more clearly if one observes that each finite verb, taken in isolation, has a meaning that is completion-requiring[35] ("dependent" in the Husserlian sense), whereas, at the very least, there can be independent nominal word meanings. This fact by itself already indicates that finite verbs are distinguished by a particular affiliation to higher units of meaning —i.e., sentences—and that taken in isolation they are the result of a particular abstraction. The completion requirement of isolated finite verbs shows itself in a peculiar element of these verbs, which constitutes an analogue to the nominal intentional directional factor. Let us turn to it now.

A verb becomes a finite verb because, among other things, as the grammarians say, it has a certain "person" and "number." Here, as we know, two forms are possible: either the simple "*amat,*" "*legimus,*" etc., or, for example, in English the customary "he writes," "we go," etc. In connection with this, we must observe, first of all, that both "*amo*" and "I think" (or "he writes") can be used and understood in two totally different ways: (1) as a sentence and (2) as an isolated finite verb. We shall deal with the first case later (in § 19). Here we must stress that it is entirely possible to take the expression "*amo*" or "he writes" not as a sentence but as an isolated finite verb, as, for instance, when I wish to clarify the difference in meaning between, e.g., the Latin forms "*amabam*" and "*amarem*" or when I am teaching someone the form of the third person singular and say "he thinks." In this case, the "he" is not the subject, nor is "thinks" the predicate, of a sentence. The words "I," "you," "he (she, it)" only explicate a determinate meaning element of the finite verb, an element that is necessarily contained in its full meaning and which remains in other languages (e.g., Latin) in an implicit

34. The form of an indeclinable participle is also possible only as a mode of the general verbal intentional development.
35. See Pfänder, "Logik," p. 312.

state. This element is not to be identified with the subject of a sentence. If there were no difference between "I think" as a sentence and "I think" as an isolated finite verb (or between the meaning of "I" in each case), we would be at a loss to explain why it is possible, for example, to say in Latin, "C. J. Caesar exercitum contra hostem misit," without implying a double subject. Likewise, one could not explain why, if the subject of the sentence is already contained in the word "*vicit*," one says "Exercitus Romanus hostem vicit" instead of simply saying "Hostem vicit." [36] If I am not mistaken, the Latin form "*venit*," taken in isolation, is more adequate for the meaning than the English "he (she, it) comes," because the latter goes too far in explicating a determinate element of the verbal meaning and, by using a particular word, gives it the appearance of a sentence-like "subject concept" (to use Pfänder's term) which is alien to this meaning element or represents an unauthorized completion of it. In fact, the full meaning of a finite verb stimulates language-formation to explicate the element contained in it—which in many languages is expressed only in the "grammatical form" of "person" or by a special word—through an indicating functional word. The reason for this is that that element which strives for explication is an immanent factor in each finite verb, one which indicates what belongs to it or, more precisely, what is concealed behind it. Here the activity developed by the material and formal content of the verb is thought of, from the beginning, as one that is executed by *any subject of the activity*.[37] This "backward"-pointing factor searches, so to speak, for *any* (passive or active) carrier (performer) of this activity. The verb "*amat*" tells us, as it were, that there must be someone who "loves" if this love is to be effected, if it is to occur. This is not to say, however, that this "search" for a subject attains its goal— that, in other words, there is such a carrier that does this, and that the given activity flows from it and is activated, effected, or sustained by it. This happens only in a sentence. In the *isolated*

36. We can, of course, find many sentences of the form "*Hostem vicit*" in Latin texts. But these are, first of all, clearly elliptical sentences, whose meaning is completed only through the complex of succeeding sentences; second, they appear as sentences, so that the reader is from the beginning attuned to those functions of the words *vicit, amo,* etc., which they can perform only in sentences. We do not deny that they can do this. We only claim that they then have a different meaning than when they are taken in isolation. And it is with the latter case that we are dealing in our study.

37. One must strictly distinguish the subject of an (active or passive) activity from the subject of features.

finite verb, on the other hand, not only is this subject not determined more specifically (it is always *some* "he," "she," or "it"), but also its existence is not conceived. The finite verb merely *requires* a subject; in a sentence the carrier of the activity is indicated as being required. At the same time, the activity being developed is still represented as being effected "purely as an occurrence," but not as "really" effected by a carrier of the activity. The dependence of every isolated finite verb is clearly seen in the existence of the searching, backward-pointing factor, which we may call the verbal directional factor. In the isolated verb, moreover, this factor is always variable and potential; it leaves the performer of the activity indeterminate, and it does not, so to speak, secure him. The subject of the activity is determined only according to number by the simple form of the finite verb—either as a single subject or as a plurality of subjects. This plurality in turn can remain indeterminate, as in "the plural," or be precisely determined, as in the dual. In connection with this, the verbal backward-pointing directional factor is also differentiated. It differs from the nominal directional factor because (1) in the case of the verb's isolation, it can never turn into a constant, actual directional factor which secures an active object (which is possible for isolated nominal word meanings), and (2) it does not direct itself at the activity developed by the material and formal content of the verb but, on the contrary, points back at something entirely different from it.[38]

We trust that we have thus presented and substantiated the difference between nominal and verbal word meanings.[39]

§ 16.   *The actual and potential stock* of the word meaning*

WE MAY OBSERVE that the same word, indeed with identically the same meaning, can be used in different situations

38. Pfänder does not distinguish the verbal directional factor, but he probably has in mind the situation that we have presented when he states that "the object intended in the action concept is apprehended as dependent in one step; and in the active form of the action concept it is coordinated to the mental subject of the activity, while in the passive form it is coordinated to the object of the activity, namely, to that object which gives it full mental support" ("Logik," p. 312).

39. Our distinctions refer solely to the differences of structure and the functions of word *meanings* and set aside the question of whether these differences concur in a genetic sense with the distinctions between word categories actually constructed in various languages.

in different ways, so that, despite the identity of the meaning, a distinct change can be ascertained in it. For example, we say, "The word 'square' means (i.e., in our terminology: has the following material content) an 'equilateral rectangular parallelogram'" (1). We can also say, however: an equilateral rectangular parallelogram with sides of any length (2); or: an equilateral rectangular quadrangle with two pairs of parallel sides of any length (3). It is in expressions such as these that we give the "meaning" of the word. Everyone would undoubtedly agree that the word "square" has these meanings. The question is, however, which of these three? All of them? Or perhaps none of them? And what does our discourse about "having" a meaning or of "meaning" [*Bedeuten*] actually signifiy? For, after all, the word "square" has its *own* meaning, and each of the various words whose manifold is supposed to explicate the meaning of the word "square" has its own meaning. We are thus dealing with not *one*[40] but a *number* of meanings, all of which, however, are "the same" in a sense that has yet to be determined. That they are not "the same" in every respect follows from the fact that the meaning of the word "square" is, at the very least, different from the meanings of expressions (1) to (3), since the latter form *compound* units of meaning, whereas this cannot be said in the same sense about the meaning of the word "square." To what, then, does the "sameness" of these meanings refer, and what does it signifiy? And finally: do we really mean by the word "square" the compound meanings of the above expressions, as, for example, when we say the sentence "The square has two equal diagonals"?

One may perhaps attempt to solve this problem by observing that there are *two different* meanings in question but that they are "equivalent" since they refer *to one and the same object.*[41] This, however, is no solution. It is true that both meanings refer to the same object in the sense that they both have an identically oriented intentional direction factor. But the expressions (1) "the square" and (2) "a parallelogram with two equal and perpendicular diagonals" both refer to an object that is identically the same—if by object one understands the *objectum*

* [I.e., in the sense of "stock of components or elements of a word meaning"; cf. *O dziele literackim*, p. 141.]

40. As is the case, for example, with the words "table," "*Tisch*," "*la table*," "*mensa*," etc.

41. And indeed, to the same object that is *transcendent* to the meaning and its intentional object.

materiale—and, despite this, have *different* meanings in a sense that is entirely different from what can be said about the above-mentioned meanings. Thus, reference to one and the same "material" object does not suffice for an "equivalence" of meanings.

Likewise, a possible recourse to the "formal objects" [42] of the meanings in question does not lend itself to a solution of the problem: by recourse to the corresponding material object we can indirectly show that the formal object is indeed identical in the expression "the square" and expressions (1), (2), or (3), in the sense that the directional factor of both meanings is identically oriented. But if by "formal object" of a meaning one understands that which exclusively possesses those qualitative properties that are explicitly assigned to it in the material content of the meaning, then the formal objects of the meanings in question are different in exactly the same degree as the meanings themselves. While the formal object of the word "square" is something constituted exclusively by squareness as the qualitative element of its nature, the "equilateral rectangular parallelogram" is constituted by an entirely different "immediate *morphē*" [43] (namely, by the "parallelogramness"), and, moreover, it is distinguished by two features: its equilateralness and its rectangularity. It is true that if anything is constituted by squareness, then in itself, due to the a priori references between the corresponding essences, it must also be a parallelogram and be distinguished by both of the above features. But this is an ontological circumstance which exists independently of the purely meaning-oriented manner of determination of the intentional object projected by the meaning. The *formal* object of the first meaning, on the other hand, is conceived differently (with respect to both its qualitative property and its formal structure) from that of the second meaning, and in this respect the two formal objects differ from each other. For this reason, the alleged "sameness" of the meanings in question cannot be reduced to the sameness of their formal objects.

One could perhaps say that the meaning of the word "square" contains implicitly "the same thing" that is explicitly meant in the second expression. One could agree to this, however, only if one already knew what "implicit" and "explicit" signify in this case and if one were sure that one could in fact "transfer" the

42. See Pfänder, "Logik," p. 273n.
43. See J. Hering, "Bemerkungen über das Wesen, die Wesenheit und die Idee," *Jahrbuch für Philosophie und phänomenologische Forschung*, IV (1921), 495 ff., and also my *Essentiale Fragen*, p. 27n.

first meaning into the second by means of a "making explicit" whose sense has yet to be determined. As I see it, it is a question of, on the one hand, two *different meanings* that belong to one and the same ideal concept of the same object and, on the other hand, two different ways in which the elements of one and the same meaning can appear.[44] For it is part of the *concept* of a square that it be constituted by squareness as the qualitative moment of its constitutive nature and that *eo ipso* it contain in its nature the doubly dependent element of "parallelogramness" and at the same time be provided with "rectangularity" and "equilateralness." Likewise, the essence of "squareness" is a derived essence that is equivalent to the determinately ordered manifold of essences: "parallelogramness," "rectangularity," and "equilateralness." [45] The meaning of the word "square" contains in its material content *actually* only part of what is contained in the concept of a square or in the idea of "the square"; in contrast, the meaning of the expression "equilateral rectangular parallelogram" contains *actually* a *different* part of the content of the *same* concept, one which, moreover, allows the object of the concept to be constituted by a manifold of essences that is *equivalent* to squareness. Further, both of these meanings contain, though now in a totally different, potential way, something which is also contained in the ideal concept of a square, namely, that the sides of a square can be of "any absolute length." This appears *actually* only in the compound meanings (2) and (3). Or, to put it differently: each word meaning of a *non*compound nominal expression which in its formal content intends something in *objective* structure is an *actualization* of a *part* of the *ideal* sense that is contained in the concept of the corresponding object, assuming, of course, that such a concept exists. Above all, this actualization creates the material and formal content of the meaning. Each ideal concept has a number of word meanings for the same object. That aspect of the ideal sense of the concept that is actualized in each case creates the *actual stock* of the meaning. On the other hand, that which is still contained in the given concept and ensues directly from the actualized stock constitutes the *potential stock* of the given meaning, i.e.,

44. Pfänder also distinguishes between the "concept" and the "meaning content" of a word (see "Logik," p. 272*n*). I cannot agree, however, with Pfänder that concepts can be meaning contents of words. It is also not clear whether Pfänder considers a concept an ideal objectivity, since his various observations concerning this are contradictory.

45. With regard to this entire analysis, see the corresponding explanations in my *Essentiale Fragen*, Chap. 5, esp. § 26.

that which can also be actualized without the already actual stock of the meaning having to be altered in any way. By converting the potential stock of a nominal word meaning into an actual stock, the full word meaning is indeed modified, but the modification is based only on an enrichment of the actual contents of its material content. A modification of its formal content may also accompany it.

If this conversion of a potential stock into an actual one occurs in such a way that each of the newly actualized elements of, first of all, the material content finds its *own* "expression," i.e., is "clothed" in a corresponding word or manifold of words, then the newly actualized stock appears "explicitly" in the meaning of the given expression. Otherwise we arrive at a compound nominal expression. The change of the potential stock into the actual can also be conducted in such a way that the meaning that still contains the potential stock and the meaning that already contains it (or at least a part of it) in actual form, are both bound to *the same* word sound (or to the same manifold of word sounds). In this case the newly actualized part of the actual stock does not find any particular expression of its own. This stock is contained "implicitly" in the corresponding word meaning. Insofar as the nominal word meaning does not refer to primary simple essences, it has both an actual and a potential stock. On the other hand, each individual nominal word or compound nominal expression can have a meaning appearing in either the explicit or the implicit form.

It seems indubitable that there can be an implicit appearance of the potential elements of the nominal word meaning. Inasmuch as we do not take into consideration the possible references to experience that an intelligent reader of the text may make but confine ourselves to the contents of the text, there arises the difficulty of how one can convince oneself, on the basis of the text alone, that the text and, in particular, the nominal word meanings entering into it contain an *implicit* potential stock. For there is no trace of this in the simple word sound. In the living language, and especially in declamation, the nonexplicit potential elements of meaning can be made known by means of intonation. None of this remains, however, in the case of silent reading. The purely literary artistic text, in which one cannot call upon cognitive results, seems to present a distinct difficulty.

Two resources may be useful in this situation. First, one can draw on the system of meanings of the given language. In this system the individual words, and especially the names, are endowed with their full meaning as a result of the various connections which the given word has with other selected words. Usually, however, only a fraction of this full meaning is actualized; the rest remains potential and implicit. But it is always possible to undertake a corresponding explication or, at the very least, to consider it as a possibility. Second, in a given literary work the individual words frequently appear in a different context, which in turn suggests, as it were, which potential elements of the meaning are, or should be, implicitly cointended with these words. These two circumstances allow us to make a distinction in the potential elements of the word meanings, i.e., between those "potential" elements of the meaning whose potentiality constitutes a mere possibility and those "potential" elements of the word meaning which are not yet actualized but which, so to say, approach this actualization in that they are "suggested." If we were to call the first the "empty" potentiality and the second the "ready" [prepared] potentiality, one could say: the greater the knowledge of the vocabulary and the possible associations of words in the given language, and the more active the support of the context in which the word meaning in question appears in the given work, the richer the stock of the "readily potential" elements of the word meaning. The problem of what properties of the contexts' activity this stock is dependent on is a broader one, and one which we cannot develop here. There is no doubt, however, that in this respect the texts of individual literary works show great differences. It is clear, at any rate, that one cannot comprehend the potential and, in particular, the readily potential stock of the word meaning if it is isolated from the context. The reference to these potentialities also provides us with a transition from the observation of individual words to the investigation of the interconnected meaning units of a higher order.

We attain the cognition of an object, and in connection with it also the comprehension of its ideal concept, in a temporally extended manifold of cognitive operations.[46] The further the cognition progresses, the more we comprehend of the contents of the ideal concept of the given objectivity. In conjunction with this, there is also a change in the accompanying nominal word meaning. Its actual stock, which at the outset is comparatively meager, is gradually enriched as the potential stock is progres-

---

46. The issue of the cognition of primary essences can be left out of account here.

sively actualized. If, in the process, one goes from the simple word meaning to increasingly interconnected word meanings, then, in lieu of the originally meager actual stock, a much richer actual stock of the same meaning takes on explicit form. If, on the contrary, the same word sound is used consistently, the meaning belonging to it will indeed be richer, yet it will always remain in the implicit form. It is easiest to comprehend the change in the meaning of one and the same word in terms of, for example, the reading of a scientific work. However, one can also trace it easily in the history of a science. In the poetic work of art, too, one can discover new phases in the course of the work, where changes take place with respect to the actual and potential stock of the individual word meanings. And it appears that, at least in many works, the stock of the readily potential elements of word meanings grows considerably in the course of the development of new phases or parts of the work. However, in this we are anticipating our subsequent investigation of the literary work of art.

Various particular manners of transformation may come about in the course of different transformations of the actual and the potential stock of word meanings. For example, it may happen that the actual stock of a meaning is the actualization of the elements of not one but two (or more) concepts which we have not yet distinguished. The potential stock of this meaning, of which we are almost totally unconscious, may thus contain content elements whose total manifold has no single ideal concept corresponding to it at all. Only the further movement of our perception and the transformation from the potential stock into the actual one that is connected with it make us conscious of the fact that what we have is not *one meaning* but *two* different *concepts*. At this point there occurs what one usually calls a "separation of concepts," which actually is based on the breakup into two or more different meanings of what had previously been considered one meaning. We then reject the original, unbroken meaning as "nonobjective" or entirely contradictory. If such a "breakup" does not occur, even though the newly actualized stock is the actualization of *different* concepts, then we are dealing with a special form of "nonobjective" or contradictory word meanings. It may thus happen that in the use of such a word only a part of the newly actualized stock is truly intended, i.e., that which belongs to concept A; another time, a different part of the newly actualized stock is meant, i.e., that which belongs to a different concept, B. The stock of content elements that recurs in both cases tempts us to perceive this fact in such a way that we remain convinced that we are dealing with one meaning, which is the same in every respect. We are then dealing with words which have double or plural meanings but whose ambiguity escapes our attention. Finally, if there is an enrichment of the initially content-poor actual stock of a meaning belonging to *one* concept, then, even after the termination of this entire process (i.e., when the perception process is arrested for a while and our nominal word meanings "solidify"), changes of the actual stock of the word meanings may still occur, whereby the same word may be used in various instances with either a richer or a poorer actual stock. In connection with this, the degree of "implicitness" of the word meaning may also vary.

It is clear that in these changes it is primarily the material content of the meaning that comes into question. However, the same thing may happen with its formal content. It must also be noticed that, while the formal content is a functional one, usually it also belongs to the potential stock of the meaning.[47] Only special reflection on the formal structure of the corresponding object or on the use of the word in a sentence causes the formal content to change into the actual stock of the meaning; with the use of the meaning, the corresponding functions are either simply consciously executed or are made intelligible in a special way. But this would lead us too far afield.

§ 17. *Word meanings as elements of sentences, and their attendant changes*

THE INDIVIDUAL, isolated word, whose semantic side was the object of our preceding investigation, appears in the literary work, as we have already mentioned, not as something isolated, but always as an element of a sentence, and sometimes—and then it is essentially changed—as an entire sentence in itself. Its isolation is undoubtedly the result of an artificial operation performed for purposes of observation. However, we have attempted to perform this in such a way that, while no essential deformation of the units of meaning would result, the basic structure of the various types of words would, at the same time, be brought out. It cannot be denied, however, that signifi-

47. This applies, above all, to isolated word meanings.

cant changes occur in word meanings when the words are isolated or when they are reinserted into the whole of the sentences. Thus it will be our next task to pursue these changes and in particular to show what changes are undergone by one and the same word with respect to its meaning when it occupies different positions in the sentence. These changes arise from the fact that the individual word does not simply appear in a sentence (as, for example, a thing in a class of things) and merely enrich the whole of the sentence by one meaning element; rather, it performs, at the same time, some *function* in the sentence. Since these functions are very numerous and multifarious, we can treat only some of them as examples.

The appearance of a word meaning in a whole sentence entails, above all, a structural change in both of them. Let us compare the following two examples:

1. The manifold of words: "Every. Body. Is. Heavy."

and

2. The sentence: "Every body is heavy."

We notice immediately that while in (1) every word meaning forms a self-contained whole, this self-containment is broken in (2). As an element of the sentence, the individual word does not cease to be what it is, yet it is significantly changed in its structure. One word meaning becomes linked in an almost literal sense to another word meaning; what is more, they *unite* with each other into *one* unit of meaning, in which they do not disappear fully but merely lose their mutual rigid delimitation. And only this union allows the constitution of something that is a "sentence." The way in which the "self-containment" of the individual word meanings is broken down in a sentence is a different question, and one which we cannot analyze here. An example of the preliminary analysis for this may be the consideration conducted above of the functions that the individual word performs in a compound nominal expression.[48]

However, the changes which the word meanings, and in particular the nominal meanings, undergo in a sentence go far beyond the purely structural. Let us juxtapose the following sentences:

---

48. We cannot deal here with the separate question of which subjective operations these structural transformations go through, since this would generally avoid phenomenological problems.

1. C. J. Caesar, the Roman consul, crossed the Rubicon.
2. In the Roman state the Roman consul exerted great influence on the course of political affairs.
3. L. Brutus killed the Roman consul himself.

Let us now compare the *full* meaning which the expression "the Roman consul" has in these sentences with the meaning it has when it appears in (4)—i.e., in full isolation. In all four cases, the material content of its meaning is fully identical. On the other hand, there are distinct differences with regard to the remaining components of its full meaning. First of all, as regards the intentional directional factor, it is variable and potential in (2) and (4), where the limits of its variability are determined by the material content of the expression. In (1) and (3), on the other hand, it is actual and constant. But even between these last two cases a difference arises with regard to the directional factor. While in sentence (1), due to the special function of this expression, it points not only to an individual, specific Roman consul but also to the one who is in fact C. J. Caesar, so that ultimately he is the terminal point of its direction, in sentence (3) it is also directed at an individual specific object, but at the same time its function seems to terminate there. To be sure, it undoubtedly follows from the content of this sentence that Brutus could kill only an individual, specific consul; but it is likewise not at all clear that it was precisely Caesar. Only if we were to take sentence (3) in connection with the other sentences (or with our historical knowledge) would the intentional directional factor of this sentence be exactly the same as the one appearing in sentence (1).

This property of the directional factor in sentence (1) necessitates the fact that both the expressions "C. J. Caesar" and "the Roman consul" ultimately refer in this sentence to one and the same object, although their material contents have almost nothing in common. In this way they build a unit of meaning of a higher order, whose constitution is based on the specific grammatical-logical function of the apposition which in this sentence is performed by the expression "the Roman consul." As a result, there occurs correlatively a remarkable identification of the intentional objects of both expressions. In the remaining instances there are no signs of this.

It can be shown that significant differences also appear in the formal content of the expressions in question. Let us observe the following. If we examine the given expression ("the Roman

consul") in isolation, we see that its formal content contains
that element which specifies the intended object as an *independent* carrier as contrasted to the properties adhering to it
(particularly that he is a *Roman* consul). In (2), this element is
modified. At issue there is still an independent carrier of
properties; but the quality of being a carrier is interwoven with
a special element which is necessarily exhibited by the formal
structure of the object as soon as the latter is treated as a subject
of an *explicit* predication directed at it, as is exactly the case in
sentence (2). The same element in expression (4) is modified
in a totally different way in (1): the object specified by the word
"consul" does continue as the carrier of properties, but in a certain sense it is no longer an independent carrier. In this case,
the expression "the Roman consul" has, so to say, lost its own
independent object. The ultimate independent carrier, which is
simultaneously the subject of the predication, is specified by the
name "C. J. Caesar"; he is also "the Roman consul"—in other
words he performs a special role which more closely determines
him as the Roman consul. This role finds in him its ontic basis;
it is ontically grounded in him.

A further different modification of the same element of the
formal content of the expression in question is found in (3).
Here, too, the corresponding object is perceived as an independent carrier of its properties, but it also exists as an object
at which an action is directed. As a result, the carrier of
properties is changed into a carrier which *bears* the activities
directed at it. This modification stems from the grammatical-
logical function of the accusative, which the given expression
performs in this sentence, and it is directly connected to the
material content and the function of the predicate "killed." This
connection is so close that the expression "the Roman consul"
would be essentially dependent if it appeared in full isolation
(i.e., not in a sentence). Thus the above modification, stemming
from the function of the expression in the sentence, is so far-
reaching that it transforms an independent nominal expression
into a dependent one and thus essentially stamps it as a part of
a higher meaning unit.

It should be noted that these modifications of the formal
content are basically its enrichment. They all stem from the
special functions performed by the nominal word meanings in a
sentence, and they are essential for these functions. If these
functions were to be eliminated, then the modifications in question would also cease to exist. The use of an isolated word for

constructing a sentence introduces into its full meaning various modifications and elements that are foreign to the isolated word. If we are dealing with a nominal word meaning which forms part of a sentence, we must distinguish sharply between the elements of its formal content that it would retain even in isolation and those that are produced by syntactic functions. This differentiation is of particularly great importance where we cross over to the intentional correlates of word meanings and analyze the formal structure of purely intentional objects as distinguished from the formal structure of "states of affairs," "facts," etc.

We will see later on that the *material* content of nominal word meanings can also undergo various changes (which we have already partially indicated above) when they are employed in the construction of sentences. But these changes usually appear only when we are dealing with a manifold of connected sentences. We shall thus defer their examination to an appropriate point in our work (§ 23).

§ 18. *Word meanings, sentences, and complexes of sentences as products of subjective operations*

THE INVESTIGATIONS conducted in the last three sections were intended not only to disclose the essential features of word meanings and their structure but also to turn our attention to a series of facts which have to be taken under consideration if the general idea of the word meaning is to be disclosed and, in particular, if the problem of its mode of existence is to be solved.

To begin with, there are, in modern investigations of the units of meaning, two radically different conceptions: the psychologistic, which was dominant among the logicians of the last decade of the nineteenth century, and—if one may call it such—the "idealistic," whose most distinguished representative is Edmund Husserl in his *Logical Investigations*.[49] His devastating

49. In the thirties, the logical-physicalist conception of language propagated by the so-called Vienna Circle gained great popularity. Actually, I had already found the main theses of this conception in Warsaw in the year 1919. It prevailed among the logicians of that city—Lesniewski, Tarski, etc. But a theoretical alliance between the Warsaw group of logicians (to which, among others, Ajdukiewicz also belonged) and the representatives of the Vienna Circle occurred only in the early thirties. The year 1934 (the Prague Philosophical Congress) was the high point of

critique of logical psychologism seems to have overcome for all time that doctrine in which word meanings ("concepts," as they were then usually called) and sentences are to be regarded as psychic states or elements of the concrete stream of existence. And yet when Husserl himself, in Volume II of the *Logical Investigations*, undertook the analysis of "meaning" by investigating the essence of the intentional cognitive act—that is, by proceeding on the path of phenomenology—his system culminated in the observation that meanings are "ideal species" of a special type. At that time it seemed that this was the only possible solution of the problem that would avoid the errors of psychologism. However, we must ask whether Husserl—at least in the period of the *Logical Investigations*—did not go a step too far.[50] For regardless of how the theory of ideal objects and "essences" developed in Husserl himself (in the *Logical Investigations*) and in his students,[51] the identification of word meanings with "ideal species" of a special type (according to Husserl's own explanation) necessarily implied their *timelessness* and therefore their absolute *changelessness*. How then should it be understood that one and the same word meaning—as we have hoped to show it—can combine at different times with this or that meaning into a unit of higher order, that it may appear in various positions in the sentence and thereby be subject to various modifications of its intentional directional factor and its

this alliance and also of the "physicalist" conception of language (with tinges of "operationalism"). After the Prague Congress, and after the publication of Tarski's treatise on the concept of reality, there came, on the one hand, a slackening of ties between the Polish logicians and the Vienna Circle and, on the other, the formation of an essentially altered standpoint in the conception of language. It would take us too far afield to go into the details of the over-all conception, as well as the various changes that have occurred in recent decades up to the most recent publications of Carnap and Wittgenstein. I first spoke out against the original conventionally physicalist conception of linguistic formations that prevailed up to 1934 (as far as my foreign publications are concerned) in a paper delivered at the Prague Congress and then in a somewhat expanded article in the *Revue philosophique*, "Essai logistique d'une refonte de la philosophie" (1936). The interested reader may refer to that. A part of my counterarguments is contained in § 9 of this book.

50. As I first learned on the basis of a letter from Husserl [in 1922] and then by personal communication from my esteemed teacher in 1927 during my stay in Freiburg, Husserl had abandoned his previous logical position and had begun lecturing in 1922 on "transcendental logic." Unfortunately, I am not acquainted with these lectures and therefore cannot say whether the assertions presented in this book are related to those of Husserl. See the preface in regard to this.

51. See, in particular, the works of W. Schapp, J. Hering, H. Conrad-Martius, and also my *Essentiale Fragen*.

formal content, and, furthermore, that it can take on various modes of actuality or potentiality, of explicitness or implicitness? Can it still be considered an ideal *species* and be placed on the same level with ideal essences or ideas? Or, on the other hand, can one, for the above reasons, consider word meanings as psychic realities, as components of psychic existence or of conscious experiences? Or can one in general deny the existence of ideal meaning units, of ideal concepts?

Neither the psychologistic nor the idealistic solution is tenable. This was clearly demonstrated by the insoluble difficulties we posed at the beginning of our work concerning the mode of existence and the ideality of the literary work.[52] Yet, how should the new positive solution sound?

Above all, the following should be noted:

1. In the various changes of the full word meaning which we have indicated above, there is no question of any psychic or subjective conscious processes which do or can take place in the thinking of a sentence or a word meaning. These subjective processes of the consciousness, which may possibly occur parallel to the changes presented, were not mentioned above in any way. They can also be very diverse in one and the same sentence. The concretely experienced contents of the consciousness can differ significantly with respect to both the degree of concrete explicitness of the material content of the given word meanings and the manner in which the formal content is cogitated, not to mention the multifarious possible modifications of clarity or vagueness. We have spoken, however, exclusively of the transformations that occur in the meanings themselves when they occupy various positions in a sentence or in different sentences and which we discover in the analysis of the total contents of the meaning of the sentence itself (or of the word) even if we know nothing of the concrete processes of the speaker's consciousness. Despite the difference between the two sets of transformations—on the one hand of the units of meaning, on the other of the concrete conscious experiences—the possibility exists that, in the case of a sentence, we are dealing with something that, according to both its mode of existence and the

---

52. These difficulties, of which I first became conscious in 1918, when I began writing a dialogue on the literary work of art, also gave me the first impulse to the insight that one has to abandon the "idealistic" conception of word meanings. But, at the same time, I went too far in the opposite direction, so that, at the time I was writing *Essentiale Fragen* (1925), I was disposed to deny the very existence of meanings or concepts.

determinants of its content and form, is assigned to the performance of determinate conscious operations. But even if this possibility were shown to be a fact, the sentence, along with all its parts and elements, forms a self-enclosed unit which cannot be identified with any concrete units of consciousness or their real parts. And it is exclusively the constituent facts that can be found in this unit that will furnish the material for solving the problem of their ideality or their changeableness and thereby also the problem of their relation to the concrete conscious operations effected in the course of time.

2. The question arises of how far we can speak, in the cases discussed, of a *transformation* of one and the same word meaning and, in connection with this, whether it would not be more correct to maintain that word meanings are absolutely unchangeable and that, on the contrary, only we, the cogitators, *switch over* from one meaning to another in the process of using word meanings in the formation of sentences. If this were in fact the case, the argument against the idealistic conception of the word meaning would become void, and the entire state of affairs would then appear (at first glance) to be much simpler.[53]

Nevertheless, this projected solution leads to significant difficulties. First of all, one would have to accept a much greater variety of meanings than would exist with our conception of meaning transformations. For example, instead of one word meaning, "table," one would have to accept as many different, though related, meanings as there are modifications of this meaning in the various instances of its application.[54] Then it would also be false that one and the same word can be used in different sentences in multifarious functions. On the contrary, one would have to agree that one and the same word sound can be "bound up" with various meanings and therefore be very ambiguous. In itself this would not yet be an absurdity. What is worse is that, to be consistent, one would have to speak of *two* meanings when it is only a question of the difference between the actual or the potential stock of a meaning. In this way one would not only arrive at a monstrous proliferation of vocabulary, but it would also become impossible to determine the individual elements of a meaning if this could be done only with the help

---

53. This is the solution which Husserl, in his *Logical Investigations*, attempted to implement with regard to "occasional meanings."

54. Thus, "the table," "a table," "I am buying a table," "I am sitting at a table," My "table is large," etc., would all be entirely different meanings.

of other and different word meanings. Likewise, a word standing in isolation would have a different, a *second*, meaning from the meaning it has when it appears in a sentence (as a consequence of the structural differences we have indicated above). Thus there would be, on the one hand, words which, according to their very essence, could appear only in a given sentence and could not be torn from its context and, on the other hand, words which could never be an element of a sentence. In connection with this, one would also have to accept an endless manifold of sentences that are "complete" in advance and only waiting to be discovered by us. It will be demonstrated, however, that the total meaning content of a sentence undergoes various and sometimes very essential modifications only because the given sentence appears in a certain place in a determinately arranged manifold of sentences. If it were to appear in another place, or in another manifold of sentences, its meaning content would be altered. As a consequence of the attempted solution we are arguing against, one would also have to speak, in this case, of two different ideal "sentences in themselves." Finally, one would have to consider those manifolds of sentences which, due to the over-all meaning content and to the arrangement of their sequence, form a meaning complex of a higher order (a complex of sentences) as complete, timelessly existing ideal formations. It is obvious that from such a complex of sentences one can create at one's discretion a great number of other manifolds of sentences by rearranging their parts. If the attempted solution we are arguing against were correct, one would have to consider the writer to be not a creator of his work but only a discoverer of complexes of sentences.

As a consequence, the thought that word meanings and all units of meaning of a higher order are ideal unchangeable formations and that only the thinking subject performs the *transition*, occurring in time, from one meaning unit to another, would not be absurd. But not everything which is not absurd is *eo ipso* true. If we could demonstrate that what is present is not merely [mental] transitions from meaning to meaning or from sentence to sentence, but truly sentence-forming operations, we would have the conclusive argument that units of meaning of a higher and a lower degree are not an ideal species.

3. If, however, word meanings and the units of meaning of a higher degree are neither elements of psychic existence or of the concrete consciousness nor an ideal species of a special type, and yet their existence is not to be doubted, then it is clear—especially since units of meaning are not physical objects—that the

usual distinction of all objects into "real" and "ideal" does not exhaust all the possibilities. Thus, it is necessary to accept yet another type of objects. On the other hand, it is not necessary to doubt the existence of ideal objects. One must only sharply distinguish them from units of meaning.

4. We cannot attempt to provide a phenomenological analysis for the subjective operations which generate the units of meaning of a higher and lower order. It will suffice to indicate the following facts.

An essential aspect of the word is that it possesses a meaning by dint of which it either intentionally designates an object and determines it *materialiter* and *formaliter* in this intending or performs determinate intentional functions with respect to the already intentionally projected object. This intentional designation, which is linked to the word sound, is not—as we have already mentioned—a phonic property of the word sound itself; it is totally heterogeneous with respect to it, yet it is linked to it. It is precisely this heterogeneity which makes it impossible for the word sound to be linked, on the basis, as it were, of its own power (i.e., due to its rightful properties), to the intentional thinking or to perform the various intentional functions. If this "linking" does occur at all, or rather, if the word sound carries any meaning at all, it is only because this function is as if externally imposed; it is bestowed upon it. This bestowal can be accomplished only by means of a subjective act of consciousness. We do in fact know acts of consciousness in which we bestow a sense, a meaning, to a word. Something which is initially meaningless, which in no sense indicates anything beyond itself, comes to be used as an external support for something that is heterogeneous to it, as, for example, when we intentionally designate an object (and, in particular, one that is not present) and, forming the phonic material into a word sound, make the latter into a "name" for the intended object. The intentional designation contained in the meaning is, as it were, a reflection of the intentional thinking [*Meinen*] contained in the meaning-bestowing act.[55] The intentionality of the word is the intentionality that is *bestowed* by the corresponding act. But while the intentional designation contained in the act of consciousness constitutes a *concrete, real* element of the act and shares with the entire act its absolute ontically autonomous mode of existence (i.e., it

55. See Husserl, *Logical Investigations*, Vol. II, First and Fifth Investigations.

exists in the same sense that the act itself does), the intentional designation bestowed upon the word is not merely fully *transcendental* with regard to the act of consciousness but is also something which exists in a thoroughly *different* mode of existence, i.e., one in which the object itself refers to some other existence, from which it draws its source and upon which it is dependent. In a real sense, the act of consciousness creates something that did not exist before, even though it is not capable of creating anything that, once created, could exist with ontic autonomy. In comparison with the existence of the real, the ideal, and, finally, the purely conscious, what is created is analogous only to "illusion," to something which only pretends to be something though it is not this something in an ontically autonomous sense.[56]

Every word meaning, taken in isolation, is a self-enclosed unit of meaning. In spite of this, the vast majority of them—as our analyses have demonstrated—conceal within themselves a manifold of various elements, in particular when it is a question of a compound nominal word meaning. These elements are selected from all the possible ones by the meaning-bestowing act of consciousness and are combined into one unit. This usually occurs in a discrete manifold of conscious acts, so that the meaning is first gradually constructed and reconstructed until the moment when it stands before us as something finished and no longer in the state of production and, in conjunction with the word sound, forms a "word" which we can use as frequently as we wish in various situations as identically the same, i.e., as having, to put it more precisely, the same word sound and the same meaning content.

To be sure, the conscious and intended formation of isolated word meanings occurs, relatively speaking, very rarely. Usually it is the case that in cogitating entire sentences and complexes of sentences we use the already extant word meanings for constructing sentences. Since we are attuned to the totality of the sentence which we are to construct, we find these word meanings without further ado; they come forward on their own and accommodate themselves to our ordering and combining grasp. Thus the primal language-forming operation is that of sentence-

---

56. We will go into this in greater detail below, p. 122. Cf. our "Bemerkungen zum Problem Idealismus-Realismus," *Festschrift, Edmund Husserl zum 70. Geburtstag gewidmet, Jahrbuch für Philosophie und phänomenologische Forschung, Ergänzungsband* (Halle, 1929), and § 20, below.

formation. That such a sentence-forming subjective operation does exist is best demonstrated in those instances where—in the course of its formation, as it were, and even at the last moment —we formulate a sentence we have already begun in a manner different from what we had initially intended, or, for example, when, having already grasped a "thought," we wrestle for the precisely appropriate, for the simplest and clearest, formulation and reconstruct the initially planned (and perhaps even recorded) sentence in various ways until the "finished" sentence is finally expressed or recorded. However, not only the reconstructed sentence, but *every* sentence is formed in a temporally extended subjective operation. For a sentence is nothing else but the correlate of an operation that allows many variations. In its execution, the operation not only uses word meanings but also forms and restructures them so that a meaning unit of a higher order may result. For at the basis of the sentence being formed there lies what one may call an empty formal schema, which is predetermined by the general type of sentence-forming operation; and only when this schema has been filled out in the course of the uniform execution of the sentence-forming cognitive operation by the corresponding word meanings, which possess material content, does the sentence become a "sensible" sentence. It is the sentence-forming cognitive operation which brings out the transformations in individual word meanings that we analyzed above, adjusts them to the basic schema and type of the sentence being formed, and constitutes the unity of the sentence. If there were no sentence-forming operation, there would be no sentences. As a result, the transformations in the individual word meanings appearing in the sentence, which go hand in hand with sentence-formation, are completely relative to the execution of this operation; they *originate* from it in the true sense of the word. But precisely for this reason, the sentence as a whole, as well as the organically interconnected parts appearing in it, forms something which has nothing in common with the purely ideal sphere of "concepts" and ideal objects in general, that is, with a sphere in which individual objects are beyond the reach of any spontaneous activity of the conscious subject and where they resist any attempt at changing them. The whole sentence, along with all the elements of meaning appearing in it, is "established" [*gestiftet*]—to use Husserl's term—and is, in a manner of speaking, maintained in its existence by this operation. In what sense one can speak of the "existence" of a sentence is a question we shall answer only in connection with other, analogous questions (see Chap. 11). For the time being, it may be clear from what we have already said that, with respect to its existence, the sentence does not have its source *in itself*, nor is it ontically autonomous in the sense that during its existence it contains in itself the foundation of this existence. But precisely because of this, sentences, and—as we will soon see—to a still larger extent, manifolds of connected sentences, are accessible to the subjective restructuring operations of the consciousness. They do not resist the attempts at transformation in the way that ideal objectivities in a strict sense do. The sentences cannot merely "originate"; they must also be changed in corresponding subjective cognitive operations, connected into higher units, or, finally, be destroyed, that is, be removed from the world in the very specific cognitive operation of "rejection." [57]

The sentence-forming cognitive operation, which according to its particular properties produces variously constructed sentences, can be performed in two basically different ways: either in the form of a primal, truly sentence-*forming* operation or only in the form of an operation that corresponds to the primal one and yet is an essentially modified, a *duplicating* or reactualizing, operation. Only the sentence-forming operation of the first kind is truly creative, and it requires for its execution a very special spontaneous activity of the conscious subject; the sentence-duplicating operation, on the contrary, only reactualizes what has already been created, and it can be effected by a purely receptive stance of the subject.

The sentence-forming or duplicating operation, however, is in most instances only a relatively dependent phase of a much broader subjective operation, from which arise not individual, out-of-context sentences but, instead, entire complexes of sentences or manifolds of connected sentences. [58] When, for example, we conduct a proof or develop a scientific theory or simply narrate an account, we are attuned, usually from the very beginning, to the whole which we are to "develop" even before we have formed the individual sentences by which it will be "developed." This adjustment to the whole may take on various forms of a

---

57. It would be the task of a noetically directed logical investigation to thoroughly study the essential structure of the sentence-forming mental operation and also to set forth the possible varieties of this operation. This would be the counterpart of the noematically oriented "apophantic of sentences" in the Husserlian sense.

58. We will consider in a later section (§ 23) what conditions must be met for a connected manifold of sentences to arise.

more or less conscious implicit apprehension (imagination) of the whole. A specific "theme" comes to mind—as "that which is to be discussed" or as "that which is to be developed"—and it combines with the impulse to execute this development. If we accede to this impulse, the theme is transposed into a manifold of sentences which we construct in sequence, yet always with reference to the whole. At the same time, a single theme can be "developed" or "represented" in multifarious ways. Every one of them requires a different arrangement of sentences, which, depending upon the chosen arrangement, must be differently "formulated." The given sentence-forming operation is thus, on the one hand, under the guiding principle of the yet-to-be-expressed and, on the other hand, is under the pressure of the already-expressed; it is thus relatively dependent and is carried by the initial impulse of developing a theme. But even when we do not have a preconceived theme which has to be "developed," a specific sentence-forming cognitive operation can be of the kind that conceals in itself the nucleus, so to speak, of subsequent formation. It carries with it a manifold of other sentence-forming operations in which first a theme is crystallized and subsequently there is the formation of a specific "story," "proof," etc. Here, too, the individual sentence-forming cognitive operations are carried by the general impulse; they are motivated by what precedes them and are adjusted in their details to the still vaguely sketched-out goal. In this case, however, no actual phase determines unequivocally which subjective operations are yet to follow. If even this goal is sketched out vaguely and indeterminately, the tendency is always present to perform the already actually executed sentence-forming operation as one which is to be followed by other operations or—if it is a question of forming the "last" sentence—to construct it precisely as the "ending" of a connected manifold of sentences. The well-known phenomenon of "interruption"—when we are addressed by someone while we are speaking, reading, or writing—is possible only because, while the actual sentence-formation constitutes only a phase of a broader operation, its successive phases, though not yet effected and, more frequently, also not predetermined, are already announced in some way and are already influencing what is actually being effected.

Each of these broader cognitive operations, whose transitional phases are formed by the individual sentence-forming operations, corresponds to a connected manifold of sentences which is a unit of meaning of a higher order: a story, a proof, etc.[59] Its structure, the type of connection of the individual sentences, the arrangement of the latter, etc., is, throughout, dependent upon and relative to the aggregate of the underlying subjective operations. One can narrate "the same thing" in various ways; but each of these narrations forms an object in itself, which exists only because it was constructed in precisely this manner and no other. And it would be laughable to believe that all these various treatments of "the same theme" have existed from all eternity as ideal objects when, during the narration, we have a definite awareness that we could easily do it in another way, that it is in our power, insofar as external circumstances do not interfere, to construct the narration in this or that way. The "narration," the "proof," the "theory" developing in this manner —i.e., understood as a unit of meaning of a higher order, as a manifold of connected sentences—can raise no claims to ontic autonomy; it can do so even less than an individual sentence. However, it does not at all follow that, in performing an initial cognitive operation which produces a complex of sentences, we are *fully* free and subject only to the creative impulse. With regard to the narrowing of our freedom, significant differences arise among the subjective cognitive operations which bring out the various possible types of sentence complexes. But as, on the one hand, we are not fully free, so also we are not fully bound, even in the framework of the strictest theory, which we can structure and restructure in various ways. And it is precisely the possibility (and the fact) of such a reconstruction that best demonstrates that the "theories" constructed by us (taken as manifolds of sentences) are not ideal objects. This will be substantiated by our subsequent investigations of sentences and sentence complexes.

The temporary solution, therefore, of the problem occupying us in these paragraphs is the following: the stratum of the literary work which is constructed out of word meanings, sentences, and complexes of sentences has no autonomous ideal existence but is relative, in both its origin and its existence, to entirely determinate subjective conscious operations.[60] On the other hand, however, it should not be identified with any concretely experi-

59. See § 23, below.
60. One may, of course, doubt whether only a pure mental operation is at issue in every sentence complex of that type, as if different factors, perhaps of an emotional nature, did not play a role. It is certain, however, that a mental operation of some kind cannot be lacking, even though in itself it may stem from deeper subjective impulses and may accommodate itself to them.

enced "psychic content" or with any real existence.[61] We are dealing here with something entirely specific, the closer clarification of which, especially with respect to its mode of existence, is yet before us.

We must go deeper into the stratum of meaning units, however, if we are to reveal their role in the literary work.

§ 19. General characteristics of the sentence[62]

WE HAVE SPOKEN previously of sentences and sentence complexes as correlates of determinate subjective intentional operations without dealing more closely with the structure of these objectivities. We shall now bring up this matter to the extent that it is germane to our purpose.

In the literary work, sentences of all possible types can, on principle, appear. Thus, even "mutilated," incomplete sentences may appear (for example, in the dialogue of a drama). Usually, these various kinds of sentences are named according to what,

61. K. Twardowski, who in his treatise *Zur Lehre vom Inhalt und Gegenstand der Vorstellungen* (Vienna, 1894) stands entirely on psychologistic ground with respect to word meanings, later attempted to modify his standpoint on this question in his *Czynnósci i wytwory* (Activities and Creations) (1911), where he conceives meaning as a formation of the psychic functions. I am not very clear, however, about what kind of formation this is to be and what Twardowski in fact means by "meaning." Thus I am not able to say what the relationship is between my conception and Twardowski's. One thing seems certain, namely, that Twardowski accepts neither the derived intentionality of word meanings (nor considers meaning as one of his "general objects," which arises from all the "common" moments of the psychic "contents" of the corresponding mental experience) nor the ontic heteronomy of the word meaning, once it has been formed. Since I cannot agree with his conception of "general objects" nor fully understand his conception of the word meaning, I must limit myself to the observation that the only relationship between Twardowski's position and mine is that, in both, meaning is considered a product of subjective operations.

62. As I was writing these paragraphs in 1927 and when my book appeared in December, 1930, J. Ries's paper "Was ist ein Satz?" (*Beiträge zur Grundlegung der Syntax*, Vol. III [Prague, 1931]) was not yet published. I read this paper only many years later, at the beginning of the last war; and, while it was written by a linguist and, in particular, a grammarian and naturally sought to perceive the sentence from a different point of view, I found much in it that was closely related to what I have argued here. I cannot go into it at greater length here.

as one puts it, they "express." [63] It may, of course, be questioned whether this is the proper basis for differentiation; for the time being, however, we can make use of it. Thus we can say that we find in a literary work sentences which express "judgments," "questions," "desires," or "commands." Furthermore, sentences may appear in various modifications, as, for example, in direct as opposed to indirect discourse, etc.

Without going more deeply into the individual types of sentences, we would like to draw, at least in outline, a general characterization of the sentence in order to describe, on this basis, its role in the literary work. This characterization must proceed in three different directions: (1) what a sentence is in itself, (2) what it performs, purely of itself, as an objectivity constructed in a particular manner, and (3) what services it performs for psychic individuals in connection with their lives and experiences.

Ad 1. Like individual words, sentences are also a two-layered formation, in which one has to distinguish (*a*) the phonetic stratum and (*b*) the meaning content. As we noted before, there is no "sentence sound" which, as a unit, may be analogous to the word sound. If the sentence does appear as a unit, this is due solely to the unity of its meaning content; this is what we must now characterize more closely.

This content is a *functional-intentional* unit of meaning which is constructed as a self-enclosed whole out of a number of word meanings.[64] Word meanings enter into it as its components, but, nevertheless, it is not a simple sum or aggregate of word meanings but rather an entirely new objectivity with respect to them, one possessing its own particular properties. Since it is constructed precisely out of word meanings, however, it is indebted to them for a number of properties. Thus it is, above all, an intentional unit, i.e., one that transcends itself and points to

---

63. Wundt, for example, divides sentences into (1) exclamatory, (2) declarative, and (3) interrogative. A. Marty, however, posits (1) assertions, (2) emotive speech, and (3) fictive speech, and so on. In this respect one finds some very interesting arguments in K. Brugmann's *Die Syntax des einfachen Satzes im Indogermanischen* (Berlin and Leipzig, 1925), especially "Die Gestaltungen des Satzes nach der seelischen Grundfunktion," pp. 187 ff.

64. Among other things, I would like to stress that we are using the word "sentence" in the narrow sense in which the so-called subordinate clause is not a sentence but only a part of it. A great many authors, e.g., Wundt, Delbrück, Marty, and Bühler, have pointed to the fact that the sentence is a self-enclosed unit. Cf. the modifications that arise in this respect from the connection between sentences (§ 23).

something different from itself. Only the way in which it points to something outside itself is different from the way that the isolated word does this. On the other hand, it is, as we said, a *functional* unit, since by its very essence it performs, as a whole, a function which arises from the functions of its components. To put it more precisely: it performs a function which specifies which functions the word meanings (or words) appearing in it must perform if they are to appear as its components. Only by determining this function and the special nature of the intentionality of a sentence can we bring out essential aspects of a sentence. More about this presently. At this point we must counter a possible objection.

We have said that a sentence [65] is constructed out of a manifold of word meanings. There are, however, so-called one-word sentences, as, for example, "Fire!", as well as "*Amo.*", etc. We do not wish to renew here the argument over "subjectless" sentences. Whatever the case may be, the sentence "Fire!", as well as "*Amo.*", contains a manifold of word meanings. It appears to consist of one word only on the purely phonetic level. For in every sentence of this kind there appear "punctuation marks," which, according to their function, are nothing other than various dependent, functional words. The word "fire" naturally does not constitute a sentence, but the expression "Fire!", taken with the "exclamation mark," does constitute—as Marty correctly noted —a full sentence. The exclamation mark performs here a special, rather complicated, and differentiated function.[66] The sentence "*Amo.*" conceals in fact three elements of meaning, since we are fully justified in this case in developing it into "*Ego amo.*" Something similar can be shown in all other cases, leaving aside the many "one-word sentences" that are clearly elliptical formations and whose sense is completed in connection with the sentences that follow it. In any case, one-word sentences usually constitute an exception and also a borderline case. Most sentences are constructed out of several words, not only in terms of their meaning content but also on the purely phonetic level. We will now turn our attention to these sentences.

In his article "Kritische Musterung der neueren Theorien des

65. Here, and frequently in the following, we are using for the sake of convenience the shorter expression "sentence" instead of the more exact "the meaning content of the sentence." This cannot produce any misunderstanding, however.

66. See, for example, F. Neumann's paper in the *Festschrift, Edmund Husserl zum 70. Geburtstag* (cf. n. 56, above).

Satzes," [67] K. Bühler distinguishes three basic kinds of sentences: *manifesting, releasing,* and *representing* sentences, and he identifies the last of these with affirmative propositions [declarative sentences]. Representing sentences "represent" a state of affairs; but with respect to the function of representation, we learn only that it is a *coordination* of words to objects, of sentences to states of affairs. Both the objects and the states of affairs are intended as elements of reality.[68] I will not argue here whether there truly are these three kinds of sentences, with each sentence performing one and only one of the functions distinguished. It appears to me that *each* sentence performs *all* these functions, or at least can perform them, and that the individual sentences differ from one another only in that, at a given time, one or another of the functions is in the foreground. It is much more important to note that the function of "representation"—correctly understood— can at no time be lacking in a sentence, since it constitutes the indispensable basis for the other functions of the sentence. It is, therefore, also necessary to set forth correctly the essence of "representation." For it does not depend on simple "coordination" with the real object and state of affairs. This is true at the very least because (1) there are many sentences [69]—indeed, declarative sentences—that exhibit no "coordination" with real (or even with ideal) objects,[70] and (2) if only this "coordination" with something objective were to be characteristic of the sentence, then in itself it would not be capable of performing this function. In other words, the sentence must have such properties as bring about its "coordination" with *some* (either really or ideally existing) determinate objectivities. From the preceding, it is clear that we must look for this property in the intentionality of the sentence meaning.[71] It must differ from the intentionality of the individual isolated word meaning, for otherwise there would be no essential difference between words and sentences. This differ-

67. *Indogermanisches Jahrbuch,* IV (Berlin, 1920), 1–20.
68. Bühler does not say this expressly, but it undoubtedly inheres in the sense of his arguments.
69. That is, sentences which, according to Bühler's own explanation, should perform the function of representing and which he therefore calls "representing sentences."
70. Strictly speaking, all false declarative sentences [affirmative propositions] belong here, but, above all, sentences with purely fictional objectivities.
71. That is, if we do not want to fall into the nonsensical position where, on the one hand, there would be meaningless sounds and, on the other, only psychic experiences, which would decide the "meaning" of these sounds.

ence appears to be the most definite result of linguistic and logical investigations thus far. This particular intentionality of sentences, however, should not be studied on the basis of sentences which claim to be true and thus have a very special reference to existing (real or ideal) objectivities. For, in that case, one could easily consider as an essential property of a sentence what would be valid only for a judgment (in the logical sense).

Every sentence—as we have already stated—is the result of a subjective sentence-forming operation. Usually this operation is at the service of other operations, which modify both themselves and their product. Thus, for example, it can be at the service of a cognitive operation or a simple exchange of information between several psychic individuals. It can also be used as the medium for influencing another psychic individual (e.g., political agitation, etc.) or simply for the purpose of fixing the results of the free play of the imagination. Finally, it can be merely the wholly unintentional sequel to the performance of specific psychic processes, one in which the latter find their conceptual-verbal "expression." If this operation appears, for example, at the service of the cognition of something real, it is usually effected on the basis of an intuitive apprehension of an objectively existing state of affairs and is adapted in its phases, with greater or lesser precision, to the content of the latter. As a result, it is bound up with various elements that are not essential to it. Thus, it is interwoven with a particular intentional moment, thanks to which the effecting subject not only "directs" himself at a state of affairs existing in reality but also believes that he has *found his mark* and that in this connecting intentional glance he has become anchored in reality. The sentence that is thereby being formed requires a corresponding intentional moment which, as we shall presently demonstrate, both transcends the purely intentional correlate that belongs to *every* sentence and appears to *find its mark* in the state of affairs existing in reality. The purely intentional correlate of the sentence is thereby intentionally tranported into reality in a characteristic manner and is not only identified with a really existing state of affairs but is also recognized as really existing along with it. In contrast, the sentence itself—as the location, so to speak, where this recognition has its source (though only a secondary one)—is enriched by yet another element: it claims to be "true." In a word, it becomes a "judgment" in the logical sense, one that is subject to evaluation according to "true" and "false." All of this becomes void if we free the sentence-forming operation from the service of cognition. If, on the contrary, we use the sentence only for an exchange of information with another psychic individual, with regard, for example, to situations whose real existence neither of us believes in (i.e., when we neither "express" nor "perceive" any judgment), then the expressed sentence is free of the moments discussed above, but, on the other hand, it gains another intentional moment: it becomes "directed" as a whole at someone. Even though nothing is changed in its meaning content, it is, nonetheless, no longer a pure sentence but an "address" or an "answer."

These examples should suffice to convince us that, if we are to investigate the sentence purely in itself, we must take it exclusively as a product of the sentence-forming operation, free of any other functions or purposes.[72]

Let us now take a very simple "categorical" sentence of the form "S is P" (e.g., "This rose is red." and "A wagon passes.") Let us not, however, take it as an "expression" of an executed judgment, but let us limit ourselves to what the sentence itself says in its meaning content, that is, as if it were not applied to a determinate state of affairs intuitively given to the subject of cognition and rooted in the sphere of reality. We said previously that, in accordance with its meaning content, this is a functional-intentional unit which conceals a particular intentionality and performs a particular function. What does this say of our examples?

"A wagon passes." In this meaning unit we distinguish, on the one hand, the name "a wagon" and, on the other, the verbal expression "passes." We have already noted that the meanings of these expressions are not loosely juxtaposed. But how are they joined into a unit? The name "a wagon" names an object and, in particular, a thing; it names it because its nominal directional factor is directed at an object. However, for this factor to be directed at it, the object must be determined; it must be projected by the material and formal content. Thus the first work done by this name consists of the nominal projection of an object. The expression "passes," taken in itself, develops an activity and points back by means of its verbal directional factor at a subject

---

72. It is questionable whether one could succeed in freeing the sentence-forming operation from the other operations and functions in which it is usually involved and have it isolated, only for itself. But this is not necessary for our purposes. It is enough to view it in itself and at the same time treat the other functions, with which, at any given time, it is bound, as changeable and arbitrary.

of the activity. As part of the sentence, however, it does not merely "search" for it—as it would if it were isolated; it has already found it, as it were, in the object projected by the name "a wagon." As a result, the following three facts occur: (1) the developed activity is now represented as effected, as caused by *this* object; (2) the object projected by the name becomes, as a result of this, a subject of the activity and, more precisely, the subject of that particular activity which is developed by the finite verb—but by this alone *it is not yet named as such;* and, what is more, (3) it becomes the subject of an activity and is conceived precisely in the execution of the given activity.[73] No longer is there a loose juxtaposition of the subject of an activity and a so-called subjectless activity, but a new unit is produced: "A wagon passes." [74]

It must be emphasized that (1) the *sentence* "A wagon passes" and (2) the *nominal* expression "a passing wagon" are not identical in meaning. In (2) an object which performs a specific activity is *named,* that is, the intentional directional factor points to an object which from the outset has been determined (i.e., by the material content of the compound meaning) as "passing." It is not stated here that it is passing, but the object appears as one that is provided with a special feature due it by reason of the activity performed and as a consequence of the performance. In the sentence "A wagon passes.", the wagon is not at all projected or named as one that is provided with this feature. It is projected and named simply as a "wagon"; and only when the activity developed by the verb gains a foothold in it, thanks to the verbal directional factor, is its activity, and thereby it itself in the performance of this activity, developed in a verbal —and, as we shall see, not purely verbal—manner.[75]

---

73. These are two different matters: simply to be the subject of an activity and to be the subject of an activity performing precisely that activity. For example, to apprehend someone simply as a teacher, and to apprehend him as a teacher performing precisely his function of teaching.

74. Recently H. Ammann pointed to the unity of the sentence (*Die menschliche Rede* [Lahr i.B., 1928], Vol. II). The mere assertion, however, will not suffice as long as one does not show how this unity is produced.

75. See Herling, *Die Syntax der deutschen Sprache:* "In the sentence the relation appears as one that is occurring, in the word as one that has already occurred. In 'The bird flies' the relationship truly occurs, in 'the flying bird' the relationship of flying to the bird is shown as having already occurred" (cited by J. Ries, "Was ist ein Satz?"). Ries adds: "Herling's formulation signifies the following: the sentence is the linguistic result of a psychic act in its current execution; the (narrow) word group, on the other hand, is the expression of the result of such a previously executed act. In a sentence the nexus of presentation is, so to speak, ex-

As we have just described it, the function of the finite verb in the sentence examined illuminates the structure of the meaning content of this sentence only from the standpoint, so to speak, of the verb appearing as a predicate. One can, however, examine the same situation from the standpoint of the name "a wagon": here it is not simply a name; in fact, it functions as the *subject* of the sentence. This signifies a twofold function: (1) "wagon" not only names an object, but it also conceives it as something that is a carrier of either a feature assigned to it or an activity that is to be performed by it. (In the sentence being examined, it is clearly only the latter that is applicable.) The name makes the named object "ready," as it were, to perform this or that function; and only because it is made "ready" can the object serve as the end point of the searching verbal directional factor. And conversely, because of this, the activity developed by the finite verb can "gain a foothold" in the object. Let us assume that a purely functional word appears in place of a name—for example, the word "and," giving us then the phrase "and passes." Here the verbal directional factor searching for support can find no object by which the given activity can be effected; it passes by the linkage formed by the word "and" and necessarily indicates something beyond the entire formation projected by the expression "and passes." It is for this very reason that the formation is

---

perienced (or reexperienced) as occurring at the time, while in the word group it is apprehended and represented as already complete and present in the consciousness" ("Was ist ein Satz," p. 69). J. Kuryłowicz sought to formulate this difference in yet another manner in his "Les Structures fondamentales de la langue: Proposition et groupe des mots," *Studia Philosophica*, Vol. III (Cracow, 1947). I believe, however, that the difference is based on something else. To that effect, I made the attempt in Volume II of my *Der Streit um die Existenz der Welt* to formulate the essence of the process according to its form, in contrast to the objects (and in particular to things) continuing in time. It then became obvious that one must necessarily distinguish the process as it develops in the course of time as a growing totality of phases, from the process as an object (as a subject of properties) constituted in this development. The difference between a sentence and a word group in which a name is connected with an adjective corresponds to this difference. The sentence grasps the process in its primary form of a developing totality of phases, whereas the word group grasps it as a particular object. Clearly, this is already the case in the difference between the purely verbal formulation "flies" and the nominal formulation "the flight of the. . . ." One can, of course, raise the question of whether the formal difference between the process as a subject of properties and the process as the developing totality of phases is primary, so that the difference between the given linguistic formations is a linguistic reflection or whether it is, on the contrary, intentionally brought into existence by the various linguistic formations. This, however, is a problem which far exceeds the subject at hand.

not independent, and the expression in itself appears as a fragment that still has to be completed by something. (2) The name that serves as the subject of the sentence also functions as the meaning factor which satisfies the need for completion of the finite verb appearing as the predicate. It enables the backward-searching verbal—and, when the verb is isolated, potential—directional factor to actualize itself and to blend with its own nominal directional factor. In this way it also enables the finite verb to perform its function of developing the activity as one *stemming from a subject of the activity.*

One can also say that on both sides—on the part of the name acting as the subject of the sentence and on the part of the finite verb acting as the predicate—functions are performed which, metaphorically speaking, only wait for each other to fully work themselves out with mutual support. Consequently, they not only establish the unity of the meaning content of the sentence but also bring to fruition the function of the *whole* sentence which is founded on them. In our example this sentence function rests on nothing other than this very characteristic *nominal-verbal development* of an activity which will be performed by a carrier of the activity. One can, of course, rightfully object that in not every case is it a question of the development of an activity—if only in another example: "This rose is red." The predicate "is red" fulfills here the function of *attributing* a trait.[76] But this predicate, too, does this in the same verbal manner that was seen in the previous example. It develops the "having" of the characteristic "red" that exists, as it were, within the object.[77] Thus, the formal content of the expression "is red" contains here, not the moment that projects the structure of the activity, but one that is essentially different, i.e., one that conceives the "red" in terms of the characteristic structure of "attributing a characteristic to something." On the other hand, the verbal-predicative function of this expression remains in force. In connection with the, in this case, different formal content of the predicate, the name carrying out

76. We are disregarding here the "assertive function" of the "copula" (see Pfänder's "Logik," p. 182), since we are analyzing only affirmative, not assertive, propositions.

77. It seems doubtful to me whether the so-called purely nominal sentence that is frequently used in some Indogermanic languages can be distinguished, according to its meaning content, from the "copula"-containing sentence now being analyzed. The only difference that I can see between them is that the predicate of a purely nominal sentence performs its verbal function implicitly, whereas it is explicit in sentences of the second type. K. Brugmann is quite correct in maintaining that the purely nominal sentence is not an elliptical formation (*Die Syntax,* p. 62).

the function of the subject of the sentence does not project any carrier of the activity but instead projects a carrier of the yet to be accepted trait. Depending on what kind of predicate appears in the sentence, there also appears a change in the function of the subject of the sentence. This is best seen in the way the elements of the meaning content of the sentence adjust to one another and how, in this adjustment, they build a unit of meaning, so that in every case the same total function of the sentence attains completion, i.e., as the nominal-verbal development of the state of affairs.

We have thus described one of the most essential functions, and for us, in any case, the most important function, of the declarative sentence. In itself, the declarative sentence is a unit of meaning whose particularity consists in performing this function.[78] At the same time, we see in it the special nature of the intentionality of the sentence meaning, one which we still have to characterize in a few words. This intentionality is neither purely nominal, directly indicative-determining, nor is it a purely verbal and developing intentionality; rather, it is entirely specific, and extensive analyses will be required to clearly set forth its particular character and make it accessible to intuitive apprehension. We must be satisfied at this point with the observation that it consists of a peculiar synthesis of the two kinds of intentionality that have been distinguished—the nominal and the verbal. However, the verbal element always prevails.[79] Its correlate is also entirely unique; this correlate is not an "object," nor is it a pure "behavior" (which could be projected without being the behavior of something) which would correspond to the isolated finite verb. It is, as it has correctly been called at various times, a "state of affairs." [80]

Ad 2. The performance of a sentence depends on its total

78. If it were a question of a complete theory of the sentence, one would have to demonstrate in detail that this function is performed by every sentence, whatever its form or content. And of course it is no easy task to show, on the one hand, the various modifications and complications of this function and, on the other, its identity in all these variations. However, this would lead us too far from our main subject.

79. F. Neumann is quite correct in this respect in claiming that the verb is the sentence-forming element. See "Die Sinneinheit des Satzes und das indogermanische Verbum," *Festschrift, Edmund Husserl*, pp. 297 ff.

80. I am unable to say who was the first to introduce this term. In any case, it had taken root in philosophical language from the time of the investigations of the phenomenologists—Husserl, Reinach, Pfänder. A. Meinong, who at any rate had occupied himself with intentional sentence correlates before Reinach, used the term "*Objektiv*." K. Stumpf, however, also used the term "state of affairs."

function: This function intentionally creates a sentence correlate, and at the same time it also "coordinates" this correlate to
the sentence. In particular, the state of affairs created and developed by the sentence is transcendent with respect to the sentence content yet, according to its essence, belongs to it. In other
words, in its existence the state of affairs is essentially relative
to the sentence or to its meaning content; it finds its ontic basis
in it. Hence, there is no developed state of affairs without a sentence, and there is no sentence without a developed sentence correlate. One must also note that the state of affairs that is developed and created by the sentence must be strictly distinguished
from a state of affairs that "objectively" exists and is rooted in an
ontic sphere that is ontically independent with respect to the
sentence.[81] Thus, we shall call the first the "purely intentional
state of affairs" or the "purely intentional sentence correlate."
We shall see later that the two can be set "in relation" to each
other and that in this way the sentence can attain a "coordination" to an objectively existing state of affairs. (see §§ 22
and 25).

Ad 3. Finally, in communicative speech, *every* sentence can
perform the function of "manifesting" or of "releasing" [82] [or
"evoking" the reactions of the person being addressed] in a manner more or less expressive or evident. However, the fact that not
every sentence must necessarily do this is best shown by those
cases where we construct sentences without "directing" them at
anyone or without manifesting them to anyone even in a wholly
unintentional way.[83] Only those sentences in which the releasing
function is prominent, due to their special meaning content, lose
their intrinsic meaning (i.e., their "purpose") when they are constructed in solitary, nonexternalized thought.

Although the purely intentional sentence correlate and the
purely intentional object belong essentially to the next stratum of
the literary work, it might be useful at this time to say something
about their structure. For in this way it will be easier to present
facts, important to our purpose, which are closely related to the
structure and the performance of sentences and complexes of
sentences. Let us turn to them now.

81. See my *Essentiale Fragen,* p. 3n.
82. See K. Bühler, "Kritische Musterung der neueren Theorien des
Satzes" (see n. 67, above).
83. This same problem, pointed at the essence of meaning, is treated
in detail in Husserl's *Logical Investigations,* Vol. II, First Investigation.

§ 20. The purely intentional object of a simple intentional act

BY A PURELY intentional objectivity [84] we understand an objectivity that is in a figurative sense "created" by an act of consciousness or by a manifold of acts or, finally, by a formation (e.g., a word meaning, a sentence) exclusively on the basis of an immanent, original, or only conferred intentionality and has, in the given objectivities, the source of its existence and its total essence. We will later (pp. 122 ff.) have an opportunity to examine more closely in what sense we can speak of a "creative" operation of an act of consciousness and, correlatively, of a "createdness" and existence of a purely intentional objectivity. For the time being, the determination made above will serve only to distinguish the purely intentional objectivity *in terms of its idea* from objectivities that are ontically autonomous [85] with respect to consciousness. It is entirely accidental that the latter objectivities (if they exist at all) become targets of conscious acts and thus in a secondary manner become "also intentional" objectivities.

The word "intentional," used so frequently in modern philosophical literature, is ambiguous. At times, that which contains an "intention" is called "intentional." In this sense, conscious acts, for example, are "intentional." Wherever there is a danger of misunderstanding, we will use in these cases the term "intent" instead of "intentional" (e.g., "an act of intent"). At other times, that objectivity is called "intentional" which constitutes the target of an intention. In this latter sense, then, one must still distinguish between "purely intentional" and "also intentional" objects. The definitions at the beginning of this section are meant to draw this distinction. Finally, among the "purely intentional" objects, one must still distinguish between the "originally purely intentional" and "derived purely intentional" objects.

---

84. With respect to intentional objects, see, above all, Husserl's *Ideen zu einer reinen Phänomenologie* (Halle, 1913), passim. [English translation by W. R. Boyce Gibson, *Ideas: General Introduction to Pure Phenomenology* (New York: Macmillan, 1931).]
85. See my "Bemerkungen zum Problem Idealismus-Realismus."

The former draw the source of their existence and their essence *directly* from concrete acts of consciousness effected by an ego; the latter owe their existence and essence to formations, in particular to units of meaning of different orders, which contain a "borrowed" intentionality. Since formations of this kind refer back to the original intentionality of acts of consciousness, even the derived purely intentional objects have their *ultimate* source of existence in these acts.[86]

Purely intentional objects are "transcendent" with respect to corresponding, and, in general, to all, conscious acts in the sense that no real element (or moment) of the act [87] is an element of the purely intentional object, and vice versa. Nevertheless, they belong to the corresponding acts from which they draw their source; and they constitute a necessary "intentional correlate" of these acts, in the sense that this correlate flows from the essence of the acts of consciousness.

A special instance of purely intentional objectivities are the originally purely intentional *objects* that belong to a simple act of intending (or to a manifold of them). Let us turn to these first.

First of all, in every purely intentional object we must distinguish between its *content* and the *structure* which characterizes it as something *purely intentional.* One could speak of its content and the purely intentional object itself or, finally, contrast the specific characters of intentionality with its content.[88] In particular, it is a question of the following.

For the sake of simplicity, let us take the purely intentional

86. Obviously, neither intentionality nor purely intentional objects were discovered by me. Without the investigations of Husserl, Pfänder, F. Brentano, and K. Twardowski, I would not have arrived at these ideas. In the following I am only trying to reveal more thoroughly the essence of the purely intentional object and to free its "concept" from various impurities. Max Scheler also distinguishes between "purely intentional" and "also intentional" objects (see his article "Idealismus-Realismus," *Philosophische Anzeiger,* II, no. 3 [1927], 255–324.

87. In the sense of Husserl's *Logical Investigations,* Vol. II. Concerning the transcendence of intentional objects, see Husserl's *Ideen,* §§ 41, 42.

88. In my *Essentiale Fragen,* where I occupied myself with the special case of the purely intentional objects that correspond to sentences (I called them formal objects of judgments or questions), instead of speaking of the contents and the structure of intentional objects I spoke of their "matter" and "form," as a consequence of which I had to struggle with the inevitable ambiguity of these terms. See *Essentiale Fragen,* pp. 3 and 8*n*.

object of a simple intentional act in which we "merely imagine" a determinate "table." To the content of this object belong: (1) the formal structure of the thing, (2) the total range of material determinations which, while partaking in this structure, qualify the whole as a "table," and (3) an ontic character of some sort, depending upon whether we "imagine" a "real" [89] or a fictional "table." Here, the main element in the formal structure of the thing is the independent carrier of the qualitatively determined properties or features, which itself is determined by a qualitative moment (the "tableness"), which is its "immediate *morphē*" [90] and which becomes the nature [91] of the given object. But this carrier of properties of the intended "table" constitutes only a distinct point, as it were, of the content of the given purely intentional object and is different from the carrier of *this object itself*. The given purely intentional object as such has its own carrier, i.e., a carrier of *its* properties or features, which are different from the properties that appear in its content and pertain to the intended "table." To the carrier belongs, for example, the fact that the purely intentional object is only "something intended" which necessarily belongs to the given act of consciousness, that it contains a "content" (i.e., this specifically determined content), etc. Thus a remarkable bilateralness and "double-carrier" quality is present in the structure of the purely intentional object, and this in itself constitutes a characteristic, formal distinctiveness of purely intentional objects as such (i.e., it does not belong to their content), a distinctiveness which, in individual objects that are ontically independent with respect to the act of consciousness, is not only absent but by its very essence is excluded.

This discussion of the two carriers that appear in a purely intentional object must be understood correctly, however. First of all, of the two carriers distinguished, the one with ontological priority is the carrier of the properties of the purely intentional object *as such*. The second carrier (the one described by "tableness") plays in the purely intentional object as such only the subordinate role of a distinct element within the framework of its content. If *having* a content is a property of the purely inten-

89. More exactly: "intended as real."
90. See J. Hering, "Bemerkungen über das Wesen, die Wesenheit und die Idee," *Jahrbuch für Philosophie und phänomenologische Forschung,* Vol. IV (1921).
91. See my *Essentiale Fragen,* Chap. 2.

tional object,[92] then the "carrier of the table" belongs to the domain of that which is possessed by the intentional object, and in this object itself it performs no role as a carrier. The "carrier of the table" performs this role only with respect to the other moments of the content (the properties of the intended "table"), and it "does" this, in contrast to the carrier role of an ontically autonomous object, for example, only in a very modified sense (about which we shall speak more precisely later).[93] Furthermore, for both of the carriers to be visible, the act of intending must be effected in a particular manner. Usually the structures and characters of the intentionality of the purely intentional object and, in particular, its carrier do not come into view at all. Primarily, we are directly focused on what we have called, above, the "content," and we have it before us, not as a *content*, but simply as something that is an object whose carrier constitutes precisely the carrier element of the content of the corresponding purely intentional object as such. And under the aspect of the "what" of this element, what is intended is not only the content of the corresponding intentional object alone (as it in fact should be) but the *entire* intentional object. In these cases, in other words, what plays the role of the *true* carrier, so to speak, of what is intended is precisely this moment that is qualified by an immediate *morphē*, whereas the authentic carrier of the purely intentional object as such remains in a latent, practically concealed state. Only a particular manner of executing the act, one which exhausts the *full* capacity of the act of consciousness, as it were, makes the true carrier of the intentional object fully visible and shifts the relation of the two carriers toward each other in the way discussed above.

One might be inclined to deny these remarkable transformations that occur only in purely intentional objectivities during a change in the manner of executing a simple act of intending, and one might, as a result, deny the presence of the pair of carriers. For in everyday life, in our natural attunement to ontically autonomous objects, we are inclined to extend the objective structure found in them to all objectivities in general and to reject as absurd the assertion of the existence of the two carriers.

92. It would of course be a mistake to consider the content itself a property of the purely intentional object. But it is also difficult to consider this content as a part of this object in the sense in which a leg is part of a table. These are quite special situations, which must be investigated separately.

93. See Chap. 7, § 33.

At most one could concede that an illusion of their presence in purely intentional objects arises from the fact that we perform a *new* objectivization, in that, instead of simply effecting an intentional thought, we intentionally direct ourselves in a second act to the correlate of the first thought. But then—the charge goes—we are dealing basically not with *one* but with *two* different purely intentional objects, each of which possesses *one* carrier.

To this one must say that, naturally, it is possible in principle to submit the intentional correlate of an act of intending to a new objectivization of a higher degree, as it were. But this is not necessary, however, for grasping the purely intentional object in its peculiar double structure. On the other hand, this bilateral structure is not created solely through a two-staged objectivization. In order to grasp the double structure, all that is needed is to effect the simple act of intending in a somewhat modified manner, one which brings the full performance of the act into view, so that the specifically intentional characters and structures are brought out of their latent and usually almost concealed state into full light. In the process, of course, attention is also devoted to these characters. The consequence of this, however, is only their clarification, and it is not to be confused with an independent conceptual act, which would project its own purely intentional object. If, on the other hand, one performs a second act of intending which is directed at an intentional object of some other intending, we then have neither *one simple* purely intentional object nor two such objects but a purely intentional correlate of two acts, constructed one upon the other,[94] which constitutes a formal structure that is much more complex than that of the simple purely intentional object.

The clarifications and transformations in the domain of the purely intentional object which occur during the change in the manner of effecting the act are the first to turn our attention to the distinctive essence of the purely intentional object. In effect, they show to what degree the purely intentional object is dependent on the acts of consciousness, when the smallest change, in both the manner of execution and the meaning content of the act, necessarily evokes a transformation in the whole of the intentional object belonging to it. In other words, it can be seen quite clearly that—despite its transcendence—the purely inten-

94. In that, along with its intentional correlate, the so-to-speak "lower" intentional act, as something essentially linked to the correlate, also becomes an intentionally meant *object,* even though it may not be considered a purely intentional object.

tional object in its total existence and essence is dependent on the existence and essence of the appertaining act of consciousness. It arises from the execution of determinately conditioned acts of consciousness which lead to its "constitution" as a whole that transcends this act. But already in this "dependence on the acts of consciousness," in this "total submission to the sphere of influence of the 'I' of the consciousness," and, on the other hand, in the lack of a genuinely creative power of the pure consciousness, of the type we humans are capable of realizing in our experiences, there lies the final argument for the fact that the purely intentional object as such is, itself, a "nothing" in terms of ontic autonomy, that in itself it can neither exist nor be capable of changing itself. We say that it is "projected," "created" by intentional thought; but, in accordance with the proper essence of the intentional act of thought, this creation is not genuine creation, it is not the kind of production by which what is "created" immanently contains the determinations assigned to it by the act. They are merely assigned to it, and this assigning is not creative in the sense that the assigned determinations can be "incorporated" into the object—especially into the content of the purely intentional object. In the mere intentional state of "having" determinations "assigned" to it, the purely intentional object contains in its content nothing that could give it its own ontic foundation. It is in a true sense ontically heteronomous.[95] To this extent as well, the two carriers distinguished by us are not carriers in a true sense. The purely intentional object is not a "substance." If one may put it this way: some of the elements assigned to the purely intentional object fool us with the outward appearance of a "carrier"; they seem to play a role which according to their essence they are truly not capable of playing, since for this role the true immanence in the given object of the proper determinations is indispensable. Only the qualitative and formal elements that in a true sense are immanent in an object can "determine" it, can form it as this or that object. The purely

95. With regard to ontic heteronomy and autonomy, see my "Bemerkungen zum Problem Idealismus-Realismus," p. 165. Where we speak of "ontic heteronomy," H. Conrad-Martius speaks of "immanent frailty." In her analysis of the mode of existence of the merely hallucinated she says: "The immanently frail, generally speaking, never comes 'into its own' but instead is embedded, in its roots and its core, in the spirit that produces it only for the sake of appearance. Thus, as something bereft of essence, it is not at all truly 'brought into existence'" ("Realontologie," *Jahrbuch für Philosophie und phänomenologische Forschung*, IV [1921], 185).

intentional object, at least in its content, is not "determined" in the strict sense of the term. In comparison with any ontically autonomous object it is an "illusion"—an illusion, however, that does not have its ontic basis in the real sphere that is transcendent with respect to pure consciousness; rather, it is an "illusion" that draws its illusory existence and essence from the projecting intention (from the "meaning-bestowal" [*Sinngebung*], as Husserl calls it) of the intentional act.[96] On the other hand, the purely intentional object is not a complete nonentity, a nonentity which has no point of contact or support in any sphere of existence. We will later have the opportunity of speaking about this.

For the present, it must be remembered [97] that every intentional act indeed "has" *its own* purely intentional object but that, despite this, a *discrete* manifold of acts can have one and the same purely intentional object. The object is in that case individually the same, i.e., the carrier of its content is intended as one that is identically the same. The content can thereby be changed, at least in the sense that, in the event of a new intention, it carries a certain "quality of being known." The changes, however, can be much broader and deeper. They may be limited to a closer and more thorough determination, or they may even lead to an other-determination, more precisely, to a recasting of the content. There is, naturally, the problem—which we cannot develop more thoroughly here—of which other-determinants of the given purely intentional object are possible if its "what" has already been established and retained. One must only note that the range of these possibilities is different for purely intentional as compared to ontically autonomous, "also intentional" objectivities. Thus, for example, there is no real "wooden iron" or ideal "round square," whereas purely intentional objects with such contents are quite possible, even though they cannot be *intuitively* imagined. If the conscious subject wishes to move in the framework of the intuitively imaginable—holding fast, only on the basis of his own resolve of course, to the already intended ("established," as Husserl called it) purely intentional object—he is bound by the determinate limits that are drawn by the *what* of the content. If he abandons this resolve, however, the limits of

96. It is inordinately difficult to describe precisely the character of this illusion, since, because of their usual application in describing ontically autonomous objects, all the expressions we can use are attuned in their meaning content to facts existing in ontically autonomous spheres.

97. See Husserl's *Ideen,* passim.

his freedom are extended, so that, for example, he can move freely within the limits prescribed by a special *type* of objectivity (e.g., that of "real" objectivities). A borderline case of these possibilities, one which should not be overlooked, is the "destruction" of a purely intentional object that had previously been established: in a particular act the object is declared to be "void," to be "no longer existing," whereby the intentional correlate of such an invalidating act contains some states of affairs that are quite remarkable.[98] Particularly interesting is the fact that an object that has already been "destroyed," already "invalidated," can again be intended as an invalidated object. In purely intentional objects that—as identically the same in terms of the "what" of the content—correspond to a manifold of discrete acts of intending, a unique "transcendence" is created, which should not be confused with the previously established (p. 118) transcendence of every purely intentional object with respect to the acts appertaining to it. This new type of transcendence is dependent on the type of object perceived from the aspect of content. For example, when projecting the plan of a novel, we imagine a young man who, because of his innate attributes, is unprepared to carry on successfully in certain difficult life-situations. In the meantime, a fateful event occurs, in the face of which he is thrown completely onto his own resources. As a result of the difficult inner and outer conflicts that he must endure, he develops a new strength, previously contained perhaps only in embryo, so that finally, completely changed, he emerges from the crisis a stronger and more mature man. In order to conceive all this in detail, we must execute a manifold of intentional acts in which the "hero" is consecutively seen in new situations; and even

---

98. In opposition to this, H. Conrad-Martius remarks ("Realontologie," p. 182): "Having been poetically created, Hamlet cannot be destroyed, since he does not possess a destructible self." Naturally, the Shakespearean Hamlet cannot be "destroyed" in the way a real man can be destroyed, precisely because he is not ontically autonomous. But this does not exclude the fact that Hamlet can be banished by an intentional "no" from his, in a certain sense illusory, precisely ontically heteronomous existence. The poet does this frequently with regard to those of his creations which he abandons or drops because they no longer satisfy his artistic will. Moreover, Mrs. Conrad-Martius makes a distinction between the poetically created Hamlet and a merely hallucinated object and sees an essential relationship between poetically created and ideal objects (e.g., a triangle) with respect to their mode of existence—in my opinion, without sufficient justification. But this can be shown only in a systematically developed existential ontology (see my *Der Streit um die Existenz der Welt*, where I have attempted to give a deeper analysis of the purely intentional object).

though in each he is somewhat changed and undergoing different psychic states, he is still intended as the same (as the same person). Moreover, in the individual acts that occur "later" in the manifold of acts, he appears not only as one who is provided with various determinations that were explicitly intended in the given act but also as the one who "previously" was "different" and who had previously undergone precisely this and not a different fate, etc. However, it is not only with respect to what he was "previously," and which properties he "had," but also with reference to the "present" properties that he is intended in such a way that the range of his properties is not exhausted by what was in fact explicitly intended in each individual act. Thus the total content of this purely intentional object exceeds in various directions that which corresponds to the explicit content of the intention of each individual act and which would constitute the content of the purely intentional object belonging exclusively to the given act (if the remaining acts were not extant). The total content of the object intended as identical in many acts "transcends" the content of the object belonging to an isolated intentional act. Or, to illustrate it differently: since in our case the individual act is not isolated, and since it stands in a determinate spot in a temporally extended plurality of acts as their member, the intentional content that is determined only by the explicit content of the intention points beyond itself to the remaining elements of the total content of the intentional object that is intended as identical in many acts. Therein lies a special *content intentionality*. Whence it comes, and how it is at all possible, are special phenomenological problems which cannot be examined here.

§ 21. *The derived purely intentional correlates of meaning units*

WE CANNOT DEAL HERE with the various types of primary purely intentional objects that correspond to variously constructed acts of consciousness. More important for our purpose are the modifications which distinguish the derived purely intentional objects created by word meanings from the primary ones.

As we have already said, both isolated words and entire sentences possess a borrowed intentionality, one that is conferred on them by acts of consciousness. It allows the purely intentional objects to free themselves, so to speak, from immediate contact with the acts of consciousness in the process of execution and thus to acquire a relative independence from the latter. Being purely intentional, the objects "created" by the units of meaning remain both ontically heteronomous and ontically dependent, but this ontic relativity of theirs refers back directly to the intentionality immanent in the units of meaning and only indirectly to the intentionality of the acts of consciousness.

Through this shift in their ontic relativity these objects gain a certain advantage over primary purely intentional objects. For while the latter are "subjective" formations, in the sense that in their primariness they are directly accessible only to the *one* conscious subject who effected the act that created them, and while in their necessary belonging to concrete acts they cannot free themselves from these acts, the derived purely intentional objects, as correlates of meaning units, are "intersubjective": they can be intended or apprehended by various conscious subjects as identically the same. This is based on the fact that words (sentences) and in particular word meanings (meaning contents of sentences) are themselves intersubjective (cf. Chap. 14).

Because of this detachment from concrete acts of consciousness, which are effected in primary vividness and richness, the intentional correlates of meaning units also undergo various other modifications, of which one in particular is important for the structure of the literary work. It inheres in a certain *schematization* of their content. The primary purely intentional objects usually acquire their intendedness in the intentional acts that are interwoven with various other conscious experiences. Thus the intentional act is usually constructed on the basis of various *intuitive* contents and is frequently interwoven with various theoretical and practical attitudes. It is also frequently accompanied by diverse emotions, acts of will, etc. As a result of all this, the corresponding purely intentional object achieves vividness and richness in its content and in time is provided with diverse feeling and value characters which surpass what is projected by the mere meaning content of the simple intentional act. But in spite of this, these characters belong to the full content of the given purely intentional object—which in this case constitutes the correlate of the total stock of the then developing conscious experiences—in exactly the same sense as the part of the intentional content determined exclusively by the contents of the intentional act.[99] The meaning content of the intentional act can, of course, be constructed in such a way that in its content the corresponding purely intentional object is intended as one that is provided with these various characters or as one represented in a particular intuitive material; it does not, however, achieve intuitive fullness and vividness by means of this *alone*. Usually these various intentional elements are not included in the content of the intentional act, but the corresponding primary intentional object nevertheless achieves its intuitiveness, fullness, and its emotional characters from the other elements of the total experience in which the given intention is embedded. It is also possible for the object to receive its intentional characters of emotion or will from the experiential basis which produces the given intentional thought. To be sure, they are not explicitly apprehended in the content, but, nevertheless, to use Husserl's term, they are "unthematically" present.

As soon as the purely intentional object loses its direct contact with experience, however (i.e., when it is a derived intentional object), and finds its immediate ontic support in the borrowed intentionality of a word meaning (or a meaning content of a sentence), it also loses both its imaginational intuitiveness and its manifold feeling and value characters, since the full word meaning, too, can contain only what corresponds exactly to the content of a simple intentional act.[100] Of the originally intended purely intentional object there remains, so to speak, only a skeleton, a schema. For the literary work of art, into which the derived purely intentional objects enter, this is a particularly inconvenient circumstance; and the question ensues of whether the loss arising from this for the literary work of art can be reversed by means of other nonsemantic elements. Later we will see that this is truly the case; moreover, we have already collected, in outline form, a part of the material relevant for that purpose.

99. Husserl had this latter content, or part of the content, in mind when he spoke of the "noematic nucleus"; see *Ideen*, § 99.

100. Insofar, of course, as it is a question of a word meaning in whose material content no characters of this kind are determined.

§ 22.   *The purely intentional correlate of the sentence*

THE PURELY INTENTIONAL CORRELATE of the sentence [101] is different in several respects from the purely intentional correlates of simple intentional acts or nominal word meanings. What we must now do is to describe more precisely the particular structure of intentional sentence correlates and especially of the "states of affairs." It is clear that here, as in many other points in our book, we must limit ourselves to an analysis of examples, without attempting to give a general theory which would take into account all the details and possible cases.

Let us limit ourselves for the moment to correlates of assertive propositions. First of all, we must distinguish, as we have already noted in § 19, between the purely intentional sentence correlate and the possibly "objective" state of affairs which in a given case appears in an ontic sphere that is ontically independent with respect to the sentence.[102] Whereas the objective state of affairs, provided that it exists at all, has its ontic locus in existing objects, enters with the given object into the given ontic sphere as a member that cannot be strictly isolated, and is only *discovered* by us in judgments, the purely intentional state of affairs not only has its ontic foundation in the given assertive proposition, by whose meaning content it is created and to which in its essence it "belongs" as its correlate, but is also—in the case of sentences standing alone—an isolated, self-enclosed whole. In contrast, this kind of "belonging," or any kind of "connection" with the sentence, does not occur in the objectively existing state of affairs. It is totally accidental for it to be "struck" by the meaning content of the sentence. There is no intrinsic, essential, or even *ontic connection* between it and the corresponding sentence. It is only for this reason that there can be sentences and, what is more, assertive propositions, to which no objective state

101. In recent decades the primary concern has been with the intentional correlates of assertive propositions, whereby one speaks of "states of affairs." Since I am looking for a term which would be appropriate for designating the correlate of any given sentence (which is not true for the term "state of affairs," e.g., in the case of the correlate of an interrogative sentence), I have chosen the general expression "the purely intentional correlate of the sentence." Special cases of this correlate would then be "states of affairs," "problems," etc. Cf. my *Essentiale Fragen*, Chap. 1, p. 10*n*.

102. In my *Essentiale Fragen* I spoke of the "formal" and "material" object of the judgment. See p. 3*n*.

of affairs "corresponds."[103] A sentence, in fact, does not "have" an objective state of affairs. It "has"—indeed, in an essential way—solely the purely intentional state of affairs or (generally speaking) the purely intentional sentence correlate, where what is "had" constitutes no part of the sentence.[104]

Objective states of affairs can directly correspond, according to their essence, only to assertive propositions. (We shall later see how this "correspondence" is accomplished and how it is possible at all.) On the other hand, such a direct correspondence is already fully excluded, in accordance with their meaning, in the case of factual interrogatory sentences.[105] The same thing is true also of imperative sentences, optative sentences, etc. If I order someone: "Give me a glass of water!" and he then actually does this, what he has done is indeed the fulfillment of the command received, but it is not the "commanded" in the strict sense. The "commanded" as such [106] cannot exist at all in any ontically

103. If this does occur in the case of an assertive proposition (a "judgment"), we are dealing with a "false" assertive proposition.

104. Among the phenomenologists, Husserl (*Logical Investigations,* passim), A. Reinach ("Zur Theorie des negativen Urteils," *Münchener Abhandlungen,* 217–35), and A. Pfänder ("Logik," *Jahrbuch für Philosophie,* IV [1921], 174–76, 185–89, 221n) in particular have worked with states of affairs. Further literature would include A. V. Meinong (especially *Über Annahmen* [Leipzig, 1902], passim) and K. Stumpf (*Erscheinungen und psychische Funktionen* [Berlin, 1907]). In none of these authors do I find a fully conscious and detailed distinction made between the objectively existing and the purely intentional state of affairs. By "state of affairs," Husserl and Reinach understand an objectively existing state of affairs. This is entirely clear in Reinach. Pfänder, on the contrary (and Meinong as well), understand by it the purely intentional state of affairs. Yet in both Pfänder and Meinong one finds places which speak for the fact that they distinguish between the purely intentional and the objectively existing state of affairs. In these cases Meinong speaks of "object in fact" [*tatsächliches Objektiv*] and Pfänder of the "automatic behavior of the object" [*Selbstverhalten des Gegenstandes*] ("Logik," p. 221n). Meinong's theory, where he uses the term "*Objektiv,*" is not consistent. As a result, it is often difficult to determine what he really has in mind. Reinach's charge that Meinong operates with an unclarified concept of the sentence and consequently arrives at a false conception of both the object and its relationship to the sentence is well taken, even though one may find various places in Meinong which approach Reinach's point of view. My subsequent arguments are an attempt to go beyond the positions already established in the critical literature, and thus they depart in several points from the existing theories. A polemic with them would, however, lead us too far afield.

105. See my *Essentiale Fragen,* Chap. 1, § 3.

106. The "commanded" as such is to be distinguished, on the one hand, from the objectively existing "ought" which arises from the person who has heard the given command and, on the other, from the experience of this "ought," and, finally, from the purely intentional correlate of this experience.

autonomous or real world. The implementation of the command is effected in the realization of a state of affairs (or a manifold of states of affairs). As one that is *realized*, it can be made into the "material object" of an assertive proposition and brought into relation with the received command—as its "implementation." Yet it is not the "commanded" as such that is realized here but a state of affairs whose realization is in fact the result of the compliance of someone who received and understood the command. The realized state of affairs, however, does not carry in itself a special stamp of "commandedness," and it is thus different from the "commanded" as such, for which this stamp is essential. Thus, there is no stamp of "commandedness" which would distinguish a *real* state of affairs totally *independently* of all conscious or propositional intentions. For it is part of the meaning of a command that that which is commanded is *not yet* existing but is still *to be realized*. With respect to the command, the commanded as such is "something that is to be realized," and in reality there is nothing that exists and at the same time is only "something to be realized." Hence the "commanded" as such cannot be truly realized. It is only the purely intentional correlate of an imperative sentence or a subjective act of intent. Consequently, there is no objective state of affairs that would correspond exactly and directly to an imperative sentence.[107]

In short: every sentence "has," according to its own essence, a derived purely intentional sentence correlate, but objectively existing states of affairs correspond only to sentences of a determinate, particular type. Later we will be satisfied that even

---

107. It is precisely in cases such as the "problem," the "commanded," etc., that one sees most clearly that the purely intentional correlates of meanings or of sentences are not arbitrary, convenient scientific constructs but must necessarily be recognized and accepted in their peculiar "being." Only now—almost thirty years after the appearance of this book —are there investigations into the various aspects of the problem of the mode of existence of various objects. Among others, Etienne Sourriau (who in 1943 published his *Les Différents modes d'existence*) published in 1958, on an essentially broadened basis, a treatise on the mode of existence of that which is "to be realized" or "to be made." His arguments are undoubtedly interesting and contain various true observations; but the entire analysis is lacking a satisfactory existential-ontological basis because the existential moments, as well as the modes of existence, are not sufficiently worked out. Cf., in this respect, the first volume of my *Der Streit um die Existenz der Welt*. An analogous phenomenon has also appeared in recent years in the United States. Problems of the mode of existence, the structure, and the identity of the work of art have been rediscovered there by various authors [cf. p. lxiii, above].

sentences which have the form of assertive propositions can be modified in such a way that, in contrast to genuine "judgments," they make no claim of "striking" an objective state of affairs.

In the purely intentional sentence correlate one must differentiate—in the same sense as with every purely intentional object—between its *content* and its intentional structure and mode of existence. This differentiation seems to us to be even more compelling than in the case of purely intentional objects of simple intentional acts (or of nominal word meanings). If one were not to do this, one would have to concede that purely intentional sentence correlates contain mutually contradictory elements. For example, the purely intentional sentence correlate as such—precisely because it is intentional—*always* has one and the same heteronomous mode of existence. Meanwhile, the ontic character of the content of a purely intentional sentence correlate is always different depending on the different type of sentence in question. Thus the content of a judicative proposition is characterized as "existing," that of an interrogatory sentence as "questionable," etc. In fact, already in assertive propositions (more precisely, in the so-called judicative propositions) there exist considerable and mutually irreconcilable differences. For example, there appears in the content of the intentional correlate of a categorical assertive proposition the ontic character of unconditional, simple existence; in contrast, in the case of hypothetical judgment, this character is totally different, i.e., the existence in question is conditioned in one way or another; in the case of a problematical judgment it is now a "possibility" or a "probability," etc. On the other hand, there appears in the correlate content of, e.g., the sentence "Freiburg is in Baden" the character of a particular mode of existence, which we call reality. This kind of character, meanwhile, does not appear at all in the correlate content of the sentence "The diagonals of a square intersect at right angles," where it is replaced, if one may put it so, by the character of ideal existence. All these are ontic characters which are strictly different from, and incompatible with, the character of intentional existence. In addition, the content of a purely intentional sentence correlate has a formal structure which is proper to it as a sentence correlate (in an assertive proposition, it is the particular structure of the "state of affairs"; in the interrogatory sentence, that of the "problem," etc.) and which is essentially different from the simple *object* structure that is also proper to the purely intentional sentence correlate *as such*.[108] If the purely intentional sentence correlate were not "two-sided"—as is every purely intentional objectivity—and if, as an objectivity, it did not have its own carrier and proper features, which cannot be placed on the same level with the moments appearing in its content, then it would be impossible for all these characters and structures to appear in one and the same object. It is only the differentiation we have made between the sentence correlate as such and its content, together with the mode of existence of the "merely assigned," the "merely intended," which is essential for purely intentional objectivities, that enables us to understand the presence of these mutually exclusive characters and structures.

In the content of the purely intentional sentence correlate we must again distinguish between its matter, its formal structure, and its ontic characters. It may happen that a state of affairs and a problem have exactly the same matter and yet are different according to their ontic characterization. When, e.g., I ask: "Is iron hard?" and then state: "Iron is hard.", the matter of the two purely intentional sentence contents is exactly the same. For it is precisely the thing whose existence was questioned that is described as existing in the given assertion. The ontic character of the corresponding correlate content is changed, however.[109] Analogously, there are states of affairs with identical content matter and different content form and, on the other hand, states of affairs with the same content form and different content matter. As an example of the first, we may use the correlates of the sentences: "The house which stands on the other side of the street is four-storied." and "The house standing on the other side of the street is four-storied."[110] The second case may be clarified by the correlates of the sentences: "This rose is red." and "This dog is brown." Throughout, the matter should be contrasted with the formal structure, and it should be kept in mind that it is only an exception when two sentence correlates with a totally identical matter differ only with respect to formal structure. The opposite is more frequently the

108. I have already pointed to this in my *Essentiale Fragen* by contrasting states of affairs and problems.

109. This state of affairs is *intended* as real, even though, as a purely intentional correlate of the given sentence, it is only something "merely intended," that is, ontically heteronomous.

110. Along with the formal differences, there still appear differences in the manner of development of the state of affairs in that, in place of the relative sentence, which sententially develops the "standing on the other side of the street," there appears an adjectival expression, which in the second sentence forms a part of the nominal subject meaning.

case: content correlates with the same formal structure have a different matter. Despite a certain variability of content matter coupled with the same content form (and vice versa), one may say that in general there is a functional dependence between the formal structure and the matter of the content. The laws which govern the individual cases do not concern us here.

Without developing a *general* view of the content form of a purely intentional sentence correlate, we would like to show, on the basis of the special example of the state of affairs, how this form differs from the formal structure of a simple *object*.[111]

If we disregard the various ontic characters in which the state of affairs occurring in the content of an intentional correlate of a statement may appear, the whole thus remaining may be specified both *materialiter* and *formaliter*. It is clearly impossible to have pure matter or pure form only in itself. Only a variation operation (to use Husserl's well-chosen term), by means of which we allow the material determinations to vary and thus make them variable, enables us to set apart the formal structure of a state of affairs.

As an example, let us take the intentional correlate of the sentence: "This rose is red." First of all, we must note that the peculiar formal structure of the state of affairs cannot be apprehended purely if one says—as heretofore has most frequently been done—that this is nothing else than the "red-being of the rose." Even disregarding the fact that this nominal expression is so formulated that the ontic moment, or, more exactly, the moment of continuance, is pushed to the foreground (as if the state of affairs were distinguished from the simple object precisely by this), this expression is a *nominal* expression, and it brings into its intentional correlate that formal moment which is characteristic of simple objects. Through this, the peculiar formal structure of the state of affairs is to a certain degree concealed or, in any case, is made impure. The state of affairs can be apprehended in its pure structure only if we do not name it but, effecting a sentence-forming operation, develop it in a nominal-verbal manner and, in doing so, glance, as if incidentally, at its formal structure without thereby objectifying it.[112] We will then see that the formal structure of the state of affairs (or,

111. Here I am using the word "object" [*Gegenstand*] in the same sense that A. Reinach uses it. As far as I understand Meinong, it corresponds to his expression "*Objekt*."

112. We are disregarding here the immediate, nonsignificative apprehension of a state of affairs, which is also possible. See A. Reinach, "Zur Theorie," p. 225*n*.

more generally, of the sentence correlate) differs fundamentally from the structure of a simply intended object.

Let us analyze this more carefully: "This rose is red." If we really execute the corresponding sentence-forming operation, we are undoubtedly intentionally directed at this rose as if at an object (and, in this instance in particular, as if at a thing), but yet not in precisely the same way as with simple purely nominal presentation or intending.[113] In the latter, the rose appears as something *enclosed* in itself, as something caught in *one* grasp "from the outside," which, while persisting in its self-containment, does not reveal itself to us. Figuratively speaking, we cannot break into the given object; we thus conceive it as a unity, which, while indeed determined by a number of different qualitative elements, is nevertheless undifferentiated, is not seen in contrast to its individual qualifications. Moreover, we are "finished" with the intending (or perceiving) in that we have it before us simply as an unopened whole. In no way does it serve as a starting point for something different, regardless of whether this other thing is contained in it or is transcendent to it. The object, "this rose," appears quite differently to us when it occurs as an element of a state of affairs developed in a sentence. To be sure, here, too, it is "presented" i.e., it remains "in sight"; and it does not lose its self-containment by being deprived of its delimitation.[114] Nevertheless, clear modifications do appear. First of all, the object [115] "this rose" serves as a starting point toward something else in the development of the state of affairs. Or, speaking purely ontologically: it functions in the state of affairs as the point of support for whatever else also appears in the state of affairs. In a certain sense it itself belongs to the state of affairs as its real component. On the other hand, we can say that the entire state of affairs (in *our* case: when we are dealing with categorical affirmative propositions of the type "S is p") [116] takes

113. See our comments, above, on the sentence, where we have stressed that the object of the subject, as we have called it, is also nominally-verbally intended.

114. Of course we are not speaking of "delimitation" in a spatial sense, even though spatial delimitation can be coconstitutive in the case of spatial objects for the delimitation that is here intended.

115. We shall presently indicate in what sense one can speak here of an "object."

116. One should point here to the great variety of types of states of affairs, the classification of which can be found in Pfänder's "Logik." The difference in the types of states of affairs naturally leads to various modifications of the formal content structure. We cannot go into this in detail, however.

place within itself, within the bounds of its own "limits." [117] This will become clear (and at the same time a certain ambiguity connected with the object "this rose" will disappear) as soon as we turn to the different ways in which the object "this rose" shows itself in the state of affairs. For the moment, however, we should note that this object, taken as an element of the state of affairs, *opens* itself to us in a remarkable way even though it still remains a delimited whole. From the beginning, it appears to us as something accessible "from within," as something that is open to us. And as we develop the given state of affairs, we simply make use of its "openness" and intentionally penetrate its interior. This "openness" is, *in general,* not an ontic moment; it is not an ontic mode of behavior of the ontically autonomous object itself. In general, this object is insensitive [118] to the differences between "openness" and "self-enclosedness," even though these differences have their basis in its ontic structure. In our case, it is only a question of the fact that we "open" the object, so to speak, as soon as we apprehend the state of affairs. The sentence-forming operation—in all its various modifications, but primarily in the one which leads to a categorical assertive proposition—is precisely one way of "opening" an object (and in particular a thing) which for the moment is given externally in its totality. When it appears to us as already "opened," however, we are sufficiently prepared to develop or apprehend a state of affairs and thus deal with it as with an object that is "opened."

117. One can validly speak of a "taking-place" of a state of affairs only when what is involved is a state of affairs of a temporally existing object. In connection with ideal objectivities or states of affairs it is only a figurative expression. But even with reference to temporal objects it should be noted that one cannot conceive of this "taking-place" in the sense of a process, for every process presupposes existing states of affairs. The fact that one can still rightly speak of a "taking-place" of a state of affairs of a temporal object has its foundation in the peculiar modifications to which every temporal, i.e., primarily every temporally existing, state of affairs is, as a temporal one, subject. In this regard, see the extraordinarily interesting observations of H. Conrad-Martius in "Die Zeit," *Philosophische Anzeiger,* Vol. II, no. 2 (1927); also published as *Die Zeit* (Munich, 1954).

118. This refers, above all, to "lifeless," "dead" things. For if it is a question, e.g., of psychic individuals, there are certainly various modes of behavior in which they can "open" themselves to, or "close themselves off" from, a cognitive individual or from another psychic individual that is involved with it. In the latter case Max Scheler speaks of "spheres of intimacy." See *Wesen und Formen der Sympathie,* 2d ed. (Bonn, 1923). For that matter, there can also be a "closing oneself off from oneself," as is shown not only by numerous pathological but also by many entirely normal cases.

At that moment it also ceases to be given to us in a purely "objective" manner. For the self-enclosedness of the object belongs to a simply objective (nominal) manner of being given, not merely in the sense of demarcation, but also in the sense that the conscious subject to whom the object is given apprehends it or intends it only "from the outside," in *one* grasp.

Here we also have a delineation of the sense in which the object "this rose" "appears" in the state of affairs and constitutes a real part of it, even though, at the same time, the state of affairs "takes place" "within the framework" of the object of the subject. In order to show this, however, we must first be better oriented with regard to the other elements of the state of affairs. We say "This rose is red." Thus, in this state of affairs there also appears the element of redness. In this state of affairs, however, and in general, redness is not an object in itself. It is something which according to its essence cannot be an *ens*—to use the appropriate Scholastic expression—but only an *entis*. As such, it is different from the "rose" itself. On the other hand, in our case, redness is precisely what is "contained" "in" the rose; it is that which—according to the sense of the sentence—"belongs to" the rose. And it can exist only as something "contained" or "belonging." As something thus essentially dependent, something which, having the point of support of its existence in something other (the rose), exists in the unity of a whole only with that other, this element of redness—just like "this rose"— constitutes a real component of the state of affairs. However, it is not merely something "belonging" or "due"; it is, at the same time, something that belongs in such a manner that it is contained in the given object as something *determining* it, as something forming and limiting it as a "red object." This "determining containedness" is characteristic of every "feature," of every "property" as such. And one can say equally well: it determines the object only by being contained in it; and: it is contained in it only because it determines it.

As what, then, does the object "this rose" appear in our state of affairs? As a "red rose"? Or as a "rose" with all its properties and features, with the exception of this single element of redness? Or, finally, in a third sense, yet to be determined?

As we shall see, it appears in all three ways; and the fact that it "does" so is especially characteristic of the formal structure of the state of affairs. If we begin for the moment with the last, the third mode, it is clear that one can speak of "this rose" in the sense that one has only the rose "itself," so to speak, in mind, i.e., as a carrier of various properties, a carrier that is already qualitatively determined, according to the nature of the object, as "rose," but with no regard for the qualitative determinations of these properties.[119] When we speak of a "carrier" (*substantia*), it is already decided that it is a carrier only as a carrier of some properties and other determinations. It is therefore not possible, while being attuned to a carrier, to disregard the properties that accompany it, those that are "carried" by it, as if they were completely eliminated. It is possible to disregard only *which* properties these are, i.e., one can disregard only their qualitative determinations. In our state of affairs, "this rose" functions primarily as a carrier that is qualitatively determined as "rose" and, in particular—in the case of a completed development of the given state of affairs—as a carrier of precisely that determination moment thanks to which the rose is, in fact, red. To this extent, then, the "rose," thus understood, appears as something contrasted to its accompanying element of redness. This contrast, which is based on the difference between the functions of being a carrier and being a property, is surmounted, however, by the essence of these two functions. And the peculiar essence of the state of affairs, which finds its full development only through the intentionality of the sentence, lies precisely in surmounting [120] this basic opposition. The fact that the rose, as a carrier factually determined according to its constitutive nature, is precisely the carrier of this determination of redness means nothing other than: this rose *is* red. When we apprehend an object in its basic opposition to its determination and, at the same time, in the surmounting of this opposition by means of the two functions we have named, we apprehend a determinate state of affairs in the explicit, fully developed form that is peculiar to it. Through this surmounting, the "red" of the "rose" becomes "peculiar" to it, it

119. On the concept of "nature" and, more precisely, the "individual constitutive nature" of the object, see my *Essentiale Fragen*, p. 27. It must be noted that, by introducing this concept, we are simultaneously abandoning the concept of a "determinationless carrier," which was correctly attacked by English empiricists. The problem is that, at the same time, they went nonsensically too far in altogether abandoning the idea of a carrier, since they saw neither the essence of the property nor the totally different essence of the nature of the object.

120. It must be specially stressed that this "surmounting" is present in the existing entity. It is only revealed in its primariness in the development of a state of affairs, but it is not created by the predicative function (provided, of course, that we are dealing with an objectively existing state of affairs). It is, so to speak, the pure expression of the two functions that are essentially constitutive for an object and are necessarily mutually relative: those of "being a carrier" and "being a property."

is drawn into the ontic sphere of the rose; and though, in this state of affairs itself, the "result," as it were, of this inclusion is not attained (whereas, if it were, it would be "included" or "contained," as in adjectival-nominal word meanings), yet everything is prepared to this end precisely by the development of the given state of affairs. In the state of affairs itself, only the inclusion is exposed—precisely as it is engaged in the execution, as it is executed in the development of the two functions of being a carrier and being a property. The peculiar function of the sentence—as we have already noted, but as it is only now, perhaps, made clear —lies precisely in the accomplishment of this exposition.

When we speak of the "function" of the carrier, we are clearly using a figure of speech; we must strictly and necessarily eliminate from its sense the element of any "activity" or of any "happening." Even though the rose *is red*, nothing "happens." If one prefers, it is a question here of a purely *static* relationship, which nevertheless, as a correlate of a sentence, attains in its pure being a nominal-verbal exposition and development. In a purely nominal "objective" intending, however, it is not visible in its development but is indicated only in the "ready" *objective* form that is constituted through its existence (i.e., in the total form of something that is determinately qualified). The object thus stands before us as a self-enclosed unit, which we apprehend only "from the outside."

The surmounting of the opposition between "rose" as carrier and "red" as its determination, a surmounting that is effected in the state of affairs, necessarily carries with it the fact that "this rose" of the given state of affairs appears in another remarkably potential-actual mode, i.e., as this "red"-*determined* rose. It is a "potential" mode, since the rose is not yet present as a "red rose" in this state of affairs; for it to appear before us as a "red rose" requires a special nominal "objectivization" which would take into account the "result," so to speak, of this state of affairs. Undoubtedly, in this objectivization a certain "logical" form is imposed on the object, a form which reflects the "adjectival" connection of the word "red" with the word "rose." One should not think, however, that this objectivization in any way ontically transforms the object or treats it in a manner foreign to it, i.e., as if the static relationship between the carrier and the property (more generally, the determination) that is characteristic of the object were characteristic of it only in that form which appears as we apprehend the state of affairs and as if the object "red rose" were to be made relative to the objectivization that "constitutes" it. That this is not so is shown precisely by that remarkable potential-actual mode in which "this rose" appears in our state of affairs. To the extent that this rose *is red,* to the extent, therefore, that the surmounting of the opposition between the "rose" as carrier and "red" as its determination has been accomplished, the rose *actually is* a red rose and was merely not specifically apprehended in this actuality; for this reason, its manner of appearance is provided with an element of potentiality.

But "this rose" appears in our state of affairs in yet another sense, that is, as a rose provided with *all* its properties with the single *exception* of the one by which it is "red." It, the same rose which is fragrant, which is delicate, etc., is red. To be sure, in our case this is not meant explicitly, nor is there an explicit development in the corresponding state of affairs. In spite of this, however, all of the rose's (known) properties are implicitly and potentially cointended when we speak first of a rose and then of this rose.[121] Consequently, but only to the following extent, the rose is potentially indicated as such in our state of affairs. From this there arises a consequence of particular importance for us: i.e., since every property of an object conceals, as it were behind it, a determinate state of affairs that—figuratively speaking—indirectly manifests itself in a compressed form in the object that is provided with the given property (thus, e.g., in the "delicate rose"), therefore, direct lines, so to speak, lead from the state of affairs which is just then attaining development to other states of affairs appertaining to the same object (this rose), and we need only follow them in order for them to be developed as well.[122] We can say that the object—as it appears to us when we penetrate its "interior"—is nothing other than a determinately circumscribed and ordered manifold of states of affairs united by the same carrier, of which we bring only one to a particular, developed exposition at any given time but, therefore, to a certain degree delimit it from the remaining ones. If we direct ourselves at an object in a *nominal* act, we intend in one stroke the total ontic range that is staked out by such a unified manifold of interwoven states of affairs and see it from the outside as a uniform *whole* that is qualified in this or that manner; and we take this

121. We are reminded here of our distinction between the "actual" and the "potential stock" of a word meaning. See above, p. 87.
122. Or—if by the expression "this rose" we understand the rose taken together with all its properties and moments—to other states of affairs immanent and compressed in it.

whole *sub specie* of the constitutive nature ("rose") which directly qualifies the common carrier of all these now compressed and invisible states of affairs. The existence of "this rose," taken explicitly, is the *coexistence* of all the states of affairs united by the identical carrier appearing in them. Only if one limits the sense of the word "object" to the carrier of properties can one say that the object of all these states of affairs serves as their basis, that it founds all of them. It founds them precisely because—and only in this sense—in each of them it "functions" as a carrier. But without these states of affairs it could not exist at all. Therefore, one can say that a *bare* carrier is as ontically dependent as an "accident." [123] Only with all of its "accidents" (properties, moments, etc.) does it form an ontically independent ontic range, an "individual," one which would not be possible if it were not performing the function of a carrier in it.

In the multiplicity of states of affairs (and to an even greater degree in the multiplicity of the intentional sentence correlates) one finds—as we have already indicated—very diverse modifications of the structure just described. We cannot dwell on it any longer. We must add one more point, however, to dispose of a possible objection. Someone may ask: is the penetration into the interior of the object—in the sense of an ontically independent ontic range—characteristic for every state of affairs? And what is the situation for the correlate of a sentence such as "A wagon passes by." or "My dog is barking.", etc.?

It must be conceded that, in these instances, the kind of penetration into the interior of the object of the subject that occurred in the earlier examples does not occur. Here the object of the subject performs an action as an enclosed, an "unopened," individual. But, nevertheless, it is not intended as resting in itself, as abiding within its own ontic bounds, as is the case with simply objective, purely *nominal* intending. We in fact do not penetrate it, but it reaches, so to speak, beyond its own ontic range; at the very least, it takes part in a happening or it per-

123. In her "Realontologie," § 14, H. Conrad-Martius writes: "The real carrier, too—that is, the one that is constituted to a real entity thanks to its factually imposed quiddity—is not something which in itself, i.e., apart from the imposed quiddity and without it, can be known and assumed to exist" (p. 169). This is of course quite correct, but the "carrier" in H. Conrad-Martius' sense is only a real form, which, naturally, cannot exist without the "quiddity" (in my terminology, the "individual nature") that is contained in it; i.e., it is ontically dependent. I would like to state, moreover, that even when the "carrier" is taken with its "quiddity" (nature), it is still ontically dependent on the determinations that are "carried" by it, that is, the properties pertaining to the object.

forms an action. As a result, a breach is made in some spot in its total ontic range through which we can break into its interior, as, for example, when we develop the state of affairs "A wagon is passing by." [124] But also—disregarding this possibility—the object qualified in this or that manner and grasped at once in one stroke, in its total qualification, appears here as a carrier of an activity performed by it, so that this activity finds in the carrier not only its ontic foundation but also its point of origin. Thus, the activity indeed does not fall into its ontic range, but it does belong to the range of its operations. Consequently, we have before us the object of the subject as one that is developing in a certain direction of its range of operations. That this possible range of operations also belongs to the object and is conditioned in its design by the object's total essence is shown already by the fact that, having postulated the sentence "A wagon passes by," we can proceed to the now fully valid "A wagon is passing by" or, in the existential formulation, "There exists a passing wagon."

Despite these noteworthy distinctions, we are dealing, in the present examples, with the *behavior* of an object, with the difference, however, that here it is not the behavior of the carrier of a property that is developed with respect to its property. We are dealing, rather, with the behavior of a carrier, no matter how qualified, of an activity in that carrier's surrounding objective world, and it is this behavior which attains nominal-verbal development in a line of operation that is contained in its total range of operations. And precisely in the same way as, in "This rose is red," a "red rose" is indicated in a potential-actual manner, so, in the state of affairs "A wagon passes by," a "passing wagon" is indicated in a potential-actual manner, so that we can immediately cross over to it and nominally intend it or develop it in terms of the state of affairs. If we really do this, we broaden, as it were, the pure ontic range by a line of its range of operations and nominally grasp the whole.

The analysis of the structure of the state of affairs that we have just completed was primarily oriented on ontically autonomous states of affairs. But the conclusions are also valid for the purely intentional correlates of predications, with the distinction that here everything refers to the formal structure of

124. This expression is not used in German, but it occurs in other languages (e.g., English). The question is not with figures used in speech but with forms of meaning and the expressions that are in principle possible to them.

the *content* of such a correlate, and this structure, as well as the material qualifications contained in this form, is only something merely intended and ontically heteronomous. However, one should not draw the false conclusion, on the basis of the parallelism we have just established between ontically autonomous and purely intentional states of affairs, that *everything* which is at all valid for ontically autonomous states of affairs is also valid for purely intentional sentence correlates and vice versa. Here we will limit ourselves to only a few examples of the differences between them, as follows.

In order to exist at all, ontically autonomous states of affairs must fulfill a series of conditions that are not binding for the contents of purely intentional states of affairs. They must not only satisfy the laws that arise in general from the essential structure of every object (i.e., the "analytical-formal" regularities, to use Husserl's term) but must also fulfill the essential laws which govern in the domain of objects to which the matter of the given state of affairs belongs. However, if it is a state of affairs that is to exist in a factually existing, and in various respects contingent, world, then various "accidental" conditions must also be fulfilled; concerning these conditions, corresponding "experience" (in the narrow sense of the word) instructs us and finds its expression in, e.g., physical, chemical, or similar laws. None of this is necessary for the contents of purely intentional states of affairs. Whereas on formal-ontological grounds, for example, it is not possible for an objectively existing, ontically autonomous state of affairs to contain mutually exclusive material elements, a purely intentional state of affairs with mutually contradictory elements is quite possible. Likewise, if it is to exist at all, a really [*realiter*] existing state of affairs must be completely, *unequivocally, determined*. This does not pertain to the contents of purely intentional sentence correlates. If a sentence is ambiguous in its meaning content, its ambiguity is reflected in the content of the accompanying purely intentional correlate in a remarkably opalescent multiplicity. Above all, the matter of the sentence is affected by this; but in connection with this, its formal structure also shows an exceptional complexity. In many cases it is very difficult to analyze these complex situations clearly, especially if the ambiguity of the accompanying sentence does not become evident and the sentence, at first sight, seems to be unambiguous. If the ambiguity of the sentence is sufficiently evident, however, the multiform or multilayered nature of the purely intentional content of the correlate is clearly drawn. As we know, the ambiguity of a sentence can be based either on the ambiguity of the individual words appearing in it or on an obscurity, and, therefore, also an ambiguity, of sentence construction. One can "read" such a sentence in various ways and thus arrive in each case at a different (and then already unambiguous) sentence; but neither the individual words nor the sentence construction empowers us to favor any one of these readings. Moreover, the ambiguous sentence is also not to be identified with the manifold of unambiguous sentences obtained through "interpretation." It is precisely characteristic of ambiguous sentences that they allow [125] a number of "interpretations" without firmly excluding or favoring any of them. But because all "possible" interpretations are allowed and *equally* justified, the purely intentional content of the correlate is also "opalescently" multiform and conceals conflicting elements within itself. Since this is impossible in the case of an objectively existing ontically autonomous state of affairs, and since one usually overlooks the sphere of purely intentional correlates, one would perhaps be inclined to take the position that ambiguous sentences have, not one correlate, but a number of them, and that their range is exactly determined by the number of possible interpretations. The individual correlates would then constitute a *discrete* manifold, each member of which would belong to a *different* sentence. In this way we would come to the assertion that an ambiguous sentence actually has *no* purely intentional correlate of its *own* but must first be made unambiguous in order to have it.

This view, however, overlooks, or attempts to remove, precisely what it is that has to be clarified, namely, the ambiguity itself. To deny an ambiguous sentence its own purely intentional correlate is basically not to look at the purely intentional correlates but at the objectively existing ontically autonomous states of affairs, which clearly cannot present such an opalescent multiformity. It also amounts to overlooking the significant differences that exist between a purely intentional and any ontically autonomous objectivity and, at the same time, facilely arriving at an erroneous conception of the *latter*. Once again it must be stressed that *every* sentence—even the absurd and the ambiguous one—has its own purely intentional correlate. In particular, however, it is not true that the purely intentional correlate of an

125. In order to make the right choice and thus remove the ambiguity, we must, if it is possible, use other connected sentences as an aid; but even then we do not always succeed in achieving unambiguity.

ambiguous sentence consists of a *manifold* of *discrete* sentence correlates. On the contrary, it is a *single* correlate, and, more precisely, a *single* content of a correlate, that "opalesces." This already follows from the fact that a sentence (and also a single word) is ambiguous only if in its meaning content it contains, in addition to the ambiguous elements, those which are *not* ambiguous. Only the interweaving of unambiguous and ambiguous meaning elements brings about an ambiguous sentence. Correlatively, its purely intentional correlate content is constructed in such a way that it possesses a foundation of "common" elements upon which the other elements, corresponding to the ambiguous expressions, are fastened in a remarkably multirayed manner. And they are only fastened, precisely because, between the unequivocally determined (the "common") elements of the content and those belonging to the ambiguous expressions, there exists only a loose, not finally fixed connection. This is the basis for the "iridescent," the "opalescent," character of the entire correlate content.

The presence of such an "opalescent" purely intentional sentence correlate is of particular importance for grasping the essence of the literary work. For the moment it should only be noted that there is a special type of literary work of art whose basic character and peculiar charm lie in the ambiguities it contains. They are *calculated* for the full enjoyment of the aesthetic characters that are based on "iridescence" and "opalescence," and they would lose their peculiar charm if one were to "improve" them by removing the ambiguity (as frequently happens in *bad* translations).[126]

These analyses of purely intentional states of affairs will enable us to understand the new circumstances and problems that will be revealed to us in a manifold of interconnected sentences. Let us turn to them now.

§ 23. *Sentence complexes; higher meaning units constituted therein*

IN PRINCIPLE, it is not impossible for a number of sentences to follow one another without having any interconnection.

126. Therein also lies one of the main difficulties of translation. The ambiguities of the original must not only be left in place; care must be taken that the translation contain the same ambiguities as the original.

If this is so, they can be freely rearranged or replaced by others; their order is in any case not determined by their meaning content. In this case, not only does every sentence contain a uniform "thought," but the "thought" is also definitely enclosed in every sentence and begins completely anew without being tied to what precedes it and without indicating what is to follow. Thus, for example, the insane can sometimes talk for hours, and no one can guess from the meaning content of the sentences precisely why such sentences were spoken in such a sequence.[127] Nevertheless, a sequence of such disconnected sentences is an anomaly. The *succession* of sentences in itself requires to a certain degree that they be treated from the first, not as inanimate pebbles lying side by side, but as *members* of a higher whole. From the beginning we are prepared not merely to understand the individual sentences but also to take them only as "measures" and, by observing the connections that prevail between them, to apprehend the unity that is founded in them.[128] Since these connections are nearly invisible, one tries to find them; and one is astonished when one does not find them, e.g., in the case of nonsensical speech.

There is no doubt that it is normal for such connections to be present in successive sentences.[129] However, the following questions arise:

1. What is a connection between sentences?
2. Which properties of the individual sentence is it based on (what brings it about)?
3. Does the presence of these connections of sentences bring about the constitution of something entirely new, and, if this is the case, what is it?
4. Are there various types of connections between sentences, and, if this is so, what are they?
5. Is the variability of the types of sentence connections recognizable in the peculiarities of the newly constituted entities, and in what manner?

127. This "why" can be sought and explained in the particular pathological psychic dispositions of the speaker. But then the spoken sentences are taken above all in their manifestation function as "symptoms" of some illness.

128. In this we see that we were correct in maintaining that in "normal" instances sentence-forming operations are only relatively independent.

129. T. A. Meyer stresses this with emphasis in *Das Stilgesetz der Poesie* (Leipzig, 1901), pp. 18 ff.

Yet the formulation of these questions assumes that the individual sentences are primary and serve as the basis for the whole—whether this is a "story," a "proof," etc.—which is built and first constituted upon them. We can also find the opposite view, i.e., that, on the contrary, it is the whole that is primary, determinant, and constituting and that the individual sentences are determined and constituted by the sense of the whole. Is it possible that our own previously expressed observations on the relative dependence of the sentence-forming operation bring us precisely to such a conception? Are we not contradicting ourselves here?

As we see it, both views—correctly understood—are correct and are not contradictory, since they refer to different situations. When we speak of "constituting," it may have a twofold meaning according to the standpoint from which we observe the whole, e.g., a story. One may observe the whole either in its "becoming," as it arises from subjective operations, or as something already *complete*, which we can apprehend solely by understanding the individual sentences contained in it. In the first case, one can admit that, in a certain sense, the whole is more primary. Not only in the creation of a literary work, but in living speech as well (especially in longer units, for example parliamentary speeches or lectures—provided, of course, that they are not written out beforehand), the so-called conception of the whole is primary; it is the first to arise. It is the thing that determines how the individual sentences are formed and in what order they are to follow. Or, to put it differently: the individual sentences, according to their content, their form, and even their phonetic expression, are composed only with a view to what the whole *is to be*. To this extent, then, the whole would be that which contributes to the constitution of individual sentences, even though, ultimately, the individual sentences must be created in themselves in the sentence-forming operations. Or, taking the subjective approach: the original impulse for creating a determinate whole (a "speech," a "story," a "drama," etc.) carries the individual sentence-forming operations and influences their execution. But, even from this perspective, what lies at the basis and is the determining factor is not the already *formed whole* itself but only its "conception," the more or less precise *outline* of what is to be formed. The work when it is finally completed usually differs considerably from what was originally felt and planned by the author. For even with a very clear and detailed conception, the whole of the work develops through the establishment of individual sentences and *departs* more or less from what was originally planned. How often it happens that the author does not know what his work will become or how it will change "in his hands." It seems to me that the only correct view of this is that the author must have a certain perspective on something that transcends the individual sentences that are formed at any given point in the work.[130]

The situation looks different when the entire work [131] is seen as a completed formation. Then the individual sentences are the basis; it is they that must "first" be there for the whole to be constituted at all. The entire work is then something dependent, which arises from the total meaning content and from the order of the individual sentences. At the same time, however, one should not forget that individual sentences appear in a determinate sequence and in determinate connections and that as result—as we shall soon see—their total meaning content (and in some cases even their phonetic side) is not determined solely by the word meanings appearing in the individual sentences (taken in isolation) but quite frequently is formed in detail and modified in various respects by the meaning contents of other (preceding) sentences.[132]

Essentially the same situation occurs when we familiarize ourselves with a literary work. What we see first, what we must fully utilize in both its content and its form if we are to attain the whole work, are the individual sentences. Moreover, these cannot be given to us all at once; on the contrary, we must become acquainted with them and understand them *in sequence*.[133] Likewise with respect to this: it is the individual sentences that are primary and determining; it is the whole work that, on the contrary, is constituted by them. But since all our analyses have for their object the *completed* literary work, and since we refer

---

130. Pierre Audiat is quite correct when he speaks of the coming into being of a literary work and requires a "biography" of this work. (As we will see later, one can speak of a "biography" in an entirely different, more appropriate sense; see Chap. 13.) He errs only when he identifies the formed work with the subjective operations from which it arises and to which it is transcendent.

131. We now speak of the "whole" work in the sense of the whole meaningful text. We will see, however, that this term is also permissible with reference to the whole work in all its strata.

132. Or—to put it differently and more correctly—the sentences that are connected with a given sentence frequently decide the sense in which words appearing in that sentence are to be taken.

133. This will subsequently compel us to an entirely different manner of treating the literary work; see Chap. 11.

back to the subjective operations only where what is found in the work itself necessitates this, we are fully justified in putting the five questions formulated above.[134] Let us now turn to the answers.

Ad 1. Let us contrast two examples:

A. 1. "Cars make an unbearable racket."
    2. "Freiburg is in Baden."
B. "My son received a good report card. He is very happy and is playing merrily in the garden."

Without thinking much about it, we can say that in A there is no connection between the two sentences; in B, however, there is one.[135] True. But what in fact occurs when there is a connection between sentences? If we take A first, we are dealing with two sentences whose meaning contents are not only independent in themselves but also form such enclosed sense units * that no meaning unit from the first sentence reaches out beyond the sense unit * of this sentence to other meaning formations, and vice versa. It is precisely this reaching-out of a meaning element beyond the meaning content of its own sentence that occurs in the *second* sentence of B. If we take this sentence as if it were totally isolated, and in particular as if it did not follow sentence B_1, we would simply have:

C. "He is very happy and is playing merrily in the garden."

In its meaning, this sentence differs very clearly from sentence B_2. Here some unknown and unspecified "he" who "is happy," etc., is intended by the sentence. In sentence B_2, on the other hand, this "he" has a totally different meaning: it points to identically the same object that is determined by the expression "my son," but, at the moment B_1 is expressed, we also know that he has received a good report card. The word "he" does not merely project in B_2 (as it does in C) an otherwise indeterminate subject element belonging *not* to B_2 (or, more precisely, to C) but to B_1. To put it differently, the meaning of the word "he" in B_2 reaches out beyond the state of affairs which would be projected by this sentence if it were isolated (as in C) into a different, an extrinsic, state of affairs. This word can do this, however,

---

134. See above, p. 145.
135. It would appear even more clearly, and be formed more tightly, if sentence B_2 were formulated as: "Because of this, he is very happy and is playing merrily in the garden."
* [I.e., sentence meaning units.]

only because its full meaning undergoes a modification, i.e., it is thought from the very beginning ("he"—the same one who is my son, etc.) in such a way that its meaning ties on to the meaning element of the preceding sentence, B_1, and by dint of this tie enters with its directional factor into the "extrinsic" state of affairs. Furthermore, in such a combination, B_2 is usually understood as containing in its sense content a potential stock of meanings which can be actualized and explicated by the addition of the expression "for this reason." Through this, one of the meaning elements of B_2, by tying into the *total* meaning content of B_1, again enters the state of affairs of B_1 and simultaneously characterizes it as *basis* and, on the other hand, characterizes the state of affairs developed by B_2 as result. Wherever the meaning content of a sentence B (either as a whole or as a meaning element appearing in it) is tied to the meaning element or the total meaning content of another sentence β and reaches out beyond its own state of affairs to another state of affairs, a first step is taken, so to speak, in creating the indispensable basis for establishing a connection between the two sentences. It would be a mistake, however, to claim that because of this a connection is already established and that it is based precisely on this tie and this reaching-out. For we can give the following example:

D. "The child is crying. It has two perpendicular and equal diagonals."

When we read these sentences, we are prepared, at the beginning of the second one, for it to continue to refer to the child that is crying. Instead, the continuation of the second sentence destroys this expectation: it becomes apparent that there is no connection between the two sentences and that they are in sequence for totally incomprehensible reasons. The seemingly outward-reaching meaning element of the word "it" is incapable of tying into either the meaning element or the entire meaning content of sentence D_1, since it is prevented from doing this by the sense of the remaining meaning elements of D_2: the "it" which has, or should have, two perpendicular and equal diagonals is certainly not a child but a square. A connection between two sentences exists, therefore, only if it truly *succeeds* in tying a meaning element of one sentence onto the meaning content of another (or onto the meaning element of this sentence) and if, as a result, the corresponding purely intentional correlates also enter into an effectively executed connection. Indeed, the connection between two sentences is nothing other than this kind of successful tying of one sentence content onto another. It is characteristic that, despite this successful tie, neither sentence content loses its unity or its character of wholeness. Even when they are connected, the sentences remain *two* different sentences, and each of them develops its *own* state of affairs. Their independence, however, turns out to be not absolute, since their "state of connection" is effected only by various modifications of their total meaning content, and these modifications are guided in each case by the meaning content of the other sentence (or vice versa).[136] The two meaning contents accommodate themselves to each other as it were, but this accommodation does not go so far as to make them cease to be sentences, i.e., particular functional-intentional meaning units.

The "reaching-out" of a meaning element can issue from either the preceding sentence or the following one or, finally, from both at the same time. On the other hand, as is frequently the case, there may be a connection of *many* sentences. The reaching-out and tying-in of the meaning elements of various sentences, the successful tying-in of many meaning contents of sentences, brings about various special complications, into which we cannot delve here. We must only emphasize that a connection can exist among *several*, at times among very numerous, sentences, but this does not preclude the possibility that, at times, groups of more *closely* connected sentences may be established and that the sentence groups thus established can enter in turn into *one* broader encompassing connection.

Ad 2. How is it possible, however, that individual sentences, which, after all, are complete units of meaning in themselves, can refer beyond themselves and mutually enter into a meaning complex? From the preceding, it already follows that they must contain meaning elements which effect this. These meaning units are, above all, some (though not all) of the purely functional words [137] observed above—for example, "and," "thus," "since," "consequently," "however," "on the other hand," "this," "the same," "nevertheless," "moreover," "insofar," etc.—and also some materially functional words—for example, "afterwards,"

136. One can best see that such meaning modifications actually do exist when one tears connected sentences from their context and studies them in their meaning content in full isolation.
137. See Pfänder, "Logik," Part II, Chaps. 8 and 10.

"behind," "as" (*cum temporale*), "during," etc.[138] Most sentences contain several words of this kind—in various combinations with nominal word meanings—and only their common function leads to the establishment of a connection between given sentences. We have a connection established by a purely functional word when an assertion, for example, is followed by another sentence (in fact, a principal sentence) beginning with "for." This "for" characterizes what is expressed in this sentence as the "substantiation" of the preceding sentence and places both sentences in a determinate, close connection. The preceding sentence, which from the first stood as a self-sufficient and fully independent meaning unit, is characterized *ex post facto* as something dependent and substantiated. This characterization, however, is accompanied by a clear modification of its meaning content: it is not that something entirely different is asserted by it, that a state of affairs is developed which is determined in a materially different manner; rather, the modification is based on the fact that the element of the *absolutely* "categorical" establishment of the state of affairs, contained from the beginning in the meaning content, is transformed into an element whose sense can be explained by the words "this is so because."

The appearance of such functional words, however, is not necessary for the establishment of a connection between sentences. For example, if the same subject, to which various predicates refer, appears in two different (and sometimes not immediately consecutive) sentences, the sentences are connected. Moreover, it is not at all necessary for the place of the subject to be occupied in both sentences by precisely the same nominal word meaning, i.e., one that is provided with the same material content. The place of the name in the second sentence may be taken by a pronoun, for example, or by a nominal expression determining the same object by means of other attributes. What is indispensable in this case is only that in both instances the intentional directional factor be directed absolutely identically. In such cases we see most forcefully that though the immediate succession of two sentences is by itself insufficient for establishing

138. A full theory of sentence connections would naturally require an exact determination of the range of the functional words that are capable of establishing a connection between individual sentences. To these one would have to contrast those that are not capable of doing this, as, for example, "is," "in," "from," "off," etc. It would also be necessary to answer the question of what properties words must have if they are to produce a sentence complex.

a connection between them, it does—in the presence of factors establishing a connection—contribute to its establishment. And it does this by leading to a very determinate modification of the meaning of the second sentence. If I say, for example, "He is happy and is playing in the garden," the intentional directional factor of the word "he" is potential and variable, and the sentence can be "applied" in numberless different cases. If, however, this sentence immediately follows the sentence "My son received a good report card," the directional factor is already actualized and stabilized and refers to precisely the same object that is designated by the expression "my son." [139] But *here* what contributes to the establishment of the connection is not simply the immediate succession of sentences but the position of the sentences in the sequence.[140] If we say, for example, "He is happy, etc. My son received a good report card," nothing in the pure expression of these sentences has changed in comparison to the case analyzed above. Nevertheless, there is now no connection between them. The directional factor of the word "he" is now purely potential and limitlessly variable, and absolutely nothing can be inferred from the meaning content of this sentence to the effect that "he" is in fact "my son." Another example in which the succession of sentences in a specific sequence contributes to the establishment of a connection is the following: "Mr. X doesn't know the first thing about driving. Moreover, he's clumsy and very irresponsible. Yesterday he took two acquaintances in his car, drove out to Y, and on the way ran over two children. Both are dead. An idiot like that can cause so much misfortune." Only the determinate order of the sentences causes the expression "an idiot like that" to refer to Mr. X and the word "both" to designate the two dead children and not the two acquaintances of Mr. X. If we were to change the order of the sentences, their meaning would be altered and the connection between them would disappear or at least be deformed to such an extent that we would hardly be aware that any connection was present. An adequate order must be introduced from the very first for the connection to be present in its rightful form and with full clarity.

It is not necessary that the nominal expressions that estab-

139. Assuming, of course, that the directional factor of this latter expression is already stabilized and thus indicates a fully determinate individual. In the contrary case (if it is not established, in some way, whose son is in question), the directional ray of the pronoun is variable to the same degree as that of the expression "my son."

140. Generally, this is not binding. There may be sentences that are connected regardless of the order of their sequence.

lish the connection should always be the subject of the sentence. For example: "The thief noticed us and tried to flee. He ran quickly. But we caught him and took our things back."

Finally, it can also be the form of the sentences which establishes the connection (the form usually being indicated by a functional word or a punctuation mark). For example, a question postulates that the sentence following it belongs to it as the "answer" (though this postulate need not always be fulfilled). The same applies to address and reply: "Give me a glass of water"—and the answer—"The water here is very bad," etc.

Ad 3. The above analyses—though they do require amplification—show us quite clearly that sentences that are in connection with one another constitute a totally new whole, which is not to be equated with a mere manifold or with an agglomerate of (isolated) sentences. In a given case, this whole can be a "story," a "proof," a "theory," etc., and in each case have its characteristic, proper attributes which cannot be reduced to the attributes of the sentences entering into the given whole and which also do not belong to an agglomerate of fully disconnected sentences. We are not yet fully prepared to give a satisfactory general determination of the whole that is being constituted in the connected sentences. Some remarks, however, will be of use. For example: every such whole possesses its own *compositional structure,* which is naturally dependent on the sentence contents and the order in the sequence of sentences and, finally, on the type of the connection. This structure is not identical with any attribute of the individual sentences, however. There is a great variety of different types of such structures. Thus, for example, at the "beginning" of a work, an "exposition" may be given which develops the "past history"; only then there follows the presentation proper of the events in, say, a chronological sequence, until the point of culmination is reached and the work ends. As a particular consequence of this or that "composition," there arises some form of *dynamics* of the work, and, on the other hand, a *transparency* and natural *simplicity of composition* or, conversely, a *complexity,* a certain *eccentricity* and *artificiality,* etc. All these are attributes of the whole and not of the individual sentences. And though it must be admitted that the individual sentence has this or that compositional structure, that it can be characterized by a given dynamics, etc., these are properties that are, nevertheless, only analogous to those appearing in the whole; they are not exactly the same, let alone identical, properties.

Ad 4. As we see from the above discussion, there are various types of possible connections between sentences. Thus there may be a loose and unsystematic connection, as, for example, in a sequence of sentences created on the basis of a loose, unrestrained, and whimsical association. On the other hand, the sentences may be very tightly knit, as in the case of a strict deductive theory. They may be direct or indirect to a higher or lesser degree; they may appear in an explicit or an implicit form, etc. This is not the place to analyze all of this thoroughly. Yet we may point to one difference, namely, the one between the purely *material* connections and those established and possibly revealed by the various *logical* functions which appear in the meaning contents of the sentences or are performed by the sentences themselves.[141] Let us take as an example two propositions from geometry: "The square is an equilateral parallelogram. Its diagonals intersect and are equal to each other." The connection between them is purely material. Even if—in order to determine this connection more closely—we interpose a third sentence between the two: "All equilateral rectangular parallelograms have two equal intersecting diagonals," the connection remains purely material, as before. Only if, after the first sentence, we introduce a second, in the form of: "Its diagonals intersect and are equal to each other because every equilateral rectangular parallelogram has such diagonals," then, on the one hand, thanks to the *logical* function of the word "because," a particular logical connection between these sentences attains explicit expression, and, on the other hand, the accompanying states of affairs gain new intentional elements which not only bring about a *necessary* connection between them but also identify their roles in the complex of states of affairs that is constituted by them. All "proofs," all systematizations (e.g., axiomatizations), of scientific results are essentially based on the fact that, thanks to logical functions and operations, the purely material connections are indicated in their greater or lesser strength and proximity and, at the same time, a logical-operative capability and the operative role belonging to the given capability are bestowed on the sentences.

Ad 5. All of these differences in the kinds of connections between sentences are meaningful for the attributes, and in general for the type, of the whole (of meaning units of a higher order) that is constituted in the connected sentences. The kind of connection that is *dominant* in a given manifold of sentences,

141. Cf. T. A. Meyer, *Das Stilgesetz*, p. 210n.

as well as the *selection* of types of connections that appear in a whole of a higher order, characterizes this whole in a peculiar way. And, conversely: if a whole of a determinate type and with determinate attributes is to be constituted, the type and range of its attributes are prescribed by the range of the types of connections "possible" to it or by the predominance of a sentence connection of a determinate type. If at a given time there are some connections in a whole which are not in accord with its type, then either the type will not attain pure expression, or a whole of a type totally different from the one intended will be constituted —a type that *will* be in accord with the individual connections. Let us imagine, for example, in a simple story about a small everyday occurrence—e.g., in the usual short short story—that at one point, to make this everyday occurrence possible, the most weighty general psychological issues are interpolated and that they are developed in a strictly logical order according to the operant logical connections (by which other parts of the story will also be carried through with great logical rigor). The character of the simple story will have been destroyed. However, the type of a strictly scientific psychological treatise will also not have been attained. We will have a variegated whole, fitted out with inharmonious attributes, a miscarriage, with which one truly does not know "where to begin."

As we see, we have before us broad perspectives on particular formations and structures of literary works, perspectives which up to now have barely been apprehended here and there in existing investigations in literary theory and in the theory of knowledge in general. Their systematic exploration is of great importance, for various reasons. Here we must be content simply to point these perspectives out.

§ 24. *The purely intentional correlates of the higher meaning units that are constituted in sentence complexes*

LET US NOW TAKE A LOOK at the purely intentional correlates belonging to sentence complexes or to the meaning units of a higher order constituted within them.

Let us take, for example, the following two sentences: "My typewriter has forty-three keys. The keys on my typewriter are easily worked." According to their contents, their purely intentional correlates are two different states of affairs, both of which, however, "refer" to one and the same typewriter. This "referring to" may have a twofold meaning, depending on whether the two sentences are taken as assertive propositions ("judgments") or as pure affirmative propositions. In the first instance, both states of affairs "refer" to one and the same *real* typewriter, to something that in its existence is ontically autonomous and is, at the same time, perhaps perceptually given. This happens because the intentional directional factor contained in the nominal expression "my typewriter" goes, so to speak, beyond the purely intentional object and strikes the corresponding autonomontically existing object.[142] However, if we disregard this "reference" and take both states of affairs as purely intentional correlates of simple affirmative propositions, then they will "refer" (indeed, primarily) to the purely intentional object projected by the word meaning "my typewriter." Indeed, the reference in our example is somewhat different in each state of affairs. In the content of the first state of affairs, it is based on the fact that in it the typewriter appears as its effective part and that it performs the function of carrier of the possessing of such and such parts. Thus the remainder of the content, so to speak, refers to the typewriter as the carrier, and, in particular, the keys are contained in the ontic range of the typewriter as its *parts*. In the second instance, however, the function of carrier is performed not by the typewriter itself but by its keys. But since the latter have appeared in the correlate content from the first as the keys *of the typewriter*, the carrier function which they perform with respect to the attribute "easily worked" is significantly modified in comparison with the carrier function they would perform if they were not parts of a whole, which is in itself not a "key," but were to constitute an ontically independent object. It is true that it is the keys *themselves* that are "easily worked"; but since they are appertaining (though removable) parts, it is ultimately the typewriter itself that has the easily worked keys. Hence there appears in the carrier function of the keys a relative dependence on that of which the keys are a part. At the same time, this modification of the carrier function points back to the typewriter itself, and, as a result, the whole state of affairs indirectly "refers" to it.

However, if, in the two sentences, only the expression "type-

---

142. In connection with this, there still appear particular properties in both purely intentional states of affairs; we will deal with them at length in the following sections.

writer," or even "my typewriter," were to appear without its being clear that the same person possesses it and that he is speaking of one and the same machine, then the state of affairs
developed by the sentences *taken in isolation* would not yet refer
to one and the same typewriter. Only because there is a connection between these sentences do they "refer" to one and the same
(intentionally meant) machine. In the process, something new
is also established, fundamentally changing their mutual relationship: a *material ontic* connection between them. With all
their differences, they exist within the enclosed ontic range of
one and the same object and therefore belong primarily to it but
to each other as well. The second state of affairs does not take
place within the framework of the first; it does not condition it,
nor is it required by it. Yet, if the first state of affairs did not
exist, the second also could not exist. For this reason, what we
have is a loose relationship between two states of affairs. Naturally, there can be very diverse types of ontic connection between
two states of affairs. But, however it may be with the individual
case, what is important for us is simply the fact that such connections between states of affairs as correlates of connected sentences occur at all and that such ontic connections are allowed,
and in most cases are required, by the peculiar structure of the
contents of the sentence correlates (and, in particular, by the
structure of the states of affairs). If there are many sentences
which, while connected, refer to one and the same object (e.g.,
in a description of an object), the states of affairs, figuratively
speaking, merge into a "net" in which the given object is "ensnared." One state of affairs is tied in this or that manner to another or is connected to it by a third, other states of affairs link
up in various ways, and thus a field of connected states of affairs
is developed. All of them exist within one and the same object
and in their connection make up the delimited ontic range of the
given object. And, conversely: the ontic range of an object
reaches precisely as far as the total manifold of the states of
affairs that "refer" exclusively to it. One must note, of course,
that, as a whole, every object can be variously related to other
objects and that, therefore, the circle of the states of affairs "referring" to it is significantly enlarged. But these states of affairs
refer not only to it but also to other objects; and thus, gradually,
an entire field of the most diverse states of affairs is developed,
in which a manifold of objects, a segment of a determinate ontic
sphere, is "ensnared." Or, to put it more precisely: a determinate
object, or a whole manifold of objects and their vicissitudes,

comes to be *represented* [143] in a manifold of connected states of affairs. When in the process of understanding (or expressing) a sequence of connected sentences we see as if before our eyes the development of a manifold of states of affairs, we enter into the "interior" of the given object and become acquainted with it, just as we become acquainted with the events in which it and other objects take part. Correlatively, it is presented to us through various states of affairs in its own essence. Here, however, it is presented to us in a totally different way than when it is simply given in a perception or in a direct (and thus *non*significative) apprehension of a state of affairs. That is to say, it is a question of the particular manner in which the purely intentional states of affairs that are developed by the connected sentences enter into a mutual bond: they do in fact unite and quite frequently remain in close and strict ontic connections; nevertheless, they are to a certain degree *separate*, and they *do not coalesce* or blend in *every* respect. Even in its original, immediate apprehension, an ontically autonomous, objective state of affairs is intentionally isolated by the act of apprehension from the uniform whole of the object in which—speaking purely ontically—it is embedded. From this isolation there follows a separation (to be sure, an intentional one—but that is precisely the point), an isolation from all the remaining essence of the given object. The remaining states of affairs existing in its ontic range escape our attention, so to speak, so that the object actually shines in the apprehended state of affairs only as a qualified carrier of the determination which is due it and which appears in the given state of affairs. It is precisely through thematic concentration on the given state of affairs, and consequently through the necessarily connected "leaving out of sight" of the remaining states of affairs, that we arrive at the above-mentioned intentional demarcation. In a primary nonsignificative apprehension of the state of affairs, however, this intentional demarcation can be removed and, at any rate—if we may so put it—made "harmless" for the final apprehension of the object. For in a *fluid* apprehension of the object it is possible to cross over *continually* from one state of affairs to another. In this crossing-over, or in the coapprehension of states of affairs which were first apprehended separately, we see that the demarcations are movable and relative to the acts of apprehension, thanks to which we are struck by their purely inten-

143. See the analysis in § 29, below.

tional character. As soon as this occurs, the demarcations appear as something not belonging to the given ontically autonomous object, and they are removed from the ontic range of the object by a peculiar canceling elimination. In this way we can advance in the primary apprehension of the objectively existing state of affairs to the structure of the *concreteness* that is peculiar to the object, that is, to the *original state of coalescence* of everything which makes up the enclosed—and, despite the heterogeneity of the individual determinations, the originally uniform—ontic range of the object and, indeed, the object itself. In this original apprehension of the states of affairs, an apprehension which at any moment is capable of changing the intentional content, the continuing processes, naturally, can also be apprehended. In doing this, we cut, as it were, a cross-section in the flowing happening and, while apprehending it, flow along with the happening in this cross-section-effecting attitude.

The situation is different if, from the first, the state of affairs is developed significatively by already established meaning contents of sentences or if we grasp them by understanding present, completed sentences. Since the meaning content of a completed sentence, standing in the once-for-all-established sentence complex, forms a rigid meaning unit, an analogous rigidity is introduced into the content of the purely intentional sentence correlate. Despite the presence of connections between sentences and despite the bonds between their purely intentional correlates, these correlates remain partly discrete units. Thus, if an object is accessible to us only through the sentence contents of a number of connected sentences, it *disperses*, like a ray of light in a prism, into a discrete manifold of distinct, though connected, states of affairs. In this, the demarcations between individual states of affairs are of the same purely intentional character as the content of the state of affairs. Thus, *of itself*, so to speak, there can *never* be an opposition between these demarcations and the factual material of the individual states of affairs, nor can there be a canceling removal of them from the structure of the object. We will later see that nevertheless, to a certain degree and in a totally new way, this does, or can, come about. But even then the track of this sentence-based, dispersing manner of representing the object is always visible in the object and can never be totally removed. Here, truly, the object is caught as in a "net." And insofar as we limit ourselves solely to an understanding of sentences, we reach the object in this "ensnarement in a net."

Or, to put it differently, the object dispersed in this way, and ensnared in a net of states of affairs, is indirectly outlined by the connected sentences and is represented in the states of affairs. There is no doubt that, when we are reading a well-written literary work, we are not conscious of this dispersion of the represented object. Hence the question arises: by what means is this dispersion removed in the literary work? Some new factor, which transcends the pure understanding of the sentence, as well as its pure meaning content, must be cooperating. We will see the nature of this factor later, since it no longer belongs to the stratum of the literary work now in question (cf. Chaps. 8 and 9).

§ 25. *The quasi-judgmental character of the declarative sentences appearing in a literary work*[144]

IF WE WERE TO COMPARE the declarative sentences [affirmative propositions] appearing in a literary work with, for example, those of a scientific work, we would immediately observe that, despite the same form and despite at times also a seemingly identical content, they are essentially different: those appearing in a scientific work are genuine *judgments* in a logical sense, in which something is seriously asserted and which not only lay claim to truth but *are* true or false, while those appearing in a literary work are not pure affirmative propositions, nor, on the other hand, can they be considered to be seriously intended assertive propositions or judgments. In order adequately to grasp the essence of the stratum of meaning units and their role in the literary work, it is indispensable to clarify this special modifica-

144. The motto to § 25, as well as the later § 52, can be taken from Breitinger's essay "Von dem Wunderbaren und dem Wahrscheinlichen": 'The peculiar art of the poet thus consists of taking the things he wishes to make pleasing through his representation and to a certain degree artistically distancing them from the appearance of reality, but always to such an extent that even in the farthest distancing one never fully loses sight of the illusion of reality." And, further, "One must distinguish well, therefore, between what is true for the intellect and what is true for the imagination; something that may seem false to the intellect may be accepted as true by the imagination, and, contrariwise, what the intellect knows to be true may seem unbelievable to the imagination; thus it is quite certain that the false is sometimes more probable than the true" (see *J. C. Gottsched und die Schweizer, J. J. Bodmer und J. J. Breitinger,* [Berlin, 1884], p. 163).

tion of declarative sentences and, as will presently be shown, of all sentences appearing in a literary work.

As we have already noted, the subjective sentence-forming operation, whose pure product in a special case is the pure affirmative proposition, can serve other subjective operations and, in particular, the cognitive operation. Among cognitive operations, one of the most important is the judgment about something. That which is judged is usually expressed in an affirmative proposition, which, as a result, becomes an assertive proposition, a judgment in the logical sense. Irrespective of the change which thus occurs in the manifestation function of the affirmative proposition, its meaning content undergoes a special modification, which now merits closer attention.

If we were to understand the sentence "My fountain pen is lying on the desk" first in the sense of an affirmative proposition and should subsequently change it into a judicative proposition, we would notice first of all that the directional factor of the nominal expression "my fountain pen," which at first is directed at the corresponding purely intentional object, *refers*, in the judicative proposition, *beyond this object,* as it were, to a real object (or one intended as real), that is, to an object which should possess precisely those determinations which are intended in the expression "my fountain pen." Through this reference of the intentional directional factor, the entire purely intentional state of affairs developed by the meaning content of the sentence is applied to the real fountain pen, and, what is more, it is treated as a state of affairs that is contained in the pen's ontic range. It is intentionally transposed into the real ontic sphere in which the given fountain pen finds itself and in which—to use H. Conrad-Martius' well-chosen word—it is "rooted." At the same time, the predicate of the judicative proposition acquires, along with the function of the verbal development which it performs in the pure affirmative proposition, yet a second function, which is the direct discharge of the judgment, so to speak, and one by which the state of affairs determined by the sentence is *set* in the given ontic sphere (in our case, in the real world) as *truly existing.*[145] Above all, in both these functions—in the *transposition* into the given (real, ideal, etc.) ontic sphere [146] and in the *existential*

145. If a copula appears in a judicative proposition, it is that which, in the first place performs the two functions distingiushed here. See Pfänder, "Logik," pp. 182 ff.

146. The function of transposition was brought to my attention by A. Rosenblum.

setting [147]—there is based what one usually calls the "claim to truth" of the judgment. In other words, the judgment makes the claim that the state of affairs determined by its meaning content does *in fact exist,* not as a purely intentional state of affairs, but as one that is rooted in an ontic sphere that is ontically independent with respect to the judgment.

The function of "transposing," however, is indivisibly bound in the *judgment* to another function that is likewise characteristic of the judgment: to the intention that the *content* of the purely intentional sentence correlate should be so precisely *adjusted,* in terms of all the material and formal determinations that are not relative to the cognitive operation, to the state of affairs existing in the ontic sphere that is ontically independent of the judgment, that, in this respect, the two can be *identified.*[148] The cognitive operation must proceed and be continued until the intentional state of affairs created in its culminating phase, in the final judgment act, is formed in such a way that it attains this degree of adjustment. Speaking purely ontically, both states of affairs must constitute—with respect to the above-named moments—two different kinds of concretization of *the same* ideal essences or ideas: the purely intentional concretization, ontically heteronomous in form and relative to the subjective operation, and the objectively existing concretization, characteristic, in form, of the respective ontic sphere and thus, in a state of affairs that exists in the real world, in the form of an ontically autonomous realization of the corresponding essences or ideas. In view of the *sameness* of that which is concretized in two different

147. These two functions are so closely connected in the judgment that on superficial reflection they could be considered to be one and the same. More detailed analyses in later sections will show that the transposition into another ontic sphere, even if it is then essentially modified, need not necessarily go hand in hand with an existential setting. Thus one must distinguish these two functions even when they appear together.

148. It must be stressed emphatically that, in the execution of a judgmental act which culminates in a judgment in a logical sense, one usually cannot find any particular subjective operation of identification of these two states of affairs. This fact, however, does not contradict our conception. For what is at issue is that in a simply executed judgment the content of the purely intentional correlate of the appertaining affirmative proposition is considered from the first as identically the same as the objectively existing state of affairs. However, there are instances in which there is a conscious identification of these two states of affairs; indeed, this always happens when we make the given judgment after deliberating whether it is really true. In this deliberation there is a very clear juxtaposition of the two states of affairs, which are thus identified only when we have compelling reasons for doing so.

ways, the two states of affairs are identified with each other, and as a result this type of ontically heteronomous concretization (the pure intentionality) of the intentional state of affairs is passed over, as it were, and the intentions of the judicative proposition point directly at that which is ontically independent with respect to the judicative proposition. Only when it is thus adjusted can the purely intentional state of affairs be intentionally transposed into the corresponding ontic sphere.[149] The consequence of all these functions is that the purely intentional state of affairs, as a purely intentional one, therefore disappears from our field of vision, so to speak; it does not attain distinctness.[150] A special attitude is then required to apprehend it in its peculiarity and to contrast it with the objectively existing state of affairs. An attitude of this kind, well known from daily life, occurs when, upon understanding a judgment and consequently following the intention contained in it, which projects a state of affairs, we simultaneously doubt the judgment and, in order to prove it, compare the state of affairs projected by the sentence with the simultaneously intuitively given objective state of affairs. But the very deferment of the claim to truth that is immanent in the judgment suffices for the purely intentional correlate to be distinguished as purely intentional. In these and all analogous cases, we are no longer dealing with a pure *judgment* but with a modified one, in which the claim to truth, having been infringed upon, is now put in question. If the claim to truth *is made seriously*, we return to the situation we have described above.

As simple and understandable as the entire situation seems to be at first glance, there can still be objections to the correctness of our conception. Thus, there emerges the following train of thought: would it not be much more correct to say that, in a

149. Pfänder claims that the "agreement" between reality and judgment, in which he sees the essence of the truth of the judgment, rests on the fact "that the judgment in its assertive setting, which it effects with respect to the object of the subject [of the sentence] coincides with the behavior of the object itself" ("Logik," p. 221). If by the "behavior of the object itself" I am to understand the state of affairs objectively existing in a given ontic sphere, it seems to me that my conception given in the text is close to Pfänder's—with the provision, of course, that the moment given by Pfänder does not exhaust the entire situation which exists in a true judgment and that the "coincidence" of the judgment should be understood in the sense that, with respect to its content, the purely intentional state of affairs is matched with the objectively existing state of affairs and that the two states of affairs are identified with each other. Otherwise, I would not know what other meaning of "coincidence" would justify our speaking of an "agreement."

150. One could say figuratively that it becomes fully "transparent."

true judgment, there is *only one* objectively existing state of affairs, which is simply apprehended in the act of judging and is set and intended in the judicative proposition as an objectively existing one? For it is an indubitable fact that, while simply judging, we do not intend *two* states of affairs—the purely intentional and the objectively existing—and then somehow "make them coincide"; rather, we simply direct ourselves at one (and indeed, the objectively existing) state of affairs and hold it, or believe we hold it, in an existence that is ontically independent of the judgment. If this conception [that there is only one objectively existing state of affairs] were true, however, then the statement about a transposition of the purely intentional state of affairs would, therefore, have to be false; and, moreover, the entire theory of the purely intentional correlate of meaning units would also be placed in question. For then we might justifiably wonder whether such a correlate also exists in the case of false judgments and in other sentences.

Nevertheless, the presence of the purely intentional correlate in the kind of formation that is a sentence cannot be doubted. Thus it would be incomprehensible why only *true* judgments should be deprived of such a correlate. On the other hand, the presence and the dissimilarity of the two types of states of affairs can easily be shown in the case of true judgment as well. This is already proven in the instances where we have reflected on the veracity of a determinate judgment. But there are cases where this can also be easily shown without "suspending" the claim to truth of the judgment, i.e., without bringing into the judicative proposition the modifications that are bound to it. Let us take as examples the following judicative propositions, which we shall assume to be true: "Every body is extended," and "This fountain pen is of German make, while that one is American." In *reality* there is unquestionably no "this" or "that" fountain pen, hence no object which would possess an attribute or any moment which could correspond to the words "this" or "that." Similarly, there is no body which would be "every." [151] To be sure, when, for example, referring in conversation to a thing we say "this fountain pen," this intentional turning to it, and its concomitant distinction from other things, produces the consequence that, in its visi-

151. A similar idea was expressed by Dr. M. Kokoszyńska, in a paper delivered before the Lvov Philosophical Society, when she stated that the expression "every S" or "all S" cannot be conceived, as she said, as an independent name and that, therefore, the "every" belongs not to the subject concept but to the predicate concept.

ble *appearance content,* the given thing attains a special moment—one that can be intuitively apprehended as well—that corresponds to this turning-to and is relative to it. This moment, however, is of a *purely intentional* nature, and in no respect can it change the given real thing—as it is, purely in itself—and thus, in particular, it cannot produce any new attribute in it. This moment also stands out clearly against the totality of the real attributes pertaining to the thing. Thus, when we say, "This fountain pen is of German make," the meaning content of this sentence determines the object of the subject of the corresponding purely intentional state of affairs, not merely as "fountain pen," but also as something provided with the intentional moment that corresponds to the word "this"; and only when the pen is so conceived does it refer the rest of the state of affairs to itself. This moment, however, is not found in the corresponding real state of affairs. Hence the two states of affairs are clearly dissimilar. But since the direction which is specified by the intentional directional factor of the word "this" coincides with the direction of the act in which the subject of the real state of affairs is apprehended, the two states of affairs can correspond to each other and be identified with each other, so that their dissimilarity does not clearly enter our consciousness. Nevertheless, from the purely ontic point of view, the identity does not extend to all the moments of the two states of affairs if we take only the really existing state of affairs in its full purity, that is, after having removed all the purely intentional characters that are relative to conscious operations, i.e., when we treat it as we should treat it in every judgment that makes a claim to truth. At that point, the purely intentional state of affairs projected by the judicative proposition in question also strikes us in its pure intentionality. Thus, in the case of true judgments as well, the existence of the two states of affairs—the purely intentional and the objectively existing—is unquestionable. This is not controverted by the equally unquestionable fact that, in effecting the meaning content contained in a judicative proposition, "we catch sight" of only one, not two, different states of affairs; for here we see only the performance of the judgment function, described above, which, among other things, brings about the identification of the matter and the form of the purely intentional state of affairs with the objectively existing one. Nor is it strange that, despite the dissimilarity of the modes of existence of the two identified states of affairs, such an identification does come about, since it is not the intentional correlate of the judicative proposition *as such* but only its *content* which is made "to coincide" with the objective state of affairs. In this content itself, however, the essence of the given object has precisely that mode of existence in which the state of affairs that exists in the given sphere appears. The purely intentional mode of existence, on the contrary, does not come into view at all, since it does not belong to the *content* of the purely intentional correlate, or else it cannot be found in it. The fact that the matter stands thus and not differently is precisely the direct result of the above-indicated functions of the judicative proposition.

Our conception of judgment functions and the interpretation of the claim to truth can thus be considered secure.

If, by way of contrast, we examine the pure affirmative proposition, we become convinced that all the functions directly connected with the claim to truth and their sequels are missing here. In the first place, the intentional directional factor of the subject of the sentence does not point, by way of the appertaining intentional object, at an ontically independently existing object but precisely at the purely intentional object itself. This, however, is only an external expression of the fact that neither the matching-intention [*Anpassungsvermeinung*], which makes the identification, nor the transposition of the content of the purely intentional state of affairs is present here. With that, the existential setting in an ontic sphere that is ontically independent with respect to the sentence is also missing. To be sure, the objects appearing in the purely intentional state of affairs, or the *states of affairs themselves, are characterized according to their mode of existence* as, e.g., real, ideal, merely possible, etc., but they are not *set* [accepted] as actually existing in the ontic mode.[152] Despite the existential characterization, the intentionally developed state of affairs is quite as if suspended in air; it is not "rooted" in an ontic sphere that is ontically independent of the affirmative proposition. In the comprehension or expression of a pure affirmative proposition the corresponding state of affairs appears much more clearly in the character of being supported by the loaned *intentionality* of the meaning of the sentence. At the same time, however—and we must stress this in order to avoid misunderstanding—the pure affirmative proposition is not to be confused with a judicative proposition that is recognized to be false or with a *negative* existential judgment. In other words, the

152. According to Pfänder's terminology, in a pure affirmative proposition there is no assertive function of the copula wherever the latter appears.

absence of the existential setting in a pure affirmative proposition is not to be identified with *cancellation* of the existential setting or with existential *exclusion* from an ontically independent sphere. In a judicative proposition recognized as being false we are dealing precisely with a sentence in which the existential setting is immanent and essential, even though it is recognized as unwarranted and invalid and therefore without power. The negative existential judgment also claims to be true and thus carries with it all the functions distinguished above. In the pure affirmative proposition, however, there is simply the *absence* of any claim to truth, and the peculiar character of the "being in suspension" of the purely intentional state of affairs is indivisibly connected thereto.[153]

Between the two extremes—of the pure affirmative proposition and the genuine judicative proposition—lies the kind of sentences that we find in the (modified) assertive propositions in literary works. In the title of this section we have used the expression "the quasi-judgmental character" of assertive propositions. By this we wished to indicate that the assertive propositions appearing in a literary work have the external *habitus* of judicative propositions, though they neither are nor are meant to be genuine judicative propositions. When, e.g., we read in a novel that Mr. So-and-so murdered his wife, we know perfectly well that this is not to be taken seriously and that, if the given sentences were found to be false, no one would be held responsible. It never even enters our mind to ask about their truth or falsehood. Yet, something is undoubtedly *asserted* in a particular manner; we are therefore not dealing with pure affirmative propositions, though to a superficial observer it might seem self-evident that we are doing so. It is difficult, however, to determine this peculiar modification of the assertive proposition, since in various types of literary works there are various modifications of this kind; some move from assertive propositions to judicative propositions, while others approach pure affirmative propositions.

Closest to pure affirmative propositions are the quasi-judgmental assertive propositions in works which in *no* sense claim

153. If I correctly understand Meinong's arguments, the particular instance of the pure sentence-forming operation in which the pure affirmative proposition is formed is the one he calls "the judgment-like assumption." However, at times it seems that he has the pure affirmative proposition in mind when he speaks of an "assumption." At any rate, in Meinong the sphere of meaning units is not clearly set forth, nor is the name "assumption" appropriate for the pure affirmative proposition.

to be "historical"—as in the symbolist dramas of Maeterlinck or the little dramas of Hofmannsthal. No doubt there does occur an ontic setting of the intentionally projected states of affairs (or of the objects represented therein), which, naturally, are also correspondingly existentially characterized. But there is a total absence of the intention of an exact matching—which is characteristic of genuine judicative propositions—of the projected state of affairs to the corresponding state of affairs that is objectively existing and that is to be found in an ontically autonomous sphere.[154] Thus, there can also be no mention of any identification with this sphere. Nevertheless, here, too, the sentence correlates are transposed, in accordance with their content, into the real world. But here this goes hand in hand only with the ontic setting and not—as is the case with genuine judicative propositions—simultaneously with the matching-intention and with the identification. Hence, in understanding the sentences that appear, we do not direct ourselves immediately at the real states of affairs or objects that are rooted in the real ontic sphere. Nor are we anchored with the intentions [of the sentences] in this sphere in such a way that the purely intentional correlate contents could pass unnoticed; on the contrary, the latter are themselves transposed and set in reality, without any diminution of our awareness that they have their origin in the intentionality of the meaning of the sentence. This setting and transposition, however—in accordance with the proper meaning of assertive propositions that are modified in this manner—are not effected in the mode of something fully *serious*, as is the case with genuine judicative propositions, but in characteristic manner, which only simulates this seriousness. For this reason the corresponding purely intentional states of affairs or objects are only *regarded as really existing*, without, figuratively speaking, being saturated with the character of reality. That is why, despite the transposition into reality, the intentionally projected states of affairs form their own world. One must also note that the transposition is not performed by means of the directional factor of the nominal meanings appearing in the sentences but that particular material data and content data are necessary for this purpose; for example, the information appears in the text that the situation takes place in

154. It should be noted that this matching should not be confused with the internal consistency of meaning contents of sentences or with the unity of the individual property qualities that are characteristic for objectivities of a given type. It may well be that the first is absent while the second is present.

some park, in *some* city, or *anywhere* on earth. It is the opalescence of this state of being transposed into the world and yet
being only suspended somewhere, of this inability to be truly
grounded in reality, that produces, in conjunction with this type
of quasi-judgmental assertive proposition, the special charm of
these works.

Another type of quasi-judgmental assertive propositions is
found, in some of the so-called contemporary or period novels
(rococo, Biedermeier, etc.), which are not "historical" in the
proper sense of the term but in which the represented objectivities refer in a totally different and, at the same time, if one may
put it so, narrower manner to the real world. This only simu-
latedly serious character of the "setting" function, as well as of
the transposition, is maintained here—as it is in all quasi-judgmental assertive propositions. If in the previous case, however,
the intention of "being matched" to an objectively existing state
of affairs was totally lacking, and if, as a result, the states of affairs (or the projected objects) intentionally developed by the
sentences would in *themselves* have to be introduced into the
world and existentially set there, in the present case, the beginning of such an intention of matching is already present. And, in
the first place, it is not a question of the fact that various material
and content elements of sentences provide the states of affairs or
objects with elements which are similar to the properties and elements that inhere in a specific temporal period and a specific cultural milieu; rather, it is a question of the *intention* with which
the assertive propositions appearing in a "contemporary" novel
are spoken. For it is with this intention that the special mode of
the quasi-judgmental assertive function of these sentences is
connected. The individual assertive propositions are given in
such a way that the states of affairs projected by them are to be
matched, not with *any* entirely *determinate individual* state of
affairs truly existing in a given epoch, but only with a *general
type* of states of affairs and objects that would be "possible" in a
given time and milieu. Sentences appearing in such a novel naturally project states of affairs which exist in or on *individual* objects or are themselves *individual*. But it is not with respect to
this individuality, or perhaps, to put it better, it is not in their
full individuality, that the intentionally projected objects are to
be matched with what is real. Nor is it a question of, e.g., a character represented in a novel being, as one usually puts it, "a literary representation" of a determinate person that really existed.
Instead, the matching-intention proper to the sentences appearing

here refers to the *type* which becomes manifest in the represented character. Indeed, here, too, the directional factors of the
nominal meanings do not point beyond the purely intentional objects to any determinate real objectivities; here, too, the direct
anchoring of the intentions of the meaning contents in reality is
lacking; but, despite this, the purely intentional states of affairs
(or objects) are not left suspended during the setting-into-exist-
ence, as was the case in the instance discussed above. By virtue
of a proper matching with the general type of objectivities, they
are transposed into reality; and, in order to strengthen the appearance of reality, they are at times even related to objectively
existing states of affairs which could also be ascertained through
genuine judgments. For example, we are told that such and such
an affair takes place in a city (e.g., Paris) which we otherwise
know to be really existing. In close connection with this, however, since it is merely a question of matching with a type, this
transposition cannot lead to a complete "transparency" of the
purely intentional states of affairs: they still remain *merely*
transposed and set, with a clear stamp of their intentional relativity to the corresponding sentence meaning contents.

When we finally turn to literary works of art which purport
to be "historical" and which undertake to be as "faithful" as possible in representing facts and objectivities known from history,
we are still not dealing with genuine judicative propositions. Let
us compare, for example, the description of a battle in a historical novel, even one in which the description is as faithful as possible to the historical sources, with the representation of the
same battle in a *scholarly* work. The difference in the character
of the assertive propositions appearing in the two cases is un-
mistakable. And it is not because here and there in the novel
there are "deviations" from what actually occurred. For not even
the strictest scholarly history—indeed, for fundamental reasons
—can provide an absolutely faithful representation. The difference again lies in the quasi-judgmental character of the assertive
propositions appearing in a literary work of art of this kind. Nevertheless, we are a step closer here to genuine judicative propositions. The reason is that the intention of matching [objects or
situations] with objectively existing states of affairs (or objects)
extends here to the strictly individual and not merely to the general type, as in the previous case. Thus, not only "such" and
"those kinds of" objects and situations that would be "possible"
in a given epoch can be represented here; rather, the assertive
propositions can project states of affairs or objects that are ex-

actly matched, since, as entirely *determinate* individuals, they are matched with once (or also "presently") existing objects (states of affairs). If, for example, the murder of Wallenstein is represented in *The Death of Wallenstein,* the purely intentionally projected events—precisely as these determinate *individual* events—should be matched with the events which once actually occurred in history in such a way as to be as similar to them as if they were "the same." [155] Yet there *should be no* identification here of the two states of affairs (or objects) that would, once again, cause the intentionally projected states of affairs, themselves, to be ontically characterized as real and set in existence in their entire multifariousness and would bring to representation the objects that have been transposed into the real world. Rather, on the strength of the far-reaching similarity between them, they should only duplicate the objects which at one time have really existed; they should, indeed, attempt to *substitute* for them, as if they themselves were these objects. If true judicative propositions were to appear in such a novel, neither such a "duplication" nor simulation could occur; instead, the intentional directional factor would ultimately have to indicate objects which at one time had really existed. The intentionally projected states of affairs would then have to coincide fully with the real ones, so that, as such, in the understanding of the sentence, they would have to disappear entirely from our field of vision. In artistic historical representation, however, it is precisely the purely intentional correlates which are visible to us in the understanding of the sentences. By dint of their far-reaching similarity—in accordance with the intention—and their matching with objectively existing states of affairs, they make the latter quasi-incarnate, quasi-present. Thus the past, long gone and turned into nothingness, again arises before our eyes in the merely intentional states of affairs (objects) incorporating it. But it, itself, is not what is ascertained here, since the last step which divides the quasi-judgmental assertive propositions from genuine judicative propositions is still missing: i.e., the identification, the setting into the mode of the fully serious, and the anchoring of the intentions of the meaning contents in the proper reality. This last step is effected only in the transition to a scientific consideration or to an immediate account of one's memory. But then one already attains genuine judicative propositions.

Since in a literary work there are only quasi-judgmental

155. See Chap. 7 for what this "as if" refers to.

assertive propositions of various types, they are not—as we have already established—pure affirmative propositions. Thus, by virtue of their described properties, they are capable of evoking, to a greater or lesser degree, the illusion of reality; this pure affirmative propositions cannot do. They carry with them, in other words, a suggestive power which, as we read, allows us to plunge into the simulated world and live in it as in a world peculiarly unreal and yet having the appearance of reality. This great and mysterious achievement of the literary work of art has its source primarily in the peculiar, and certainly far from thoroughly investigated, quasi-judgmental character of assertive propositions. Other factors of the literary work of art, yet to be discussed, only contribute to this.

In order to complete these considerations, I must add one further observation to avoid a false interpretation of my position. That is to say, one must distinguish two different uses of predicative sentences in a literary work of art. Some of them, as it is usually said, are spoken by "the author," whereas others are expressed by the characters represented in the literary work. This appears in both the epic and the novel, and it is especially clear in every dramatic work, where these sentences form a special text, which, as we shall see, is the main text.[156] Thus, if a sentence is spoken by a represented character as a judgment directed at another represented character, then, if the first character is truly judging and is sincere, this sentence is undoubtedly a judgment in the strict sense; but at the same time it is a judgment that is valid or true only in the domain of the represented world and in regard to the objects of this world and, finally, only for the represented characters speaking with each other. And indeed this is true regardless of whether it is an individual and particular or a general judgment. It is not permissible then—as is frequently done by critics and historians of literature—to carry the judgments spoken by the represented characters beyond the bounds of the world represented in the given work and to interpret them as judgments concerning the real world or as the author's opinions about certain questions pertaining to the real world. Such a procedure deforms the peculiar sense of such sentences and falsifies the peculiar structure of the work. For they are statements which are intended only as judgments by the represented characters, statements which themselves belong to the represented objectivities within the represented world and, for

156. See below, §§ 30 and 57.

both the author and the reader, are only putative, not genuine, judgments.

If, on the other hand, a predicative sentence belongs to the text which develops the representation of the represented world, if it forms a part of the "story" relating the vicissitudes of the represented characters and things and thereby performs the function of the intentional formation of the represented as such, then it is only a quasi-judgment, which the author uses precisely for the purpose of simulating this world. If it were then also to have the external form of a judgment about represented objects —as, for example, sentences describing the external appearance and demeanor of a determinate represented character, e.g., Herr Senator Buddenbrook—it is nonetheless not a judgment but forms instead one of the modifications of a judgment described above—a quasi-judgment of this or that form. In reading and interpretation, such sentences must be taken only in these special modifications and functions, and they may not be changed into true judgments, that is, to judgments which refer not to represented objectivities but to real, nonartistic things. This would likewise be a falsification of the peculiar sense of these sentences and consequently of the work itself, in particular if these sentences were to be taken as "the truth" which the author offers the reader for his cognizance. I will come back to this again in § 52, which is devoted to the problem of so-called truth in the literary work of art.[157]

§ 25a. *Are there no quasi-judgments in a literary work of art?*

IN HER *Logik der Dichtung* Käte Hamburger has protested against my conception of quasi-judgments and their role in the literary work of art.[158] In their place she attempts to find other linguistic means by which to explain how it is possible that in a literary work of art real truth does not constitute the subject

157. It cannot be denied, of course, that authors often use their works to smuggle through their own opinions about various problems pertaining to the real world. But this only shows that they misunderstand the essence of a work of art and misuse works of art for various extra-artistic ends (political, religious, and so on).

158. See Käte Hamburger, *Die Logik der Dichtung* (Stuttgart, 1957), pp. 14 ff. and passim.

of discourse, i.e., it is not the represented as such that constitutes it, but only a manifold—in my terminology—of purely intentional objectivities which in general only simulate or duplicate a reality. Thus she first directs a series of objections against my conception and only then develops her own theory. I would like to give some attention to the former.

The arguments Mrs. Hamburger makes against me are the following:

1. "In the last analysis, Ingarden does nothing more than label the cognitive and linguistic phenomena that are under consideration here."

2. In the attempt "to distinguish the mode of existence of poetry from the 'prose' of the truth statement [*Wirklichkeitsaussage*]" the "differentiating concept" employed by me was "taken too narrowly."

3. Too narrow a concept of the literary work of art has been used by me. In fact, it has been "applied only to epic and dramatic poetry," ("something that was all too tacitly assumed in the book, and which in any case was adapted only to English terminology"). Besides, it was a question of nothing more "than the proof of the phenomenon, and the experience, of the 'nonreality' of these kinds of poetry."

4. For the purpose of proving this "unreality," I am charged with using an instrument of cognition "which at the very least has proved to be weak, namely, the concept of the quasi-judgment."

5. The argument gets sharper from line to line, for soon thereafter I read that "this reduction of the character of nonreality of mimetic poetry to the sentences from which it arises nevertheless seems to be a by no means satisfactory explanation of this phenomenon. Indeed, in the final analysis, it is nothing more than a circular argument. The sentences or statements of a novel are constituted as 'quasi-statements' only because of the fact that they are in a novel" (*Logik der Dichtung*, p. 15). And, furthermore: "The designation of the sentences of a novel or drama as quasi-judgments, however, signifies nothing more than the tautological fact that when we read a novel we *know* that we are reading a novel or drama, i.e., we know that we are not in a reality context."

6. Soon thereafter, however, it is no longer a question of a "tautology," but the discussion turns, on the one hand, to the disregard of an important factor in the literary work and, on the other hand, bluntly to the incorrectness of my conception.

Namely, I am charged with having falsely represented the difference between a historical novel and a scholarly historical work; this error then compelled me to alter my concept of the quasi-judgment in its application to the historical novel, and the falseness of my entire conception thus became apparent (*ibid.*, pp. 15, 26).

7. Finally, yet another, entirely different charge, namely, that "with the concept of the quasi-judgment the linguistic-literary structure and specific form of appearance of the novel are in no way described; rather, what is described is nothing but the indeterminate (?) psychological attitude of the author and, correspondingly, of the reader" (*ibid.*, p. 17).

This criticism is followed by an extensive investigation in which Käte Hamburger's own position is developed. I will briefly attend to that at a later point. What is the story with the criticism, however?

First of all, we must note that in the space of a few pages a number of different charges are made which contradict one another. The criticism begins with the reproach of "labeling" and of certain weaknesses ("too narrow," "insufficiently strong," etc.); next the argument of "tautology" is raised, and finally the reproach of falseness is leveled against my standpoint. At the very end, it is again observed that I have somehow missed the mark and that, instead of analyzing the literary work itself, I have described only the "indeterminate psychological attitude of the author or the reader." The inconsistency of the offensive against my position points to its weakness. Either my standpoint is "tautological" or it is false; it cannot be both. And, if it is false, it cannot also be "insufficiently strong." If, on the other hand, it refers to the psychological attitude of the reader or the author, then it appears to be correct but sent, so to speak, to the wrong address. What, then, is the real meaning of the criticism?

I will now turn to the individual objections.

Ad 1. "In the last analysis," I do "nothing more than label." This reproach, however, could be raised only if I had merely given a new name (label) and had not troubled myself with the clarification of the properties of what I called quasi-judgments. But this is by no means the case. The reader of the preceding sections can easily ascertain how I have labored to clarify the way in which a judgment is distinguished from a quasi-judgment; and subsequently—i.e., in the treatment of the situation in a historical novel (see § 25, p. 170)—there is a continuation of my attempts to elucidate this new concept and the modifications in its content. To be sure, it is not easy to apprehend this modification of assertive propositions and also bring it, in its specificity and its modifications, to the reader's attention. And I would not have been surprised if Mrs. Hamburger had said that my efforts at clarification were insufficient and that the whole matter requires further analysis. But this is certainly not mere "labeling." Indeed, Mrs. Hamburger herself cites a series of determinations and descriptions that I give and thereby shows that in my work there is no question of mere "labeling."

But I am not surprised that it is not easy for Mrs. Hamburger to grasp what is at issue in my work. She reproaches me with occupying myself with "indeterminate" *psychological* attitudes, and she counterposes for me—supposedly as something unknown and new to me—the need for an analysis of linguistic formations (or, as she says, "phenomena"). She herself, however, in determining the concepts of "judgment," "sentence," and "statement," invokes Sigwart (!)—Sigwart, who as everyone knows, represents the height of psychologism in logic—and thereby orients these concepts in a psychological direction. But it is I who have been struggling precisely against psychologism, and indeed exactly in the sphere of the study of linguistic formations and functions, and I have made every effort to apprehend the literary work of art as something which, though it certainly arises from subjective conscious operations, is transcendent to all consciousness and to everything psychic. Thus, it is inappropriate to counterpose Sigwart's views to mine, because from the very beginning I have been building the structure of the sentence and the judgment out of purely linguistic elements and have been on my guard against any psychologization. In my method I feel myself to be quite close to Husserl and Pfänder, and I do not deny this kinship. But in their method of freeing themselves from psychologism, Husserl and Pfänder are not yet sufficiently pure for me.

The concept of the quasi-judgment has for its background Pfänder's distinction between the two functions of the copula in the sentence: the assertive function and the predicative function. For the "quasi" refers precisely to a modification of the assertive function (the assertion according to Russell), which, on the one hand, is counterposed to the categorical judgment and its simple "categorical" (unconditional) assertive function, and, on the other hand, to the "neutrality modification"—as it was designated by Husserl—or, finally, to the complete privation of the assertive function, as in pure affirmative propositions (predicative sentences without any assertion, pure "assumptions" [*An-nahmen*], according to Meinong). If someone does not know and does not take into consideration these investigations by Husserl and Pfänder (or Meinong), then my analyses are also hardly accessible. At the same time, I have attempted to go beyond what was considered by Pfänder and have sought—partly with the cooperation of Mrs. Conrad-Martius—to explain the sense or, if you will, and insofar as this is possible, the function.

Clearly, linguistic formations—like sentences, literary works, and so on—are accompanied by the speaker and his linguistic functions, cognitive operations, etc. In living speech, the function of the copula, for example, as well as the assertive function of the judgment or its various modifications, is picked up from the speaker and effected. Thus we have assertive acts, predicative operations, etc. Thus we also have correspondingly modified acts of quasi-judging, and it must be shown how these subjective operations run their course *in concreto*. All of this, however, belongs to an entirely different study from the one conducted in this book. I have also investigated it in itself from one aspect— that of the reader—in the book *The Cognition of the Literary Work*,* which I published in Polish in 1937. I have taken pains to contrast sharply the two interrelated spheres of investigation; I have certainly not sought to confuse them. Here I require no admonition from Mrs. Hamburger.

Ad 2 and 4. I am not going to take up the charges that my concept of the "quasi-judgment" is too narrow or insufficiently strong; for me they are meaningless.

Ad 3. According to Mrs. Hamburger, my concept of the "literary work of art" is too narrow since it does not encompass all of lyric poetry. I ask the reader to refer to the page where the range of initial examples is determined and where, alongside epic and dramatic works, lyric poetry is also named. Thus it is not true that I have "all too tacitly" eliminated lyric poetry from the scope of the concept of the literary work. It is only true that *in concreto* lyric poetry was not analyzed in my book, but only because I feared at that time to take examples from this sphere, since errors arise most easily in the analysis of lyric poetry written in a foreign language. If Mrs. Hamburger knew my Polish works, she would find sufficient examples of lyric poetry as well as a detailed consideration of the lyric as such. During the war

* [*O poznawaniu dzieła literackiego* (Lvov, 1937). English translation by Ruth Ann Crowley and Kenneth R. Olson, *The Cognition of the Literary Work of Art* (Evanston, Ill.: Northwestern University Press, 1973).]

(1940–41) I had to work as a Germanist in Lvov University and, among other things, lecture on the theory of literature; at that time my lectures were to a great extent oriented on the lyric poetry of Rilke. To be sure, I arrived at an entirely different conception of lyric poetry from Mrs. Hamburger's (and, for that matter, E. Staiger's). For me the lyric is no less "mimetic" than epic or dramatic poetry, and what is represented in it is "unreal" to the same degree as the world represented in a dramatic or an epic work; only it is represented differently, and what is represented is different. But again, this would lead us too far from the matter at hand.[159]

Ad 5. What, now, about the charge of "tautology," of the "circular argument"? It could be justified only if my descriptions of the quasi-modifications of judgments (N.B.: in my view there is not one modification but several different ones, which I have likewise clearly distinguished in the considerations given in this book) contained a *circulus in definiendo.* This does not occur, nor has Mrs. Hamburger demonstrated it. The charge—as it is formulated—stems, as I see it, from a confusion by Mrs. Hamburger of two totally different problems: (1) What is a quasi-judgment or the modification of its assertive function? What is its sense and function? And (2), on what basis does the reader recognize, in an individual case, that he is dealing with a quasi-judgment and not a judgment (or, as Mrs. Hamburger says, a reality statement)?[160] Here the context plays an essential role: when it is isolated, an individual judgment does not differ in its "form"—says Mrs. Hamburger—in any respect from what I call a quasi-judgment. One recognizes that one should read (or understand) it as a quasi-judgment from the fact that it is a sentence of a novel (in my terminology, a literary work of art). But, on the other hand, one distinguishes literary works of art (especially novels) from nonnovels (literary scholarly works) only because (Mrs. Hamburger says, or puts the "only" in my mouth) they consist of pure quasi-judgments. From this we have the alleged "circular argument." The fact is that if by "form" one

<hr>

159. See *Studia z estetyki* (Studies in Aesthetics), 2 vols. (Cracow, 1957–58). This is a collection of works which for the most part appeared much earlier.

160. Naturally, we are not permitted to use the term "reality statement" [*Wirklichkeitsaussage*] in place of the word "judgment" [*Urteil*] as long as by "reality" we understand the real spatiotemporal world. There are judgments that are not "reality statements," that is, do not refer to the real world and yet lose nothing of their judgmental character —all mathematical propositions, for example.

understands the manner of writing (or articulating) the sentence, we have *no particular sign* in colloquial speech which could distinguish a pure proposition from a judgment. And for this reason, when we know from the outset that we are dealing with poetry, we also know—if I am correct—that we are dealing with pure quasi-judgments as well. It is known that Bertrand Russell brought in the assertion sign in logic or in a logical system precisely for this reason, so as to distinguish the so-called theses of the system from mere "statements," i.e., pure propositions which are indeed predicative formations but are bereft of the assertive function. It would be easy to introduce a special sign for quasi-judgments as well, which one could put before each sentence of this kind in order to distinguish a quasi-judgment from judgments, on the one hand, and from pure propositions, on the other. In fact, we do have such external linguistic signs, and we use them to indicate that we are dealing with a quasi-judgment: thus, when we read aloud the sentences belonging to a literary work of art, we give them a different *intonation (frequently it is a pronounced declamation)* which is visibly different from the intonation we give to scientific sentences. It is true that graphically we do not set any "quasi-judgment sign" before individual sentences (although we could do this), but, on the other hand, the title or subtitle informs us that we are dealing with a novel or a drama. Thus, it is frequently explicitly said: "contemporary drama," "historical [novel or play] from the time of Charlemagne," etc. There is a type of title that is used for literary works of art. If, for example, one reads titles like *The Magic Mountain, Buddenbrooks,* or *Death in Venice,* etc., one does not expect to find a scientific book but instead is prepared from the first for a literary story. Naturally, there are also titles (in the absence of an informative subtitle) which do not sufficiently inform us with what kind of work we are dealing: with a "poem" or with a scientific (and, in particular, a historical) work. For example, *Wallenstein* can be either "history" or Döblin's novel, especially if the manner in which the book was written can also leave us in doubt. However, these are extraordinarily infrequent cases. For, above all, *one thing* that Mrs. Hamburger asserts and puts in my mouth is not true, namely, that *only* the quasi-judgments distinguish the work from a corresponding historical work. I have taken great pains in my book to work out a series of *other* differences between works of art and scientific works (the reader will find them below, in the later chapters of this book): a different style of language, different composition, the appearance of manifolds of aspects held in readiness, the duplication and representation functions of represented objectivities, the presence of aesthetically valent qualities, and, in particular, the appearance of metaphysical qualities, to whose revelation the literary work of art is keyed. Although these may also sometimes appear in a scholarly historical work, basically they have nothing to do with the cognitive function and with the function of the transmission of scientific results; they are present only by chance. All of these, together with the quasi-judgments, are what decides that the given work is a literary work of art and not a scientific work or a propaganda piece. I am in total agreement with Mrs. Hamburger that one must look for "linguistic functions" which distinguish literary works of art from nonartistic works. This is not, however, anything new for me, and I myself have laid great stress on their determination. But I do believe that the quasi-judgment, as a very special "linguistic function," will be determined more closely by the characteristic elements of the literary work of art that I have just enumerated.

But this entire problem—i.e., on the basis of what external signs ("forms") one distinguishes quasi-judgments from judgments, and thanks to what circumstances one knows that one is dealing precisely with a quasi-judgment—has nothing in common with the totally different problem of what is the real *sense*, and the *function* based on the sense, of, on the one hand, a judgment and, on the other, a quasi-judgment. And this is the problem that I have dealt with exclusively in the preceding sections. It is only the dissimilarity, based on their modified assertive function, of quasi-judgments from judgments that brings about the fact that they also have a different function in the framework of the literary work: they bring about the constitution of represented objectivities which in their content simply simulate, or, if one will, "play," a *habitus* of reality and in themselves are not and cannot be real. That is to say, the function that quasi-judgments perform is such that we end up dealing with—as Mrs. Hamburger calls it—"fictional" mimetic poetry.

In this whole set of problems one question is crucial: according to Mrs. Hamburger, do literary works of art (fictional poems) constitute pure judgments (pure "reality statements," in Mrs. Hamburger's terminology) or not? It seems to me to be beyond doubt that Mrs. Hamburger must say: No, in no case. Poetry is not composed of judgments. Fine. Then I ask: What, then, are those propositions that are components of poetry? In a general sense, they are predicative sentences (sometimes, of course, they are interrogatory sentences as well—but more about this later). Are they then pure "assumptions," in Meinong's sense? Or are they somewhat "neutralized" affirmative propositions? Both seem false to me, and I believe I have provided arguments to that effect. There must be something else, therefore. In my opinion it is precisely the "quasi-judgments." If Mrs. Hamburger doubts this, she must provide another theory, another clarification of the sense and the function of every "poetic" sentence. Or does she believe that they are in fact quasi-judgments and that it is only a question of what linguistic or grammatical means are used to effect their constitution? In that case my conception is correct, and the only question is one of elaboration. Whether Mrs. Hamburger is correct in her elaboration is something I cannot go into now.

§ 26. *An analogous modification of sentences of other types*

IN THE LITERARY WORK, however, it is not only the declarative sentences that are subject to "quasi-modifications." Instead, all sentences, of whatever kind, are modified in an analogous manner when they belong to the text representing the represented world, i.e., when they are spoken, as one usually puts it, "by the author." Thus when we are dealing, for example, with an interrogatory sentence, it is no longer a genuine question, but only a quasi-question; sentences which express a wish or a command are not genuine wishing or commanding sentences but are only quasi-wishes, quasi-commands, etc. Likewise, the value judgments appearing in the representing text, regardless of whether they pronounce an ethical or a social or, for that matter, an aesthetic valuation, are not genuine value judgments but are only quasi-evaluations, even though, in their purely external form, they do not differ from genuine valuations. Their function consists solely in the intentional projection of certain ontically heteronomous objectivities, which can at most give themselves an appearance of reality but can never attain it.

However, if in the text of the literary work of art there appear questions, wishes, or valuations which are expressed by *represented* characters, the situation with them is the same as with the already discussed assertive propositions which are expressed in a drama by a represented character. For example, if a represented character asks his acquaintance: "Did you go to the theater yesterday?" and adds "That is a marvelous play, and it is excellently acted," in his opinion this is a genuine question and a genuine valuation; but clearly these sentences refer exclusively to objects and states of affairs belonging to the represented world, and they cannot be held by the reader to be questions or valuations of extra-artistic real objectivities. And insofar as they contribute to the constitution of this or that unit within the represented world, what is constituted by them is only an ontically heteronomous intentional objectivity; and, in this respect, they still differ from questions and valuations which we put in full earnestness with regard to real objects. As questions or valuations posited by represented characters, they themselves belong to the represented objectivities and are themselves ontically heteronomous. They only pretend to be genuine questions and genuine valuations, while in reality they are only intentional objectivities—to be sure, from the sphere of linguistic formations.

This is a remarkable double-natured character of theirs, which they share with the assertive propositions spoken by represented characters.

Naturally, there may be sentences spoken by represented characters that are not at all seriously meant by them and may thus themsleves be only quasi-judgments or quasi-questions, etc., for these characters, when, for example, they write poetry or read poetic works or play at theater, etc. Then the intentionally projected world is many-leveled, as it were, and, in the reading of such works, it produces particular artistic phenomena. But we need not analyze this more closely at this time.

One thing more must be noted. The interrogative sentence performs, along with other functions, the function of manifestation, thanks to which the interrogatory act of the questioner is "expressed." For the person being questioned, if he perceives the question intelligently a fact which takes place in the questioner is thus revealed in a very special way. Usually, no particular attention is paid to it, but it reaches—even if only peripherally— the consciousness of the person being questioned, and it can also be apprehended purely thematically. As something that has been manifested, it belongs in essence to the question that has really been posited. Let us now consider that a character in a novel puts a determinate question. In that case it is not only the interrogatory function of the interrogative sentence which is subordinate to the "quasi-modification" but also its expressive function and—concomitantly—that which itself is manifested. In effect, the questioner, with all that pertains to him and with all that he does, is certainly intended as being real; but he is still only intended. Consequently, his experiences as well, and, in particular, the "duration" of the articulation of the interrogative sentence, are questions effected by the same character. This "duration" is thus modified here in a twofold way: (1) as that which belongs to the world that is simply represented in the literary work, not in a really genuine sense but only as really intended, and (2) in its interrogatory function—as indicated above. But the articulation of the question also belongs to the simply represented world. The manifestation connected with it is, therefore, modified in the same twofold way: (1) as the merely intended manifestation and (2) as a notifying which informs not about an objectively existing fact but only about one that is intended as real. In this the situation can still be viewed from two different standpoints: (1) from the standpoint of the interrogated person represented in the given work, for whom the function of manifestation is really effected and for whom what is manifested is real, and (2) from the standpoint of the reader, who observes both the questioner and the person questioned and for whom both are modified in the sense indicated above.

All of this, however, concerns not only the manifestation function of spoken interrogative sentences but also the wishing, commanding, and, among others, naturally the assertive propositions as well, provided they are spoken by a character represented in a literary work of art. And precisely therein lies the necessary completion of the investigation performed by us in the preceding sections.

Considerations of the manifestation function and its modification lead to an important consequence, however; i.e., it is quite possible (and this occurs very frequently in literary works) that one of the characters utters this or that sentence and in the process undergoes a certain experience without our being informed about it by any *particular* sentences in the text; we learn of this much more by the simple appearance of sentences uttered by this character. For example, there is a simple interrogative or assertive sentence in the text, and it becomes apparent from the mere sequence of sentences that it should actually be in quotation marks. Such an "adduced" sentence performs a peculiar twofold function: (1) as one that is expressed, it properly does not belong to the *text* of the work but to the "represented" world projected by the text, since it is the quotation marks (which, by the way, are frequently absent) which properly belong to the text; (2) as an *adduced* sentence, however, it enters into the text, and, while merely represented, attains thereby an actuality which is properly not due it, since it is something which is merely represented. From the manifestation function which comes to be performed by the mere appearance of the adduced sentence there arises a projection of a fact belonging to the simply represented world, the fact of the manifested questioning, asserting, lying, etc. Thus at the outset it seems as though there could be, in the world that is intentionally projected by the meaning contents of the sentences, elements which are not determined by *any* meaning content and are thus independent of the stratum of meaning units. If this were truly so, we would be faced with a significant difficulty. For our whole intention in these analyses is to show that in the stratum of represented objects there is *no* materially determined state of affairs or object at all which would not have its ultimate source in one of the two strata which together constitute the language element in the literary work, i.e., that of phonetic formations and that of units of meaning. Closer consideration, however, shows that this danger does not exist, since the meaning element which is for the moment missing here is replaced precisely by the function of the explicitly provided or only implicitly cointended quotation marks. In effect the quotation marks tell us that the following words or the following sentences are spoken with full intent and meaning by a given person and are only repeated or given here. As something that is "really" uttered, it carries with it the manifestation function. The function of the quotation marks, therefore, projects in a particular, but still intentional, manner a state of affairs, that of manifesting. And only this state of affairs, in connection with the meaning and the character of the just then articulated sentence, leads, of itself, to the projection of a new intentional state, namely, the one that is manifested. The manifested state of affairs which belongs to the world represented in the work is thus also, if only indirectly, dependent here, in its state of being projected, on a meaning element of the stratum of meaning units. Despite this, however, it must be added and stressed that the manifestation function is radically different from the purely intentional projection which comes into existence through the meaning units. Although the meaning of the articulated sentence is not totally irrelevant for the function of manifestation, it is still not the meaning, but the fact of the articulation of a given sentence, which brings about the revelation of what is expressed (the question, the assertion, the lie, etc.). We cannot continue here with a more detailed clarification of manifestation. What is important for us is only that among the states of affairs which come to be developed in the literary work there may be those which, like the expressive function, are dependent on the states of affairs that are directly projected by the meaning content of the sentence and are themselves only indirectly determined by the meaning elements of the stratum of meaning units.

6 / The Role of the Stratum of Meaning Units in the Literary Work. The Representation Function of the Purely Intentional Sentence Correlates

§ 27. *The differentiation of the various functions of sentences and sentence complexes*

IN ORDER TO SIMPLIFY the following reflections, let us restore the unity of the sentence as a whole in which we can distinguish a phonetic and a meaning aspect. To be sure, we will have to concentrate primarily on the performance and the various functions of the meaning contents of the sentence in order to allow its role in the literary work to become evident; but it will also be necessary to have frequent recourse to the role of the phonetic stratum, since it remains in close connection with the role of the meaning units and in various respects supplements and supports their performance.

Sentences and complexes of sentences perform—as do their phonetic aspects—two basically different roles in the whole of the literary work. They are, first, the role which inheres in the performance of the sentence meanings, in the creation ("projection"), or merely in the more precise shaping, of the remaining strata of the literary work, and, second, the role in which the meaning units appear as a particular material in the heterogeneous material of the literary work and partake through their particular properties and value qualities in the polyphony of the work, enriching it and influencing the shaping of the total characters or—if one prefers—the forms and values of the whole based on this polyphony.

As far as the first of these roles is concerned, there are still various functions which the meaning units can perform: (1)

Above all, it is a question of the (direct or indirect) intentional *projection* of the represented objects according to their nature, their qualitative constitution, as well as their formal and existential structure, whereby these objects can be, not only things and persons, but also the destinies, states, and processes in which they partake. (2) However, it is not merely the represented objects themselves but also the *"how" of their representation* that is precisely determined by the sentence meanings, and this determination also belongs to the work performed by the meaning contents of the sentence. In some instances the phonetic aspect of the sentences also takes part. (3) As our preceding considerations of the phonetic stratum have shown, the meanings of individual words as well as meaning contents of whole sentences influence the more detailed shaping of the formations and characters occurring in this stratum. We will not occupy ourselves further with these. (4) The meaning units lead to a predetermination of manifolds of aspects in which the represented objectivities will appear, and in this the phonetic aspect again plays an essential role. We will go into this in detail in Chapter 8. (5) Finally, the role of the meaning units for the constitution of the "idea of the work" can be dealt with only when we have clarified what we understand by the "idea" of a work. In any case, the source of this "idea"—if there is such a thing—must likewise be sought in the stratum of meaning units and perhaps in the stratum of phonetic formations as well.

§ 28. *The projection function of sentences; states of affairs and their relation to represented objectivities*

THE MOST IMPORTANT of the differentiated functions is based on the fact that the meaning content of sentences is the *decisively determining* factor for the objects and their vicissitudes which are represented in the work and which belong in essence and immanently to it. Their existence as well as their collective essence has its direct or indirect source in the derived intentionality of the meaning contents of sentences and is essentially determined by them. It is for this reason that in our analysis of the sentence we have concentrated upon their "work performed" [*Leistung*], i.e., on the fact that from themselves they develop states of affairs or, more generally, purely intentional sentence correlates. For only this performance can help explain how something like represented objects can exist at all in the literary work and in what manner this comes about. Our preceding considerations have attempted to clarify this. Nevertheless, what is intentionally *directly* projected by the meaning content of a sentence is the developed state of affairs. So the question arises of how one goes from the intentional development of states of affairs to the constitution of objects, and, in particular, things, persons, processes, etc.—always as only purely intentional correlates.

As we have shown previously, there exists a very close connection between purely intentional sentence correlates, especially purely intentional states of affairs, and purely intentional objects. Both the former and the latter *are transcendent* with respect to the meaning contents of the sentence and belong to what is intentionally created by the meaning content of the sentence or its elements, the word meanings. As such, the purely intentional sentence correlates and, in particular, the states of affairs already belong to the "object stratum" of the literary work. If the states of affairs—always taken purely intentionally—exist, then the objects in whose ontic range the respective states of affairs are contained or which partake in an occurrence (in the event we are dealing with a state of occurrence) also exist *eo ipso*. But also, conversely: if, in a given work, objects exist in their purely intentional manner, then *eo ipso* the corresponding states of affairs also exist. Indeed, in the case of an *ontically autonomous* object it is a question of all the states of affairs which in a given temporal moment[1] lie in its ontic range; in the case of a purely intentional object, on the other hand, it is a question only of those which are actually developed in the given literary work.[2] Speaking figuratively, both aspects of that which exists—whatever the mode of existence—belong to each other inseparably. In the case of an ontically autonomous object it is impossible to say which of the two is the "constituting" factor and which is the "constituted." A *reciprocal*, essentially necessary founding takes place here, though perhaps this is already claiming too much. If we limit ourselves solely to the

1. This limitation applies, of course, only to objects existing in time; it does not pertain to ontically autonomous ideal objects.

2. We shall leave aside for the moment the questions of whether this limitation to the respective "actual" moment of time applies also in this case and whether and in what sense one can speak of the respective actual moments of time in which represented objects exist.

content of the objects projected in the literary work and disregard both their purely intentional mode of existence and structure as well as their constitution by means of meaning contents, then the above also refers to these objects and the corresponding states of affairs, provided, of course, that it belongs to this content and that we are dealing with ontically autonomous objectivities. It is only the consideration of the intentional constitution of these objects that shows that here the situation is, after all, somewhat different.

Let us imagine that we are dealing with a sentence that mentions, *for the first time* in a given literary work, something about an object X. This X is projected by the meaning of the subject of the sentence. From the point of view of the constitution [of the object], it [X] forms the first constitutive basis for the corresponding state of affairs and the objective units constructed upon it, i.e., as *a thusly and only thusly determined* object, which results from the full meaning of the subject.[3] Usually it is determined as a thing only with respect to its nature and its object structure. At the same time—thanks to the special function of the subject of the sentence—it functions as the carrier of the property (or activity, etc.) assigned to it in accordance with the meaning content of the sentence. It is only on this basis—assimilating this property or activity in a special way—that the given state of affairs is constructed. Because the given state of affairs, however, is developed as an "existing" one by the sentence (though in the literary work the sentence is only a quasi-judgmental assertive proposition), the object which is constituted in it shows itself in the previously indicated potential-actual manner along with the property A assigned to it in the sentence (or as an object performing a given activity). In its actual-potential appearing, it becomes quite evident that, as the object furnished with property A, it attains, so to speak, its constitution on the basis of the given state of affairs. If the sentence is an assertive proposition (even if only a quasi-judgmental one), it is expected of object X that it will already be provided with attribute A "before" it is *apprehended* as such by the sentence. After the sentence is all there, as it were, and the next sentence begins, the object X (A) appears as one which only reveals, only represents, the given state of affairs, although it is the latter that constitutes and determines the object. If the

3. Cf. my earlier observations on the state of affairs, where I said that the object of the subject [of the sentence] appears in the given state of affairs.

next or some later[4] sentence refers to the same object X (A), then $X(A)$ in turn becomes the constitutive basis for the new state of affairs, to which, for example, the attribute B may be allotted, and which in its turn becomes the constitutive basis for the object X (A, B) and, on its own completion, represents it as an X (A, B), etc.[5]

Thus the intentionally projected states of affairs play an essential role in the constituting of represented objects, and, after all, in doing so they themselves require for their own constitution the *first* nominal projection of the same objectivities as they were "at the beginning." Thus it depends upon them—and, in the final analysis, upon the meaning contents of the sentences—which objects, how created, and subject to what vicissitudes attain constitution in the given work. Herein precisely is revealed the fact that in *terms of constitution* the stratum of sentences plays the *central* role in the literary work. At the same time, however, the states of affairs bring these objectivities to representation. In both of these functions [i.e., constitution and representation], the position of the states of affairs with regard to the objects can be figuratively determined in the following way.

The intentionally projected "stratum of objects" of the work can be considered under two different aspects, as it were: (1) If, in the course of a theoretical study of the structure of the work, one searches for the constitutive connections, then the states of affairs lie "beneath" the objects respectively constituted in them, and the stratum of meaning contents lies at the very bottom. (2) If, on the other hand, while apprehending the work, one reads the sentences with comprehension, the state-of-affairs aspect of the "stratum of objects" lies "on the outside." We must first, as it were, cross through the state-of-affairs aspect before we can reach the objects and their fates. In and through the manifold of interconnected sentence correlates (and, in particular, of states of affairs), objects, and their connections and fates, become "revealed." Since the same object can be revealed in various differently constructed states of affairs—since the states of affairs are like many windows through which we can look into one and the same house, each time from a different standpoint and from a different side, into another part, or, finally, for a second time through the same window—a certain

4. What this means will be discussed later (Chap. 11).
5. Naturally, we are taking the simplest example possible. Usually there are very diverse complications and modifications.

cleavage occurs in the "stratum of objects" of the literary work. In their representation function the states of affairs are that which represents, while the objects constituted within them are the represented. But since the state of affairs is at the same time something which belongs to the proper ontic range of the object (constituted within it), this representation is in the final analysis a *self*-representation of the object in what belongs to it.[6]

In the process, however, something else occurs which justifies the window analogy and at the same time is essentially necessary: in the performance of its representation function the state-of-affairs aspect of the stratum of objects is noticed by the reader only to the extent that it is necessary for reaching what is represented. It is like a medium through which we must cross in order to arrive at the represented objects and have them as a *given*. This medium, however, is usually not thematically apprehended in itself, especially when we are dealing with meaning contents.[7] Instead, the states of occurrence enter more into the thematically apprehendable foreground; but in the final analysis they too represent the "facts" that are realized in this occurrence or the transformations in the objects that are produced by this occurrence. And it is no accident that our gaze is usually directed straight at the represented objects, scarcely touching the corresponding states of affairs. For it is in the nature of that which represents as such, that in the performance of the representation function it disappears to a certain degree from our field of vision in order to facilitate, above all, the illumination of that which it represents.[8]

§ 29. *The representing and exhibiting function of the states of affairs*

WE HAVE OBSERVED in § 27 that not merely the represented objectivities but also the manner of the representation

6. "Representation" as the revealing function of states of affairs is only one of the many possible concepts of "representation." The other concepts of representation will be developed later (§ 37).

7. Of course, there is the possibility of attitudes on the part of the reader in which the states of affairs themselves are thematically apprehended; but then they cease to represent the objects that are constituted in them.

8. For this reason Husserl speaks of objectivities that "represent" something as—in a very broad sense—"transitional objects" [*Durchgangsobjekte*].

itself is exactly determined by the meaning contents of sentences and the meaning units of higher order based on sentences. What manner of representation is at issue here, and what is the role of sentences in this respect?

It is known that assertive propositions can be divided into various groups according to their states of affairs.[9] For our purposes let us direct our attention to the following three groups of states of affairs: (1) states of essence [Soseinsverhalte], (2) states of thus-appearance [Soaussehensverhalte], and (3) states of occurrence [Geschehensverhalte] (examples: "Gold is heavy," "In winter my room is dreary," "My dog is running away quickly"). As we shall see, states of affairs belonging to the individual groups are suited for a particular mode of representation, but, nevertheless, they can still perform various representing functions according to the particular elements appearing in them and according to the priority of individual elements in one and the same state of affairs.

A sentence which develops a state of essence can be used, if the occasion arises, in two different interpretations, depending on the elements appearing in it. For example, the sentence "This rose is red" may, to begin with, be understood as saying that the given rose is simply so constituted. However, one can also understand it so that it almost takes on the sense of the sentence "This rose appears red," whereby this "appearance as red" [Rotaussehen] is not understood in the sense of being contrasted to the rose's being red [Rotsein] and construed in the sense of "only thus appearing." On the contrary: precisely because the rose is red and because "red" belongs to its visual properties, it also appears (other conditions being favorable) as red. The same thing holds when I say: "The road to X is very bumpy," or "This piece of marble is very smooth," or "The cry of the mob was very loud." All of these sentences may be construed as dealing with a "thus-appearance." Here we take the expression "the thus-appearance" in a greatly *broadened* sense, where it can be applied not only to the visual but to all immediately phenomenally apprehendable properties of objects, processes, activities, etc. If, on the other hand, I say, "Wood is a bad conductor of heat," this sentence cannot be construed as dealing with the thus-appearance of wood. Here the property attributed to wood can indeed be discovered by experience, i.e.,

9. See Pfänder, "Logik," *Jahrbuch für Philosophie und phänomenologische Forschung,* IV (1921), 141.

it can be proved to exist in experiential connections, but it does not belong to the *phenomenal, immediately* perceivable properties. A noteworthy distinction can therefore already be found in sentences that develop states of essence, a distinction that is closely connected with distinctions in the mode of the representing function, which we shall soon discuss. Let us now take such sentences as, e.g., "In the weak candlelight the room looked dreary," "My wool jacket is soft to the touch," "This pear tastes sweet," "This load is so heavy to carry," "This rose smells sweet," etc. In each of them it is a question of a "thus-appearance" of the given object—"object" taken in the broader sense. Thus, for example, the sentence "The room appeared dreary" is not to be taken in the sense that the room appeared thus to someone, for whatever subjective reasons, but that in reality it had a totally different appearance. The usual sense is precisely that in the given objective conditions the given room *really* had such an appearance.[10]

Sentences which develop the "thus-appearance" of objects can also be used, however, in such a way that in them we are not, or at least are not primarily, dealing with the thus-appearance but with the essence of the given object revealing itself in this thus-appearance. Just as with a particular application of certain propositions of essence one can steal a glance at the "thus-appearance," so, conversely, here we steal a glance at the corresponding essence of the object.

The contrasting of the two types of sentences and their possible twofold application allows us to recognize that their states of affairs may "represent" the objects being constituted within them in two different ways and that, consequently, different concepts of representation should also be set apart. In one sense —the *more common* one, which we have already discussed— *all* the states of affairs mentioned here represent the objects belonging to them in that they "reveal" the latter in some aspect or other. At the same time, this "revelation" signifies nothing more or less than the fact that it *acquaints* us with the given object. Where previously—before the state of affairs was developed—there was something unknown to us, in a sense a closed, concealed ontic sphere where—as is precisely the case with a literary work—simply nothing was present, we now enter [this sphere] by means of the state of affairs developed by the

10. Of course, the given sentences can also be taken in the other sense.

sentence; now it is something "opened" and "revealed" to us, we attain *knowledge* about something previously unknown or in general nonexisting for us, in the course of which it is totally irrelevant whether we can apprehend this something *intuitively* or not. No one will be likely to dispute the fact that this general function of representation is performed by the intentional states of essence. However, if someone were to doubt this in the case of states of appearance, he might note that the "true" thus-appearance of an object is something which belongs to it just as its properties do, with the only difference that here, as opposed to the properties, a conscious subject is necessary to apprehend the thus-appearance and maintain it in actuality. Regardless of whether it is the essence of an object or its thus-appearance, we become acquainted with something about the given object. But even more than that. The states of thus-appearance indeed show us thematically and primarily the appearance of things. As soon as the appearance (conditions being favorable) is *real*, however, the corresponding essence of the object shows itself in it. It is only for this reason that the different interpretations, given above, of the corresponding propositions are possible. Thus, the "state of thus-appearance" also "reveals" to us—though indirectly—the essence of the given object.

Against this general representation function of the states of affairs we must set another special function, which is performed by either the states of thus-appearance or the states of essence or occurrence (with which we shall deal directly), which assign to the object named by the subject of the sentence a phenomenally perceptible property (or occurrence). It is here that stealing a glance at the "thus-appearance" of the object can take place. Here it is a question of something more and, at the same time, something other than merely becoming acquainted with something. Here there is a representation in which the object is *determined* in its *phenomenal* (directly perceptible) content, and therefore it is capable of *showing* itself without further ado in its phenomenal raiment. The state of affairs prepares, as it were, all the conditions on the part of the object aspect so that, after the subjective conditions have been fulfilled, the object can be phenomenally directly perceived. The particular manner of the representation function consists here in the *phenomenal stock* of the given object (or at least one of its aspects) being placed before, being "exhibited" before, *a possible subject.* Naturally, at the basis of the "exhibiting" there is always a "representation" in the general sense of the term. The exhibiting is only a special mode of the latter. Strictly speaking, all of this is of course valid only in the case of ontically autonomous states of affairs which are of the kind that can in themselves be directly apprehended by a conscious subject.[11]

The exhibiting can be performed to a greater or lesser extent by materially different states of affairs, depending on whether the latter are richer or poorer in directly perceptible elements of objects or whether they are so structured that there exists a greater or lesser clarity and transparency of their structure and of the objects represented in them. Likewise, in the directly perceptible elements of objects there are still differences with respect to the expressiveness, the "plasticity," of the individual features, as well as with respect to those elements which one has in mind when one says that something is "striking," "especially conspicuous," etc. The magnitude of the exhibiting function is dependent on all these factors. Therefore, states of occurrence frequently have the capacity to exhibit the objects partaking in the respectively developed occurrences to a much greater degree than do pure states of essence. This capacity is also connected to the verbal manner of development, which is better expressed in pure states of occurrence, and to the fact that many properties of the object are manifested only (or at least are manifested more forcefully) when the corresponding objects are apprehended in an occurrence. Moreover, states of occurrence—as something which is happening in a world of objects, as something which *takes place* there—to a certain extent *exhibit themselves*.[12] Simultaneously, they exhibit the facts being realized within them in which the respective occurrence culminates and which create a system of "realized" mutually interconnected states of essence (even though these are distributed among various objects). Thus, by means of states of occurrence—especially when they are projected by connected sentences—not only objects (things, persons) partaking in the given occurrence can be represented and exhibited but also other states of affairs which accrue to the given objects in this occurrence. The states of occurrence are then like connecting links between the states of essence existing within the ontic range of the individual objects, and they thus contribute in an

11. See below, p. 196.
12. "To a certain extent," since, strictly speaking, one can speak of "exhibiting" only when an *A* "exhibits" a *B* that is different from it.

essential way to the representing, and frequently also to the exhibiting, of entire segments of the world of objects.

For a more precise apprehension of the exhibiting performed by the purely intentional sentence correlates, the following must still be noted: above all, the exhibiting cannot lead by itself, i.e., without the support of other factors, to an *intuitive givenness* of the given object. For it is only an "exhibiting" and, therefore, not yet an intuitivization. For something to be brought to intuitive apprehension, two series of conditions must be met: (1) objective and (2) subjective. The first of the objective conditions is that the object coming to our attention must have among its attributes those that contain qualitative moments that are *self-presenting*. All so-called sensory qualities—but not only these—are self-presenting. On the other hand, the moment that comes into question when one speaks, for example, of silver as a "good conductor of heat" is not self-presenting. The subjective conditions in turn lie in the execution of quite determinately constructed acts of consciousness which bring with them [13] the actualization of the "aspects" in which every object that can be intuitively apprehended "appears." These latter conditions naturally cannot be fulfilled by the states of affairs projected by the sentences. But also with respect to the fulfillment of the above objective condition, the situation is different with ontically autonomously existing states of affairs and with the ones only intentionally projected by the meaning content of the sentence. Only the ontically autonomously existing states of affairs can be the "exhibiting" ones in the strict sense of the term, and only when elements containing self-presenting qualitative moments occur in them. In the case of purely intentional states of affairs, on the other hand, even if they do contain such elements, the containing of these self-presenting qualitative elements is only a quasi-containing, one which only *simulates* the containing appearing in ontically autonomous states of affairs or objects. And though we usually do not, in our attitude toward the content of the purely intentional sentence correlate, bring the pure intentionality of this correlate into our consciousness, though we almost succumb, as it were, to the deception that its content has ontically autonomous components, nothing is changed with regard to the essential fact of the pure intentionality of the entire correlate and of the circumstances that are

13. We shall deal with this later. See Chaps. 8 and 9.

essentially connected to it. Herein lies the basis for the fact that the exhibiting function cannot be performed by purely intentional states of affairs in the true sense in which it is performed by ontically autonomously existing states of affairs. Nevertheless, even in purely intentional states of affairs there is, as it were, a predisposition for their performance which would suffice for the intuitive givenness of the represented objects if only the subjective conditions of the intuitivization were fulfilled. And since there is no doubt that in reading a work we frequently apprehend represented objects in an intuitive manner—even if only imaginatively and not observationally—and in this imaginative intuitivization we are *channeled* by the text of the work (if, of course, we want to be true to the work), we must search for a factor in the literary work which, along with the displaying states of affairs, makes possible an intuitivization—if a reader is present —and thereby channels him. We shall find this new factor in the stratum of "aspects" that belongs to the entire structure of the literary work and, it being precisely a work of art, plays a significant role in it. The *phonetic* stratum is also instrumental in this.

§ 30. *Other modes of representation by means of states of affairs*

THE CONTRAST, clarified in the preceding paragraphs, between representation in a general sense and its particular mode—exhibiting—does not exhaust all the differences that occur in representation through states of affairs. On the contrary, there is a very rich variety of different types of representational modes. We shall discuss only a few as examples in order to illustrate more clearly the role of sentences, which are the ultimate source of the various representational modes. One should note, moreover, that the representational modes that we shall now discuss can occur in both the purely representing and the simultaneously exhibiting states of affairs.

1. The mode of representation by means of states of affairs depends primarily on *which* of the possible states of affairs that can belong, in accordance with the total stock of its properties, to a given object are determined and thus selected by the meaning content of the sentence. If we take, first of all, an ontically

autonomous temporal object,[14] we see that an infinite and indeed a doubly infinite manifold of states of affairs belongs to it. Doubly infinite because (1) to each temporal moment of its existence there belongs an infinite manifold of fused [15] states of affairs and (2) there is an infinite manifold of temporal moments in which the given object exists. All of these states of affairs constitute the original unity of the object and form its total ontic range. If, on the other hand, we can specify an object only by means of purely intentional sentence–projected states of affairs, we must—as we have already pointed out in § 24—divide this original unity into individual states of affairs (occasionally also into groups of states of affairs) and only then, by applying complexes of sentences, restore it to a certain degree. But since the manifold of states of affairs applicable to this end is infinite in principle, we are forced to choose only individual members from this manifold—and thus always only a finite number. We have, therefore, the possibility of a *varied* selection. At the same time, however, there is the possibility of representing the objects in various ways by means of states of affairs—though this assertion requires a word of caution. Namely, one and the same intentional object can be represented or exhibited in various combinations of properties, states, etc., depending on which manifold represents it. The object is shown here from another side—as it were, in another perspective—and, figuratively speaking, in other perspectival foreshortenings, since, in the various manifolds of properties of an object, one and the same property seems capable of taking on a different role and importance in its total essence. The discussion about "one and the same" object that is only represented in various ways must be taken with a certain proviso, however. For we must not forget that in this case the object is first constituted in the respective manifold of states of affairs, i.e., it obtains among other things those determinations—and strictly speaking only those—that were established in the states of affairs by the corresponding meaning contents of sentences. The difference in the composition of two state-of-affairs manifolds can also bring with it corresponding differences in the objects represented in them, if the states of affairs in question do not mutually require each other; thus, a discussion of "one and the same" object must be taken here *cum grano salis*. For the same reason, the literary theorists' customary discussion

14. We can limit ourselves here to temporal objects since in literary works we are concerned almost exclusively with objects of this kind.
15. In this respect it is not entirely appropriate to speak of a *manifold*.

of one and the same "material" that is only "differently formed" by different poets, as well as the discussion of the "material" itself, is, strictly speaking, incorrect, insofar as by "material" we understand, not a *real* object or a real event known from experience, but merely a fictional object projected by sentences. Despite this dissimilarity of objects, which may stem from a dissimilarity of the states of affairs, a discussion of one and the same object that is only differently represented is not entirely groundless. For although the intentional object possesses explicitly and, as it were, *actualiter* those, and only those, properties that are assigned to it by the meaning contents of the sentence, the potential components of the word meanings appearing in the sentences are not to be ignored. Their presence occasions the intending of the intentional object (according to its content) as one which, besides the explicitly and actually intended determinations, possesses still *some other* properties that belong to a certain type but are not further determined. For this reason the manifold of states of affairs developed in the manifold of sentences attains the character of a *selection* from the total stock of states of affairs—that are at times only blankly cointended and are, explicitly, imprecisely determined—which appear to constitute the ontic range of the given object even though, for the most part, they do not attain intentional projection at all. This stock of states of affairs only blankly cointended by the potential meaning content can, if necessary, be the connecting link, so to speak, between—as we may have expected at the outset— two objects that are represented by two state-of-affairs manifolds and can thus enforce their identity. Hence, with the above proviso, the discussion about different modes of representation of one and the same object is not groundless, even though in this case the modes of representation are simultaneously modes of formation.

Among these modes it is possible to distinguish various types, the exact determination of which would require special investigation. To substantiate our thesis that there are such various types, we will now point out some examples of them. For example, a work can be written so that its text predominantly projects the states of affairs of the thus-appearance of the object and in only a few cases the states of affairs which represent the object in its "internal," not directly intuitively apprehendable, properties. Here, too, there may be differences of the following kind: in one work, states of affairs are predominantly projected in which visual properties play the most important role, while, in others, tonal or tactile moments are more prominent; or, finally, there is a veritable profusion of heterogeneous elements which are developed in all their variety and richness. Analogous differences can also be found in the representation of characters: a character may be directly represented through the states of affairs of his physical constitution or thus-appearance and later, but only indirectly, in his spiritual life as well. But it is also possible to represent him in purely spiritual occurrences and properties, so that his physical appearance does not come directly to light at all and must be reconstructed indirectly. Moreover, sentences can project through their meaning content wholly unessential and accidental states of affairs of the given object, where what belongs to its essence is concealed behind them. The contrary can also be true. Another difference is found when, in one instance, states of affairs of relation are *predominantly* projected, on the basis of which the objects standing in these relations are supplementarily determined, while in another instance "internal" states of affairs are predominantly projected, which only then lead to relations between the objects, and so on.

2. From another point of view, the various modes of representation depend on whether the meaning contents of sentences project states of affairs which, in a manner of speaking, exhaust their role by showing the object to be determined as such and such *within themselves* or whether the states of affairs are intended in such a way that, although they indeed represent this object as being determined within them, their role is basically only incidental, and their fundamental representational function consists, on the contrary, of indirectly revealing *other* states of affairs which are not *directly* determined by the meaning contents of sentences. This kind of indirect determination of the state of affairs occurs quite frequently. But it leads to a particular type of representation only when the projection of determinate states of affairs is *calculated* from the very first at fulfilling this role of indirect development of other states of affairs, and if, at the same time, in the stratum of represented objects, only that which is indirectly determined is truly important in the work, i.e., is what the given work is truly all about. If such a mode of representation is utilized in a work as the main representational mode, it brings about a particular type of literary work. See, for example, on the one hand, purely "naturalistic" works, which in principle will not say anything more, or anything other, than what is directly determined in the meaning content of the sentence and which avail themselves

of entirely simple, purely "factual" expressions, and, on the other hand, those works which make full use of metaphors and the whole range of figurative and metaphorical ornamentation, and, finally, *symbolic* works *par excellence,* in which what is directly projected by the meaning content of the sentence plays only the incidental role of a bridge to what is to be symbolized, as in, e.g., Maeterlinck's "dramas." [16]

3. Another series of representational modes arises with regard to the *meaning material* utilized for the construction of sentences. To be sure, it is *primarily* a question of the modes in which the states of affairs themselves are determined by the meaning content of the sentence; but the modes of representation of objects by states of affairs are also closely connected to this. To a certain degree it is possible to project "the same" state of affairs by means of two different sentences—"the same," but still modified in various respects. At the same time, the sentences can be different in a twofold sense: (1) with reference to the pure meaning material, (2) with reference to the word sound of the words used. We can, for example, conceive "the same" thought at one time primarily in so-called abstract words and at another time "clothe" it in words which contain purely "concrete" meaning intentions. The state of affairs is "the same" in the two and yet different, as is shown at once by the fact that the former is capable of performing only the function of representing, while the latter also performs the function of exhibiting. As far as that goes, the difference in meaning material is reflected in the mode of representation by states of affairs. The differences in the phonetic aspect of sentences can work in the same direction with the same or nearly the same meaning content. Here it is not primarily a question of "the same" sentence—and indeed, with precisely the same meaning content—being expressed, for example, in two different languages. For a difference in the mode of representation need not necessarily be tied to this. In fact, however, it is a relatively rare case if a change in the phonetic aspect of sentences does not carry with it any consequences for the constitution of the object stratum of the literary work. Usually the opposite is true. This occurs above all when,

---

16. The symbolizing function should not be confused with the function of expression, which some states of affairs, i.e., those which constitute the thus-appearance of animated bodies, perform by virtue of the fact that this appearance is the "expression" of spiritual life. Likewise, the symbolizing function should not be confused with the function of reproduction of represented objects, which we shall discuss later.

e.g., a word which according to its word sound is "dead" is replaced in a sentence by one with the same meaning but with phonetic vitality. The replacement of individual words by others has much greater meaning if, in the presence of the same actual stock of meanings, the new word sound carries with it a different potential stock of meanings and thereby also brings forth a different emotional coloration. This emotional, mood-setting coloration is usually of the greatest importance [17] for the literary work, so that frequently the very genre of the work—e.g., whether it is a "lyric," a "dramatic," or an "epic" work—depends upon it and upon the manner of its appearance. It can be bestowed upon the states of affairs and the objects represented in them by the *potential* stock of meanings of words (which is actualizable only to a certain degree), as well as by the various previously discussed properties of phonetic formations, and in particular also by the manifestation qualities of word sounds. The replacement of a single word by another within a whole sentence complex can completely destroy this emotional coloration or [at least] bring about its transformation.[18] This will appear even more clearly when we discuss the role that the meaning content of a sentence, as well as its phonetic aspect, plays in predetermining the "aspects" that belong to the represented objects. When the work is being read, the peculiar, indefinable emotional coloration covers the actualized points of view and also envelops in its glimmer the represented objects that have been made to appear. If this glimmer were to disappear, then, at least in many cases, the objects appearing in the aspects could remain "the same"; but the total character of the work of art would undergo drastic change, and its value could be totally destroyed.

The importance of the word material for the mode of repre-

17. We will return to this in the section on the "idea" of the work. As far as the emotional coloration—or, as O. Walzel says, the "content" —is concerned, one can find appropriate commentary in his "Das Wesen des dichterischen Kunstwerks," *Das Wortkunstwerk* (Leipzig, 1926), pp. 100 ff. One may doubt, however, whether Walzel is correct in claiming that this emotional "content" cannot be determined or evoked by the sentence meaning. Here there is an absence of a deeper insight into the essential structure of the literary work of art as well as into the essence of meaning units. W. Conrad also stresses the significance of the "element of mood" in a literary work ("Der ästhetische Gegenstand," *Zeitschrift für Ästhetik und allgemeine Kunstwissenschaft*, III, no. 3 (1908), 492.

18. This is particularly critical when literary historians tell us what a poet really wanted to say in a lyrical poem and reconstruct the content of the poem "in their own words." This is also the reason why literary works whose principal value lies in their indefinable emotional coloration are nearly untranslatable.

sentation, and the importance of the appearance of objects in manifolds of actualized aspects closely connected with it, can be seen even more clearly if we observe that there are complex and frequently essentially determined connections and dependences among the emotional colorations themselves and also among them, the aspects, and the represented objects, and that the word material of the individual sentences must be arranged correspondingly among them if that kind of determinate connection is to come about.

4. The kind of connection between projected states of affairs that has its foundation in the sentence structure and the type of sentence complex leads to characteristic differences in the mode of representation. Interesting examples of this may be found in Fritz Strich, who, however, is not entirely conscious of what is actually at issue here. Strich contrasts the sentence structure of Kleist with that of Novalis in order to reveal—as he believes— a difference in the apprehension of time in these two poets and, in turn, in Goethe, with whom he contrasts them.[19] He says:

> The form of Goethe's sentence takes its content out of time. From the serene standpoint of an observing spirit, everything is equally distant and past, and in the sequence of the story only the continuity of the line and the equal measure of distance are telling. Kleist, however, abandons this position and plunges himself into the abyss of time. He moves and manipulates things in such a way that their pure and continuous sequence becomes transformed, as it were, into the three-dimensionality of time. A moment from the past becomes present and a standpoint for him. In it, however, another part is even more past, another more contemporary, and another future. *His sentence forms these temporal dimensions.* One could try, and it could be possible to develop the same content in a pure sequence. But then it would lose all charm for Kleist, since it would have lost all movement. As Hölderlin once said of himself, Kleist had to put himself "in the middle of time" and, while observing it, could not let it pass by at a distance. It is this in particular that one perceives as something plastic in his art.
>
> For the language of Novalis also shapes [reality] in the form of time and history. Only it does this more in the spirit of the Gothic than the Baroque. For when it is totally without this Kleistian

19. See F. Strich, *Deutsche Klassik und Romantik*, 3d ed. (Munich, 1928), p. 199. Walzel also brings this to our attention in the article cited above (n. 17).

involution and depth, the language proceeds entirely in small and quite simply constructed sentences.[20]

For us it is a minor matter that what is at issue here are two different modes of representation precisely of *time* (and, in fact, according to Strich it is a question of two different *conceptions* of time). Likewise, Strich's arguments with regard to Goethe's conception of time do not interest us here. The only thing that is important for us is that Strich had a sharp eye for seeing how the formation of the stratum of objects of a literary work was essentially dependent on the structure of the sentence. He overlooks, to be sure, the sphere of the states of affairs and thus the representation problem that is important to us here; but there is no doubt that he has clearly in mind the role of sentences in the structure of the literary work of art. Other discussions of his, which we cannot go into here, clearly prove this. But since he does overlook the sphere of the states of affairs, he misses the very important difference between Kleist and Novalis, even though his other arguments are interesting and to the point.[21] For the difference in sentence structure and in the complex of sentences leads primarily to differently constructed individual states of affairs and to a different kind of connection between them. The difference in the *temporal perspective*—as I would prefer to call it—stems first of all from the yet to be discovered differences between the states of affairs. While the Kleistian sentence develops a *total* state of affairs, an entire *complex situation,* in which the various partial states of affairs are in a certain

20. Strich, *Deutsche Klassik und Romantik,* pp. 199, 200. By way of explanation, let us add the following examples, chosen by Strich: "The Forest Warden asked him whether he thought the man the Marquise was looking for would appear. 'Without a doubt!' the Count retorted, as he bent over the paper and greedily devoured what it said. *Then, after* going to the window for a moment *while* folding up the paper, he said, 'Now everything is all right! *Now* I know what I have to do!' He turned around and courteously asked the Forest Warden if he would see him again soon, said goodbye, and went away fully reconciled to his fate" (Kleist) [English translation by Martin Greenberg, *The Marquise of O—— and Other Stories* (New York: Criterion Books, 1960), p. 69]. "Henry was aglow and got to sleep only towards morning. The thoughts of his soul flowed together in strange dreams. A deep blue stream shimmered up out of the green plain. A skiff floated on the smooth water. Mathilda sat in it and rowed" (Novalis) [*Henry von Ofterdingen,* translated by Palmer Hilty (New York: Frederick Ungar, 1964)]. Cf. Strich (1928 ed.), pp. 202–4. The emphasis in Strich's text is mine; that in Kleist's text is Strich's.

21. For this reason I am not comparing the texts of Kleist and Goethe (as Strich does, who is interested in the contrast between classicism and romanticism) but rather those of Kleist and Novalis.

sense taken *at once*, in one grasp, in their mutual involution and conditioning and for this reason lose nothing of their mutual coalescence into *one* situation, in Novalis we see in each individual sentence only the very simplest state of affairs, one that has been *torn out* of the total situation. If we limit ourselves to a single sentence, the corresponding state of affairs is one that is enclosed within itself, one that does not coalesce directly with the other states of affairs. Only the sequence of a *number* of sentences constitutes a connection between the individual states of affairs, and indeed a connection of an entirely particular type. First of all, an all-encompassing frame is projected whose blank spots are filled out in sequence and concentrically by wholly simple states of affairs. "A deep, blue stream glistened on the green plain," constitutes such a frame. Now a new, and at first self-enclosed, state of affairs is introduced, and it attains connection with the first only because of this insertion: "A boat was riding on the smooth surface." And again, at first one does not know whether anything else is to be seen in this boat—it is a blank spot which is to be filled out again by the state of affairs projected by the following sentence: "Mathilda was sitting and rowing." If "rowing" were not added, one would not know whether Mathilda was sitting in the boat or somewhere else. For all this, one does not know how Mathilda looked or what she may have been doing. Only the following sentence completes this: "She was adorned with garlands, she was singing a simple song and looking at him with gentle melancholy." Since she was looking *at* him, it is to be assumed that he was at a certain distance from her. But, for the time being, we know nothing about this. Instead, we again receive a new totally self-enclosed state of affairs: "His heart was heavy," etc. Thus we see that every sentence projects an uncomplicated state of affairs that forms a whole in itself, a single feature of the total state of affairs that in the final analysis is constituted from these features as if it were composed of isolated pebbles. These isolated states of affairs are set down, so to speak, *side by side in a patchlike manner*—as soon as they are all there, of course. Thus, in the beginning one must jump from one state of affairs to another, especially since at first we obtain visual, then acoustic, and finally purely psychic states of affairs. But we do have the time for it, as it were; for since the individual sentences or states of affairs are entirely simple and transparent, the whole situation can develop quite calmly, without the strained gaze that attempts to grasp everything at once. How different it is in the case of the sentence we have quoted from Kleist, which leaves us no time but creates instead a total state of affairs which, in its involution and complexity, with its view on what has already happened and on what is yet to happen, and in its simultaneity, its quick succession, constitutes the unity of *a single* situation and attempts to develop it all at once. If only we are equal to the exertion required of us, it compels us to a vital perception of the entire situation in its straightforward primality.

In short: the difference in the structure of the states of affairs and in the nature of their connection carries with it a difference in the mode of representation of the corresponding objects and their vicissitudes. What is represented is, of course, also not unaffected by these differences. And thus it is only natural that the differences in time perspective, and perhaps also in the perception of time, worked out by Strich also stem from this. But the source of these latter differences [i.e., of time perspective and perception] lies in the various modes of representation by means of states of affairs, which for their part—and this is also noticed by Strich—have their ultimate source in sentences.

There is, of course, a very great number of differences of this kind. Their thorough examination would show us many works in a totally new light. Here we must satisfy ourselves with examples and with merely indicating their existence.

5. Very specific differences in the mode of representation, which are independent of those discussed above, arise with respect to whether and in what manner the "narrating" subject belongs to the work by virtue of the particular formation of the meaning content of the sentence. Indeed, T. Lipps asserts that in each sentence we read, a speaking—in his words, an "ideal" —I is given. This view, however, strikes me as being not quite correct.[22] To be sure, we are usually attuned, while reading, to letting the author tell us the whole story, but this attitude is in many cases not at all required by the meaning content of the sentences and therefore is also not in keeping with it. Usually the meaning content of the sentences says nothing about the "narrator" or whether the sentences are spoken by anyone as component parts of a narration. The manifestation function can, indeed, be performed by any sentence; but it is precisely characteristic of works written "impersonally" that this function is not

22. See T. Lipps, *Grundlegung der Ästhetik* (Leipzig, 1903), p. 497: "The ideal I which I empathically introduce into what is represented is already given to me by the nature of the language."

performed. And even if the sentences are purely intentional formations, and as such refer back [23] to some subjective operation and its I, this fact is still not to be confused with the totally different situation where the speaking or "narrating" I is really *cogiven*. In other words, if the meaning contents of the sentences or the circumstances under which they appear do not indicate the author as the narrator, the entire work is, so to speak, beyond the reach of the author; he himself does not belong to the work as a *represented* character. It is different when the author represents himself as narrator in the corresponding states of affairs. Then the narrator (it is of no essential significance whether it is the author himself or a character created by him) is cogiven to us as the narrating person.[24] He himself then belongs among the objects represented in the work, i.e., to the object stratum of the work. In connection with this, the entire work gains a new two-layered structure. There the corresponding states of affairs are remarkably boxed within one another. We have, as it were, a complex of states of affairs extending through the entire work from beginning to end, in which the individual phases of the narration are represented, and frequently exhibited as well, and where it is important that the narration has precisely *this* content. Through these states of affairs, which themselves are already intentionally projected, new states of affairs—new precisely because they are states of narration—are projected, in which what is the "theme" of the narration comes to be represented. In this, a further complication in the structure of the literary work of art may come about (as is the case in the Platonic dialogues) if the "narration" itself becomes a dramatic "representation," as one usually says—a "scene," a situation in which different characters appear, engage in conversation, and thereby, themselves, project new many-layered formations: the speech itself and the twofold stratum (involving the state of affairs and the "objective" in the narrower sense) of what is meant as such. When simple, impersonal sentences appear in a work, such complications are not to be found. To be sure, in these cases, too, characters may be represented who speak various sentences and thus in themselves project a new object stratum. But even then, the structure of the whole work is simpler, at least in the sense that here there is no complex of states of

23. If, in the given sentence, Lipps had merely this fact in mind, we must agree with him.

24. See Plato's favorite mode of writing, for example. Among modern writers, Joseph Conrad frequently used it, particularly in his novels.

affairs that extends, as it were, the length of the work and represents the narrator and his narration.[25]

6. On this basis we can clarify an important feature of the difference between the "dramatic" and the "nondramatic" form of literary works. If we take a "drama," we must note, first of all, that the drama that is *read* cannot be identified in every respect with the one that is *staged*, i.e., with the "stage play," as we shall come to call it (see Chap. 12). Without examining this difference for the moment, let us limit ourselves in the following argument to written or read drama and contrast it to a novel or to any lyric poem.

What is most conspicuous in a "written" drama is the existence, side by side, of two different texts: the "side text" or stage directions—i.e., information with regard to where, at what time, etc., the given represented story takes place, who exactly is speaking, and perhaps also what he is doing at a given moment, etc.—and the main text itself. The latter consists exclusively of sentences that are "really" *spoken* by the represented characters. Because we know which character is speaking, the sentences belonging to the main text acquire, so to speak, "quotation marks." These sentences themselves, as well as the characters that are indicated as speaking and, finally, the states of affairs of what is spoken itself, become what is *represented* by the elements of the stage directions: they belong to the "object stratum" of the "side text." But the sentences belonging to this stratum are, after all, sentences, and they therefore project by themselves a new object stratum, i.e., that of the objects and vicissitudes that are being spoken of in these sentences. Thus, there appears here a "boxing" of the intentional states of affairs similar to the one we have already discussed. It must be noted, moreover, that in the projection of the states of affairs the two texts work *together*, to the extent that the represented, expressed sentences project, by means of their manifestation function, the state of affairs of the speech, as well as the manifold states of

25. I am aware that the difference between a purely "objective" mode of representation and one that introduces a narrator has long been noted. The new element which I mean to introduce consists in merely pointing out that in both of these cases, different though they are, there is, so to speak, a double projection of states of affairs. It is possible to point this out only after one has sharply differentiated the sphere of purely intentional states of affairs from the represented objects, on the one hand, and from sentences on the other. N.B.: I recently learned, in an issue of *Deutsche Vierteljahrschrift für Literaturwissenschaft und Geistesgeschichte* (1959), that W. Kayser was the first to discover the narrator in the novel.

affairs of psychic occurrences which the speaking characters "express," thus supplementing the function of the stage directions. On the other hand, the "side text," by indicating what the "acting" characters are doing, frequently completes the state of affairs projected by the main text. At the same time, it is usual that many—if not necessarily all—objects that are represented by the state of affairs belonging to the main text are *identical* with those that are projected by the side text. None of these occurrences is excluded in the novel, although there is never so sharp a division between the main and the side texts as in the "drama." Nevertheless, there is an obvious difference between these two types of literary works. There may be novels in which there is never a reproduction of the words of a represented character and thus no "boxing" (or, to use another image, no double projection) of the state of affairs. A drama that is read, however, would be totally impossible if this double projection were missing. Yet at the same time—and this is characteristic for the dramatic mode of representation—the *spoken* sentences, which are characteristically given in direct speech and never in indirect discourse, constitute the *main text* of the work. This is primarily the basis for the fact that these sentences must be formed in such a way that—at least in principle—the entire story to be represented arises from their meaning content. The states of affairs projected by them constitute the main means of representation for the objects and vicissitudes that are *actually* in question in the given work. In other words, we should learn virtually everything that is essential for the given drama from the words that the characters speak. And, in a way, it is only a way of making things easier for the poet and the reader if one makes frequent use of the side text to obtain short-cut information about certain matters that in the main text are mentioned only in passing or not at all. This information, however, can almost be omitted if there is a suitable arrangement of the main text. The one thing that must not be missing is the information that the sentences belonging to the main text are indeed "truly" *spoken* sentences. In other words, from the start, the "boxing," the double projection of states of affairs, cannot be absent. In this respect, the side text of a written drama can never be entirely removed. It is essential to this type of literary work. But it always remains only a *side* text, which in itself cannot constitute even the skeleton of a work. If we picture a work without a main text, we are left with an incomprehensible heap of rubble. If the side text is present along with the main text, however, it leads not only to the "double projection" of states of affairs but also to the *direct* determination of some states of affairs which properly belong to the "reality" projected by the spoken sentences.

§ 31. *The role of meaning units as a special material in the structure of the literary work*

WE ARE NOT going to occupy ourselves further with this extremely interesting and, to our knowledge, hitherto uninvestigated question of the various modes of representation by states of affairs. The sample analysis conducted above, which undoubtedly can be extended in various directions and supplemented in essential ways, will suffice to place in a proper light the decisive role of the stratum of meaning units, which is extremely important for the constitution of the other strata of the literary work. But this does not exhaust the role of this stratum in the structure of the work. For the sentence meanings and the entire complexes of meanings constitute—as we have already indicated—a separate material stratum in the literary work. This stratum possesses its own particular properties, and these do not depend on the effect the stratum has on the constitution of other strata; they "have their own voice" in the polyphony of the work and influence its design.

To be sure, there comes to mind the view that the stratum of meaning units is totally consumed, as it were, in its effect on the constitution of the other strata and is lost in the whole of the work as something unnoticeable in itself. In living speech as well as in the perception of a literary work we make use of meaning contents of sentences for the purpose of devoting our thematic attention to the state of affairs or the object to which the sentence refers. And one might think that the meaning content of the sentence as such is usually of no further interest for us; we pass it by, as it were, without its entering our consciousness. While this fact cannot be doubted, it does not contradict our conception. For, in the first place, while reading, we frequently turn to the meaning content of sentences; and second, even when we concentrate mainly on its intentional correlate, it never disappears fully from our field of consciousness but always appears in it, even if only peripherally and unthematically. It is a general characteristic of that which appears unthematically that it modifies in various respects that which appears thematically.

Finally, what we are concerned about here is not what aspect of the literary work comes to our attention during the reading; rather, it is a question that is to be understood purely ontically, i.e., the question of what the stratum of meaning units contributes to the whole of the work. And from this standpoint it must be observed that this stratum brings out unique moments that are characteristic of the entire work and that appear in its polyphony.

The presence of the stratum of meaning units [26] in the literary work of art attains expression primarily in the fact that this work—and this is also true of a purely lyrical poem—can never be a *totally* irrational formation, as is quite possible in other types of artistic works, especially in music.[27] This moment of *reason*, even if it resonates only vaguely, is always contained in even those literary works of art that are oriented entirely on mood and feeling. Thus there is always, in the aesthetic perception of the work, a phase in which we pass through, as it were, the atmosphere of the rational, since we must first "comprehend" the work, and indeed "comprehend" it in the sense in which *only* the meaning units are comprehensible. Precisely the most significant difference in the attitude we take toward the literary work of art as compared to our attitude to works of art of other types (music, painting) is that the transition through the sphere of the rational is quite *indispensable* for arriving at the other strata of the work and for submerging ourselves, if need be, in an irrational atmosphere. Naturally, the degree of rational contribution and the type of rationality can vary greatly in different works. There are works and entire styles where this contribution is so great that in the whole of the work it not only appears distinctly in itself, but the remaining strata, especially the object stratum, appear *sub specie* of this rationality. This "appearance *sub specie* of rationality" is to a certain degree present in every literary work, as we have already seen from our discussion of the structure of the purely intentional sentence correlates and their differences with regard to the initially [*originär*] apprehended states of affairs. But there may be different degrees of expressiveness. In this respect, the comparison between impressionistic (but also romantic) and "classical" works is quite

26. In contrast to the widespread use, especially in humanistic psychology, of the term "meaning" [*Sinn*] in the most varied and usually uncoordinated senses, I use the term only with reference to meanings, sentences, and complexes of sentences.

27. In a figurative sense there is, of course, also a "rational" music.

instructive. Likewise, the contrast between a purely lyrical poem (e.g., one by Verlaine) and an objectively treated story in a "naturalistic" novel can convince us of this. On the other hand, there is obviously the type of reader who, so to speak, takes from the whole of the work primarily this contribution of the rational and discovers in it the particular values of the work of art.[28] In contrast to this, other types of readers are to a certain degree blind to this aspect of the literary work of art and, if they do coapprehend it, push the rational aside as something intrusive, valueless, or even negatively valuable. This only shows, however, that not every reading does justice to the work.

The participation of the meaning stratum in the polyphony of the literary work of art is also shown by the fact that *unique* aesthetic values have their origin in this stratum. There is also the beauty of a pure meaning content, and indeed a particular type of beauty (or ugliness). Before we proceed with that, however, we should point out several properties of the meaning contents of sentences that are of particular importance in the investigation of a literary work.

1. The first thing that comes to our attention is the difference between "clarity" and "obscurity." Both the sentence structure itself and the type of connection between sentences and the order of their sequence contribute to the fact that the whole is at one time "clear" and at another time "unclear." It is obviously very difficult to describe the phenomenon of rational clarity, since here we come upon something primal. But we all know the difference between a clear and an unclear text, and in reading we frequently sense it in a very acute way. It is only a question of distinguishing this phenomenon of clarity (or obscurity) from other phenomena and thus making it more vivid.

First of all, we must note that "clarity" (or obscurity) is a character of the *sentence* itself, in whose structure it has its ontic foundation. Therefore, it is not something that is introduced by the reader into the work. Naturally, the *judgment* as to whether a work is clear or unclear frequently depends on the subjective capabilities and the attitude of the reader. But if the structure of the sentences, the type of meaning material that appears in them, and, finally, the type of sentence complexes produce a situation in which even the most capable reader still finds the whole to be, e.g., "unclear," then he rightly finds it so, since

28. It seems to me that this applies especially to the works of French classical literature and to the attitude of the French reader.

the given work *is* indeed unclear. We can thus leave aside the subjective conditions that must be fulfilled for the work to be correctly judged according to the degree of its clarity.

Furthermore, it must be noted that, when we are dealing with the clarity of a sentence, it is not a question of the property (characteristic of some sentences) by which the reader is *immediately* and *effortlessly* directed at what is intended by the sentence and by virtue of which he can imagine it *vividly* and *intuitively*. It is rather a question of something that is evoked primarily by the *structural* features of the meaning content of the sentence and the sentence complex. By "structural features" we mean those that depend on (1) a *sharp separation* of the individual component parts or, better, members of the meaning unit (in their precise contours, if one may use the term here) and (2) such a particular ordering of these members into a whole that they lose nothing of their quality of being members and yet allow us to see at once through the whole in its articulation and to apprehend it in its unique structure. It is only a question of a different word if we say "transparent" instead of "clear." But it is precisely this "transparency" that best enables us to reveal the phenomenon of "clarity." If a work is "clear," it is like a crystal in whose structure we can orient ourselves without further ado. The fact that we can orient ourselves through and through in the whole, that we can attain such "penetrating perceptions" at all, and that nothing impedes us in this—the fact that one perception does not cover another and thus prevent us from attaining in one glance a "survey" of the *whole* in all its parts, structures, and elements—all this seems to be involved in the peculiar phenomenon of clarity. It is founded, as we have said, on the structural features of sentences and sentence complexes. But obviously these features must still be supported by the *unambiguity* of the individual words appearing in the sentences. Of itself, however, the unambiguity of even all of the words appearing in a sentence or a sentence complex is incapable of producing clarity in a text.

The opposite of a "clear" text occurs when either the order of the parts or the general construction of the entire "thought" is such that no distinguishable parts are present, where everything is hazy, where one cannot measure the weight of the individual components in the structure of the whole, in short, where the sentence or the sentence complex is "opaque." Here we have something that is unclear from the standpoint of reason. But if we do have this kind of obscurity before us, it is not always based on the vagueness of the individual members of the whole. The "opaque" (as we often say) order of sentences which in themselves are clear and are precisely delineated from one another can produce obscurity in the whole. Finally, ambiguity, and particularly the hazy plurisignation of individual words, produces obscurity. There are different types and gradations of clarity (or obscurity), depending on what factors evoke the phenomenon of clarity or obscurity.

2. Besides those already discussed, meaning units indicate still many other differences, which we cannot review in detail, since our present purpose is simply to show that the stratum of meaning units does have characteristics peculiar to it which do not allow it to be lost in the whole of the literary work. Thus, we have differences of unambiguity and ambiguity, simplicity and plainness, or complexity and involution of sentence structure and sentence complex, and, after that, the difference of "lightness" and "heaviness" of both the individual sentences and the whole text, and so on. Frequently, these various properties of the text are quite closely connected. Thus, e.g., obscurity and complexity of a text usually go together. Ambiguity—as we have already observed—leads to obscurity. Different combinations of these properties also give the stratum of meaning units as a whole a total character that in itself can frequently be only observed but not conceptually determined. In many instances, moreover, this total character cannot be reduced to a manifold of various properties and elements on which it is founded but in relation to which it is something entirely new. It is precisely this total character that constitutes the style of the text of a literary work of art or even the style of a poet. It is indeed possible to distinguish—by means of an analysis of sentence structure, the order of sentences, the meaning material which the poet utilizes —the individual properties of the stratum of meaning units in which the style of the work is founded. But what is unique, what is inimitable, what makes up the particular "charm" of the style, can be perceived only in immediate contact with the work itself. And it is precisely this style that introduces a particular value into the polyphony of the whole work. There may, of course, be a nearly unsurveyable manifold of "beauties" and "uglinesses" of style. But all the types of beauty or ugliness that come into question here remain within a rigid framework bounded by a general type of beauty of rational meaning-formation. This type of beauty is distinguished primarily by a particular coolness and

lightness. Thus it follows that in aesthetic enjoyment of this type we cannot be deeply moved. We experience only a joy, but a joy that does not enrapture us. Deep in our spirit we remain fully calm, since we take joy in this beauty in a somewhat playful and cheerful attitude. This characteristic coolness of the beauty that we find only in the sentence stratum of the literary work is not present to the same degree when we encounter ugliness or unloveliness in the same stratum. In the ugliness, not only of individual sentences but of entire sentence complexes, an irritating element is always contained, which may at times work so powerfully that the given work evokes in us a sharply emotional aversion to that work.[29] It is just this cheerful, cool, joyful peace, this satisfaction which we experience in the enjoyment of the beauty of a beautifully constructed sentence, a satisfaction evinced so frequently by classical philologists, which is lost in the reading of a work that is negatively valuable in this respect. However, if, in this latter case as well, the value qualities of the text are not as characteristic as in the positively valuable works, it is indubitable that they too are founded in the stratum of meaning units and that we find them to be something that has its locus in them. Thus, we see that in every instance the stratum of meaning units commands its "own voice" in the polyphony of the literary work of art and takes a significant part in its construction. This manifests itself perhaps most fully in precisely those instances where the stratum of meaning units is so "characterless," so "average," so "faceless" that its positive contribution of any particular value qualities is *palpably* lacking. There appears then a certain deficiency, an absence of something which, according to the nature of the thing, as it were, should "properly" belong to the work. Finally, the particular participation of the value qualities characteristic of this stratum will also be clearly distinguished when the features of the style are not at all suited to the represented objects and their vicissitudes and where they lead to unpleasant—if sometimes intentional—disharmonies. This disharmony can go so far as to hinder the development of the exhibiting of objects which has been prepared, so to speak,

29. For that matter, it should be noted that the ugliness of individual segments of the sentence stratum need not necessarily be something negatively valuable in the whole of the work. As intended dissonance, it can ultimately play a positively valuable role in the whole. Even as a particular means for characterizing given characters and situations represented in the work, it can at times be irreplaceable.

by the meaning content of the sentences, and it can hamper or make totally impossible the vitalization of the aspects belonging to the represented objects.

The detailed study of all this, setting forth the particular value qualities and contrasting them with others, can naturally be done only by a special investigation based on positive literary study. But this inquiry would have to find its theoretical basis in the study of the ontology of the literary work, whose basic outline we are attempting to give here, and which can proceed only on the basis of correctly constructed guiding principles.

7 / The Stratum of Represented Objects

§ 32. *Recapitulation and introduction*

WE NOW COME to the analysis of the objects represented in a literary work. They appear to be the best known of all the strata, and in fact they are usually the only factor in the literary work of art to be apprehended thematically. To the extent that the reader follows the meaning intentions of the text, they are always the first thing that comes to his attention in a simple reading of the work. Usually he stops with them and their vicissitudes.[1] Likewise, the great majority of literary studies devote their attention primarily to this stratum of the work. Nevertheless, the *scientific* apprehension of these issues—as it concerns the essence of the elements of this stratum of the literary work, their structural features as well as their role in the whole of the work—is also unsatisfactory. This is due on the one hand to a psychologizing conception of literary works, on the other to the fact that the average reader, thanks to the natural functions of the meaning intentions understood and effected by him in the course of his reading, is interested only in the material makeup of the *contents* of the objects that come into question. As a result, the structures and features of real objects are transferred without further ado, and as a matter of course, onto represented objects, with the peculiarities of the latter being overlooked. In order to bring these into full light, a different, investigatory, and not

1. See W. Conrad's observations on "distribution of interest" ("Der ästhetische Gegenstand," *Zeitschrift für Ästhetik und allgemeine Kunstwissenschaft,* Vols. III–IV [1908–9]).

aesthetically perceptual attitude is required. The whole purpose of this attitude, however, is only to bring into prominence and to clarify something that is already unthematically present in ordinary intercourse with a literary work and influences its aesthetic apprehension.

Objects represented in a literary work are derived purely intentional objects projected by units of meaning. Hence, everything that we have asserted about objects of this kind—in particular in §§ 20, 21, and 24—is valid for these. Some of the discussion must be recapitulated, however, so that our subsequent arguments can be connected to it.

In every represented object, therefore, the content must be distinguished from the purely intentional object-structure. In an aesthetically perceptual reading of a work we turn toward its content and usually direct ourselves primarily to the carrier appearing in the content. For that reason, we should examine this content somewhat more closely.

As we have seen, purely intentional correlates of connected sentences can enter into manifold relationships and interrelations. And since among the sentence correlates there are also states of affairs which occur in the ontic range of one and the same object, as well as states in which events and interconnections between individual objects are represented, the represented objects also do not lie isolated and alien alongside one another but, thanks to the manifold ontic connections, unite into a uniform ontic sphere. In doing so they always constitute—quite remarkably—a segment of a still largely undetermined world, which is, however, established in accord with its ontic type and the type of its essence, that is, a segment whose boundaries are never sharply drawn. It is always as if a beam of light were illuminating a part of a region, the remainder of which disappears in an indeterminate cloud but is still there in its indeterminacy. For instance, if in a small poem a single object is represented in a single state or in *one* situation, it is still always represented as something existing in an extensive objective whole: a more or less determined background, which, along with the represented objects, constitutes *an* ontic sphere, is always present. This situation, of course, is produced by corresponding moments of meaning contents and subsequently by corresponding moments of states of affairs. We can take as an example the situation in act 1, scene 1, of Lessing's *Emilia Galotti*. There we find a prince in his study, attending to various petitions. These petitions already present to us objectivities that are to be found outside the visible room. But the room itself is apprehended from the first as a part of the princely palace. What is represented does not stop at the walls of the study but extends further, into the other rooms of the palace, into the town, etc., even though none of this is directly given to us. It is, in fact, a background. Moreover, this background need not be explicitly projected by the actual stock of word meanings. On the contrary. It is much more common for it to be brought about by the potential stock of the word meanings that appear in the sentences.[2]

The objective sphere that is represented here is usually uniform. It is not precluded, however, that, within its bounds, objects of fundamentally different ontic types may also be found. This is the case if, e.g., in a given novel, a mathematician is represented as dealing with certain mathematical objects, which are also explicitly represented. Naturally, then, the world in which the mathematician lives and performs his actions is real (or, more precisely: quasi-real), while, in contrast, the world of the mathematical objects is ideal. Nevertheless, both spheres as correlates of *one* literary text form a total sphere, which divides, to be sure, into two different ontic domains, between which, however, a relationship is established on the basis of the fact that the mathematical objects constitute the theme of study of the represented mathematician. As we shall later see, the heterogeneity of represented objects can go much further. At present it is only a question of establishing the fact that a uniform objective sphere corresponds to the uniform literary text and that in a certain sense that sphere surpasses what is explicitly represented by the states of affairs.

In order to eliminate possible misunderstandings, I would especially like to emphasize that the expression "represented object" (or objectivity) that I am using is to be understood in a very broad sense, encompassing, above all, everything that is *nominally* projected regardless of objectivity category and material essence. Thus it refers to things as well as persons, but also to all possible occurrences, states, acts performed by persons, etc. At the same time, however, the stratum of what is represented can also contain the nonnominally projected, as, in particular, what is intended purely verbally. For the purpose of

---

2. Cf. Husserl's theory of the horizons of perceptually given objects (*Ideen zu einer reinen Phänomenologie* [Halle, 1913], pp. 49 ff. [English translation by W. R. Boyce Gibson, *Ideas: General Introduction to Pure Phenomenology* (New York: Macmillan, 1931), pp. 101 ff.]), which suggests itself here. We are now dealing with an analogue of these horizons.

simplifying terminology, the expression "represented object" is meant to encompass—in the absence of express restrictions on this usage—everything that is represented as such. At the same time, it must be noted that "objectified" objects need not necessarily find themselves in the stratum of "represented objects." And this is true in various senses. In the first place, it is not necessarily a question of the particular form of the *objective givenness* in which the object remains distinctly "distanced" with respect to the observer (although in the great majority of instances this is exactly the case).[3] Second, what is represented does not necessarily have to possess "objective" properties, i.e., those that are intended as being free of every existential relativity. On the contrary, the objectivities in a literary work can be represented in such a way that they move toward the reader in a pronounced *rapprochement;*[4] on the other hand, they may be encumbered with and appear in various existentially relative, merely "subjective" moments, emotional characters, emotional illustrations, etc.[5] All possible manners of givenness that appear in various ways in primal experience may recur here as well, with the only proviso that they be subject to all those modifications that are produced, first, by the representation by means of states of affairs and, second, by the imaginative mode of appearance. Representation by means of states of affairs is not necessary with all objects, in particular not with those that are directly projected by names and nominal expressions.

§ 33. *The* habitus *of reality of represented objects*

IN CONNECTION WITH the quasi-judgmental character of assertive propositions, as well as with the modification, discussed above, of all the remaining propositions in a literary work, the

3. With regard to the "objective" mode of givenness (in the narrower sense) and the "distancing" that is characteristic of it, see H. Conrad-Martius, "Zur Ontologie und Erscheinungslehre der realen Aussenwelt," *Jahrbuch für Philosophie und phänomenologische Forschung,* III (1916), 470.
4. This mode of representation through *rapprochement* is characteristic of pure lyric poetry. After World War II Emil Staiger used this difference to contrast epic and lyric poetry. See his *Grundbegriffe der Poetik* (Zurich, 1946).
5. Naturally, this always refers only to the *content* of the intentional meaning correlates and with the provision that one disregard the pure intentionality of the represented world.

ontic character present in the content of represented objects undergoes a correlative modification. If in a novel, for example, there are people, animals, lands, houses, etc.—i.e., clearly objects whose type of existence is *real* existence—they then appear in the literary work in the character of reality, even though the reader is usually not explicitly conscious of it. This character of reality, however, is not to be fully identified with the ontic character of truly existing real objects. In represented objectivities there is only an *external habitus* of reality, which does not intend, as it were, to be taken altogether seriously, although, when the work is read, it can often happen that the reader takes quasi-judgmental propositions for genuine judgments and thus considers to be real intentional objects which only simulate reality. But the transformation connected with this does not belong to the work itself but rather to one of its possible concretizations.[6] If the represented objectivities are apprehended in their peculiar essence, then—according to their content—they do indeed belong to the type of real objectivities; but nevertheless, from the outset, they do not belong there as if they were "rooted"[7] in the real world and as if they could find themselves *of their own accord* in real space and real time, i.e., quite independently of whether a conscious subject performed an act directed precisely at them. A peculiar modification of the character of reality takes place here, one which does not remove it, yet almost reduces it to a mere claim to reality. For it would obviously be a mistake to assert that represented objects possess no character of reality at all or that perhaps they take on the character of another ontic mode (e.g., of *ideal* existence). On the other hand, this modification of the ontic character cannot simply be identified with the "neutrality modification,"[8] in the Husserlian sense.[9] It is rather something so unique that it can hardly be

6. See below, Chap. 13.
7. See H. Conrad-Martius, "Zur Ontologie und Erscheinungslehre der realen Aussenwelt," passim.
8. See Husserl, *Ideen*, §§ 109–11.
9. Under Husserl's influence, I myself did this in my "Essentiale Fragen," *Jahrbuch für Philosophie und phänomenologische Forschung*, VII (1925), 125–304; also published as *Essentiale Fragen* (Halle, 1925). I now find it necessary to abandon the position I took there with regard to "fictional" objectivities. I was also at a loss for the concepts of the various ontic characters, without which one cannot do justice to the existential situations that are at issue here. On the other hand, I went too far in *Essentiale Fragen* in the direction of pure ontology, without sufficiently appreciating various existential relativities with respect to conscious operations.

adequately described.[10] Moreover, it is remarkable that not only the character of reality but, if need be, also the characters of all other ontic modes may be subject to it. This is seen quite distinctly if within the represented world there is a contrasting of "real" objectivities with objects that have only been "dreamed" by a represented person. In this instance we see not only that ontic characters are distinctly present in the represented world but also that the world that is "dreamt" here is not truly but only quasi-dreamt. Hence, *that which* is dreamt here, which is juxtaposed to the quasi-real world as "dream," is also subject to the peculiar modification of existing in a "quasi" manner, which has its source in the previously described modifications of sentences.[11]

§ 34. *Represented space and "imaginational space"*

IF IN A LITERARY WORK there are represented objects that are "real" according to their content, and if their reality type is to be preserved, they must be represented as existing in time and space or even as being spatial in themselves. However, the space that comes into question here is not the *real* world space, which is unique, nor is it the "orientational space" that necessarily belongs to the perceptible primary givenness of things and

---

10. Max Scheler attempted to describe it this way: "Thus all aesthetic values are by their very essence values of (1) objects, (2) objects whose acceptance as reality (in whatever manner) is suspended and which thus appear as 'illusion,' except, as in the case of a historical drama, if the phenomenon of reality is the partial content of the graphically given object of the illusion" "Der Formalismus in der Ethik und die materiale Wertethik," *Jahrbuch für Philosophie und phänomenologische Forschung*, I (1913), 487; English translation by Manfred S. Frings and Roger L. Funk, *Formalism in Ethics and Non-Formal Ethics of Value: A New Attempt toward the Foundation of an Ethical Personalism* (Evanston, Ill.: Northwestern University Press, 1973). I believe that the question of the ontic character of what is represented in a work of art arises not only in the case of aesthetic values but refers to everything that is represented. One cannot make do here with the concept of "illusion" and the "graphically given." The situation is much more complicated.

11. Quite naturally, different variants of the previously mentioned modifications of the ontic character of represented objects correspond to the various types of modifications of assertive propositions discussed earlier (see § 25). It would take us too far, however, to show this in detail.

that forms a constitutive substratum of the appearance of unique real space and, as such, shows in itself an existential relativity with respect to the perceiving subject.[12] On the other hand, it is also not an *ideal*, homogeneous, geometric space, a pure three-dimensional manifold of points. Finally, it is also not "imaginational space," which essentially belongs to every intuitive *imagining* of extensive objects and can never coincide or become one with real space. Instead—if one may so put it—it is a unique space which essentially belongs to the represented "real" world. In a certain sense it is related to all these other kinds of space because it exhibits a structure that allows us to call it "space" even though its possession of this structure is only a simulated, make-believe possession. In its structure it is comparatively closest to objective real space (or perceptible orientational space). But even in this respect it should not be equated with it without further qualifications, though it might appear to be equated at first glance, when we merely think that the represented objects existing in it are intended as real objects. That is, it differs from real space by the particular feature that, while it is not positively limited and finite, it is at the same time not unlimited in the sense that real space is. Let us consider that in a novel, for example, a situation is represented as taking place in a given room and that there is no indication, even by a *single* word, that there is anything outside this room. Surely one cannot say that outside the segment of space that is bounded by the walls of this room there is absolutely *no* space and hence complete nothingness. Yet it would also be false to say that there is space surrounding this room which is *determined* by corresponding units of meaning or positively *represented* by corresponding states of affairs. If the actually represented space (within the room) does not end at the walls of the room, *it is only because it is the essence of space in general not to have any discontinuity.* It is only through this impossibility of spatial discontinuity that the space outside the room is corepresented; in turn, the space within the room consequently becomes a *segment* of space. Thus, when the author of a novel "transports" us from place *A* to place *B* without showing us the entire distance between *A* and *B*, the intervening space between *A* and *B* is not positively determined and represented but again is only corepresented, by

12. We cannot elaborate here on the concept of "orientational space" —which is actually a Husserlian concept. Cf. O. Becker, "Zur phänomeno-logischen Begründung der Geometrie," *Jahrbuch für Philosophie und phänomenologische Forschung*, Vol. VI (1923).

virtue of the impossibility of spatial discontinuity.* Explicitly, truly represented space is as if pocked with gaps, which show up as, so to speak, spots of indeterminacy. These are all circumstances which are quite impossible in real space. Here we come upon a characteristic trait of represented objects in general, one which we shall discuss more thoroughly in § 39.

Represented space does not allow itself to be incorporated either into real space or into the various kinds of perceptible orientational space, even when the represented objects are expressly represented as "finding" themselves in a specific location in real space, e.g., "in Munich." This *represented* Munich, and in particular the space within which this city—as one that is represented—"lies," cannot be identified with the corresponding segment of space in which the real city of Munich actually lies.[13] If it could be, then it would have to be possible to walk out, as it were, from represented into real space and vice versa, which is patently absurd. Moreover, nothing can change the fact that the segment of space in which the real city of Munich is *constantly* and invariably situated has a pronounced existential relativity with respect to cognitive subjects (even though it does not yet coincide with the orientational space that is existentially relative to a particular cognitive subject), since this real city quite evidently constantly changes its position in the one, objective, homogeneous cosmic space—if that at all exists—and therefore, in this latter sense, there is actually no segment of space in which it could constantly and invariably be found.† The segment of space represented in the literary work is not to be identified even with the "always the same" existentially relative segment of space in which the real city of Munich lies. They are entirely separate kinds of space, between which there is no *spatial* cross-

* ["This, of course, is true only in Euclidean space. But space in the real world—as it is given to us in everyday experience, and on which space in literary works is modeled—is, or at least seems to be, Euclidean space. We are so accustomed to this understanding of space that when we hear of curved and closed Riemannian space, which—according to modern physics—is the space of the real world, it is very difficult, if not impossible, to imagine this type of cosmic space, especially if we hear, in connection with the theory of an expanding universe, that this closed though infinite space expands along with the cosmos" (*O dziele literackim* [1958], p. 288n).—Trans.]

13. Mrs. Käte Hamburger now wishes to convince me that this is so—as if I had not known it.

† [I.e., because of the movement of the planet and the general expansion of the universe, noted above.]

ing. Later (in § 37) we shall see how the relation between them should be positively determined.

Of special interest is still the fact that, despite the dissimilarity between represented space and the "imaginational space" of a particular imagining conscious subject,[14] there exists the possibility that in reading the work we can see, by means of a lively intuitive imagining, *directly* into the given represented space and can thus in a way bridge the gulf between these two separate kinds of space. In connection with this, there is also the fact that in a lively spiritual relationship with the literary work we are capable of viewing the represented objects directly—even though clearly not in the perceptible corporeal self-givenness that is fundamentally precluded here.[15] This undoubtedly quite remarkable fact has its basis in the manner of exhibiting represented objects, a manner that is realized in the course of the actualization of the aspects belonging to them. We shall deal with this in Chapter 8. We indicate it here, however, in order to stress that this fact does not argue against the difference between represented and imaginational space, as it may appear to some superficial observers to do. The danger of confusion of the two kinds of space compels us to deal extensively with the difference between them, as well as with the dissimilarity between represented and imaginational objects.

What, exactly, is meant by an "imaginational object"? When, for example, I "imagine" my friend, who is currently in a distant city, he himself is not an imaginational object. He is a real, ontically autonomous object, for whom it is accidental that he happens to be intuitively imagined by me. Likewise, when I intuitively "imagine" a centaur, who never really existed, this centaur is not an imaginational object. He too—though he is only a "fiction"—is only imagined by me and is precisely as transcendent to my imaginational experience, and never to be found in it itself, as the really existing friend whom I imagine.[16] Beyond this object that is transcendent to my experience there is still my imagining, as an act that is quite determinately constructed and effected by "me." This act, as an intentional act of thought, has its particular, indeed *unintuitive*, content. This content is con-

---

14. We shall speak of this presently.

15. T. A. Meyer, *Das Stilgesetz der Poesie* (Leipzig, 1901), p. 185, also points to the direct apprehension of represented objects, in the course of which he speaks of their "self-presence."

16. As Husserl noted many years ago.

tained in the act itself, in the imaginational intending. It is the total stock of primary intentions that make up the given imaginational intending. Every imaginational intending—regardless of whether it is clear or unclear, ambiguous or unambiguous—is laden with content. But the total imaginational experience is not exhausted by this content or by the remaining elements of the act and its performance features.[17] There is still something there which makes the entire experience an intuitive experience: a flowing manifold of intuitive data, which in their type differ radically from the data experienced by sensory perception but which possess intuitiveness in common with them.[18] These flowing and ever changing data show yet another noteworthy heterogeneity. That is to say, in visual imagination—to which we will here limit ourselves—there are, on the one hand, qualitatively different color data, which in general belong together and are subject to the indirect directive [19] of the intentional elements of thought contained in the act of imagining, and, on the other, a nebulous medium—usually unnoticed by the person imagining —in which these data appear. Like the color data themselves, this medium is a thoroughly positive phenomenon of a unique kind. In particular, in those cases where the imagining is done with closed eyes, it has nothing to do with so-called subjective visual grayness.[20] The latter is only a special case of perceptible data or objects. The medium of which we are speaking, however, occurs only in intuitive imagining. It is not a color datum, nor is it an imaginational color datum. It is something that is spatial, yet it should not be identified with the structure of perceptively seen space. It creates "space," so to speak, for the imaginational data that are here contrasted to it, that extend within it and are encompassed by it. Here we find nothing of the *distinct* dimensions, e.g., of a distinct depth, that can occur in vis-

17. See Husserl, *Logical Investigations,* Vol. II, Sixth Investigation.
18. See, among others, H. Conrad-Martius, "Zur Ontologie und Erscheinungslehre der realen Aussenwelt."
19. By this expression we wish to indicate that the intuitive imaginational data that are merely experienced but not intended are nevertheless sensitive to changes in the content of the imaginational act: they change according to the content of the act; they can also be intentionally changed by us to a certain degree, although in general they appear independently of our intentions. Usually they come into existence without our intention. Cases are possible, of course, where they are intentionally evoked by us.
20. See D. Katz, "Die Erscheinungsweisen der Farben," *Zeitschrift für Psychologie,* supplement 7, later published as *Der Aufbau der Farbwelt* (Leipzig, 1911).

ual perception as well as in subjective visual grayness.[21] And yet it is a *spatial* medium, in which the color data appear as if coming to the surface; yet, on the one hand, it is not limitless and, on the other, it has no sharp boundaries. Nevertheless, figuratively speaking, it can be said that at its "edges" (which as such are not present here) it begins to dissolve beyond recognition (so that the dissolution itself is usually not at all apprehended); and "continuing" in its peculiar way in this dissolution, it loses itself in nothingness. At the same time, it is always marked by a certain nebulous obscurity and vagueness. This obscurity is present even when the data appearing in the medium are themselves composed, e.g., of bright color qualities and when the object which we are imagining is imagined in a bright space (e.g., a landscape in bright, sunny weather). It is precisely this medium which is "imaginational space" in the strict sense of the term, and it must be sharply distinguished from *imagined* space and, even more, from *represented* space in a literary work.

In contrast to imagined space, imaginational space is strictly immanent in imaginational experience; it is its genuine "real part"—to use Husserl's term from the *Logical Investigations*—and it cannot be removed from intuitive imaginational experience.

The imaginational data (e.g., color data) appearing in imaginational space are usually subject to the "directive"—as I have expressed it—of the intentional thought contained essentially in the act of imagining. To put it more precisely, the following is at issue: imaginational data have their own qualitative determinations and their own order, which is not imposed upon them, so to speak, from outside by the intending. They can also appear in imaginational space when the I conducts itself absolutely passively and performs *no* intentional acts and therefore also does not imagine but instead simply possesses this or that imaginational datum. Under these circumstances, however, the "play" of these data is entirely different from what it is when the I

21. This must be understood correctly, however. It certainly extends in a two-dimensional manner. But since in normal cases this medium is not noticed by us, its dimensions are also not expressly apprehended. The nonexplicitness of these dimensions is based precisely on their state of not being apprehended, of being merely experienced or felt. At the same time, one cannot say that the medium is flat or superficial, even though it has no explicit depth. Flatness, surface, depth, volume, etc., are all characters or formations of the imagined object or imagined space but not of the merely possessed and felt, but never objectively intended, spatial medium that is immanent in every imaginational experience.

executes a determinate *act* of imagining. In the first instance, it is quite accidental, irregular, and to a large degree independent from the I; in the latter instance, however, the qualities of the color data, the arrangement of spots, if one may so put it, their sequence and transformation, are dependent on the respective intentional acts and are more or less exactly matched with their unintuitive content. Leaving aside pathological cases, it is in the power of the person imagining to have exactly these or those intuitive data in his imaginational space, even though he is usually not at all prepared to let exactly these and not other data appear. Instead, he simply effects a determinate intentional act, the execution of which results in a corresponding ordering of data. In other words, the data are subject to the directive of the respective imaginational act. This directive, however, can go to different lengths. First of all, it is possible that the arrangement and the flow of the data may be dependent to a greater or lesser extent on other and, after all, quite diverse factors of spiritual and emotional life and may consequently submit in varying degrees to the directive of the imaginational act. On the other hand, this directive may be limited to the appearance and sequence of determinately qualified data, in which case the intention of the imaginational act, bypassing the data as it were, directs itself *straight* at the *imagined* object; or it may happen that the imaginational data are themselves "animated" by the unintuitive content of the imaginational act, correspondingly ordered, and made into a *particular objective* whole, which, on the strength of its similarity to the imagined object, may possibly "represent" it. It is exclusively this particular object, ontically and directly grounded in imaginational data, and possibly performing the function of representation, that may in the strict sense of the term be called an *"imaginational* object." [22] It should not be confused with the intentional object which is *imagined* and upon which the intention of the act ultimately rests. If it is constituted, this imaginational object is an inseparable immanent "real part" of the corresponding imaginational experience. If one considers the entire imaginational experience as psychic, then it, too, is psychic. It is just as concrete and real as the entire experience, an experience which does not have to be true at all in the case of the *imagined* object. If it performs the function of

22. If I correctly understand H. Conrad-Martius, she has this somewhat more precisely described situation in mind when she speaks of "imaginational type I" (see "Zur Ontologie und Erscheinungslehre der realen Aussenwelt," pp. 364–70).

representation, the intention of the imaginational act conceives it as a *proxy* for the actually imagined intentional object and effects a certain similarity between it and the latter. However, as we have said, the constitution of the imaginational object does not always have to occur. Consequently, not every imagining has its imaginational object.[23] If the latter is absent, then at most—though not necessarily—it may happen that the imaginational data are applied toward the actualization of the aspects of the imagined object and are thus also subject to a corresponding arrangement and animation: the intention of the intentional moment contained in the imaginational experience directs itself at that point *straight* at the intentional imagined object, which is then observed in the raiment, so to speak, of the actualized aspect. Thus there occurs here a *presentation* of the given object, though it is obviously not the perceptual presentation which brings the object to a corporeal *self*-givenness.[24] This latter kind of givenness is excluded by the particular imaginational character of the data appearing in imaginational space. The purely intentional object at which the imaginational act is directed necessarily "belongs" to this act, but it is essentially transcendent to it and to all conscious experience in general. Moreover, nothing is changed here by the fact that it attains presentation in the imaginational experience. As such, it also cannot be psychic merely on the grounds that the imaginational experience is psychic. It can be psychic only when its content is psychic, i.e., when, for example, we imagine someone's psychic state. But if we are dealing with intentional imagined objects from another content, there is no basis for considering them psychic. And it is totally inadmissable to identify them with imaginational objects or even with the total imagination. Only some very crude notions of "imagining" could lead to such an absurdity.

Even less are we permitted to identify derived intentional objects, projected by word meanings or by meaning contents of sentences with "imaginational objects," i.e., with something which constitutes a real component of concrete psychical experiences. *Ipso facto*, space represented by states of affairs likewise has nothing to do with imaginational space.

23. But an intentional *imagined* object belongs to every imaginational act.

24. This is perhaps the reason why Husserl also considered acts of the imagination, *Phantasieakte*, to be *originär-gebende*, i.e., acts in which objects are "primarily given." See also his 1922 lecture, "Einleitung in die Philosophie." During my stay in Freiburg in 1927 Professor Husserl lent me the manuscript of this lecture, for which I am most grateful.

§ 35. *Various modes of spatial orientation of represented objectivities*

LET US RETURN, however, to the spatial relations of the objective world represented in a literary work.

If things, animals, and men are represented in a literary work, the space that is represented along with them is not abstract and geometric, or homogeneous and physical; rather, it is the kind of space that corresponds to perceptually given space. It must then be exhibited, so to say, through the medium of orientational space. In particular, orientational spaces must thus be used which belong to the represented psychic subjects "perceiving" this represented space. If this is the case, the question arises where the center of orientation ("the zero point of orientation," as Husserl calls it) is to be found. That it is always to be found within the *represented* world is indubitable, but it must be observed that different instances are still possible. This depends on the mode of representation. If the representation is such that the poet himself "tells" us a "story" and thus as narrator belongs to the world represented in the given work, the center of orientation lies, so to speak, in the I of the poet himself—not the real one, but the represented narrator. All the represented objects (things, animals, men) are then represented as if they were seen (touched, heard, etc.) by the narrator, and in this perception they are related to his center of orientation.[25] If the narrator does not expressly belong to the represented world, the orientational space may be chosen in such a way that it is indeed found in the represented world but at the same time is not localized in any of the represented objects, so that *all* the represented objects are again exhibited as if they were seen from a determinate point (which sometimes changes in the course of the representation). It is as if an invisible and never determinately represented person were wandering through the represented world and showing us the objects as they appear from his point of view. In this manner the narrator is nevertheless corepresented.[26] Other cases

25. In this case Theodor Lipps's assertion about the "ideal I of speech" is justified (*Grundlegung der Ästhetik* [Leipzig, 1903], I, 497).
26. There are some interesting and useful observations on this problem in Franz Stanzel's *Die typischen Erzählungssituationen im Roman* (Vienna, 1955). Stanzel, however, concentrates not so much on the prob-

may occur, however. For instance, the center of orientation may be found in the zero point of the I of a represented person and move with every change of place he makes.[27] If, in our reading, we want to apprehend the world exactly as it is represented, we must, so to speak, fictitiously transpose ourselves into the represented center of orientation and wander about in the represented world *in fictione* with the given person. A good representation itself forces us to do this. We have to forget to a certain extent our own center of orientation, which belongs to our perceived world and wanders everywhere with us, and assume a certain distancing attitude toward the world. This would naturally be impossible if the represented objects were "imaginational objects" in the sense specified above and if, as such, they were the subject of our study. They would then have to be perceived by internal perception, where in each case the center of orientation would necessarily have to be our own.

In fiction, it is frequently the case that the center of orientation of a work is not located consistently in a single person but in a *number* of persons. The center of orientation may, for example, be located in the person that plays the *main* role in a *particular* section of the represented story; the center of orientation then changes from chapter to chapter. However, it may also happen that one and the same objective situation (or phase of a developing story), in which a number of persons are taking part, may be exhibited, so to speak, "at the same time" from various centers of orientation. If, in the process, the things, bodies, etc., which come into question are not represented in corresponding

---

lem of represented space and the center of orientation as on the various types of narration and the presence of the narrator in the novel. He distinguishes three types of novel—the "authorial," the "I novel," and the "personal" novel—and attempts to construct a typology of the novel. On the whole, I can agree with his arguments, although I might speak of the "author" in a different sense. I dealt with this problem in the last years before the war in order to provide a critique for the assertion then being argued by J. Kleiner that the author is immanent in, and necessarily belongs to, every literary work of art and that literary criticism, therefore, must necessarily take the author as the starting point of its study. There are places in Stanzel where it becomes evident that he, too, is inclined to distinguish various concepts of "the author."

27. Pierre Audiat investigates these situations in *La Biographie de l'oeuvre littéraire* (Paris, 1924), pp. 226–29, where, for that matter, he indicates no knowledge of a "center of orientation" or of "orientational space." In addition, he makes the mistake of treating this whole question as one of the linguistic style of the work, whereas it is a question of the peculiarities of the represented world or of its manner of representation, which is dependent only on the arrangement of the stratum of meaning units.

perspectival foreshortenings, so that the individual foreshortenings of perspective belonging to the various centers of orientation do not "agree," there occurs, as a result, a nonuniformity in the represented world. It is then impossible to identify the individual things that are simultaneously seen by various characters. If the intention of the work is to represent a quasi-real world perceived exclusively by psychically sound persons, such a nonuniformity of the represented world signifies a fault in the mode of representation. In principle, however, such a mode of representation need not be faulty. On the contrary, it may be intended quite consciously and serve as a special means of artistic formation and aesthetic effect.

A special case of where and how the center of orientation is located in the represented world is created by the state of affairs that is found in "drama" that is read. If, for example, we read in the stage directions of a drama: "To the left are two large windows, next to them is an old-fashioned, heavy desk, in front of it a stool . . . ," we are given a center of orientation, or at least the direction in which it is to be found. This center of orientation is here shifted to a possible spectator, who, after all, is not really present in a dramatic work which is only read. It would also be a mistake to think that this possible spectator is one of a number of real spectators who would be present at a performance of the drama and that it need only be determined which of them is the one in question. Quite on the contrary. Like the invisible narrator before, here the invisible spectator belongs to the represented world, with the difference that he does not attain *explicit* representation. The space in which he finds himself is *represented* space and is in no sense a segment of space from the auditorium. Still, the fact that a spectator attains even nonexplicit and indirect corepresentation is not without influence on the remainder of the represented world. For what exists and occurs in the represented world attains thereby the character of something *presented,* of something displayed for someone, regardless of whether this is explicitly indicated in the text or in the directions.[28]

One could perhaps think that this is the way that the "boxing" of represented states of affairs, of which we have spoken earlier, occurs in the dramatic mode of representation, i.e., in the sense that all the remaining states of affairs are boxed within the state

28. See W. Conrad, "Bühnekunst und Drama," *Zeitschrift für Ästhetik und allgemeine Kunstwissenschaft,* VI, no. 2 (1911), 249–77.

of affairs that is presented to the spectator. This view, however, seems to go a bit too far. In reality, the represented states of affairs are simply enriched by yet another state of affairs, which, like all the others, belongs to the object stratum of the work and whose presence results in the objectivities represented by the remaining states of affairs taking on the above-mentioned character of something "displayed." The represented world is, in a manner of speaking, supposed to be seen. In other words, the particular structure of a dramatic work is such that every drama attains its full validity only as "theater," and, in order to achieve vital communion with it, the reading also requires a particular mode of perception, one that is not required for other literary works. If this requirement is fully met, that is, if the drama is performed, it becomes *theater* and thus goes beyond the realm of purely literary works or constitutes one of its borderline cases.[29]

§ 36. *Represented time, and time perspectives*

IF THE REPRESENTED OBJECTS are of the nature of real objects, then, as we have already observed, they are to be found in a particular represented time, which must be distinguished from both the "objective" time of the real world and the "subjective" time [30] of an absolute conscious subject. The reasons for this are various.

We are first of all compelled to make this distinction by the fact that the events in which the represented objects take part are by their very essence temporal and, moreover, are represented as consecutive or simultaneous. Hence, a temporal order is established among them. This temporal order already brings about the fact that individual temporal phases and moments attain representation. But they too are quite frequently intentionally projected by the corresponding elements of the meaning contents of sentences in exactly the same way as the objects existing within them. Thus in *this* respect there is no basis for making any

29. Cf. Chap. 12, below.
30. See Husserl, "Vorlesungen zur Phänomenologie des inneren Zeitbewusstseins," *Jahrbuch für Philosophie und phänomenologische Forschung*, IX (1928); English translation by James S. Churchill, *The Phenomenology of Internal Time-Consciousness* (Bloomington: Indiana University Press, 1964).

distinction between represented objects (things, persons, events) and represented time.

In order to counter, however, those tendencies which still attempt to psychologize the literary work or any one of its strata, the following should be added: it would be fundamentally wrong to believe that the moments and phases of represented time are identical with those temporal moments in which the author wrote his work or with those in which a given reader is reading the work, even if the represented events take place "contemporaneously." As we know, it is necessary to distinguish among (1) homogeneous, "empty" physicomathematically determined world time, (2) concrete intuitively apprehendable intersubjective time, in which we all live *collectively*, and (3) strictly subjective time.[31] It is self-evident that in literary works only an analogue of *concrete* intersubjective or subjective time is represented and not empty physical time. It is also well known that neither intersubjective nor subjective "filled" time is strictly homogeneous in its individual phases, nor does it constitute an empty medium of points which is insensitive to the events occurring within it. Each of the many presents through which we consecutively pass in our life has its peculiar irreducible coloration, to which it may lay claim by reason of the fact that something quite determinate occurs in it and because it itself follows another, now vanished, present that was characteristically colored, both as that which was present and as that which is "now" past, and because it precedes another, future, "present," which is accessible to us primarily only in expectation.[32] Concrete (intersubjective or subjective) time also has—as Bergson has already shown—various tempi in its different phases, and these tempi are dependent on what occurs in the phases and on the experiences we have while perceiving the objective events and, finally, on the mode of the experience. If an analogue of subjective or intersubjective time is represented in a literary work, then its individual phases are likewise characteristically colored. And this coloration depends exclusively on what in the *represented* world occurs "previously" or "now" and, in particular, on what is experienced by the represented persons. This coloration is obviously different from those colorations that are characteristic for the temporal phases of the concrete life of the author or for the temporal phases of the read-

31. One can leave aside here the distinction between *constituted* subjective time and the temporal primary forms of the "constituting temporal consciousness" in the Husserlian sense. See *ibid.*
32. H. Bergson was the first to point to this.

ing by the given reader. *Eo ipso,* the phases of represented time cannot be identified with the corresponding phases of "real" intersubjective or subjective time.

But, also in its *structure,* represented (intersubjective or subjective) time differs from real time in quite determinate ways, so that it constitutes only an *analogue,* a modification, of the latter. Each *present* of *real* time (and again both intersubjective and subjective) has a decided ontic advantage over the "real" past and—to a still greater degree—over each future.[33] And indeed, each "now," as well as that which is really present in the "now-moment," delineates a pronounced *actuality,* which inheres in neither the past nor the present. This actuality, however, should not be understood in the sense of any particular vitality or urgency, although these elements likewise characterize the present, but rather in the sense of an *in actu esse.* This *in actu esse* in a strict sense inheres only in the present and in what really exists in the present. At the same time, it is in its essence characteristic of real existence as such. Nothing that is of the nature of a real objectivity can exist if it does not pass through the phase of *in actu esse.* On the other hand, a real object *exists* only within the range of this *in actu esse.*[34] It is from here, from the "now-phase," that what is past and the past itself are determined and, in the other direction, the future and what is in the future: only that can be past which at one point in the "now-phase" has undergone the *in actu esse.* Likewise, that which is in the future and the future itself are future only to the extent that at some point—at least in principle—they will enter into the "now-phase" and be *in actu*—to the extent that this *in actu esse* has not yet been attained. Moreover, it need not be attained in every case, since not everything that is awaited as being in the future is "fulfilled." But according to its essence it is something that tends toward this fulfillment in the *in actu esse.* And one more point: if there were no "now-phase" at all and no genuine *in actu esse,* there could be no past (or that which is in the past)

---

33. See H. Conrad-Martius, "Die Zeit," *Philosophische Anzeiger,* II, no. 2 (1927); also published as *Die Zeit* (Munich, 1954).

34. Now (1960) I would not be able to put it that flatly. In my book *Der Streit um die Existenz der Welt* (Tübingen, 1965), Vol. I, I gave a comprehensive analysis of concrete time as belonging to a particular ontic mode of reality which the descriptions given here cannot characterize with sufficient precision. However, I cannot provide these new analyses here. All the more so since they will not undermine the distinction that is being made here between the time pertaining to reality and the time merely represented in a literary work of art.

or future (or that which is in the future). Precisely therein lies the ontic priority of the present over both the past and the future. And, in fact, wherever the corresponding objectivities, in accordance with their essence, cannot be *in actu* in the strict sense of the term, there is also no now-phase and likewise no past or future: the corresponding objectivities—as, for example, individual ideal objects, ideas, and essences—are altogether outside of time.

Now, objects represented in a literary work are derived purely intentional objectivities, which are essentially characterized by ontic heteronomy even though, according to their content, they are usually of the nature of real objectivities. Their ontic heteronomy, which allows them only to pretend real existence in their content, necessarily also brings about the fact that the time belonging to the represented quasi-real world is only an analogue of real time. Naturally, here too one must distinguish between present, past, and future; but this distinction stems from a reciprocal *order* of represented events and not from the fact that they all pass through a distinct phase of *genuine in actu esse;* this, precisely, is impossible for them in the strict sense of the term, for then they themselves would have to be real. Only a simulated *in actu esse,* a simulated "present" (and thus also a past and a future), is possible here; and this, too, only on the condition that, while reading the work, we contribute, as it were, to the development of the represented events and, as each is viewed, bestow upon it the semblance of our respective actuality. By being limited solely to what is contained in the literary work itself, the represented present has none of the preeminence of the genuine present over the represented past and future. As a result, there is a certain leveling of all the represented time moments similar to the leveling that occurs when erstwhile now-moments of real time "already" belong to the past. Thus it is no accident that, in the vast majority of literary works, events and objects are represented in terms of the past. But this equalization of represented time moments is also maintained when a "story" is presented in the "present" form, with the difference that in this case, perhaps, the equalization of time moments does not attain so clear an expression. Herein, too, lies the basis for the fact that the "present" form of representation is chosen whenever the character of reality of the represented world is to be made more evocative for the reader (e.g., in drama).

The difference between represented and real time will become more apparent when we take into consideration the mode of temporal representation by means of states of affairs projected by *sentences*. Real time is a *continuous* medium, showing absolutely no gaps. Without going into the question of whether it is possible in principle to represent *explicitly* such a continuous medium in a literary work, one must assert that such a representation of time does not occur in any larger work. Leaving aside those instances where temporal relations or individual time moments or phases are directly specified by particular words (e.g., by words like "earlier," "later," "at that moment," etc.), time is represented through the development of states of occurrence representing temporally extended events. In most cases, what is primarily represented is, not the time phase in and of itself, but that which *fills out* a time phase. Only the representation of that which fills out time evokes the representation of the time filled out by it. Nevertheless, the time-filling events are never represented in *all their phases*, regardless of whether it is a single event, constituting a whole, or a plurality of successive events. Neither an individual, isolated sentence nor a manifold of interconnected sentences can develop states of affairs which could effect this. It is always only *isolated* longer or shorter phases, or, simply, only momentary occurrences, that are represented, and what takes place between these phases or occurrences remains *indeterminate*. It is always—to echo Bergson—only *isolated* "segments" of "reality" that are represented, a reality which is being represented but which is never representable in its flowing continuity. The reason for this lies precisely in the fact that the represented world has the source of its existence and essence solely in a *finite* number of sentences.[35] Consequently, the represented time phases never combine into *one* uniform, continuous whole. And if, in the reading of the work, we do not notice any gaps in the represented time, and if we are usually inclined to treat certain events of which the author does not inform us as simply *unknown* to us, so that the corresponding time phases are considered as existing but "merely" not represented,[36] it is for a reason analogous to the one we indicated in our discussion of spatial

35. We have already pointed to this in our analysis of the constitution of a "net" of interconnected states of affairs (see § 23). If Bergson had had only this in mind when he made his assertion about the inability of intellectual cognition to apprehend concretely flowing reality, he would have been entirely correct.
36. See, for example, Thomas Mann's *Buddenbrooks*.

representation: [37] like space, time—by its very essence—allows of *no discontinuity*. Wherever a time phase is represented, it appears as one which extends directly and continuously in both directions—to preceding and succeeding time phases. If two "separate" time phases are represented, one of which is "earlier" and the other "later," then, precisely because of the impossibility of any temporal discontinuity, the entire time segment lying between these two phases is taken by the reader as existing: the time gaps which correspond to the time phases that are not explicitly represented disappear from our view. Nevertheless, if we go strictly by what is *explicitly* represented in the literary work, these gaps do exist. Their presence is to a certain degree concealed by what is corepresented, by virtue of the impossibility of temporal discontinuity; but it is still discernible, because simply corepresented time phases are "empty" phases, qualitatively *not colored* by that which fills out the time. Their qualitative coloration remains *indeterminate* (at best it is intended as being *something*), in direct contrast to those phases which are represented explicitly. Here, for the second time, we come upon a remarkable property of represented objectivities, with which we shall deal more closely in § 39.

This property of represented time reminded us of an analogous situation in represented space, and the analogy can also be pursued in another direction. Just as, in the exhibiting of space, there is always a center of orientation, which can be introduced in various ways into the represented world, so in represented time there are analogous zero points of orientation and perspectives.[38] In time that is really experienced, each present is the primary zero point of orientation of time perspective, a zero point which—like the spatial center of orientation during a train ride —is in constant displacement, which, by its very nature, can never be brought to a standstill and which is always progressing in one and the same direction. This displacement is accompanied by an indispensable constant transformation of the particular time perspective, one in which past experiences or external oc-

37. There are still other, particular reasons for this—reasons that are connected with the conditions of the reading of the work and with the properties of its concretizations. We shall go into these later (Chap. 13).

38. Husserl also speaks of "temporal perspectives" in connection with really experienced time. See "Vorlesungen zur Phänomenologie des inneren Zeitbewusstseins." Mrs. Hamburger now calls these zero points of orientation the "I origin."

currences appear in direct retention or recollection.[39] As Husserl rightly observed, there is an analogue here to perspectival fore-shortening in space: the "farther" an event or a time span lies in the past, the "shorter" it seems to be in our recollection, provided we remain grounded in the given *present* and look back into the past *from there*. We can, however, *step back*, as it were, into a specific time moment in the past and from there—moving forward—recollect past events (or experiences); in that case, the perspectival foreshortening of time of which we were speaking disappears. But we can *never really* leave the actual "now." Even when we have intentionally transposed ourselves into a past "now," we are continually flowing on with an ever new present and are in fact putting more distance between us and the erstwhile event which we "now" apprehend in our recollection. This continual increase in the temporal distance escapes our consciousness in this kind of recollection: by the intentional transposition into the past, the time perspective has become fundamentally altered.

It would take us too far afield to explain everything in detail and to consider the various possibilities that occur in this connection. What is important for us at this point is the fact that analogous phenomena are not only possible in the *represented* subjective world; they are in fact frequently represented. At the same time, however, different modifications are possible, modifications which are excluded from really experienced time. In part they are linked to the fact that the represented present has no ontic priority over the past and the future. Consequently, if a represented person in a given moment of represented time intentionally transposes himself into the past (e.g., remembering something or telling a story to a friend), this transposition succeeds to a much greater degree than would be possible in the real recollection of a real person. Here the represented person can, so to speak, leave his actual present. Thus we obtain the representation of a "former" event just as if it were another present: the "past," the "no longer" existing, event is here—despite indications in the text which should effect a separation—no longer separate from the direct present by the kind of gap that exists in the real situation. In connection with this there remains the fact that one and the same event can, in a manner of speak-

39. On the concepts of retention and recollection, see "Zeitbewusstsein," p. 391*n*; English trans., p. 52*n*.

ing, be represented from two different standpoints of temporal orientation. If, for example, a series of events is reported as if it were taking place "now"—and in a continuum of such "nows"—and then, suddenly, an illumination, as it were, from a "much later" time moment is thrown on what is "just now" taking place, so that it immediately takes on the aspect of something "long existing" that is being remembered from a much later time moment, then we are dealing with the phenomenon of a double temporal orientation, one which is possible only in a represented world. This double time perspective (or, if we will, time illumination) appears particularly frequently in the novel; see, for example, the narrative mode of Joseph Conrad (e.g., *Nostromo*) or Part II of Bernanos's *Sous le soleil de satan*.[40]

Another series of different time perspectives is opened up when the mode of representation reveals the perspective of "simultaneous existence" within a given present. The previous example (taken from F. Strich) from Kleist and Novalis may help to explain the question. In Kleist this perspective is produced by the particular sentence construction. Yet it can also attain representation as a result of the fact that the narration—as long as we are speaking of the novel—is spun with many "threads," i.e., with regard to various events that occur "simultaneously," we are informed, in sequence to be sure, but in such a manner that their simultaneity is clearly represented. But whenever only *one* line of occurrences, events, or actions is represented, from among the profusion of simultaneously occurring events, the time perspective of simultaneity contracts, as it were, and we get simply a one-dimensional continuum of occurrences in a time perspective which is oriented in only two directions—the past and the future.

Still another mode of representation of temporal occurrences which carries with it a particular modification of represented time occurs primarily in the novel. If we take Thomas Mann's *Buddenbrooks* as an example, we notice that in the entire length of the narration two different types of both narrative and representational modes can be clearly distinguished: on the one hand we have short "accounts" concerning the vicissitudes of the Bud-

40. On the other hand, cases of the following kind—where, in a "later" part of a work, something is represented which should have occurred before the events represented in an earlier part of the work—do not belong to the phenomena of the double time perspective. What is represented does not, as such, achieve thereby a different time perspective or indeed a different temporal order; there simply occurs a determinate order of sentences or representations. We shall deal with this in Chap. 11.

denbrook family over long periods of time, sometimes a whole year. On the other hand, special events, of comparatively short duration, are described thoroughly, phase by phase, in all possible detail, and are represented in a particular sense (see, for instance, Thomas Buddenbrook's election to the senate). Whereas in the former case it is merely the main lines of a long development that are drawn summarily, and only here and there the more important events, the turning points, are briefly *named*, in the latter case a segment, a scene, a situation is slowly developed and shown in its *entire concrete fullness* and its *entire concrete course*. As a result, represented time appears in two different modifications. In the first it disappears quickly and is practically imperceptible in its concrete coloration: compressed in a particularly characteristic way, weeks, months, and years pass before us like almost *empty* intervals that are only here and there colored and filled out with concrete life by an event that is almost punctual in its appearance, and we are not allowed to grasp in its entire continuity and observe phase by phase the time that is unfolding. Here time sinks nearly to the level of an empty schema which merely provides us with an orientation in the temporal order of the indicated events. Only when a scene is shown in its concrete fullness and in its entire temporal extension are we again dealing with qualitatively determined, represented time. Or, to put it differently: only in the latter case are the concrete time phases represented, or exhibited, in *their individuality*. In the other cases, however, represented time is represented as time—or as a time phase in a determinate position in the time continuum—only in its *general* structure and not as a simple individual *in its individuality*. It is indeed intended as something individual even then; but it is not *positively* determined by those simple individual elements which, as something individual, it would have to have. These elements remain in a state of indeterminacy precisely because they are intended as being only of *some* kind.

Here we again come upon something that is possible *only* in represented and not real time, and through it we obtain a new argument for the difference between the two times. But along with these two different types of temporal modes of representation, or of represented time itself, we have two different types of temporal perspective. In the simple "informational" narrative mode, the time periods represented are always conceived from a "later," though in other respects indeterminate, time moment as something that is in the past. Thus, there clearly appears a characteristic temporal *distance*. On the other hand, time represented in its simple individuality, running its course phase by phase, can, in fact, also be conceived as being in the past. Nevertheless, it appears in characteristic proximity: the zero point of temporal orientation is transposed to that moment in the past where the represented scene begins and then, as the events develop, constantly shifts in each segment of the temporal continuum up to the "last" moment of this scene. Thus, in a characteristic manner, past time phases are—successively—made "present," and we, the readers, seem to become witnesses to the given events and to live "then" or, more exactly, in the "erstwhile" "now." If the whole work is projected in the mode of the present, we are dealing with a manner of representation that is characteristic of "dramatic" works.

The reflections developed here naturally do not exhaust the very numerous and complex situations that are possible in represented time and in the mode of its representation. But, in the guise of temporary models for analysis, they may serve as starting points for further investigations. They certainly suffice to convince us that there is something like represented time in the object stratum of a literary work and that it plays a significant role in its structure.[41]

§ 37. *The reproduction and Representation* functions of represented objects*

ONE OFTEN HEARS the observation that the literary work is, or at least should be, a "representation" of life or reality. What

41. It seems to me that it is through an analysis of represented time that one can show essential differences among genuine lyric, epic, and dramatic poetry, although, naturally, the differences among these literary genres are not exhausted thereby. As regards pure lyric poetry, I believe that in my book *The Cognition of the Literary Work of Art* [English translation by Ruth Ann Crowley and Kenneth R. Olson (Evanston, Ill.: Northwestern University Press, 1973)], which first appeared in Polish in 1937, and in the article "O tak zwanej 'prawdzie' w literaturze" (So-called Truth in Literature) (1938), I have shown that the appearance of time in literary works is limited to the experienced, fulfilled present, even when what has happened belongs to this present in the form of a memory and codetermines it in a characteristic manner.

* [In this section, and later, in § 57, below, Ingarden distinguishes between representation in the sense of "depicting" or "presenting" (*Darstellung*) and representation in the sense of "standing in for" or "imitating" something (*Repräsentation*). Both senses are conveyed by the English term, and, therefore, where necessary, *Repräsentation, repräsentieren*, etc., are given as Representation, Representing.—Trans.]

is the actual situation in regard to this? First of all, it is clear that this observation does not refer to the *entire* literary work but merely to its object stratum. On the other hand, when we speak of the "representation" of life, it is obvious that we mean something quite different from the representation of objects by means of states of affairs, which we have already discussed. Only the precise determination of the sense of this observation will enable us to distinguish whether the "representation" of reality, in a sense that is yet to be determined, must occur in *every* literary work.

If we were to look for a case where objectivities represented in a literary work can themselves be viewed as a "representation of something," we would come, first of all, upon the so-called historical novels and dramas, e.g., Schiller's *The Death of Wallenstein*, or Shakespeare's historical dramas. In all of them we are "dealing"—as we are wont to put it—partly "with" persons and events which, as the reader knows from history, have at one time actually existed. This expression "dealing with," however, has a particular meaning. For if it were to mean as much as "something is intended in the sentence," then the literary work would always be "dealing" only "with" *represented* objects in our sense of the term. According to our analysis, however, these objects are always different from *real*, at one time really existing, persons (things, events). And yet, "historical" literary works do "deal"—in a different sense of the term—"with" real, and at one time existing, objectivities. For example, persons "appearing" in literary works do not merely carry such names as "Julius Caesar," "Wallenstein," "Richard II," etc., but are also in a certain sense supposed to "be" the persons who were once so named and who once actually did exist. In other words, despite the fundamental dissimilarity between them and the historical persons, they must be determined—in terms of their content—in such a way that, if we may so put it, they can "play" real persons, that they can "imitate" the given persons, their characteristics, their actions, their life-situations, and behave "just like them." Thus they must be primarily "reproductions" of persons (things, events) that once existed and acted; but at the same time they must *Represent* what they are reproducing. If they were simply reproductions, they would not only clearly contrast with what is being reproduced; they would also have to be reduced to the role of "mere images" of the "original," of the "model," of the very thing to which they refer—reduced to the role of something which is not what is being reproduced, which cannot occupy the same ontic position, but is rather, by comparison, only a "phantom." [42] In contradistinction to this, literary "figures" in "historical" literary works must be something more: they must, as we have already said, "Represent" what is being reproduced, i.e., they must reproduce it so well that one forgets, at least to a certain degree, that they are "mere reproductions" and are not that which is being reproduced. As we said in § 25,[43] they are striving to "incorporate," to "make present" in themselves, that which is being reproduced (i.e., the objectivities that once really existed). By virtue of the corresponding intentional characters, whose ontic basis lies specifically in quasi-judgmental assertive propositions, they should *conceal*, as much as possible, both their intrinsic essence as contents of purely intentional objectivities and their actual heterogeneity with respect to what is reproduced, and thereby show only those properties by which they approach, and, as we have said, Represent, that which is reproduced. If this concealment of the properties of the reproduction as such succeeds, then the Representing objectivities hide what is reproduced, take its place, and, in a manner of speaking, try to be what in a true sense they are not.

Representation in this sense of the term ["*Repräsentation*"] is also an "acquainting" [the reader] with something, but it is radically different from the representation [*Darstellung*] of the object by means of corresponding states of affairs. For it is that kind of "acquainting" with a given something—a something that is different from that which represents it—in which the representer "imitates" the represented while concealing itself as the representer; it does this in order to show itself, at the same time, as supposedly represented and in this way bring up from a distance, as it were, the other which it represents only *de facto* and let it, itself, speak in its own form. It is a representing [*Darstellen*] in which the representer is not truly the represented, and yet at the same time it simulates the genuineness of the "original existence." As a consequence of this, what is represented comes into the *direct* view of the observer (insofar as he gives credence to this merely simulated authenticity), even though *de facto* it is by its very essence not present for him.

And furthermore: the function of Representation [*Repräsentation*] is based on the reproduction function of represented [*dargestellten*] objects (in our earlier sense of the term). Thus, in

42. As, for example, in a photograph.
43. See above, pp. 170 ff.

this respect it is radically different from the representation function of states of affairs. For while states of affairs are not "images" of represented objects but only "reveal" them precisely by being the states of affairs that exist in corresponding objects, the representing objects, i.e., objects Representing something, are, by virtue of the similarity arising between them, reproductions of that which is reproduced.

In *literary* "historical" works, therefore, the situation is the direct opposite of what is true for *scholarly* historical works. In the latter, the purely intentional objectivities are matched, in accordance with their content, with corresponding real objects and are identified with them; as a result they become—as we have put it—entirely transparent, so that the meaning intentions strike directly what is real, and what is purely intentional disappears from view. In the literary work, on the contrary, the purely intentional object—being supposedly "real"—appears in the foreground and attempts, as it were, to conceal the corresponding, real, Represented object by passing itself off for it.

Quite obviously, the manner in which the work is conceived determines whether the function of Representation performed by the represented objectivities is truly apprehended. If the reader's understanding of the work is in accordance with its intrinsic essence, then, despite the tendency of the Representing object to replace that which is represented, to pass itself off for it, the *complete* concealment of the Represented object never occurs. There always remains a reference to that which is Represented; and that which passes for another object is always coapprehended in its inauthenticity, in its "mere representation of another," as long, of course, as the reader does not consider (falsely) that the quasi-judgmental assertive propositions are genuine judgments and does not turn a work of *belles lettres* into a factual account or a scientific work.

There is no doubt that represented objectivities do not perform their function of reproduction and Representation in every literary work. If one asserts the contrary, it is true only if something else is meant by "representation." In that case, one usually means that, in virtue of their content, represented objectivities are in some respect *similar* [44] to determinate real objects known to the author or the reader from experience. This similarity is then frequently interpreted by the reader in the sense of a repro-

44. On the difference between "being similar" and "being an image," see Husserl, *Logical Investigations*, Vol. II, Sixth Investigation.

duction function. In effect, the reader frequently approaches the reading of a work with the expectation that the author will "tell" him something interesting from the sphere of his experiences. He frequently searches in the literary work for objectivities and situations that are similar to those he knows from his own life, and he considers the work to be "true" if he in fact finds such objectivities in the work. By the same token, the naïve tendency of the reader to judge [45] the work from the point of view of "truth" and "untruth" leads to the reading of reproduction and even Representation functions into the object stratum. This sort of thing, however, is occasioned by inappropriate readings and has very little to do with the real structure of the given work itself.

§ 38. Spots of indeterminacy of represented objectivities

IT IS NOW TIME to discuss an essential property of represented objectivities which distinguishes them radically from real objects. We have come across two special instances of this property in our discussion of represented space and represented time. It appears with particular clarity wherever the represented objectivities are, in accordance with their content, of the nature of real objects, and it arises from the fact that these objectivities are projected by a *finite* number of meaning units of different degree.

The essential nature of every real object contains, among others, the following [formal characteristics]: (1) every real object is *unequivocally, universally* (i.e., in *every* respect) *determined.* Unequivocal, universal determination means that in its total essence [*Sosein*] a real object cannot have any spots where in itself it would not be totally determined, i.e., either by A or by non-A, and indeed where it would not be so determined that, as long as A was its determination in a given respect, it could not, at the same time, in the same respect, be non-A. To put it briefly: its essence does not show any *spots of indeterminacy.* This is part of the intuitively apprehendable essence of real objects, and it would be absurd to claim the contrary. (2) All determinations

45. Whether and in what sense one can speak in a literary work of art—despite the quasi-judgmental modification of assertive propositions—of "truth" and "untruth" will be seen later (Chap. 10).

of real objects jointly constitute a *primary concrete unity*. Only when they are distinguished from among others by a perceiving subject and are apprehended in themselves are they *intentionally* fetched forth from their primary state of fusion, and only then do they constitute an infinite, i.e., inexhaustible, manifold. The series of cognitive operations in which the individual determinations of one and the same real object are successively apprehended is essentially limitless: however many determinations of a given object are apprehended up to a given moment, there are *always* other determinations still to be apprehended. As a result, in primary cognition, which occurs in a finite manifold of actions, we can never *know* how a given real object is determined in *every* respect; the great majority of its properties is always concealed from us. However, this does not mean that in itself it is not unequivocally, universally determined; it merely means that in this kind of cognition, which proceeds along the path of apprehending the object's individual determinants, it is possible, in accord with the object's essence, to apprehend it in a finite series of cognitive operations only *inadequately*. (3) Every real object is *absolutely individual*, i.e., if the determination A is to pertain to it at all, it must be individual. This signifies two things: (I) It is not at all impossible for a determination B, which with respect to its quiddity is a concretization of a "common," general, ideal essence, to pertain to it; if B, however, is to pertain to a real object, the essence which comes into question must be "individuated." For example: if a real object is "colored," this "state of being colored" is such that any number of real objects can be "colored." The essence "color" is itself a general, generic essence, but in the individual real object it appears—as Husserl would say—only as its individuation. (II) No real object can contain such a general (individuated) determination unless, at the same time, one of the *lowest* differentiae (the "eidetic singularities" of Husserl's terminology) of the "genus" in question is concreticized in it. E.g., if a given real object, in a given time, is "colored," then the color quality is also unequivocally determined and is no longer differentiable. Thus, by its very nature it is impossible for a real object to be "colored" without being either "red" of a very specific shade or "yellow" (likewise in a very specific shade), etc. Moreover, this applies to *every* general determination which at any given moment of time may actually pertain to it.[46]

46. If we put so much emphasis on all of this, it is not only to show the contrast between real and represented objectivities but also because, in various contemporary philosophical works with an idealistic tendency,

In all three of these respects, the situation is fundamentally different in the case of objectivities represented in a literary work and, in general, in the case of all purely intentional objectivities. This difference, however, applies only to their content. In a literary work they are intentionally projected in a twofold manner: by nominal expressions and by entire sentences, in which the latter develop determinate states of affairs in which objectivities are represented and constituted. Completion of each state of affairs leads—as we have shown previously—to the constitution of an absolute or relative determination of the object of the subject [of the sentence], or of objectivities partaking in the given state of affairs. If the determinations of represented objectivities were to have the basis of their constitution solely in the completed states of affairs, their number in each literary work, which contains a finite number of sentences,[47] would likewise have to be *finite*. Yet represented objectivities are also projected by nominal expressions appearing in sentences. Consequently, it seems possible that—according to their content—an infinite manifold of determinations would pertain to them. This is all the more probable since, by virtue of their formal content, nominal expressions project their objects as primary units. Undoubtedly, the *form* of a nominally projected object is the form of a primary concrete unit which potentially contains an infinite manifold of essence determinations. But in the case of represented objectivities, this form is only a schema which—in contrast to the form of real or, more generally, ontically autonomous objects—can *never* be *entirely* filled by material determinations. For in the case of simple nominal expressions, e.g., "table," "man," etc., the appertaining intentional object is projected explicitly and actually with respect to its material makeup only in *one* moment of its constitutive nature, so that, e.g., the indispensable material determinations ap-

---

the opposite has been asserted of real objectivities and *eo ipso* the way has been opened to reducing real objects to purely intentional objectivities (see Husserl, *Ideen*, p. 49). Whether the existential acceptance of a real object thus constructed is at all valid is an epistemological question; its solution, however, presupposes a formal-ontological distinction concerning the formal structure of the real objectivity. Our statements here are to be understood only in the sense of a formal-ontological assertion. In this regard, see our arguments in "Bemerkungen zum Problem Idealismus-Realismus," *Festschrift, Edmund Husserl zum 70. Geburtstag gewidmet* (Halle, 1929).

47. Every factually existing literary work contains a limited number of sentences. Whether this is essentially necessary, however, is something we do not want to investigate here.

pertaining to mankind are already cointended only implicitly and potentially. If an individual object is called "man," is intentionally projected in this naming, and is materially determined as such, then all of its (innumerable) properties are still not positively, unequivocally determined thereby. Most of them are cointended by the potential stock of the nominal word meaning only as *some* of the determinations from the range of possible instances of a given type; at the same time, however, they are not unequivocally established in their quiddity. For this reason they are *altogether absent in their concrete quiddity* in the given purely intentional objects. And precisely because this object is simultaneously formally intended as a concrete unit containing an infinite number of fused determinations and, consequently, intentionally created as such, "spots of indeterminacy" arise within it, indeed an infinitely great number of them. These spots of indeterminacy in principle cannot be entirely removed by any finite enrichment of the content of a nominal expression. If, instead of simply "man," we say "an old, experienced man," we do remove, by the addition of these attributive expressions, certain spots of indeterminacy; but an infinite number still remains to be removed. They would disappear only in an infinite series of determinations. If, e.g., a story begins with the sentence: "An old man was sitting at a table," etc., it is clear that the represented "table" is indeed a "table" and not, for example, a "chair"; but whether it is made of wood or iron, is four-legged or three-legged, etc., is left quite unsaid and therefore—this being a purely intentional object—*not determined*. The material of its composition is altogether unqualified, although it must be some material. Thus, in the given object, its qualification is *totally absent*: there is an "empty" spot here, a "spot of indeterminacy." As we have said, such empty spots are impossible in the case of a real object. At most, the material may, for example, be unknown.[48] Here, where the purely intentional object contains in its content only those moments which have the basis of their projection and therefore also their existence in the full word meaning, the ontic

48. This was written at a time when Heisenberg's uncertainty principle of quantum mechanics, which was later to be so famous, was quite unknown. As is well known, this principle arises not from the finiteness of the number of physical propositions but from the principles of quantum mechanics themselves, especially given the attitude of modern physics of accepting as real only what is determined by physical propositions. It is still to be demonstrated in what sense this principle is related to the "spots of indeterminacy" in purely intentional objects.

basis of the material qualification is lacking in our example precisely as long as this qualification is not projected by a special meaning element.

Thus, in its content, the represented object is not universally, unequivocally determined, nor is the number of unequivocally specified determinants that are positively assigned to it, and are also only corepresented, infinite: only a formal schema of infinitely many spots of determinacy is projected, but almost all remain unfilled.[49]

In the content of the represented object, however, "spots of indeterminacy" are present for yet another reason, which is connected with the individuality of the real object. For the object which is only intended as real differs from the genuinely real one also with respect to individuality. Indeed, again by virtue of the corresponding moment of the formal content of a nominal word meaning, it is intended as "individual," and, in order to mark this, it is at times even given a proper name. But this in itself is not enough to cause every "general" determination that is assigned to it also to have a corresponding "individual" determination (a determination which is the concretization of an "eidetic singularity") that is coordinated to the "general" one. The material content of a nominal word meaning cannot in general effect this. The majority of nominal expressions used by us are *general* names. In descriptions of things we are satisfied with such particulars as, e.g., an "oak" chair or a "red" ball, etc. The precise specification of, e.g., the shade of red is very troublesome and frequently quite irrelevant both for us and for the context of the literary work. This is usually true when general nominal expressions are used; but it is because of this that the "individual" determinations of the given represented object remain indeterminate. Undoubtedly, they are "some" of the determinations from the range of variables of a "general" determination. And it is precisely the "variables" [50] in the material content of a given nominal expression which intentionally project these "some" determinations of a particular type. But exactly *which* ones is something

49. Despite his over-all psychologism and a considerable faultiness in his analysis of language, T. A. Meyer sees quite clearly (and indeed stresses) that units of meaning of various degree can determine only such "fragments" of reality—only a "selection" of objective features, as he puts it (*Das Stilgesetz*, pp. 14, 23, 42, and passim). On the other hand, Meyer was not conscious of the peculiar structure of objectivities represented in a literary work, nor did he consciously make a distinction between the individual strata of the work.
50. See our earlier arguments in Chap. 5, § 15, pp. 63 ff.

that remains entirely open. And only a supplementary nominal word meaning or a projected state of affairs can determine it more closely. Thus again, a spot of indeterminacy is contained in the content of the represented object, even though it is of a different type than the one discussed above. The basis of its presence, on the other hand, lies in a different property of the meaning stratum of a literary work.

In consequence: the represented object that is "real" according to its content is not in the strict sense of the term a universally, quite unequivocally determined individual that constitutes a primary unity; rather, it is only a *schematic* formation with spots of indeterminacy of various kinds and with an infinite number of determinations positively assigned to it, even though formally it is projected as a fully determinate individual and is called upon to simulate such an individual. This schematic structure of represented objects cannot be removed in any finite literary work, even though in the course of the work new spots of indeterminacy may continually be filled out and hence removed through the completion of newer, positively projected properties. We can say that, with regard to the determination of the objectivities represented within it, every literary work is in principle incomplete and always in need of further supplementation; in terms of the text, however, this supplementation can never be completed.[51]

The situations discussed above constitute a feature of the literarily represented world which makes it radically different from every real as well as every ideal ontically autonomous object. At the same time, they constitute the basis and possibility for what we shall later, in a closer analysis, call the "life" of a literary work.[52] This feature is also something which precludes a strictly accurate realization—though in no sense exceeding the textually established realization—of the represented world—for example, in the stage play.

And yet—one might counter—while reading a work we are not conscious of any "gaps," of any "spots of indeterminacy," in the represented objects. These objects appear in our aesthetic apprehension just as if, in terms of what was discussed above, they were real objects, the only difference being that—as we know—they are "merely phantasized." We do not want to contradict this

51. If we note that every scientific work is also a "literary work" of a particular kind, this has very important consequences for the theory of science.
52. See below, Chap. 13.

fact at all. Yet it does not alter anything in our assertions. On the contrary. It is quite obvious, in our conception, that we are not conscious of the spots of indeterminacy. This is because, first —figuratively speaking—represented objects are visible to us only from that aspect which is positively determined by the units of meaning. Only a supplementary reflection concerning the constitutive conditions of represented objects, as well as the fact that some questions concerning their individual determinations are in principle unanswerable,[53] allows us to become conscious of the presence of the spots of indeterminacy. Second, however, some of the spots of indeterminacy are concealed by aspects held in readiness which are predetermined by the units of meaning and are actualized by the reader as he reads.[54] And, finally, a third factor working in this direction is the fact that, during his reading and his aesthetic apprehension of the work, the reader usually *goes beyond* what is simply presented by the text (or projected by it) and in various respects *completes* the represented objectivities, so that at least some of the spots of indeterminacy are removed and are frequently replaced by determinations that not only are not determined by the text but, what is more, are not in agreement with the positively determined objective moments. In a word, the literary work itself is to be distinguished from its respective concretizations, and not everything that is valid [55] for the concretization of the work is equally valid for the work itself. But the very possibility that one and the same literary work can allow any number of concretizations, which frequently differ significantly from the work itself and also, in their content, differ significantly among themselves, has its basis, among other things, in the schematic structure of the object stratum of a literary work, a structure which allows spots of indeterminacy.

We must still note the following, however: among the spots of indeterminacy one must distinguish between those which can be removed purely on the basis of textual supplementation and those for which this does not occur in the same sense. In the former, the representing states of affairs designate a strictly circumscribed manifold of *possible* completions of the spots of indeterminacy, from which we may choose some in the course of reading if we wish to effect this completion in accordance with

53. Precisely, all the questions that relate to the determinations a represented object would possess if some of its spots of indeterminacy were *removed.*

54. See below, Chap. 8.

55. See below, Chap. 13.

the already established determinations of the represented objects. In the latter, on the other hand, the textually established states of affairs are not sufficient for designating a strictly circumscribed manifold of possible completions. In that case, each "completion" or approximate completion actually effected in this way is fully dependent on the reader's (or in a stage play—the director's) discretion.[56] But in the former, too, the reader is not forced to choose a particular one of the possibilities predetermined by the representing states of affairs. The literary work does not necessarily have to be "consistent" or to be contained within the bounds of what is possible in the actually known world. Both what is "improbable" in terms of a pregiven type of object or situation and what is impossible in a specific ontic sphere can in principle be intentionally projected and represented, even though frequently it cannot be exhibited. At the very least, the results of our investigation of the previously analyzed strata of the literary work in no sense preclude improbable and impossible objects and situations, insofar as it is only a question of the possible *existence* of represented objectivities or of the possibility of their being projected by meaning contents of sentences. In principle, there can be literary works which do not trouble themselves at all with staying within the bounds of a particular type of object; but precisely because of this, they can make a particular aesthetic impression by representing a world that is actually impossible or one that is full of contradictions, going beyond the limits established by the regional essence of reality. We are then dealing with a grotesque dance of impossibilities. To what extent such an "impossible" world can be exhibited, and what aesthetic value qualities and values it affords, are questions that introduce entirely *new* points of view, which without doubt require strictly regulated bounds for the allowable completions of the spots of indeterminacy. Only a special investigation of this, however, could bring out the various details and patterns within a general consideration of possible styles. Here we have to be content with this outline.

On the other hand, a component part of our discussion is the fact, already touched upon, that textual ambiguity or plurisignation produces a duality or multiformity of the intentional correlate. As we have seen, the direct sentence correlate (the purely intentional state of affairs) itself already shows in this case an

56. The very fact that a "director" is possible and indeed indispensable again proves the correctness of our conception.

opalescing duality. Since it performs in the literary work the role of constituting and representing objects, its duality is reflected in what is represented. Naturally, there may still be different cases, depending on the degree and the nature of the given ambiguity. It may happen that the duality of the state of affairs does not split the identity of the represented object but rather attributes to it, as it were, two different properties, though in such a way that neither of them definitively pertains to the object but, instead, both simultaneously claim to pertain to it; consequently, neither of them is capable of fully entering with it into the primary unity of existence. From this there stems a certain tension in the object, a state in which equilibrium is destroyed. The object is inclined, so to speak, to possess both properties; but it cannot do so, since the properties that are to pertain to it mutually repel and attempt to supplant each other. Here, too, we see the phenomenon of opalescence that we have previously tried to describe. Basically, this phenomenon remains even when textual ambiguity goes so far that the identity of the object cannot be retained. Only in this case it is as if two *objects* were pretending for one place in the represented world, and neither of them could really establish itself therein. It may also happen that ambiguity is sustained in a number of sentences with a certain consistency; then this opalescence applies to entire spheres of objects, so that, in a manner of speaking, two different worlds are struggling for supremacy, with neither of them capable of attaining it. Naturally, these are also phenomena which are possible only in the sphere of purely intentional, ontically heteronomous objectivities. As such they are particularly suitable for bringing out the properties of this sphere in contrast to the ontic realms of ontically autonomous objectivities.

Before we proceed to the further properties of the stratum of represented objectivities and to a discussion of their role in a literary work, it will first be useful to analyze in detail the aspects through which these objectivities appear.

8 / The Stratum of Schematized Aspects

§ 39. *Introduction*

WE HAVE INDICATED previously that represented objects can be exhibited by states of affairs but can never really attain intuitive apprehension through them, and that, in a literary work, still another special factor is needed to prepare the ground for the intuitive appearance of represented objectivities. This factor—as we have already mentioned—is constituted by the aspects [1] of represented objectivities. They constitute a special and, as we shall see—precisely because it is a question of a literary work of *art*—a very significant stratum. It is time now to turn to a consideration of them.[2]

If we leave aside here the question of whether those objects that, according to their content, are not of the nature of real objects can also be exhibited in a literary work of art, there is still, above all, the fact that in historically existing literary works of art it is primarily "real" objectivities that have been represented. Hence it is true, at least for these works, that they must reckon with the conditions under which the objectivities that are repre-

---

1. It will soon be shown that we are dealing, not with concrete aspects, but only with certain schemata of these aspects.
2. Throughout this chapter we should be reminded of Lessing's consideration of what he called the "poetic image" in his *Laokoon*. What he condemns is not the presence of schematized aspects in a literary work of art but merely determinate, artistically flawed methods of introducing the intuitive moment into the literary work of art, and he points to the essence of the "poetic image." In this he approaches only that moment of the literary work of art that we are calling here the stratum of schematized aspects.

sented in them, which are "real" in accordance with their content, can become intuitively given. And since the manner in which they are given is attuned to the characteristic features of the *primary* perceptual reality of real objects, we must turn primarily, at least for the major points, to the perceptual modes of appearance of things.

§ 40. *The perceived thing and concrete perceptual aspects*

AMONG THE REAL OBJECTIVITIES that are under consideration here, we can contrast, on the one hand, real things and processes occurring in the "external" world [3] of a given psychic individual and, on the other hand, his "own" psychic experiences, states of mind, and constant traits of character. These differing objectivities are given in very diverse modes of appearance.[4] There is thus a very wide field of phenomena, only a small part of which has been investigated in the phenomenological works that have appeared to date. Since we cannot conduct special investigations of these phenomena here, we must select from among them only what is quite indispensable for our purposes.[5]

First of all, there is the question of external "sensory" perception. From the very complex total stock under consideration, let us direct our attention only at those "aspects" [6] in which the perceived thing attains corporeal self-presentation.

When we visually perceive a red sphere and apprehend it in its corporeally appearing sphericity, we are informed by a corresponding change of attitude that during the perception we are *experiencing* constantly changing, extrapersonal, and yet not ob-

---

3. By which, along with purely physical things, we shall also understand other individuals' bodies and their spiritual states as given in corporeal-expression phenomena.

4. See below, § 43.

5. A special publication must subsequently be devoted to a more detailed substantiation of a series of assertions that we are making in this chapter. For the rest, we refer our readers to the well-known works of Husserl, Schapp, H. Hofmann, H. Conrad-Martius, and O. Becker.

6. Husserl frequently used the expression "aspect" [*Ansicht*] in his Göttingen period. Subsequently he used a number of other expressions, e.g., *Aspekt* and *Abschattung*. I prefer to stay with the old expression. W. Conrad also used it in the article we have cited above, "Der ästhetische Gegenstand," *Zeitschrift für Ästhetik und allgemeine Kunstwissenschaft*, Vols. III (1908) and IV (1909).

jectively given intuitive "aspects" of one and the same sphere.[7] The aspect is not the sphere itself, although the latter appears in it. The sphere—taken precisely as it is perceived—is there in "space"; it is spherical, and hence it also has a side that is quite hidden from the perceiver, and an interior. It is given to us as such. It has—if it exists at all—its own existence, and it is something entirely accidental to it that it is perceived by someone. It suffers no changes due to its being perceived, and it is given to us as something which continues to exist in space after we have closed our eyes and are no longer perceiving it. In contrast, the aspect, or, more precisely, the continuous manifold of aspects that are constantly merging into one another, remains in its existence and essence in continuous reference to "me," the perceiving subject, even though it is not dependent solely upon me and is therefore not purely "subjective." Likewise, it is not an "I"-occurrence in my mind; on the other hand, it is not to be found "in space," at least not the space in which the perceived sphere is. This relativity of the experienced aspect to the perceiving subject shows itself primarily in its essential dependence on the behavior of the subject. It is enough to close one's eyes for the flowing continuum of aspects to be cut short, to be simply reduced to nonexistence. It is enough to stare out into "space" (or, conversely, at something very close) for the aspects to be considerably altered. Finally, to catch an aspect by an appropriate intentional act suffices, at least in some cases, to evoke radical changes in it, which sometimes are so far-reaching that the same thing is no longer seen in the changed aspect. Aspects, therefore, are, so to speak, in continuous contact with the simultaneously effected acts of consciousness of a perceiving subject and are sensitive to a high degree to changes occurring in acts and manifolds of acts. A continuous manifold of aspects is, on the other hand, subject to its own transformation, which is connected to its own particular time structure. The actual content of a present aspect is functionally dependent on past and no longer actual aspects. "The same"—if one may so put it—aspect would be different in various respects if those aspects which actually

7. With regard to the distinction between "objective givenness," "experiencing," and "undergoing," see my paper "Über die Gefahr einer Petitio Principii in der Erkenntnistheorie," *Jahrbuch für Philosophie und phänomenologische Forschung*, Vol. IV (1921). Objective intending and sensory givenness were thoroughly investigated prior to that by H. Conrad-Martius in her work "Zur Ontologie und Erscheinungslehre der realen Aussenwelt," *Jahrbuch für Philosophie und phänomenologische Forschung*, III (1916), 345–542.

preceded it had not done so. This series of dependencies of aspects is different from the series of dependencies occurring among the states of the thing which appears in the aspects in question, though it is not independent of these states.

In their content, too, aspects are very different from the object given by them. For example, the perceived red sphere is spherical, but no aspect in which it appears is itself spherical, nor does it contain sphericity in its content. All it contains—if one may put it incorrectly—is a "red disk," with, of course, an altogether characteristic reference to sphericity. This difference between the content of an aspect and the properties of the corresponding thing will appear even more clearly if we take as an example a ring or a steering wheel, which, among other things, is circular in form: the corresponding aspects show in their contents all possible ellipses, always of course with a special reference to circular form. Or another example: if a sphere is perceptually given as uniformly red, then the "circular disk" appearing in the contents of the corresponding aspects is filled out by various continually merging shades of red, as well as shades of other colors, again of course with an analogous reference to the uniform coloration of the sphere. Parallel railroad tracks running off into the horizon are given to us as such, while we experience an aspect of them in the content of which the given color data very markedly run together, and the like.

The above examples force us at the same time to make an important distinction in elements appearing in the content of an aspect, a distinction which once again indicates the difference between aspects and perceived things. This is the distinction between "fulfilled" and "unfulfilled qualities." E.g., we see a *fully* enclosed and determinate sphere, which has an interior and a side that is hidden. In the corresponding aspect, however, we find only the "anterior" side, the one directly facing us, as well as only a "surface" presented by the given color qualities. No one who is unbiased, however, can doubt that what is given is not an "anterior side" of a sphere that *has no* posterior side and *no* interior but rather a fully determinate sphere and that, therefore, its hidden side is also cogiven. The fact that it is merely *cogiven*, however, is reflected in the corresponding aspects in such a way that the anterior side of the sphere appears in the aspects by means of fulfilled color qualities, while the hidden side of the sphere appears only on the basis of a *special intuitive character* which *indicates* that the sphere possesses a hidden side determined in such a way that, e.g., it also possesses a spherical surface which is red, etc. This special character, which we shall call an "unfulfilled quality," naturally can appear in the content of an aspect only because there are other aspects of the same sphere, aspects which make the side now hidden appear for us, like its "anterior side," in fulfilled color qualities and because the content of each actual aspect is partially specified by the content of the preceding aspects. The transformation of one aspect into appropriate successive ones reflects the transformation of the erstwhile "anterior side" into the now "hidden, posterior side" and leads to the appearance of that character which is not really fulfilled by any quality but which nevertheless indicates a determinate quality (of color, form, etc.). It is precisely for this reason that we call it an "unfulfilled quality." [8] An unfulfilled quality can cause the appearance of a property of a thing that is not precisely determined, e.g., when I see a colored thing without apprehending the precise shade of color of its hidden side. There are, however, also those unfulfilled qualities in the aspect of a thing which bring us fully determinate properties. If, for example, I perceive my desk, which I have known well for many years, it is given to me as one which has on its hidden side an entirely determinable form and an exactly determinate color. I do not "see" this color at the given moment, but its unfulfilled quality is present in the aspect that is experienced by me; hence the hidden side of the desk is cogiven *in its qualitative determinations*. And only because I experience an aspect which conceals within itself an entirely determinate unfulfilled quality is the desk given to me as one that is determined in such and such a manner. As a matter of fact, every perception which cogives a determinate "hidden side" of a thing can be false in this respect. I.e., I can perceive, for example, the same desk from the other side and unexpectedly notice that it now has a large inkstain which was not previously given to me and which therefore was not presented by any unfulfilled quality of the aspect. But it is precisely these instances of disappointment, and the surprise that they occasion, which show most clearly that the respective "hidden side" is truly cogiven by an unfulfilled quality (or a manifold of them). Less surprising are those instances where the originally unfulfilled quality is filled by exactly corresponding color and form qualities when one walks around the thing in question. But these, too, argue for the correctness of this

8. Husserl speaks here of particular "intentional" moments, a terminology that is not convenient for us.

interpretation. And it is precisely the exact determination and the identity of the quality that appears in two different ways in the aspects, and causes the appearance of the same objective property, which compel us to speak of the indicating character of the aspect as a *quality*, even though an "unfulfilled" one. It is something which is phenomenally present and not merely significatively intended.

In every aspect of a thing that is experienced by us there is a whole series of such unfulfilled qualities of various kinds. An unfulfilled quality, however, does not always have to cause the appearance of those determinations of a thing which refer to its hidden side or to its interior. Many properties of the side of the thing that we do see can also appear for us in unfulfilled qualities of an aspect. Thus, for example, the uniform red coloration of a sphere is made to appear in an unfulfilled quality. For in the corresponding aspect there appear fulfilled color data of *various* shades of red which only by virtue of their form and arrangement and by virtue of a characteristic gradation of qualities bring about the constitution of the moment indicating a "uniform red coloration of the sphere." The only way a uniform coloration of a sphere can appear is through an unfulfilled quality. The same holds true for, e.g., the smoothness of paper that is *seen* or the softness of silk that is *seen*, etc., except that, in these cases, there is still tactile perception, which adequately gives the above-named properties of things through fulfilled qualities. The above examples show, at the same time, that both the *degree* and the *kind* of unfulfilledness of a quality can be very different in the content of an aspect. The highest degree of unfulfilledness and indeterminacy appears, for example, in a perception in which a heretofore entirely unknown thing is presented to us. We apprehend it as having a "hidden side" and an "interior" though we are given no further qualification of this side (or of the interior). Between this and the other limit—where a quality is truly fulfilled in an aspect—extends an entire manifold of gradations of fulfilledness and determinacy.

This opens up various problems that are highly significant for the theory of sensory experience. Nevertheless, we must confine ourselves here to the stated issues. The only thing that was indispensable for us was the emphasis that unfulfilled qualities appear in an aspect, since failure to notice these qualities leads to an erroneous conception of the essence of the aspect of a thing.

Aspects that we experience in the course of the experience

of one and the same thing change in various ways, and something which in a previous aspect appeared only in the form of an unfulfilled quality is present in a later one in the form of a fulfilled quality, and vice versa. But fulfilled and unfulfilled qualities are present in *every* aspect of a thing, and in principle it is impossible to have the unfulfilled qualities disappear altogether.[9]

For the sake of simplicity, we have limited ourselves in this discussion to the visual aspects of things. There are, however, various aspects of one and the same thing, e.g., tactile, tonal, etc., in which corresponding properties of things attain their appearance. On closer examination, there are no *purely* visual (or purely tactile, etc.) aspects of things. It is always special syntheses that come about, so that, e.g., in the content of a visual aspect of a thing, various moments arise which cause the appearance of corresponding, originally only tactually given, properties of things; these moments hence also refer to corresponding moments of tactile aspects.

Every visual aspect of a *thing* constitutes a *part* of a homogeneous *total aspect* of the entire *surroundings* that are perceived in the given moment by the subject, and it is primally fused with the remaining elements appearing in the content of this total aspect, even though it is usually clearly distinguished from them. But the *primary* concrete whole constitutes the visual total aspect at any one time. The unity of an aspect of a given object is usually constituted, not by means of a sharp, contoured delineation of its content from the remaining elements of the total aspect, but rather by a common membership of elements contained within it, a common membership which itself is a consequence of both a succession of diverse, quite determinately ordered aspects and the execution of accompanying acts of perception that are correspondingly determined in their content.

9. Closer analyses show that very complex situations still exist here, leading to much deeper strata than that of aspects. The stratum of aspects we are describing here is, so to speak, only the surface, which shows what is occurring in the depths. Here one should have recourse to Husserl's investigations (especially to those in the "Vorlesungen zur Phänomenologie des inneren Zeitbewusstseins" [*The Phenomenology of Internal Time-Consciousness*, trans. James S. Churchill (Bloomington: Indiana University Press, 1964)]). In addition, one should consider the treatise of H. Conrad-Martius, cited above, and some chapters of Becker's work, "Zur phänomenologischen Begründung der Geometrie," *Jahrbuch für Philosophie und phänomenologische Forschung*, Vol. VI (1923), in which he reports on a series of yet unpublished Husserlian investigations [dealing with the so-called constitution of real space].

§ 41. *Schematized aspects*

IN THE PRECEDING SECTION we attempted to show as simply as possible the difference between the perceived thing and the aspects in which it appears. This must suffice for now. However, we must still note the following. A more thorough analysis will show—as Husserl correctly observed and proved—that there is a *strict affiliation* between every perceptually given property of a thing and the manifold of aspects, strictly ordered according to rules, in which the given property appears. And conversely: as soon as we experience a given manifold of aspects, a determinate property of a thing or a determinately qualified thing must be corporeally self-given. To show this in detail and to search for the laws governing it would require very extensive and difficult analyses, which, despite the groundbreaking investigations of Husserl and his students, are still not completed. Here we are only interested in the changed sense—compared with previous usage—of the term "aspect" that comes into question when one establishes such affiliations and laws and their patterns. If we attempt to understand precisely Husserl's assertions, stated above, we will see that what is in question here are not aspects that are experienced once and then lost for all time but certain *idealizations,* which are, so to speak, a *skeleton,* a *schema,* of concrete, flowing, transitory aspects. There are, in fact, *no* two concrete aspects of the same thing, perceived from the same side, experienced *successively* by one and the same conscious subject, which would be *completely similar in every respect.*[10] Both their fully concrete contents and the manner in which they are experienced must always differ in varying degree. Meanwhile, when speaking of a regular affiliation of a given manifold of aspects to a given property of a thing, we assume the repeatability of the aspects in question. Thus it is clear that (1) if this regular affiliation is actually to exist, then what is at issue are not aspects taken in their full concreteness but only certain schemata, contained within them but still forming only

10. We can only assert this here. The full universality and justification of this assertion arise only from the essential structure of concretely experienced aspects which in their foundations reach into the depths of the primary constituting sense data (in Husserl's sense) as well as into the manifold connections and dependencies that exist between the aspects and the simultaneously experienced acts of consciousness.

a skeleton of them, which may remain as such despite the various differences that occur in the contents of the concrete aspects and in the manner of their experiencing; and (2) there really exists the idea of such schemata or schematized aspects. If we assume this, it can be claimed that every moment of a thing determines a manifold of schematized aspects which constitute the skeleton of the concrete aspects in which it appears. By "schematized aspect," therefore, one should understand only the totality of those moments of the content of a concrete aspect whose presence in it is a sufficient and indispensable condition for the primary self-givenness of an object or, more precisely, for the *objective* properties of a thing. And in fact, not every moment of the content of an aspect and not every difference in the manner of its experiencing performs a differentiating role in the presentation of objective properties (existing in themselves and pertaining to the given object itself) of a perceived thing. In other words, it is possible for two aspects, experienced in different moments of time and differing in both their content and the manner of their experiencing, to cause, nonetheless, the primary appearance of *one and the same* property of a thing (or one and the same object in the same combination of unaltered properties), provided that these two aspects contain only concretizations of the same schematized aspect. Naturally, connected with this is the fact that indeed, in every concrete aspect, all elements of its content form a fused unity in which each element is colored by the remaining ones, though a change of this coloration has no influence on the identity of at least some of the elements appearing in the aspect's content. Consequently, these elements are relatively independent of the remaining elements appearing in the aspect, and hence they may maintain themselves in a continuous manifold of changing aspects. Their totality is thus repeatable in various, even temporally discrete, aspects and constitutes what we have called above a "schematized" aspect. The remaining elements of a concrete aspect are thereby conceived, not as being absent, but only as being *variable* within those limits in which they can be variable if the continuing, relatively independent elements are still to be maintained. Only a concrete aspect can be experienced, of course. But a determinate object in a determinate manifold of corresponding properties prescribes only a determinate manifold (or manifold of manifolds) of *schematized* aspects in which it can be directly given as it itself and as one that is determined in a particular way. The question of the further filling-out of these schemata in given individual instances in part no longer depends on the object itself and on the selection of its properties but rather on various factors of a subjective nature that change from case to case.

§ 42. Schematized aspects in a literary work

SCHEMATIZED ASPECTS, which are neither concrete nor at all psychic, belong to the structure of a literary work as a separate stratum. They can appear in it only as schematized. This is because they are not generated by the experience of any psychic individual but instead have the basis of their determination and, in a certain sense, their potential existence in the states of affairs projected by the sentences or in the objects represented by means of the states of affairs. It is not only this theoretical reason, however, that speaks for the fact that in a literary work only schematized aspects can appear, although in the reading they allow of various actualized aspects—though within predetermined limits. We can convince ourselves of this practically, so to speak.[11] It is frequently the case that represented objects are supposed to portray determinate real objectivities. For example, the story in Romain Rolland's novel L'Ame enchantée "takes place"—as we usually say—in Paris. Various streets of the French capital are represented here. Let us assume that a given reader of this novel does not know Paris from his own experience. In reading, he naturally actualizes, among other things, the novel's predetermined aspects of the given streets. However, since he has never concretely experienced these streets in primary perception, their actualization never succeeds in such a way that the contents of the aspects actualized by him could be similar in detail to the aspects he would have experienced had he once really seen the streets. Predetermined schemata of as-

---

11. T. A. Meyer does not make use of the concept of the aspect, in particular the schematized aspect. He speaks only of "sensory features," "internal perception images," etc. But it seems to me very probable that what he has in mind here are the aspects of sensorially perceptible things. In particular, Meyer sees quite clearly that here it can be a question only of schematized formations (see Das Stilgesetz der Poesie [Leipzig, 1901], pp. 45, 139n, 191, 196, etc.). In this fact, however (which, correctly, he closely relates to the essence of language), he believes that he has found an adequate argument against the appearance of something "intuitive" in the literary work. I cannot agree with him in this.

pects are always being completed and filled out as one reads by various details which actually do not belong to them and which the reader draws from the contents of other, formerly experienced concrete aspects. To a certain degree this also happens when represented objects engaged in a function of reproduction refer to a prototype known to the reader from his direct experience, since aspects of the same object which are experienced by various psychic individuals must in principle differ in various respects. Thus it is impossible for the reader to actualize with complete precision the same aspects that the author wanted to designate through the structure of the work. Here we see once again that a literary work is a *schematic* formation. In order to see this, however, it is necessary to apprehend the work in its schematized nature and not confuse it with the individual concretizations that arise in individual readings.

Speaking purely theoretically, to the represented objects "belong" *all* the schematized aspects in which these objects may generally be given. But then this "belonging" signifies only *a coordination*, arising on the basis of a strict predetermination, between *possible* schematized aspects and corresponding represented objectivities. For such merely coordinated aspects to be actualized, however, other factors, lying beyond represented objects, are necessary.[12] Some of these factors can be evoked by various properties of the literary work itself; on the other hand, others inhere in the experiencing psychic individual, so that schematic aspects can be concretized and actualized only by the reader (or by the author). If a literary work is so constructed that the former factors of aspect actualization are present in at least some of its parts, the latter aspects, though they are not yet actualized (since an experiencing individual is still indispensable for this), are, so to speak, *prepared* for this actualization, so that they are forced upon the reader in the event of a reading. We are saying that here the schematized aspects are not merely coordinated to the represented objectivities but are at the same time "held in readiness." Thus, to *every* literary work there belong schematized aspects that are merely coordinated to represented objectivities, but only *some* literary works contain (at least in some of their parts) aspects that are held in readiness.

The factors which hold aspects ready in a literary work inhere in part in some of the properties of intentional sentence

---

12. We shall soon discuss what these factors are based on.

correlates, discussed above. We have distinguished between states of affairs in which the essence of the object is represented and those in which its "thus-appearance" is represented. On the other hand, we have contrasted the exhibiting and the simple representation of an object. Exhibiting, and in particular exhibiting the thus-appearance of an object, also brings with it a holding-in-readiness [*Parathaltung*] of the aspect or manifold of aspects belonging to the represented object. Schematized aspects that are held in readiness pass from the state of mere possibility, in which they find themselves by virtue of a simple coordination with represented objectivities, into a mode of a certain actuality, which, however, is not the actuality of a concretely experienced aspect, nor is it simple potentiality.[13] To a holding-in-readiness of aspects contribute, on the other hand, various "images," "metaphors," "similes," etc.,[14] of poetic language in which objectivities that are totally *different* from the ones that were just represented are projected, and indeed are projected merely to make objects that are to be represented appear in corresponding held-in-readiness aspects. It is not only appropriately selected intentional meaning and sentence correlates (and, primarily, appropriate meaning contents of sentences) that contribute to the holding-in-readiness of aspects; word sounds and phonetic formations of a higher order are also especially suited to it.[15] We have already referred to this when speaking of the role played by the stratum of phonetic formations in the literary work. If appropriate aspects are to be held in readiness by the literary work of art and imposed on the reader in the reading, then the sound stratum must above all contain

13. It is very difficult in general—and in particular within the framework of our study—to provide a precise conceptual determination for this and to correspondingly elucidate it, since to this end a detailed analysis of the various possible ontic modes and existential characters would be required—an analysis which, to my knowledge, no one has yet seriously attempted, let alone performed. At any rate, it is clear that the primitive and flat distinctions between existence and nonexistence, actuality and potentiality, etc., with which one is usually satisfied cannot do justice to the great manifold of existing differences. Primitive dialectical arguments can, of course, only obfuscate the situation. See, in this regard, my book *Der Streit um die Existenz der Welt*, Vol. I (Tübingen, 1965) (first published in Polish in 1947), where the various possible ontic modes are set forth and conceptually determined. For a short résumé, see the *Acts of the Tenth International Congress for Philosophy, Amsterdam, 1948.*
    14. Here again we have a broad field for special investigations.
    15. In this regard, see T. A. Meyer's arguments on the "sensory tone" of words and its meaning in literary works (*Das Stilgesetz der Poesie*, pp. 160 ff., 171).

words which not merely are drawn from the vocabulary of the living language (from an abstract terminology) but also show, in their word sound, either a similarity to the corresponding objectivities (onomatopoetic expressions), or conceal "manifestation qualities," [16] or, finally, evoke, by constant usage in determinate, concrete life-situations, fixed associations with aspects of various kinds. Appropriately selected phonetic formations of a higher order, e.g., various speech melodies, rhythm, etc., also work in the same direction. The concurrence of all these factors brings about the fact that aspects are formed less schematically and more concretely than would be possible with the use of words that are already "dead" or with the projection of inappropriate (e.g., purely abstractly determined) states of affairs. This "making it more concrete" also contributes to what we have called the "holding in readiness" of aspects.

To avoid misunderstanding, let us stress one more thing: it would be entirely false to believe that represented objectivities appear in full vividness when aspects belonging to them are *themselves described* in the text of a literary work. In fact, it is quite the opposite. If the aspects were described, then what is represented in the work would be, not the objectivity that is to appear in them, but the aspects themselves (which is of course not precluded), and the corresponding object would either totally disappear from the realm of the given work or would belong to the work only as something that is indirectly represented. In any case, it could not appear through the aspects *described* in the work. It is the *objects*, their vicissitudes, their "thus-appearance," objective situations, etc., which must be represented or described. Aspects which belong to them and effect their appearance can only be held in readiness, in the manner already indicated, if they are at all to perform their function of effecting the appearance [of objects] or if, in the reading, they are to be evoked only in such a way that they are not given to the reader thematically but are only experienced by him and, in this state of being experienced, effect the appearance of the corresponding object.

In the holding-in-readiness and determination of aspects, two circumstances play a particularly important role for the structure and the aesthetic apprehension of the literary work. With the means we have mentioned, it is impossible to hold in readiness *all* the manifolds and, simultaneously, entire *continua* of aspects

16. See above, p. 55.

which, according to their meaning, belong as possibilities to represented objectivities. The very fact that represented objectivities necessarily contain spots of indeterminacy produces the situation that only *that* manifold of aspects can be predetermined which belongs to the *explicitly* represented side of the objectivities. To be sure, there frequently occurs here the previously discussed phenomenon of the spots of indeterminacy being concealed by aspects that are held in readiness (and possibly actualized in reading), since these aspects are held in readiness in a different manner, e.g., by appropriate phonetic structures. But these structures are not capable of removing the gaps in the manifolds of aspects. Moreover, it is impossible to represent objects solely in those states of affairs that will exhibit them and thus prepare their appearance in manifolds of aspects. In connection with this, the number of gaps in the aspect manifolds is increased. It is always only a few, and frequently not directly connected, aspects that are held in readiness, so that, as one reads, objects appear vividly only from time to time in momentarily actualized aspects. A certain *stabilization* of held-in-readiness aspects is connected with this; and though it is not necessary for every work and for every part of a work, it is very frequently present. By stabilization of an aspect we mean the fact that both the fulfilled and the unfulfilled qualities in the content of an aspect appear as something unchanging or only imperceptibly changing. The situation is entirely different with respect to concrete perceptual aspects. Here the aspects are in permanent flux and in continuous transformation into one another, indeed even when there occur—to use a Husserlian term —"jumps" in the individual qualities of their contents. To put it more precisely, sensory data,[17] which constitute the substructure of an aspect and which as such normally do not enter our consciousness during our experiencing of an aspect, are changing constantly and to a much greater degree than the fulfilled and unfulfilled qualities of the aspect content which directly present the object.[18] But the latter are also apprehended in

17. With regard to sensory data, see Husserl's *Ideen zu einer reinen Phänomenologie* (Halle, 1913), passim; English translation by W. R. Boyce Gibson, *Ideas: General Introduction to Pure Phenomenology* (New York: Macmillan, 1931).

18. Bergson would say here that every aspect constantly vibrates in its depths and is crystallized on its surface. In his analysis of external perception (see *Matière et mémoire* [Paris, 1896], Chap. 1) he undoubtedly had in mind, in one of the two systems of "images" he was comparing, the sphere of perceptually experienced aspects. He did not succeed,

continuous change and are continuously being transformed, one into another. In fact, there are continuous transitions, not only between simultaneously experienced aspects of different objects, but also between aspects that cause the appearance of one and the same object and are experienced *successively* by the perceiving subject. However, since the (schematized) aspects of a literary work are held in readiness by incompletely determined objects or by noncontinuous manifolds of exhibiting states of affairs, they are units separated from each other *by jumps*. Along with the continuity of their transitions, the mobility of their content is also lost to a great degree. To overcome this stiffness and to get the whole started again, there is first the need of the reader's help and the unfolding operation of reading. But the jumpiness of the succession of aspects can never be entirely removed. Even when it is overcome to a certain degree, that which causes this overcoming, and the overcoming itself, do not belong to the literary work itself but to one of its concretizations, which in their essence relate to a given reading and a given reader.[19]

The second fact which must now be taken into consideration constitutes, to be sure, only a property of a literary work's concretization, but it does follow from its essential structure; i.e., aspects that are imposed on the reader in the reading can never be actualized as genuine perceptual aspects but can be actualized only within an imaginational modification, even though in the work itself they are commonly determined as being perceptual. They are, however, suggested to the reader only by artistic means, and they belong not to truly real, but to purely intentional, objectivities, which, according to their content, are quasi-real. Imaginationally actualized aspects have for their substructure only a quasi-sensory material which, despite its actuality, is essentially different from genuine sensory data. Consequently, an imaginationally actualized aspect can never have, among other things, the vividness and vitality of a perceptual one. Nor does it usually possess the sharpness and precision of the latter. In addition, this kind of aspect actualization is marked by a characteristically *pulsating* mode of experiencing: as a result, a reader can never experience an entire continuum of aspects with equal vividness and sharpness. There are always phases, in which actualized aspects disappear altogether and then

however, in descriptively apprehending it in a pure manner or in correctly determining its relationship to perceived things.
  19. See Chap. 13.

suddenly again come to light. Finally, perceptual aspects differ from imaginational ones in the manner in which the aspect of an attentively perceived thing is fused with aspects of our total surroundings. In perception the latter are indeed much more blurred than the central segment, which presents to us the thematically perceived object; but they do effect the appearance of *things*.[20] As a result, a leap or a continuous transition of the intention from the object just perceived to the one lying in the background is possible at every moment, and the corresponding aspects are naturally altered in various respects. While keeping one's gaze on the object of perception, one may also shoot a glance at objects lying in the background and apprehend them precisely as background objects. In this case, too, the background aspects undergo a change, but the *nature* of the aspect is maintained. They are still background aspects which co-produce for us the appearance of things, the same things, in fact, which would be given thematically in the event of an appropriate turning of attention to them. All of this is *lacking* in the imaginational actualization of aspects of things. Here the actualized aspect emerges from an undifferentiated murky cloud (this, of course, is only a metaphor) that in its essence is of a different nature than the reactualized aspect itself. Among other things, it is not capable of imaginationally presenting or representing any *thing* at all. For this reason, things appearing imaginationally are necessarily encompassed by nonobjective surroundings, which do not belong to the apparent objective world in question at all and which *conceal* the objective surroundings belonging to the imaginationally appearing object. That which appears imaginationally can naturally be an entire manifold of objects merging into one "region." But even then the murky, cloudlike surrounding band is present. This emergence from an essentially heterogeneous medium is especially characteristic for the mode of appearance of objects in the reading of a literary work. This is also a point in which the literary work itself differs essentially from its concretizations. Since, as we have already noted, aspects that are predetermined and held in readiness in the literary work itself are generally designated as perceptual objects. Only the special conditions of the actualization of these aspects in the reading bring about the modifications discussed above.

Thus we have described the nature of living access to the

20. See Husserl, *Ideen*, p. 62.

objectivities represented in a literary work. In this nature there is, on the one hand, a boundary that we cannot cross when we are reading, i.e., we can never perceptually apprehend represented objects; on the other hand, the existence of this boundary shows us the way in which it can be crossed, though no longer in a *purely* literary work but in one of its special modifications, where some of its strata are "realized" to a certain degree. There are literary works that are particularly predisposed to such "realization," i.e., "dramatic" works. The mode of their "realization" is theatrical performance. We will have occasion to discuss it in § 57.

§ 43.   *"Internal aspects" of one's own psychic processes and character traits as elements of a literary work*

UP TO NOW we have confined ourselves to aspects in which inanimate things and their properties appear. Yet there are also aspects of various other objectivities, which not only appear in literary works but in fact play particularly important roles in some of them. A special case of this is, first of all, aspects in which we are given living foreign *bodies*. They undoubtedly have for a substratum contents of aspects in which mere physical bodies appear. This substratum, however, does not exhaust the content of an aspect of a living body; moreover, it must have a particular content, since not every conceivable thing has properties that are characteristic of a living body. Functioning thus as a substratum, it undergoes essential modifications, since at least some of the fulfilled or unfulfilled qualities appearing in its content enter into the function of referring to other properties already characteristic of the living body as such. Finally, there appear in the content of an aspect of a living body (or of its property) constructed on this substratum totally unique qualities, which cause the appearance of properties characteristic of a (living) body. If, for example, a greenish facial color is given as "unhealthy," or if, in general, a surface color is given as the color of *skin*, if small red spots are perceived as a "rash," etc., then what we are witnessing throughout the corresponding aspects is the appearance of totally unique qualities, which would make no sense in an aspect of a simple physical body.

The form of the content of an aspect becomes much more complex if it effects the appearance of corporeal properties and characteristics as an "expression" of *mental* and *spiritual* processes and properties of a psychic individual. No matter how difficult it is to clarify and to describe these complex facts—especially after the failure of the "inference by analogy theory" and Lipps's theory of empathy—the presence of such aspects can hardly be doubted. The fact of their being held in readiness, as well as their possible actualization, is of the greatest importance for the literary work, and in particular for the literary work of art which deals primarily with psychic and spiritual reality.

Likewise, when we are effecting an "internal" perception and turning to our own character traits, psychic states, and changes in our soul, we apprehend all these objectivities, not "immanently" (as with our own conscious experiences), but always in unique "internal" aspects in which these objectivities *appear*.[21] Here, of course, the word "aspect" has a totally *metaphorical* sense, since, according to its content, an "aspect" which makes our soul [i.e., our psyche] appear in a given determinate state can in no way be compared to the content of "external" aspects. However, if we retain this word for these cases as well, it is not only to have a single term that would permit us to span the entire stratum of the literary work but for purely factual reasons as well. The decisive factor is that (1) that entity in which our own psychic (and possibly also spiritual) properties and states happen to appear is different from these properties and states;[22] (2) it is capable of effecting *self*-presentation of that which is different from it; (3) while engaged in this function, it is *not* given objectively to the conscious subject who is apprehending his psychic properties and states but is only experienced by him. In these three points an "internal aspect" is totally analogous to an aspect of a "sensorially" given thing.[23] A

---

21. With regard to the difference between "internal" and "immanent" perception, see Husserl, *Ideen zu einer reinen Phänomenologie*. See also M. Geiger, "Fragment über den Begriff des Unbewussten und die psychische Realität," *Jahrbuch für Philosophie und phänomenologische Forschung*, Vol. IV (1921), and E. Stein, "Beiträge zur philosophischen Begründung der Psychologie," *Jahrbuch für Philosophie und phänomenologische Forschung*, V (1922), 18 ff.

22. A question that is entirely different and independent of this is whether the sphere of concretely experienced aspects of external and internal perception is itself to be found within the realm of the psychic. We cannot decide this matter here.

23. Naturally, the internal aspect should not be identified with the total stock of internal perception.

different analogy between these two basic kinds of aspects rests on the fact that the *content* of the aspect should be distinguished in both cases from its structural moments, which characterize it as a special objectivity, and this content possesses a stratum structure that is analogous in the two cases. This is not to say that sensory data must necessarily appear in the substructure of an internal aspect. If they are present, however, they are at any rate entirely heterogeneous to those appearing in the substructure of an aspect belonging to external perception. Above all, these are data localized in "my" own body, largely of a kinaesthetic nature; they are also "emotional sensations" (in the Husserlian sense),[24] e.g., pain sensations, sexual sensations, etc.— all of them data that are altogether different from color, tone, touch, or olfactory data. Furthermore, they are data which do not seem to inhere in any part of the body and yet are "bodily," as, for example, a feeling of fatigue, of freshness, etc. The remaining basis of the data goes beyond the purely bodily and is quite varied, depending on which psychic sector is engaged in the excitation and which is absent and on the mode of the excitation itself.[25] The content of an internal aspect depends on the nature and the variety of the established data. But the manner of appearance of these data also plays a significant role here. If, e.g., someone's emotional sensations are wont to appear with great violence and precipitous intensity, it is an indication of his impulsiveness, instability, and the like. Again, it depends on the content of an internal aspect as to which of our states, processes,

24. See *Logical Investigations,* Vol. II, Fifth Investigation, § 15.
25. Internal aspects have, until now, been almost entirely overlooked. One reason for this is that nineteenth-century psychology, under the influence of English empiricism, considered under "psychic" only conscious experiences and rejected everything not experienced as being "metaphysical construction." As a result, the internal aspects that are directly fused with experience have also lost the function of "bringing to appearance" psychic states and character features and cannot be recognized as aspects. It is only the investigations performed by the phenomenologists (Pfänder, Scheler, Geiger, E. Stein), as well as some tendencies in psychoanalysis, which have again opened the way for studying what is psychic in the true sense. A second reason for overlooking internal aspects stems from the fact that it is truly difficult to perceive and describe them in themselves and in their function. For in both simple awareness and internal perception of psychic events, internal aspects, as well as the corresponding sensory material—in correspondence with their particular essence—are only experienced, never objectively apprehended in themselves; this makes their analysis essentially difficult. A very special attitude is necessary for such an analysis, one which would bring to our attention both the sensory substructure of the aspect as well as the aspect itself. Internal aspects are apprehended more easily in a clear recollection.

and character traits appear in internal perception. On the other hand, one and the same character trait can appear in various internal aspects having a heterogeneous sensory substructure. The same brutality, for example, can manifest itself in either an outburst of anger or sexual excitement, and totally different aspects, and the sensory data establishing them, are present in the two cases.

There are, of course, psychic states (or processes), as well as character traits, that appear in such internal aspects but have no sensory substructure. If any internal sensations are experienced, they constitute only a "secondary phenomenon" and do not partake in the function of presenting psychic facts. If, for example, any of my purely spiritual faculties are made manifest to me in one or another aspect, the internal sensations that may be potentially present perform no essential role in the process. On the contrary, it is in the manner of effecting subjective operations or acts that this spiritual faculty is manifested. If I have difficulty in making up my mind, then this is a characteristically hesitant way of deciding, one in which this personal attribute becomes apparent to me. Here, experiential situations —the decision to be taken, my position with regard to myself and to what is to be decided—can all be quite different. And it is precisely this diversity which conditions the fact that one and the same irresoluteness confronts me in various aspects. It is this that is identical and apparent, and it is the various experiential situations which form the aspects in which it manifests itself.

In addition to the differences between internal aspects that we have already indicated, there remain various modifications stemming from the different modes of internal perception: i.e., whether the given psychical state is precisely the main subject of the perception or whether it is grasped only peripherally, whether it is more or less attentive and clear, etc. A special mode of appearance of the psychic (and therefore also a special type of internal aspect) occurs when no internal perception exists as a special reflective act of consciousness and, in spite of this, we simply become aware of the psychic processes that are just then developing. A process or a psychic state arouses us here in a certain way and thereby becomes apparent. The completion of an internal perception of this state can be a sequel of this arousal only if this completion is, for some reason, of interest to us. It may also happen, however, that at the moment we become aware of a psychic state, without yet having perceived it, we sidestep the state that is arousing us and even to a certain degree repress it into our unconscious (cf. Freud). This again implies other modes of appearance of psychic processes.

All of this is intended to provide sketchy examples to support our contention that psychic occurrences and objectivities also appear in manifolds of aspects. Appropriately schematized internal aspects enter into a literary work just as much as "external" aspects do. The poet's great art consists precisely of not *merely speaking* about the psychic states and character traits of his "heroes" but representing them in such states of affairs that the experiential situations and aspects in which they manifest the given psychic realities are determined and imposed in their presentation function upon the reader. If this mode of representation is lacking, if the appropriate internal aspects are not held in readiness, and if the given psychic individual is also not shown in his "external" mode of behavior, then one has to deal with lifeless, "paper" figures.[26]

26. We feel that through our consideration of schematized aspects in literary works we have, by placing it on a new basis, solved the old problem, frequently considered since the time of Lessing, of the participation of intuitive elements in literary works. As is well known, T. A. Meyer (see *Das Stilgesetz der Poesie*) correctly challenged the extravagances of "intuitive aestheticians" (in particular Vischer's position) and came out very strongly against the presence of intuitive elements in literary works. At the same time, however, he collects, in §§ IX and X of his interesting work, rich material that not only argues for the presence of schematized aspects (in our sense) in literary works but can also serve as a substantiation of our conception that schematized aspects can be held in readiness by, among other things, the various phonetic formations and characters. He then attempts to remove this inconsistency by his theory of the "illusion of the uniform image" (*ibid.*, pp. 186 ff., 22). All of these difficulties and false constructions stem from the fact that Meyer has not fully analyzed the literary work in its stratified structure and its polyphony, nor has he contrasted it to its concretizations and to the subjective experiences of the reader. Meyer's interesting book is perhaps the best example of how the psychologistic tendency can mislead even an outstanding author.

9 / The Role of the Stratum of Schematized Aspects in a Literary Work

§ 44. *The differentiation of the basic functions of schematized aspects in a literary work*

THE ROLE WHICH THE STRATUM OF ASPECTS plays in a literary work is twofold: (1) aspects held in readiness enable us to intuitively apprehend represented objects in predetermined types of modes of appearance. At the same time, they gain a certain power over represented objects by influencing their constitution. (2) Aspects have their own properties and constitute their own aesthetic value qualities, which have their own voice in the polyphony of the whole work and which play an essential role in the aesthetic reception of the work.

It is now time to discuss in greater detail what particular modifications and types of these two functions of aspects are possible. This will show how differences in aspects also influence differences between works. Our contention that aspects resonate within the polyphony of a work (and, in particular, in a literary work of *art*) will find therein its substantiation and elucidation. In our discussion we will confine ourselves to a few typical cases.

§ 45. *The determining function of aspects; the influence of aspect variety on the total character of the work* [1]

THE FIRST AND MOST SIGNIFICANT FUNCTION of aspects in a literary work is based on the fact that, through them, repre-

1. Where there is no danger of misunderstanding, we will for the sake of brevity, say "aspect" instead of "schematized aspect."

sented objects can be made to appear in a manner *predetermined* by the work itself. If aspects were totally lacking in a work, represented objects would have to be blankly intended in the reading; they would have to be *thought* in a thoroughly unintuitive manner, provided, of course, that the reader adhered strictly to what was offered by a work thus understood, i.e., as one containing no aspects. Represented objects would then be empty, purely "conceptual" schemata, and one would never have the impression that one was dealing with a unique, live quasi-reality. Concreteness, strict individuality, vitality, corporeality can be brought out only by an actualization of aspects held in readiness. Wherever this concreteness and vitality are of decisive significance—as in a literary work of *art*—aspects held in readiness are altogether indispensable; otherwise the work is more of a dry treatise or chitchat on paper than a work of *art*.[2] One may assume, of course, that, even if aspects were not held in readiness in a work, the reader would actualize, in the course of his reading, various aspects on his own initiative, as it were. But in doing this he would not be bound at all by the work, and it would be entirely a matter of chance as to what aspects were in fact actualized. The fact that he is bound to a high degree, that quite determinate types of aspects are imposed on him, best indicates that they are predetermined and held in readiness in the work itself.

As we have said, however, the role of aspects goes even further. If they were predetermined and held in readiness only by the pure meaning content of sentences (or by corresponding states of affairs), they would merely cause the appearance of represented objectivities but would have no influence on their constitution. Meanwhile, the readiness of aspects is also brought on by various phonetic formations;[3] and it happens, for example, that by using two words identical in meaning but different in word sound *different* aspects can be held in readiness, or one aspect may at one time be *held in readiness* and at another time be only predetermined by the meaning of the word but not imposed on the reader. It may also happen that, by virtue of its word sound, a word may hold in readiness a *different* aspect

2. In this respect, Max Dessoir seems to be of a different opinion. See his *Ästhetik und allgemeine Kunstwissenschaft* (Stuttgart, 1906), pp. 359 ff.

3. That this is possible is best shown by the fact that in music one can "represent"—as musicians say—certain objective situations by means of purely tonal formations; that is, strictly speaking, by these means one can hold certain aspects in readiness.

than the one predetermined by its meaning, or an aspect held in readiness by a word sound may *exceed* the objective "something" that is determined by the meaning. It is for this reason that finding the "right" word, one that not only is fitting in accordance with its meaning but also, with respect to its capability, holds appropriate aspects in readiness, is of such great importance for poetic art. Consequently, aspects held in readiness can contribute not only to intuitive appearance but also to the constitution of represented objectivities, in the sense that, as one reads, the given objectivities appear to take on moments, or properties, to which, simply on the basis of what is represented by states of affairs, they are *not* entitled. To this extent one may also speak of the determining function of aspects.

Here we must distinguish sharply between two different situations: (1) The represented object is determined *primarily*, and in a proper sense, by the intentionality of the units of meaning or by corresponding purely intentional states of affairs, by virtue of their representation function. (2) On the other hand, aspects held in readiness fulfill the determining function with respect to represented objects only *secondarily*, for the most part only in the sense that they effect their appearance. If they are precisely matched to the content of corresponding sentence correlates, they do not perform any *particular* determining function with respect to the object, or the component of the determining function that is contained in the function of effecting appearance runs parallel to the component of meaning intentionality. Yet, wherever particular properties of phonetic formations produce a holding-in-readiness of aspects and in turn cause the appearance of new properties of an object, properties not represented by intentional sentence correlates, the aspects attain, as it were, a particular determining function: they add something new to the object, but only because, as aspects, they perform the function of effecting appearance. In a certain sense a special kind of illusion occurs here, in that something appears which has neither an autonomous nor a purely intentional existence based on the intentionality of meaning units, hence something which also does not exist in the sense of heteronomous existence. And yet it *seems* to exist, since it appears in an aspect.

The significance of this for the properties of the total work, that is, when schematized aspects appear in it, can be illustrated most easily if we show, on the basis of at least a few examples, how a difference in aspects modifies the whole of the work and how the work assumes different characteristics depending on the nature of the predominant aspects.

In principle, aspects of every possible content can be held in readiness in a literary work. Thus, in the representation of one and the same objective situation, visual, acoustic, and tactile aspects can, for example, be employed. The psychic state of a "hero" can be made to appear, e.g., by means of external aspects of his bodily behavior as well as by internal aspects, etc. On the other hand, there can be schematized aspects held in readiness which are all taken from a single point of view, so to speak. It is also possible, however, to employ aspects belonging to entirely different points of view, aspects which are quite jumbled, so that the given object appears in various ways almost simultaneously. The reader is then unable to observe these objects calmly and, as it were, systematically but must allow a swarm of aspects (which in their cooperation produce special opalescing phenomena) to work on him impressionistically. For this same reason the represented world is not only shown from various sides but also attains a quality of restlessness and vitality which possesses a special aesthetic charm.

It is much more frequently the case, however, that in one and the same work a particular kind of aspect predominates, and this gives the work a characteristic imprint. For example, predominantly "external" aspects of people behaving in such and such a way are used in a work in order to express their psychic processes; in another work the same purpose is served by various "internal" aspects. On the other hand, there are works in which visual aspects predominate to such an extent that the represented world is essentially only a *seen* world, in which events that are purely acoustic or have acoustic elements are either entirely eliminated or are determined only in visual terms. For example, if a door is slammed shut by a man transported by rage, we *see* in this case how the door is *pushed* by a violent movement and how it looks in this movement, but we do not hear the sound it makes when it is slammed. If the shouting of this same raging man is described, we do not hear the shrill sounds forced from his throat into space, in a certain sense piercing that space. Instead we are shown his facial muscles straining violently from the shouting, the appearance of his face; we see how the man suddenly opens his mouth and how in a sense he cannot close it, since his raging anger forces him to hurl ever new imprecations at his adversary, etc. In a different work a similar situation can be expressed in predominantly acoustic aspects, so that we *hear* the man rage and shout though we never get to see him do so. Even if, in both instances, we are dealing with the same situation, it will be modified not insignificantly—if we treat it as something purely intentional—by the use of other states of affairs and by the holding-in-readiness of various series of aspects; if it were to be determined and apprehended from another side, it would contain other spots of indeterminacy, and perhaps it would also possess a different aesthetic valence. And it is only because when we read we usually *go beyond* what is simply presented in the work and overlook the spots of indeterminacy [4] that we believe that in both cases we are dealing with a represented situation that is entirely "the same." If, e.g., one were to translate a literary work of art in such a manner that the represented objectivities were indeed constituted in the same states of affairs and would possess entirely the same moments as the "original" but that, at the same time, the aspect stratum were changed by the use of a different phonetic material in such a way that, e.g., the previously predominant visual aspects were largely replaced in the translation by acoustic aspects, the total character of the work itself would be essentially altered. We could then justifiably ask whether we were still dealing with the same work of art.

Another more important difference between works stems from the fact that in one work the aspects that are predominantly or even exclusively held in readiness are, so to speak, the common property of us all, or at least of a specific circle of readers, in that they are not only generally known but are an everyday and average mode of appearance [of objects], while in another work appear aspects of a kind that we have only rarely and under extraordinary circumstances perceived.[5] Unknown and unusual aspects show us an entirely new "visage" of the represented world; they allow us to discover new details in long-known and boring situations, even though, in the beginning, they may have made a correct seeing of the represented objectivities difficult. The use of such aspects gives the represented world a sheen of newness and interest that in itself is a positive, if only transitory, aesthetic value. Frequently, the appearance

4. In doing so, however, we go beyond the given literary work and are then dealing with one of its possible concretizations.

5. *Mutatis mutandis*, this difference also plays an important role in painting, in particular in portraiture, especially in assessing the "likeness" of the portrait to the model.

of new literary movements can be reduced to the fact that represented objects are expressed in totally new, previously unused, manifolds of aspects. In this, of course, it is not only the uncommonness of these aspects that is active; it is rather the already-mentioned circumstance that a change in the nature of the aspects on the one hand produces a modification in the represented objects and, on the other hand, effects the appearance of new, if one may so put it, *decorative* moments of aspects.[6]

This difference may intersect another one, which, while related, is not to be identified with it. If some aspects have become better known to us than others, and if at the same time a habit has been formed of perceiving and imagining[7] given things primarily in them, the basis for this may reside in the fact that, by chance, some things were frequently given to us in a determinate selection of aspects and that for some practical consideration it was of interest to us to perceive these things precisely in such aspects. The familiarity of some typical aspects can have another basis, however; as closer analysis will show, not all the aspects which in principle belong to an object have the capacity to present it clearly in—if we may use the word— its unique *essence*, in the *particularity* of its qualitative makeup

6. Insofar as one considers the literary work of art to be an "expression" of the author's or his contemporaries' relation to the world, this change can reflect a change in the way of seeing and perceiving the world and also a change in the nature of the aesthetic taste of the author and his time.

7. This habit can go so far as to cause remarkable obscurations: if it is deeply rooted, it may happen that we are nearly incapable of experiencing an unusual aspect in a pure manner. We are then unable to bring unknown objective properties to an apprehending perception; instead we interpret, unconsciously and unintentionally, as it were, the actually experienced aspects in terms of what we have previously frequently experienced, and we take the actually given thing *sub specie* of the already known. What is actually experienced and perceived is obscured to a large degree by what was previously experienced. Certain practical attitudes, in particular, often lead to such obscurations. In this sense Bergson was correct in speaking of "practical schemata." But both Bergson and, more recently, Heidegger are in error when they think that practical schemata are something primary. Heidegger, in particular, is mistaken when he asserts that the purely cognitive attitude is founded on the practical one. In this he overlooks, first, the fact that the practical attitude is formed on the basis of primitive modes of cognition and leads precisely to the obscuration we have just mentioned, and, second, the fact that this obscuration must be *removed* and not made the basis (as the word "foundation" seems to indicate!) if we are to return to *pure* perception. In this latter respect, one must agree with Bergson. Unfortunately Bergson failed on many points in his conception of both practical and pure intuitive cognition.

[*Sosein*]. In experiencing some of these aspects, the particularly characteristic [element] that expresses the entire essence of the thing "catches our eye," while other aspects are not at all capable, or at least are less capable, of opening for us a cognitive access to the essence of the same object. In the first case, the object's *own* countenance, as it were, is established, while in the latter we perceive only the accidental, the superficial, the average, the everyday. This difference in aspects is particularly clear in the direct perception of psychic states and character traits of others. In view of the complexity of this kind of cognition, it may indeed seem doubtful what the actual basis is for the fact that sometimes we immediately apprehend the total man in his most essential features in *one* facial expression while at another time we can guess nothing at all or only very little of his spiritual structure and of his then-unfolding psychic states. Many investigators would be willing to agree that this revealing or concealing function is performed primarily by the facial expression itself. Though this is true, one must not overlook the fact that the choice of aspects in which one and the same facial expression is given is also of great importance. It is enough, for example, to observe a man's face and the play of his features in an unusual, strongly foreshortened perspective, e.g., from above or from below, to become convinced that a change of aspect frequently makes the facial expression itself unrecognizable, and, as a result of that, the corresponding character traits (or psychic states) are unrecognizable. The same holds true for the manner of appearance of inanimate things. Hence it is most important for the literary work which manifolds of aspects are held ready in it. If the represented world is really to have some "fresh blood" in it, if the work is to reveal what is most peculiar and essential to it, aspect manifolds of great revealing power must be held in readiness in it.

Still another difference in the manner of appearance of represented objectivities that we might point out comes to mind when we compare older works of "narrative" literature, but also Thomas Mann's *The Magic Mountain,* for example, with works of the later expressionistic period. As we noted above, it is fundamentally impossible to hold in readiness *all* manifolds and unbroken *continua* of aspects. Among individual works, however, there may be significant differences in the degree of incompleteness or in the manner of interconnection of individual aspects. When we read, for example, the first chapter of *The Magic Mountain* (a work which is particularly instructive in this respect), we not only find a manifold of successive, closely inter-connected states of affairs representing an almost uninterrupted story, but, at the same time, closely interconnected aspects of corresponding objectivities are imposed on us. For example, if we walk with the hero from his room along a corridor, down the staircase, and into the dining hall, we see almost continuously before our eyes the pertinent objects in appropriate aspects: first the room, then the corridor, etc. As we pass by, we see everything as it would appear sequentially in reality. This is not only Mann's great art [8] but a characteristic feature of a literary direction which here achieves its high point. And we should not consider it either a shortcoming or an inability to form appropriately the appear-ance-effecting function but rather a different artistic intention leading to unique new effects which can also be "great art" if, in expressionistic literary works, objective situations that are not directly connected are not only largely represented momentarily but appear in aspects which are *torn*, as it were, from the con-tinua in which they are transitory phases and which follow upon one another in sudden leaps. Every aspect of this kind is almost like a momentary photographic flash—suddenly illuminated and just as suddenly extinguished. If a new aspect emerges, it is not a continuation, a directly successive phase of the same aspect continuum, but something disconnected from the preceding as-pect, something separated from it by a gap which is the *absence* of aspects. Perhaps because of this sudden illumination and ex-tinction, this jerky succession, the individual "flash pictures"—if we may use the term—have great illuminating power and, simul-taneously, the great power of revealing the objects that appear in them. This is the basis for one of the essential features of literary expressionism, though this does not exhaust its essence.

This difference that we have just indicated in the manner of appearance is not without consequence for represented objec-tivities. In the first example, we see a nearly continuous oc-curring; in the second, however, there is only a loose succession of momentary situations, of *turning* points, whose transitory phases are not directly represented and, in this sense, are alto-gether lacking in the work. The turning points are so determined that they are, so to speak, "self-sufficient" and do not tend, either generally or only in part, to provide an indirect representation of the missing phases. Undoubtedly, this mode ultimately has its basis in the manner in which states of affairs are projected by

8. In this respect, the beginning of the short story "Herr und Hund" is quite brilliant.

sentence meanings, but aspects held in readiness do reinforce the momentariness of the world thus represented and incarnate it in a characteristic *imprint.*

As we see, the nature of the predominant aspects in a given work not only gives it a characteristic imprint but also produces stylistic differences between works. Special investigations of these issues could shed an entirely new light on the differences between literary movements. Subsequent considerations will support us in this conviction.

§ 46. *Decorative and other aesthetically relevant properties of aspects*

IN THE PRECEDING SECTION we have discussed differences between aspects with respect to their appearance-effecting function. In addition to these, still other differences appear, which are connected to elements and properties of aspect contents that are carriers of aesthetic values, and it is these that we now wish to pursue.

To begin with, let us make use of an analogy. If an artistically gifted photographer wants to make a good photograph, he will first of all select from the many possible aspects of the given object the one which not only will, comparatively speaking, best bring out the similarity of the picture to the given object but will at the same time contain special aesthetically relevant features, e.g., lighting, lines of perspective, emotional shadings, etc. For this reason he must first of all become aware of the visual aspects that normally are simply experienced and not observed and judge them with respect to their lighting effects, etc. At the same time, he must be particularly sensitive to the aesthetic values (largely decorative) that are based on these light, color, and line effects. That which follows—the reconstruction of the chosen aspect by photographic means [9]—is only more or less skilled technique. Sculptors, for instance, keep in mind similar moments of aspects when, in designing a monument—e.g., of a human form which is to stand on a high pedestal and thus

9. Naturally, the patches of shade and color that arise on a photographic plate as a result of chemical action are not to be identified with an experienced concrete aspect. Only what is evoked by these patches in a viewing of the image is an aspect which is or should be similar to an aspect of the photographed object.

be seen from below and from a given distance—they do not adhere to purely anatomical proportions but fashion the figure in such a way that, seen from below, it can evoke the intended "impression" (i.e., nothing other than an aspect provided with special aesthetic value qualities). In other words, among visual aspects there are those whose content, with respect to the choice of colors and color combinations and the choice of their form and sequence, conceals within them positive (or in other instances) negative aesthetic value qualities.[10] It would take us too far to analyze in detail the various possible types of value qualities.[11] We must confine ourselves to the assertion that the aspect stratum of a literary work contains its own aesthetic value qualities and can constitute its own aesthetic values according to the type of aspect and the nature of its content and that, within one and the same kind of content, various mutually harmonious systems of value qualities are still possible. For their part, these systems constitute what one may call a *style* of a manifold of aspects, which is a value-possessing form which constitutes itself in the elements and the types of aspects, as well as in value qualities appearing in them. These features and differences of style—whether in concrete experiencing of perceptual aspects or in their imaginational actualization—are not usually apprehended in themselves as properties of aspects but instead transform themselves into special stylistic features and stylistic differences of *objects* appearing in them. But they belong to these objects only when these are *apparent* objects. Or, to put it differently, *when* these or other objects *appear* in aspects that are determinately characterized with regard to style, they themselves exhibit particular valuational stylistic features. But since, from the purely ontological point of view, a manifold of aspects neither constitutes nor essentially conditions ontically autonomous and, in particular, real objects, the stylistic features in question would fall away altogether if manifolds of aspects were altogether absent. These stylistic features do not constitue anything that would pertain to real objects in the way of real attributes.

With appropriate modifications, similar situations can be found in the schematized and held-in-readiness aspects of a literary work. It is possible, by appropriate means which cannot

---

10. *Mutatis mutandis*, this is valid also with references to aspects of other sensory realms.
11. A closer study of this is a broad subject for art theoreticians and historians but especially for the study of literary theory.

now be analyzed in detail, to hold in readiness in a literary work aspects which would contain the above-mentioned value-quality moments—primarily of a decorative nature—and which, by consistent implementation, would impress—not only on the objects partaking in individual situations but, in general, on the entire world represented and portrayed in a given work—a particular aesthetic style which is dependent on the type of its mode of appearance. In this, aesthetically relevant moments of schematized aspects play a much more important role in a literary work of art than they do in the concrete aspects in which real objects appear to us. The reason is, first, that in their ontic constitution represented objects are dependent on held-in-readiness aspects by virtue of the determining function of these aspects, which we have already discussed. This is not true of real objects. As a result, their content is enriched, through the activity of aspects held in readiness, by appropriate value-quality moments and stylistic features. Second, this enrichment is particularly important in a literary work of *art*. For, in many works, objects are represented *primarily* for the purpose of appearing in value-qualified aspects and thereby carrying special stylistic features. If they were to be totally deprived of these features, they would, in some works, be quite indifferent as elements of a work of art, and the aesthetic value of the given work would be seriously impaired. Finally, we may take many different attitudes with regard to real objects, but only one of them is an aesthetic attitude. If it is present, and if it causes us to perceive aesthetic values, it has its own meaning and its own place in our lives. Nevertheless, it is only a secondary thing, only an ornament, a luxury in practical life. Real, active life gives precedence to other attitudes toward objects and to other value systems. Thus, when aesthetically relevant stylistic features of objects are apprehended, it is more likely to be accidental. The situation is entirely different in the case of a work of art and, in particular, of a literary work of art. To be sure, here, too, various attitudes toward the represented objects are possible, but here the aesthetic attitude is primary in the sense that this is what it is ultimately all about, this is what the work of art is "designed" for. In a certain sense, however, this attitude requires that the objects appearing before us be possessed of aesthetic value qualities and hence, among other things, that they be provided with those stylistic features which accrue to them from aspects which are appropriately constructed according to their content. In other words, these value qualities and stylistic features belong *by their very essence* to represented objects, since they are aesthetic objects. This clearly does not imply that there could not be a literary work in which represented objects would be provided with *no* value qualities stemming from aspects. This only signifies that *if* a literary work is to be a genuine *work of art*, the aspects held in readiness must impart some moments and stylistic features of the kind mentioned above to the objects appearing in them. Again, it is not necessary for them to distinguish *every* object represented in a literary work in *each* of its situations. But in the over-all course of the story being represented, there are always phases which in a certain sense are culmination points of the work, and alongside them there are also phases which constitute only a preparation or a transition to a new culmination phase.[12] If a literary work is to be a work of art, then, at the very least, the culmination situations must contain objects which appear in aesthetically valuable aspects.[13] For their part, the preparation and transition phases can be indifferent in this respect, though they cannot conceal any value qualities that conflict with the successive culmination phases, and therefore they must at least be so constructed as to make possible the development of value qualities in the successive culmination phases.

The above considerations show the importance of the role played by the stratum of aspects held in readiness in a literary work of art. It is *de facto* an essential element, whose removal would transform a literary work of art into a mere written work.

12. This observation brings us to the idea that the literary work must be analyzed in still another direction, one which we have not yet taken. See Chap. 11.

13. O. Walzel seems to approach this when he says: "All poetry is indistinguishable from science as long as it limits itself to conceptual words. It becomes art only if, and to the extent that, it expresses its contents of cognition, wish, and feeling in a sensorially effective manner, only if it transforms content into form" (see O. Walzel, *Gehalt und Gestalt im Kunstwerk des Dichters* [Berlin, 1923], p. 178). Walzel is correct, of course; but as long as one does not analyze more exactly the "sensorially effective manner" of expression and does not uncover the entire stratum of aspects held in readiness, little is achieved.

10 / The Role of Represented Objectivities in a Literary Work of Art and the So-Called Idea of a Work

§ 47. Does the object stratum have any function whatsoever in a literary work of art?

WHEN WE ATTEMPT to apprehend the various strata of the literary work of art in the role they play in the whole of the work, it immediately becomes apparent that all other strata are present in the work primarily for the purpose of appropriately representing objects. The object stratum itself, on the other hand, appears to exist within the literary work solely for itself; and it is thus not only the most important element, the focal point of the literary work of art, for the constitution of which all the other elements exist, but it appears to be something which has no other function than simply to be. In fact, in reading a work, our attention is likewise directed primarily at represented objectivities.[1] We are attuned to them, and our intentional gaze finds in them a certain peace and satisfaction; whereas we pass by the other strata with a certain degree of inattention, and, at any rate, we notice them incidentally, only to the extent that this is necessary for the thematic apprehension of objects. Some naïve readers are interested solely in the vicissitudes of represented objects, while everything else is nearly nonexistent for them. In works in which represented objects are engaged in the function of representation,[2] such readers wish only to *find out*

1. Here we have an instance of the "distribution of interest" of which W. Conrad speaks.
2. For that matter, this function is already something which conflicts with the alleged self-sufficiency and lack of function of the object stratum. But we are not concerned with this function now.

something about the *represented* world. And since the represented world, usually the real world, which then constitutes the main focus of interest, is conceived as something existing only for itself and performing no function, the world represented in a literary work of art is also conceived in the same sense. It is quite in keeping with this that works of literary history on the whole deal mainly with represented objects and, after some analysis of the properties of the "language" or of the nature of "images" used by the author, go into various problems of the work's genesis.

However much this can be explained by the various circumstances of reading and by the role that literature plays for the practical man, there is no doubt that this is a false conception of the literary work of art. It is false for two reasons: (1) of all the strata of a work, only *one*, with prejudice to the remaining, appears, as it were, to take the place of the entire work; (2) as a result, one overlooks something which is directly dependent on the object stratum and which in a literary work of *art* constitutes its *core*, for the sake of which everything else in it—and thus represented objects, too—constitutes, to a certain degree, the "accessories," a means (even if not *merely* a means). It has been said often enough that objects are represented in a literary work so that something else may be attained. And in the course of time this something else has multiplied greatly. Thus, it was thought that represented objects (even though one had never fully worked out their pregnant concept) should arouse in us some emotion or mood, or instruct us, or influence us ethically, or, finally, "express" the author's experiences and the author himself. Our purpose is neither to contest nor to approve any of this, but merely to put it aside, since it broaches an entirely different question, the question, namely, of the role of the literary work of art in the totality of man's cultural life, or the question of the relationship of the work to the author. We, on the other hand, are interested in an altogether different problem, namely, whether the object stratum does something in the *structure of the literary work of art itself* whereby another element—and perhaps the most important—emerges in it, or whether its role is exhausted by its mere presence.

By following the theories we have mentioned, one would frequently go much too far and believe that represented objects serve *only* for effecting something, e.g., the expression of an "idea" apprehended by the author. A discussion of means and ends is indeed out of place here, where it is a question of roles

290 / THE LITERARY WORK OF ART

or functions of elements of an organic whole with respect to that whole. But even in terms of this false aspect it must be said that the object stratum, regardless of its functions, still constitutes an end in itself. It should be created, so to speak, in the work, made to appear, and, as something created, simply *be*. But at the same time, it still "should" do something. It only remains to be asked what this performance consists of, and what it should effect.

Considering first of all the theory already mentioned, according to which represented objects are a means for expressing an "idea," one must note that it is erroneous inasmuch as the word "idea" is used in a false, or at least in a very trite, sense. One means by that nothing other than a *true* proposition, a "truth," as one usually puts it, which the author in principle could say much more clearly and briefly without, for example, writing a play. In other words, one means by that a *purely rational meaning*, and one also assumes that it is *true*. Historians and critics of literature also attempt, with much effort, to work out (or better, *construe*) this "idea"—this allegedly true rational meaning—from the texture of the work of art, and they believe that they have performed something valuable. There undoubtedly are literary works and authors which suggest this line of approach (i.e., tendentious literature). However, this effort is misdirected precisely with those works that are genuine *works of art* because it apprehends the literary work from a side which, while it allows such "truths" *on the basis* of the work, has subordinate significance in it. Moreover, this conception overlooks the most significant element of the literary work of art, the one that is directly evoked by the function of the object stratum, even though in the final analysis this element is dependent on the other strata and has its ultimate ontic basis in them. What is at issue then, and where does the sought-after function of represented objects lie? That is the question. To answer it, we must first proceed to different ground.

§ 48. *Metaphysical qualities (essences)*

THERE ARE SIMPLE or "derived" qualities [3] (essences) as, for example, the sublime, the tragic, the dreadful, the shock-

3. According to my terminology in "Essentiale Fragen," *Jahrbuch für Philosophie und phänomenologische Forschung*, VII (1925), 125–304.

ing, the inexplicable, the demonic, the holy, the sinful, the sorrowful, the indescribable brightness of good fortune, as well as the grotesque, the charming, the light, the peaceful, etc. These qualities are not "properties" of *objects* in the usual sense of the term, nor are they, in general, "features" of some psychic state, but instead they are usually revealed, in complex and often very disparate *situations* or *events*, as an atmosphere which, hovering over the men and the things contained in these situations, penetrates and illumines everything with its light.[4] In our usual, everyday life, oriented on "small" practical ends and their realization, situations in which these qualities would be revealed occur very seldom. Life flows by—if one may say so—senselessly, gray and meaningless, with no regard for the great works which might be realized in this antlike existence. And then comes a day—like a grace—when perhaps for reasons that are unremarkable and unnoticed, and usually also concealed, an "event" occurs which envelops us and our surroundings in just such an indescribable atmosphere. Whatever the particular quality of this atmosphere, whether it is frightening or enchanting to distraction, it distinguishes itself like a shining, colorful splendor from the everyday grayness of the days, and it makes of the given event life's culmination point, regardless of whether the basis for it is the shock of a brutal and wicked murder or the spiritual ecstasy of union with God. These "metaphysical" qualities—as we would like to call them—which reveal themselves from time to time are what makes life worth living, and, whether we wish it or not, a secret longing for their concrete revelation lives in us and drives us in all our affairs and days. Their revelation constitutes the summit and the very depths of existence. Whatever their metaphysical position may be, whatever role their revelation and realization may play in human life or in life in general—all of them problems that we are not prepared to deal with here and that do not belong to the subject at hand— the following may, in any case, be said. (1) Independently of whether in themselves they have positive or negative value, their revelation is a positive value in contrast to gray, faceless, everyday experiences. (2) In their unique form, they do not allow purely rational determination, and they cannot be "grasped" (as, for example, one "grasps" a mathematical theorem). Instead they merely allow themselves to be, simply, one might

---

4. See D. von Hildebrand, "Die Idee der sittlichen Handlung," *Jahrbuch für Philosophie und phänomenologische Forschung*, III (1916), 167.

almost say "ecstatically," *seen* in the determinate situations in which they are realized. Moreover, they are perceivable in their specific, simply incomparable and indescribable, uniqueness only when we ourselves live *primarily* in the given *situation* or, at the very least, when we feel as one with someone who lives in such a situation and do not search out metaphysical qualities. These qualities are closest to us, and perceivable at their most elemental, when we do not deal with them thematically but are simply gripped by them. (3) Whatever the particular nature of these qualities, they are also characterized by the fact that—to use a frequently stated but not overly significant expression—they reveal a "deeper sense" of life and existence in general and, what is more, by the fact that they themselves constitute this usually hidden "sense." [5] When we see them, the depths and primal sources of existence, to which we are usually blind and which we hardly sense in our daily lives, are "revealed," as Heidegger would say, to our mind's eye. But they not only reveal themselves to us; in looking at and in realizing them, we enter into primal existence. We do not merely *see* manifested in them that which is otherwise mysterious; instead, they *are* the primal [element] itself in one of its forms. But they can be fully shown to us only when they become reality. Thus the situations in which metaphysical qualities are realized and shown to us are the true high points of unfolding existence, and they are likewise the high points of the spiritual-psychic essences which we ourselves are. They are high points which throw a shadow on the rest of our lives; that is, they evoke radical transformations in the existence which is immersed in them, regardless of whether they bring with them deliverance or damnation.

Their realization, however, is, as we have phrased it, a "grace." This is not to say that they are realized and manifested suddenly and without cause or that they are given, for example, in a mythological or religious sense by some power (God, angel, or devil, etc.) as a gift or a punishment. [6] This is only to establish the simple fact that we cannot evoke deliberately, for their own sake, the situations or experiences in which these meta-

5. In this case, of course, the word "sense" has nothing in common with the meaning that we have in mind when we speak of the sense [meaning] of a sentence. It is also inappropriate since the word "sense" usually signifies something that is rationally apprehendable. I would be happier to avoid it here, but I cannot find any other word that is appropriate.

6. Whether this is possible or not is something that I can in no way decide.

physical qualities are realized. And it is precisely when we are awaiting and desiring their realization and the opportunity to behold them that they do not appear.

In real life, as we have said, situations in which metaphysical qualities are realized are relatively quite rare. Moreover, their realization affects us too strongly for us to experience fully the totality of their contents. There is a secret longing in us for their realization and contemplation—even if they are to be frightful. But when the moment that they become real arrives, their realization, or better, they themselves in their own countenance, become too powerful for us, they grip us and overpower us. We do not have the strength, and we do not have the time, as it were, to lose ourselves in contemplation; yet there lives in us, for whatever reasons, an inextinguishable longing for precisely this losing ourselves in contemplation. This longing is the secret source of many of our acts. But it is also the ultimate source, on the one hand, of philosophical cognition and the drive for cognition and, on the other hand, of artistic creativity and satisfaction in it—the source, in short, of two psychic acts that are totally different and yet ultimately directed at the same end. Art, in particular, can give us, at least in microcosm and as reflection, what we can never attain in real life: a calm contemplation of metaphysical qualities.[7]

§ 49. *Metaphysical qualities in a literary work of art*

LET US RETURN NOW to a consideration of the object stratum of a literary work of art. The most important function that represented objective situations can perform is in exhibiting and manifesting determinate metaphysical qualities.[8] That this is possible is best shown by the fact that metaphysical qualities are seen by us in many represented situations. In addition, the

7. In the preface to his *Maria Magdalena* (Hamburg, 1844), Friedrich Hebbel said: "But art is not merely something infinitely greater; it is something entirely different, it is realized philosophy."

8. The word "revelation" [*Offenbarung*] is not to be understood in this context in the sense in which it is used in religious or religio-philosophical discourse. It merely indicates the opposite of "being hidden," of "obscuration." One could also speak, perhaps more adequately, of "self-showing," if the expression were not too awkward. As we shall see, this revelation is only potential in the work itself.

work affects us most deeply when this is the case. The literary work of art attains its high point in the manifestation of metaphysical qualities.[9] The uniquely artistic, however, is based upon the *manner* of this manifestation in the literary work of art. Precisely that which, from an ontological point of view, constitutes a shortcoming, a deficiency of represented objectivities, namely, that they do not have a real, but only an intentional, ontically heteronomous mode of existence and that in their content they only feign a *habitus* of reality, enables them to manifest metaphysical qualities in a manner that is peculiar to the work of art. Naturally, the metaphysical qualities cannot be *realized* here; this is precluded precisely by the ontic heteronomy of the represented situations. But they are *concretized* and revealed, and they share their mode of existence with represented objectivities; ontically heteronomous and purely intentional in themselves, they simulate their own realization. This, however, does not impair their concreteness and total determinateness. They are qualitatively totally determined, and as concretizations of ideal essences they can appear only as qualitatively totally determined. In this respect, too, they do not differ from the realizations that they attain in real situations. Their ontic heteronomy, however, enables us to contemplate them relatively calmly, since in this concretization they do not have the richness and power that they attain in a full realization. No matter how much we are "gripped," "enraptured," and perhaps even transported beyond the level of everyday life by the metaphysical qualities in an aesthetically modified viewing of them, their actual unreality, the fact that they are concretized only to the extent required for their manifestation, still allows a certain calmness in apprehending them and a distance [10] between the reader and the con-

9. S. I. Witkiewicz, a Polish painter and art theorist, stated in his *Teatr* (The Theater) (Cracow, 1923) that all art has its source in metaphysical *feelings* and that dramatic works in particular should evoke such feelings in us. By "metaphysical feelings," however, he understands the "experiencing of the secret of existence as unity in variety," which has nothing to do with our "metaphysical qualities," insofar as it is at all possible to understand something quite determinate by "metaphysical feeling." But it is certainly true that a metaphysical factor comes into play in a work of art. Despite various shortcomings in Witkiewicz's arguments, it must be stressed that they contain much that is interesting and valuable.

10. A "distance" that of course has nothing in common with the "distance" that occurs in the case of purely cognitive, objective apprehension. To be sure, in our case, too, a beholding, and thus a knowing, takes place. But it is only a pure beholding of particular qualities, which contains no claim to truth and, in particular, no assertion of existence

cretized metaphysical qualities. It allows a viewing which is not at the same time a true perceiving of qualities, as pressing reality is for us. As a result, concretizations of metaphysical qualities attain specific aesthetic value. We can observe them, be enraptured by them, enjoy fully everything they qualitatively offer without being, in the true sense of the term, afflicted, depressed, or transported by them.[11] In connection with this, their observation does not evoke those changes in us that true realizations do.[12] After a truly tragic situation or after an experience of true happiness, we cannot in our essence remain entirely as before, and accordingly we cannot subsequently behave entirely as we choose. In contrast, after seeing a play that moved us "to the very bottom of our heart," we can calmly go home and occupy ourselves with inconsequential or vital or altogether different matters. Undoubtedly, an echo of the shock experienced during the play is discernible for a while; but real life is much stronger, and it demands its rights.

---

and, at the same time, no "objectivization," all of which are characteristic for purely cognitive operations. The "distance" of which we speak here rests only on the unique phenomenon of "not belonging to the same world" and brings with it the impossibility of genuine participation in the represented situation, a genuine transposition from our life-situation into the one represented in the literary work. If, e.g., I see a tragic situation in the theater, I do not belong to it; no matter how much I am moved by it, I remain "outside" it and thus cannot find the tragic as something fully realized in *my* life. It is like a breath that comes to me from a different world, one that is brushed aside as soon as my real life comes into play, when, for example, I am "awakened" by the applause of the spectators or by a fire that breaks out in the theater. There is no doubt that the experiences we have during the reading of a work are real and that various changes can be evoked in us under the influence of the reading. Despite their reality, the evoked experiences and aftereffects are not genuine, but "poetic," experiences, which enter into our real life in a quite remarkable way and indeed become interwoven with it, without being "ours" in a true sense. (Cf. A. Pfänder's interesting arguments in "Zur Psychologie der Gesinnungen," *Jahrbuch für Philosophie und phänomenologische Forschung*, Vols. I [1913] and III [1916].)

11. See R. Lehmann, *Deutsche Poetik* (Munich, 1908), p. 246: "Here [i.e., in life] one reaches quickly indeed the boundary where passion brings only suffering; it is different in art, where the certainty—which lies dormant in our unconsciousness—that everything that is seen and heard is only illusion accompanies even the strongest emotions and thereby mitigates them to such an extent that they can become pleasures."

12. In closest connection with this aesthetic manner of observing metaphysical qualities is what Aristotle had in mind when he spoke of "catharsis." Viewing them in an aesthetic attitude not only fills us with pleasure and bliss but also gives us that specific relief which we experience after all difficult events requiring the exertion of all our powers. It appears that precisely this relief and inner calm after an aesthetic apprehension of a metaphysical quality is what Aristotle meant by catharsis.

We must also note that the manifestation of metaphysical qualities in a literary work of art permits various modes and degrees. There are preparatory phases in which a specific metaphysical quality is only indicated; its approach is announced, as it were; then there comes a moment, a culmination point, when it is fully developed. It may also happen that, due to an unforeseen change at the very last moment, the culmination point never arrives at all; the given quality emerges only halfway, then again disappears from view, like a threat or a promise. All of this must be left for further detailed analysis.

§ 50. Is the manifestation of metaphysical qualities truly a function of the object stratum?

THE MANNER IN WHICH represented objective situations can manifest metaphysical qualities, the way they must be constructed for this to be possible at all, and the question of what the situations are in which a specific metaphysical quality can be manifested are naturally separate problems in themselves. They are all subjects for special investigations which we cannot conduct here. What is important for us is only the fact that metaphysical qualities in literary works of art are manifested and that, as a result, the object stratum of the work can perform the function of revealing them. Hence it is not, at least not in every work in which metaphysical qualities appear, a pure end in itself. One could, however, challenge our position by asking whether metaphysical qualities are not simply moments of the represented world which are determined by sentence meanings and are represented by intentional sentence correlates, just as the represented objects themselves are. If this were really so, it would of course be impossible to speak of the special function of the object stratum.

It is undoubtedly correct that metaphysical qualities appear on the basis of represented objective situations and objects and do not constitute a special stratum of the literary work of art. This does not contradict at all the fact that they are carried precisely by represented objectivities, that they have their basis in them, and that the objectivities consequently perform this function. However, they are *not directly* determined by sentence meanings. What is remarkable is precisely the fact that, although metaphysical qualities can quite easily be intended in pure meaning units, this in itself, however, is *not* enough for them to be *manifested*. Only when the appropriate objective situation is determined and made to appear with reference to the elements that are essential in this instance can an appropriate metaphysical quality likewise be manifested in it. Thus, for this to occur in a literary work of art, there must be, along with the object stratum, the cooperation of those strata of the work whose end product is above all the representation and appearance of the object stratum; these are the stratum of phonetic formations, the stratum of units of meaning, and finally, also, the stratum of aspects. Only when the represented world is constituted by their cooperation, and when it appears before our mind's eye in living form, are the appropriate metaphysical qualities also revealed. We are correct, therefore, when we assert that it is the object stratum which performs the function of revealing metaphysical qualities, but we must add that this function can be performed only by represented objects *that have been constituted and made to appear*. For the manifestation of metaphysical qualities naturally depends not only on the purely objective attributes of represented objects and situations but also on the manner in which they are represented and made to appear or, to put it differently, on the structure and the cooperation of all the strata of a literary work of art that we have listed. If, for example, we read in our morning paper a police report of an event which is tragic by its nature, then the metaphysical quality of the tragic does indeed belong to this situation; but the official tone and style of the report make it impossible for the tragic to be manifested. In reading of it we can only *think* that the reported event is truly tragic, but we cannot see this unless we transcend the simple police report. Taking the matter purely objectively, the same event, if represented in a literary work of art, though represented in other states of affairs and in other aspects (and therefore, strictly speaking, not "the same" in every respect), can be such that the tragic is genuinely manifested. In the first instance we read the report with perfect composure over our morning coffee; in the second, we are deeply moved by what is represented, even though it may be something that never really occurred.

If the manifestation of a metaphysical quality is effected by the cooperation, not only of the object stratum, but also indirectly of all the remaining strata of a literary work of art, this again shows that, despite the stratified structure, the literary work of art forms an *organic* unity. And obversely: if the manifestation of a metaphysical quality is to occur, the strata must cooperate harmoniously in a determinate way and fulfill specific conditions. In particular, the polyphony of value qualities must not merely show a harmony that permits the appearance of a metaphysical quality; instead, it must be harmoniously compatible with it, so that the given metaphysical quality is *required* by the harmony as a complementing element.[13] If, however, the manifestation of the metaphysical quality is dependent, among other things, on the stratum of aspects held in readiness, then one must say that the metaphysical qualities are not explicitly manifested in the work *itself* but rather are only *predetermined* by objective situations and are *held in readiness* by the above-named aspects. For they can be manifested only in an objective situation that is truly apparent, that is, only in a concretization of the work in reading. In the work itself they constitute only a predetermined element whose manifestation shows a potentiality similar to the one that takes place in aspects held in readiness.

The manifested metaphysical quality, as well as the manner of its manifestation in the concretization of a literary work of art, constitute an aesthetic value.[14] If this manifestation does not attain fruition, or if the manifested quality is in conflict with other qualities manifested in earlier or later situations, so that not even a dissonant polyphonic harmony happens to occur in the course of the work, then the given work of art may perhaps

13. Here we again have extremely important problems, in particular the essence of artistic form and its connection with the "content" [Gehalt], to use Walzel's term. But to provide their correct formulation, one would first have to establish, on the basis of our results, the true concept of the form of a literary work of art, which is something that would exceed the subject of our study. I have concerned myself with this problem in a larger treatise entitled "O formie i treści dzieła sztuki literackiej" (Form and Content in the Literary Work of Art), appearing in Vol. II of my *Studia z estetyki* (Studies in Aesthetics) (Warsaw, 1958).

14. When Susanne Langer speaks in her book *Feeling and Form* (New York, 1953) about "feeling" and considers it to be essential for art, she basically has in mind the appearance of metaphysical qualities in a work of art, but she has not distinguished this group of qualities from other emotionally accessible qualities, nor was she conscious of their special manner of appearance in works of art. At the same time, it must be stressed that there are other specific aesthetically valuable qualities without which the mere appearance of a metaphysical quality in a literary work is incapable of making it into a fully developed work of art. For it is the essential nature of works of art of this kind, and perhaps of works of art in general, that, if they are to be positively valuable works of art, they must contain a manifold of different aesthetically valuable qualities which together must constitute a particular polyphonically formed harmony.

possess other values, constituted in the remaining strata, and thus have secondary value, even though as a whole it cannot achieve perfection.

§ 51. *The symbolizing function of the object stratum*

STILL ONE MORE OBSERVATION—a not unimportant one. One should not confuse the function of the object stratum that we have mentioned above with the *symbolizing* function which this stratum performs in some works (a typical example being Maeterlinck's dramas)—a function which does not absolutely belong to the essence of a literary work of art.[15] The symbolizing function undoubtedly has its ontic source in represented states of affairs or in sentence meanings. But it is performed only by represented objectivities. In other words, sentence meanings or intentional sentence correlates must be appropriately determined if represented objectivities, generally speaking, are to be symbols. Once they are constituted as symbols, however, then it is *they* which perform this function.

The difference between these two functions can be summed up as follows: whereas manifested metaphysical qualities attain *self*-revelation on the basis of represented situations and appear as already revealed qualities [i.e., in a concretization] in precisely the same sense as does the objective world, it is part of the essence of the symbolizing function that (1) what is symbolized and that which symbolizes it belong to *different* worlds—if we may so put it (at the very least what is symbolized is a different object, state of affairs, or situation than the symbol itself); (2) what is symbolized is in fact only "symbolized" and cannot attain self-presentation. As something symbolized, it is, according to its essence, *directly* inaccessible, it is that which does not show itself. Naturally, an object to which a symbol refers and which it made into "something symbolized" can itself be given under certain circumstances, but then it ceases to be something that is symbolized. And symbols or symbolizings are indispensable precisely whenever, for one reason or another, we cannot originally know the symbolized object or at least at a given moment are not

15. Susanne Langer seems to commit this very error. In doing so, she broadens the concept of symbol (under the influence of Cassirer) to the extent that everything possible is included. But then the concept of a symbol loses all the valuable functions it can perform in the study of art.

in the position to do so. It is for this reason that symbols are used most frequently in religious life and, for that matter, in all things mysterious and inaccessible. (3) If a determinate real, or merely represented, situation brings a metaphysical quality to self-manifestation, the ontic foundation of the latter lies in the situation itself, and both—the quality and the situation that serves as a foundation for it—play a significant role in the literary work of art. It is entirely different in the case of a symbol: the symbol is *only* a means. The concern is not with it, itself, but with what it symbolizes; only in retrospect can the symbol attain a certain meaning, provided that what is symbolized is significant. The role of the symbol, however, is exhausted in its function, and everything else that may appear in it but that plays no role in its symbolizing function is quite irrelevant—in contrast to the situation we find in the object stratum and its function of revealing metaphysical qualities.

Another, and related, function that can, but need not, always be performed by the object stratum is the already discussed function of reproduction or representation [*Repräsentation*]. But we need not go into this any further.

§ 52. The problem of the "truth" and the problem of the "idea" of a literary work of art

IN CONNECTION with these last considerations, we can now attempt to solve two problems raised previously. The first is the question of whether, and in what sense, one can speak of "truth" in a literary work of art. It arises, on the one hand, from the assertion made previously that no sentence in a literary work of art is a "judgment" in the true sense of the word and, on the other hand, from the frequently made assertion that the poet seeks to give "reality" in his work and also from the charge of "unreality" that one makes against some works. Is our point of view therefore false, or are these charges misdirected, or is it, finally, a question of ambiguity? We should like to show that the last is the case.

By "reality" in the strict sense of the term we understand a determinate *relationship* between a true *judicative proposition* and an *objectively existing state of affairs* selected by its meaning content. If this relationship exists, then the given judicative proposition is characterized by a relative quasi-feature,[16] which we express by the word "true." In a *figurative* sense, then, the true judicative proposition is itself called a "truth." Sense transformation (and alteration) go much farther when by "truth" we mean the *purely intentional* correlate of a true judicative proposition; and it seems entirely inadmissible when the word "truth" is frequently used as meaning the appertaining *objectively existing* state of affairs. In *none* of these meanings of the word can we reasonably speak of truth in a literary work of art. In the last, the fourth, sense, we cannot do so, since objectively existing states of affairs in no way constitute an element of a literary work. But neither can we do this in the remaining three meanings, since no individual proposition in a literary work is a judicative proposition in the true sense of the term. Thus, if the frequently heard contrary assertions are not to be false, the word "truth" must be used in an entirely different sense. In fact, this word is used in a number of other different meanings.

Above all, there is that sense of the word "truth" which may be applied to the function of reproduction that is performed in some works by represented objectivities. We then call "true" a represented objectivity engaged in the function of reproduction (or the sentences effecting its constitution) if it is the *truest* reproduction of an appropriately reproduced real objectivity, i.e., when it is a "good" copy, a "good," close "portrait." This concept of "truth" can be applied in a strict sense only to "historical" literary works of art in which the function of reproduction is truly present and intended. "Historical" literary works can also be true works of art, but they constitute only a special case of literary works of art in general. Hence, what holds for them need not hold for all literary works. Therefore, the charge that "untruth" is to be found in a work is not meaningful for all works. Moreover, the question of whether more or less accurate reproductions occur in a "historical" literary work of art has no effect on its purely artistic value. After all, as we have already established, there can be no literary work in which the reproduction is *entirely* accurate. In this sense, therefore, every such work is to a certain degree "untrue."

We speak of "truth" in a literary work of art in another sense when we have "objective consistency" in mind. For the time being, the author is bound in his creation only by the consider-

16. See "Essentiale Fragen," *Jahrbuch für Philosophie und phänomenologische Forschung*, VII (1925), 125–304, Chap. 6, with regard to relative quasi-features.

302 / THE LITERARY WORK OF ART

ation that his work be understandable and that it constitute a unified whole. He operates with sentences and complexes of sentences and is thus bound by all the laws stemming from sentences and their complexes. As far as the content of the objectivities represented in the work is concerned, it can in principle be largely formed in an arbitrary manner and, in particular, without regard to the degree to which it is similar or dissimilar to objectivities known to us from experience. However, once represented objects are established by the meaning contents of sentences as objects of a determined ontic type (e.g., as real objects and, in particular, as real psychic individuals), a consistency must be maintained in their further determination if they are to be constituted in the over-all course of the work as identical and if they are to appear in the *habitus* of the given type. If this consistency is broken, their identity, if we may so put it, is disrupted, or at least the given ontic nature (e.g., real) is not simulated. This consistency, however, can be maintained only if the content of represented objects is formed, at the very least, according to the a priori essential laws of the given ontic region.[17] If the represented objectivities are determined by sentences in such a way that all of these laws are fulfilled and, at the same time, the various empirical rules that hold true for objects of this nature are satisfied, then one usually says that they are "true" and consequently attributes positive value to the work in question. Naturally, this has nothing to do with truth in the strict sense. "Objective consistency" obviously must be maintained in every work whose object stratum is engaged in the function of reproduction, but maintaining this consistency need not carry with it a reproduction or representation function [*Repräsentationsfunktion*]. If the representation function is successful, it bestows on the given work—provided it is "intended"—a positive value (even though, in other respects, the work may be "bad"); and, therefore, objective consistency, too, is either itself a positive value or at least a condition for other values of literary works *of this kind*. On the other hand, however, objective consistency need not be maintained in every literary work. It is neither an indispensable condition of a literary work's *existence* (clearly there are works that exhibit no, or only defective, objective consistency, precisely those which are criticized for this very reason),

17. If we are dealing at all with *objects* in a work, then, naturally, the laws of formal ontology must be observed. Similarly with all possible categorical modifications of objective structure (e.g., structures of things, processes, etc.).

nor is it a condition of the total value of a literary work of art. On the contrary, there are literary works of art whose artistic value is in fact closely tied to an objective inconsistency of a certain degree and is conditioned by it—works, that are deliberately constructed in such a way that the represented objects produce no semblance of reality; it is an art that draws, and wishes to draw, on the realm of the improbable and the impossible. Therefore, in this sense, too, there are "untrue" literary works and works of art.

Finally, there is still another sense in which one speaks of the "truth" or the "untruth" of a literary work—though one is not fully conscious of the sense of such a statement. For reasons that inhere in the mode of representation and appearance, there may be, despite scrupulous observation of objective consistency, no manifestation of the metaphysical qualities that properly belong to a specific situation. In other instances, however, this manifestation may occur (which is possible even when objective consistency is violated, as long as the mode of representation and exhibition is appropriately implemented). In the latter case, we frequently hear it said that the given work is "true." Thus by "truth" one means here either the given metaphysical quality itself or its manifestation in the given work. Whatever the influence of the presence or absence of metaphysical qualities on the artistic or aesthetic value of the literary work of art may be, it is evident that, in this case as well, the "truth" of a work is not a condition of its existence.

After these considerations, it is clear that the recurring search for an "idea" of a work in the meaning of a *true proposition* is, at least in all shallow and tendentious works, wasted effort, which ultimately rests on a misunderstanding of the basic character of a literary work of art. Such a proposition cannot be found in a literary work of art, nor can it be deduced from sentences that are contained in it. For a true proposition cannot follow from sentences that are not genuine judicative propositions. But just as the word "truth" is used in so many different meanings,[18] the term "idea" of a work also has various meanings. It would take us too far to distinguish and determine all of these meanings. The most important of them is the one by which we take into consideration the metaphysical quality that manifests itself in the culmination of a work. Not alone, of course, but

18. I have made a more extensive analysis of the various concepts of "truth" in the article "Des différentes conceptions de la vérité dans l'art," *Revue d'esthétique*, II (Paris, 1949).

with the total situation in which it is manifested. It is the first to reveal the role that the given situation—as the culminating phase of represented events—plays in the total work. It bestows upon the work the mysterious "sense" concealed in the complex of represented events, a sense that cannot be determined purely conceptually. Or, to put it differently and more exactly: in this sense the "idea" of a work is based on the *essential connection,* brought to intuitive self-givenness, that exists between a determinate represented life-situation, taken as a culminating phase of a development preceding it, and a metaphysical quality that manifests itself in that life-situation and draws its unique coloration from its content. In the revelation of such an essential connection, which cannot be determined purely conceptually, lies the poet's creative act. Once this essential connection is revealed and perceived, it allows us to "understand" the internal connection of the individual phases of the work and to grasp the whole work of art as a creation that is of one piece.

§ 53. *Conclusion of the analysis of the strata*

THE LONG CHAIN OF OUR INQUIRY has shown us the stratified structure of a literary work of art in its main features; at the same time, it has developed and substantiated more precisely the assertions that were made at the beginning of our positive arguments. We have also pointed out the heterogeneity of the individual strata, their manifold roles and functions, and finally their close connection and cooperation. In this way we have cut a cross-section through the structure of the literary work and have shown simultaneously a framework whose exposition will enable us to answer future questions. This cross-section, however, does not permit us to apprehend the total nature of the literary work of art. Our analysis of the metaphysical qualities, the "idea of the work," and the various meanings in which one can speak of the "truth" of a literary work, but also our earlier consideration of the phonetic formations of a higher order, as well as the relative dependence of sentences and sentence complexes, have opened up perspectives on the structure of the literary work that are different from the ones seen in the various strata and their interconnections. It is these perspectives that we must now follow up, at least by way of outline. The cross-section of the structure of the literary work must now be followed by a longitudinal section.

11 / The Order of Sequence in a Literary Work

§ 54. *Introduction; alteration or destruction of the work through the transposition of its parts*

WE MUST NOW TAKE UNDER CONSIDERATION another system of organic connection in the literary work, one which is predicated by the presence of the strata. This has to do with the particular structure of the literary work inhering in it from its "beginning" to its "end." The very fact that the literary work has something like a "beginning" and an "end" indicates a specificity of structure that it shares perhaps only with a musical work. Usually one says that the literary and the musical work are both works of "temporal" art [1] and means by that they are *temporally extended*. As plausible as this may appear at first, it is false, and arises from the confusion of the literary work itself with its concretizations, which are constituted when the work is read. It is indeed no accident, no peculiarity or fault of our psychic organization, that we can apprehend literary works only in a temporally extended process and that the concretizations of the works arising thereby are likewise temporally extended. This manner of concretization of a literary work is dictated by its very essence, just as the essence of a painting requires that it be apprehended at once, in one glance. But to draw the conclusion from this that the literary work *itself* is temporally extended is wholly unjustified. That temporal extension is not an attribute of the literary work itself is already shown by the fact that, if this conception were true, one would have to attribute *different* temporal extensions to one and the same work according to the length of given

1. W. Conrad still claims this in "Der ästhetische Gegenstand," *Zeitschrift für Ästhetik und allgemeine Kunstwissenschaft,* III, nos. 1 and 3 (1908), 71–118, 469–511; IV, no. 3 (1909), 400–455.

readings. Significant differences could occur here. In the spirit of this interpretation, one would also have to admit that some parts of a literary work are "earlier" than others and that, the moment the "later" parts are read, they cease to exist (which, with reference to the parts of a work's *concretizations*, is undoubtedly true). With reference to the work itself, however, it is evident that, once it has come to exist, it exists *simultaneously* in *all* of its parts and that none of these parts is "earlier" or "later" in a temporal sense. Thus the work itself is not a formation that develops and is extended temporally on the axis of its "beginning" and "end." [2]

And yet we do speak, not without reason, of a "beginning" and of "earlier" and "later" parts of the *work* while thinking, not of its concretizations or of the beginning or the later phases of events represented in the work, but rather of the individual parts of the *entire work*, taken together in *all* its strata. Only this "earlier" and "later," this "beginning" and "end," are *not* to be understood in a *temporal* sense. The question then is, in what sense? That is the problem. Here we confront a specific structure of the work, a structure which is grounded in the *order* of the parts of a work and which, for want of a better expression, we shall call the "order of sequence."

In order to show that such an order, still to be detailed, exists at all, let us try mentally to reverse or remove the order of parts in a given work. Let us try, for example, to read a given novel, e.g., *Buddenbrooks*, "backwards." This can be done in various ways: with only the sentence order being reversed, but with every sentence being read "forwards," or with the order of the word sequence simultaneously inverted, or, finally, with only the second and not the first being inverted, etc. [3] Let us do this consistently from the "end" to the "beginning" and think, not of the

2. The fact that the work *as a whole* can last a certain length of time is an entirely different matter, which we shall discuss later.

3. The idea of such an inversion is not new. I am acquainted with it from the novel *Der Zauberlehrling*, by H. H. Evers, though there, to be sure, it is applied to a cinematographic representation. Here the inversion produces many comical situations and in many cases changes the content of what is represented. Eating, when shown cinematically in a reversed sequence, looks like vomiting; descending a ladder is changed into climbing it. Lighting and smoking a cigarette become an almost incomprehensible happening. But since in cinematography, as we shall see, finished instantaneous aspects of total situations which depict things are reconstructed, and since the individual images on the film strip are not destroyed by the inversion, things as they appear are still given to us in the inversion, and thus absurdity need not be transformed into nonsense. The situation is quite different with literary works.

course of the concrete reading, but of what is constituted by this "backward" reading. In each case we obtain, in comparison with the original work, *new* formations, which, depending on the kind of inversion, differ from it to a greater or lesser degree. Indeed, in a "work" read in this way, all of the same words, without exception, appear as in one that is read "forwards"; the inversion, however, has changed, if not everything, at any rate so much that it is no longer a question of whether we are still dealing with "the same" work but whether, ultimately, the formation we obtain is still a literary work at all. The fact that a specific work *A* is entirely changed, if not destroyed, by a radical inversion of the word order is seen above all in the appearance of entirely new phonetic formations of higher order (as, e.g., rhythmical properties, etc.) and the consequent destruction, or at least the alteration, of all those functions performed by the phonetic stratum of the work, which have decisive importance for both the constitution of sentence meanings and the holding-in-readiness of aspects. It may happen—and it is usually the case—that a sentence read in reverse order is no longer a sentence at all and that we can understand the manifold of words as a meaningful sentence only if we mentally reinstate the original order (e.g., "Table the upon lying is book the"). Indeed, the various grammatical rules of so-called word order are to a high degree accidental and are traceable to the various nonlogical peculiarities and sympathies of peoples and races; but nonetheless, there is a core of necessity in them, so that their *total* removal produces sometimes only a change in meaning ("Father beats son," "Son beats father") but more frequently its total destruction (as in the earlier example). If the sentences are changed by inversion into disconnected, irrationally strung-together words, they cannot develop an intentional sentence correlate and, in particular, an intentional state of affairs. But then the object stratum of the work is also absent, or at least does not form a unified represented world. And even if some aspects could be held in readiness by individual words, they would still be indiscriminately intermixed. After such an inversion, all that would remain of a total work would be a heap of words.

We need not introduce such an extensive destruction of the work to convince ourselves that every literary work possesses an order of sequence of its parts and, in particular, of its *sentences* that is unique to it. The above considerations of the relative dependence of the sentence and the sentence complex already provide us with sufficient evidence. But it is also enough, e.g., in a drama, to reverse the order of acts or to jumble up individual scenes to change the drama into a grotesque play of disconnected situations. Its unity is thus destroyed, provided, of course, we do not mentally reconstitute the original order. In a well-constructed drama every scene is prepared by preceding ones; it flows, so to speak, from the preceding scenes as their result, it presupposes them. This pertains not only to external events in which represented things and persons take part but, above all, to internal changes in persons, changes that occur in consequence of actual events. Every event leaves a more or less visible mark on the soul of the man partaking in it. And conversely: every event takes on a totally determined form due to the fact that persons with precisely these and not other internal transformations take part in them. Transposition of acts or individual scenes must consequently have the result that determinate situations that are constituted by the meaning content of corresponding sentences and the persons partaking in them are suspended in air, as it were. Transposition causes either a different determination for them with respect to those moments that were the precondition for the given situation and that are now missing, or it makes the given situation "impossible," since now the basis in past history is entirely or partially lacking. For, as we already know, represented objectivities draw their content only from the structure of all the remaining strata of the work, in which units of meaning play the most significant role. If, as a result of transposition, interconnected sentences are missing up to a specific phase of the work, or if they follow only after a given sentence, the corresponding objectivity cannot be fully constituted. It is like a "torso," whose completion is impossible as long as the reader does not go beyond what is given in the text. Naturally, in a literary work of art we find ourselves in the realm of "free imagination," but this freedom—as we have already shown—is not unlimited. There is always a limit beyond which the "impossibilities" possible in a literary work of art can no longer provide the desired effect. The whole—if it is still a whole—would then represent an unbearable, senseless hodgepodge of facts lumped together; the work would be a heap and no longer a work of art. *Mutatis mutandis*, one could speak similarly about the remaining strata of the literary work. If, as a result of this transformation of sentences, such extensive alterations were to come about in the individual strata, the polyphony of qualitatively valuable moments based on them would be thoroughly altered if not totally destroyed.

This attempt at destroying the work proves satisfactorily that every literary work of art contains an *order of sequence,* a determinate system of phase positions, in which every phase consists of corresponding phases of *all* the interconnected strata of the work and attains determinate qualifications because it occurs in precisely one and not another place. On the strength of these qualifications, the constituent strata of the work of art can perform functions for the other strata and for subsequent parts of the work, functions that would be impossible if they were to occupy another place in the work.

§ 55. *The meaning of the sequence of parts of a literary work*

WHEN WE SPEAK of a "sequence" of individual parts of a literary work, the word should not—as we have already pointed out—be understood in the usual sense, where we speak of the sequence of real events in concrete *time.* On the other hand, we have to contrast the order before us with, for example, that order which, as an ideal objectivity, rules the elements of a geometric figure. In the latter, an attempt to speak, even figuratively, of an order of sequence would be quite absurd. Nevertheless, the structure of the literary work requires this, due to the place system of its individual phases. For example, determinate states of affairs must be "already" projected so that others may be constructed upon them. The same also applies to the remaining strata of the literary work. It is certainly very difficult to give the exact meaning of this "already" or of this "sequence"; this difficulty is connected with the fact that the essence of the time that is to be contrasted here has not as yet been satisfactorily clarified. At any rate, if it is essential for concrete time that there always be a distinct "now"-phase in the developing time continuum, one that attains by itself, and along with other already existing objectivities, a particular actuality of existence (or better, real existence in the true sense) only to lose it the moment the "now" is transformed into a "past," then, in regard to the parts of a literary work, which is a formation constructed from *all* the strata, one cannot speak of a "now"-phase, and hence of time, in the true sense. None of the literary work's "phases" is distinct in this manner from the remaining ones, provided, of course, that we observe the work itself and not any of its concretizations. In connection with this, the literary work taken as a whole likewise does not show the other time forms of "past" and "future." [4] Yet, despite this, we cannot avoid speaking of a "sequence" of individual phases of a work and, therefore, of "phases" themselves. If we attempt to clarify for ourselves the meaning of this "sequence," we are struck by the fact that in every case it is a question of a *one-sidedness of conditioning* in the constitution, which, without exhausting its essence, is also present in temporally developing existence but which, on the other hand, is not possible in an entirely extratemporal existence, e.g., in an ideal geometric object. Every phase of the literary work (except for the first) shows moments within it which have their foundation outside themselves in moments of a different, "earlier" phase. At the same time, every phase contains within it a system of elements that requires *no* foundation in elements of a different phase. Finally, it contains moments that constitute the basis of foundation of determinate moments of a different, "subsequent" phase.[5] "Earlier" is what we call the phase that contains founding[6] moments that are founded for another phase, while "later" is what we call the one that contains elements that are *founded* in elements of another phase. Indeed, this "earlier" and this "later" are quite relative. At the same time, however, it is impossible for the phase that is "later" with regard to another also to be "earlier" with regard to it. That is to say, if a given phase *B* contains elements that have their basis of foundation in another phase *A*, then (1) no moment of phase *A* is founded by any moment of phase *B;* (2) if phase *B* contains founding elements, they function either as the basis of foundation for other elements of *the same* phase or as the basis of foundation for elements of a different phase, *C,* which is then later than *B.*[7] Mutual founding can occur only between elements or moments of one and the same phase. It is precisely through these properties of foundation that the order of "sequence" of phases in a literary

4. As we have established earlier, all of these time forms belong to the content of the intentional objectivities represented in a work. One should not, however, confuse the time form of what is represented with the particular order (now being investigated) of the sequence of parts of the whole work.

5. The latter can belong either to those elements that require no foundation or to those that are themselves founded in elements of another phase.

6. On the concept of founding, see Husserl, *Logical Investigations,* Vol. II, Third Investigation.

7. Detailed analyses will show that various complications are still possible, that one can, e.g., speak of indirect founding, etc.

work is established, and we use this word since there are analogous foundation relationships in the real sequences of concrete
time.[8] With regard to "sequence" in the sense being analyzed
here, the following in particular must still be emphasized, since
it was only partially indicated in the above determinations. (1)
Founding elements and elements founded by them that are to
establish the sequence of two phases must belong to *two* different
phases. (2) Every phase must contain elements that have no
founding requirement with regard to elements (or moments) of
another phase. Otherwise it would not be possible for *two* different "phases" of a work to exist at all. Elements of a phase
that have no founding requirements with regard to elements of
another phase simultaneously serve as the basis of *ontic* foundation for *all* elements (or moments) of the given phase and bestow upon it an ontic independence which is, however, for other
reasons, relative in a twofold sense. First, despite this ontic independence, the given phase (provided it is not the "first") contains elements (or moments) which at the same time have the
basis of their foundation in a different, "earlier" phase. The
latter elements (or moments) are also doubly founded, first,
in that they are *ontically* founded in the founding elements of
the same phase and, second, in that they are founded in *essence*
in the elements of the earlier phase. This relativity of the ontic
independence of a phase causes it to be, *not* an *absolutely self-
enclosed* whole, but only a phase, a part of an encompassing
whole, namely, of the given literary work. Its ontic independence,
however, causes it not to be a *part* of the other phases but only
to be in close *connection* with them, a connection which in fact
consists of the founding relationship between some of their elements or moments and the elements (moments) of "preceding"
or "subsequent" phases of the same work. In a second sense, a
phase of a work is only relatively ontically heteronomous and in
this sense also ontically relative to subjective conscious operations and, as we will show later, to another ontically autonomous
entity; therefore, in our terminology it can be ontically dependent.[9] (3) Any "earlier" phase of the work exists *simultaneously*
(in a temporal sense) with any "later" phases of the work. It is

8. To the sequence in time belong still more distant moments, which
make it a *temporal* sequence and which stay in the closest connection with
the ontically superior position of the "present."
9. See my arguments in the article "Bemerkungen zum Problem
Idealismus-Realismus" in *Festschrift, Edmund Husserl zum 70. Geburtstag
gewidmet* (Halle, 1929).

precisely a question here of the order of founding and not of the order of arising and disappearing in time.

In the "order of sequence" of the individual phases of a work lies the basis for the fact that the concretization of a literary work can develop only in a segment of concrete time.

In order to remove possible misunderstandings, we must stress that the order of sequence of phases of a work should not be confused with either the world corepresented in the object stratum or the time in which the literary work itself exists. We will speak about the latter somewhat later (see Chap. 13). With reference to the former, however, the following should be noted: that one should distinguish between them follows already from the fact that a "later" phase of a literary work frequently represents a situation *which is earlier in time* (that is, in represented time) than another, "already" present situation, as, for example, when we learn from the narration of a represented person the "prehistory" of the situation just then being represented.[10] The temporal order of what is represented and the "order of sequence" of individual phases of the work are, within broad limits, independent of each other, though it would require special investigation to establish whether this independence is total or whether it is limited and, if so, to what extent. To be sure, represented time shows various significant modifications in comparison with time in the real world, but it is still a time in which the basic structures of present, past, and future, even if modified, are present. In contrast, these basic structures have no meaning in the sequence of the phases of a work.

The presence of a "sequence" of phases of a work has the consequence that every work has a determinate line of development and thus an *internal dynamics*. There are preparatory phases of a work which lead to a culminating phase, and there are the culminating phases themselves. In *one* work, e.g., a drama, there may be a *number* of such phases, as well as phases that may be compared to a fadeout, a unique increase and decrease of tension that in itself constitutes a particular asethetic value quality. On the other hand, it is of course possible for the culminating phases to be the conclusion of the work, for it to

10. At first glance this seems to conflict with the one-sidedness of the direction of founding that in our earlier discussion we found to exist among the phases of the work. However, it is a question, not of founding what is represented "earlier" by what is represented "later," but only of the completion of the determination of what is represented "earlier" in order to remove "previously" existing spots of indeterminacy.

break off at just that point, etc. It must be noted, however, that *each stratum* of the literary work of art can present its *own* internal dynamics, so that the culminating phase in *one* stratum need not necessarily correspond to the culminating phases of the other strata. Various combinations are possible here, leading to a complete range of possible polyphonic harmonies and disharmonies. As in many other points, we must limit ourselves here to the establishment of the basic fact and to indicating the directions for specialized investigations. For here, as everywhere, many problems open up and, in particular, the most important problem, that of "composition," which, like many others, can be resolved in a satisfactory manner only on the basis of the structures and complexes we have set forth here.[11]

We have thus presented, at least in their main features, the basic structures of the literary work. It is now time to supplement our discussion and to draw our conclusions.

11. See O. Walzel, *Die künstlerische Form des Dichtwerks* (Berlin, 1916).

PART III

Supplementation and Conclusions

12 / Borderline Cases

§ 56. Introduction

IN OUR INVESTIGATIONS so far we have directed our attention to a determinate series of works in which, following our original and as yet unclarified intuition, we could see examples of literary works with a degree of certitude. In the course of our investigation it became clear what it is that we are dealing with in these cases. At the very beginning of our study, however, we indicated the danger that limiting our analyses to these examples would presuppose the ultimate validity of our original, unclarified intuitions and opinions and could therefore lead us to a false conception of the essence of a literary work (or a literary work of art). In order to guard against this danger, we must turn to the more important of the questionable cases, those whose specificity and affiliation to literary works (or literary works of art) was previously unclear.

§ 57. The stage play [1]

WE GO TO THE THEATER to "see," for example, Schiller's *Don Carlos*. Are we dealing in this case with a literary work, or do special properties occur here which draw a sharp line

1. With regard to § 57, see, among other things, R. Lehmann's arguments in his *Deutsche Poetik* (Munich, 1908), especially "Dramatische Dichtung" (pp. 163–81).

between the cases studied above and the "stage play"? [2] What, in fact, happens when we attend a play? Is the *Don Carlos* we read identical with the one we "see" on the stage?

We must first of all draw a distinction here between individual theatrical performances and the play itself, which is performed many times.[3] Each performance is an individual event which, even though it cannot be designated as real in every respect, still has its indispensable foundation in real events. Each performance differs from the others in various details, even though, in every performance, one and the same play is "performed" and, indeed, even when it is performed "badly." To be sure, the performance must not be too bad, for then the given play would not attain expression at all.[4] But it is precisely in a "bad" performance that we see clearly the difference between the performance and the play itself. The very postulate that the "good" performance *should* be formed in such and such a way presupposes this difference. The question is only whether what is counterposed to the individual performance is the corresponding "written" literary work or a "stage play" that is different from it. If it is the latter, we will have to contrast literary works of a certain kind ("dramatic" works) with stage plays, which will then be seen as heterogeneous to them; if it is the former, we will have to accept only a special kind of concretization of "dramatic" works, namely, the kind that is realized in a "performance."

If we observe a given drama (e.g., *Don Carlos*) as it appears to us in various individual *readings* and then compare it with "the same" drama (which is what, with a certain degree of validity, we usually call it) as it is given to us in various individual stage *performances,* we are struck by both the difference and the connection between them. The difference lies primarily in

2. For the sake of brevity we shall use the term "play" for everything that is staged in the theater, regardless of whether it is a "drama," a "tragedy," or a "comedy." We shall not consider so-called musical drama or musical comedy (operetta), since the presence of musical elements introduces complications which constitute, it would seem, a special form of art work.

3. This has already been done by W. Conrad, "Der ästhetische Gegenstand," *Zeitschrift für Ästhetik und allgemeine Kunstwissenschaft,* III (1908), 470; IV (1909).

4. A special case of this are those performances from which individual scenes (parts) of the work have been deleted for one reason or another. Here one can say either that only some parts of the work were performed or—if the deletions are extensive and a certain tradition has arisen of always making the same deletions—that a different work has been performed than the one created by the author. In that case, this new work must be contrasted with the individual concrete performances.

the way represented objectivities are represented in the two cases by the states of affairs and in the way they appear in their aspects. In a *written* drama there are, as we have already established,[5] two different texts: the main text, i.e., words and sentences spoken by *represented* persons, and the side text (stage directions), i.e., "information" given by the author. In a stage play the stage directions are eliminated as *text*. Consequently, the "double projection" of states of affairs that we discussed earlier is also eliminated, and the sentences constituting the main text cease to belong to what is represented by the stage directions and lose the character of being "in quotation marks." The function of projection, which in a drama that is read is performed by the stage directions, is taken over in a stage play by determinately qualified *real objectivities*,[6] which appear in corresponding aspects but which are not unequivocally determined [7] with respect to their individuality. These objectivities "play a role," as it is usually said, or, more precisely, perform the function of reproduction and *representation*.[8] Indeed, they represent those objects which, in a "drama" that is read, are *intentionally* projected by both the stage directions and the main text.[9] These representing objects need not be precisely those real things and men that in a given performance really find themselves on stage. But they must be constituted in such a way that they can perform, at least in part, the function of reproducing and representing objectivities represented in a stage play and of making them appear in appropriate visual and acoustical aspects.[10] At its most basic, it is primarily a question of having their

5. See above, pp. 208 ff.
6. T. A. Meyer does not see this. Nevertheless, his arguments concerning drama contain a number of valuable observations that agree in part with our analyses (see *Das Stilgesetz der Poesie* [Leipzig, 1901], pp. 105 ff.).
7. They are fully individualized only in a determinate performance. Here, among other things, we see the difference between a play itself and its individual performances.
8. See above, pp. 242 ff.
9. But not the real things and persons that are perhaps reproduced by the represented objectivities. As a result, in the case of a historical play, a special, interesting complication occurs here.
10. For the result of these functions, i.e., the represented objects, to be apprehended in a concrete performance, a "spectator" must be present and must effect special apprehending experiences. These experiences do not, of course, belong either to the play itself or to its concretizations (performances). It must be noted that these experiences are not true perceptions, even though, with respect to the nature of their intuitiveness, they are similar to perception. L. Blaustein, a student of K. Twardowski

determinate thus-appearance appropriately form the corresponding aspects so that the represented objectivities can appear in *concrete* aspects that can be experienced by the "spectator." Thus the stage play differs from a *purely* literary work, as we will call it from now on, in that entirely new means of representation, precluded by the essential nature of a purely literary work, appear in it: (1) real objects engaged in performing the function of reproduction and representation and (2) aspects appropriately formed and predetermined by the properties of these real objects, in which represented objectivities are to appear. These aspects are not merely held in *readiness* by various artistic means, as in a purely literary work, but instead are determined *concretely*—to the extent that their content is dependent on the objects that appear—by representing objects as aspects of represented objects, so that only the spectator is needed for them to be actualized in their full concreteness.

One should not think, however, that *all* the details of objectivities presented in a stage play are represented by real representing objects. This applies fully only to what is intentionally projected by the stage directions of the given purely literary work; it applies partially, also, to those physical objects and situations, determined by the *main* text, which are to be found (or which take place) "on stage." In contrast, the psychic processes of the "heroes"—which are either "expressed" by the manifestation function of actually spoken sentences (unless this is done directly by the mimicry of the "representer") or are spoken of "on stage"—are represented and made to appear as in a purely literary work. Moreover, the means of representation and depiction (purely intentional states of affairs and schematized held-in-readiness aspects projected by sentences) characteristic of a purely literary work likewise do not lose their function in a stage play as long as they are projected and predetermined by sentences in the main text. The function of these states of affairs, however, is changed significantly in a stage play. In a purely literary work, they form the essential and most important means of representation, so that the constitution of represented objectivities depends *primarily* and *essentially* on them and at most is supplemented by aspects held in readiness. In a stage play, on the contrary, these states of affairs do not

---

and myself, concerned himself with these apprehending experiences and included them among what he called "imaginational representations." See his *Przedstawienia imaginatywne* (Lvov, 1930).

first have to primarily constitute the things that are represented, since this constitution—which at any rate is only incipient—is effected by the real objects that perform the function of reproduction. Things and people that represent are present here from the start, whereas those that are represented are constituted as things by virtue of the corresponding properties of the former and by virtue of their representation function, so that represented things and human forms are given to us from the start (provided there is an appropriate attitude [on the spectator's part]). Even those intentional states of affairs which constitute the action that takes place "on stage" and that is performed by represented persons share the constituting function with representing objects, the "actors," since these acts, at least in their purely physical components, are produced by the actor's "play." And as far as those states of affairs that fall into the sphere of purely psychic existence and events are concerned, they also share their function of representation, at least to a certain extent, with the manifold phenomena of expression of the acting "stage player" and, in particular, with manifestation qualities of words and sentences actually spoken by the player. In this respect, the role of intentionally projected states of affairs is one of secondary, auxiliary significance; they facilitate interpretation of the phenomena of expression (which are frequently not fully expressed and not sufficiently unequivocal) and, through this, the lively apprehension of the represented psychic states. Thus, in a stage play an element which in a purely literary work is not even present takes over part of the function of representation. Only when objects and events are only talked about and reported, objects that are situated or take place "off" stage, is the manner in which they are represented and depicted fully the same as in a purely literary work. But it is precisely a drawback in a stage play to have too many such "stories" and reports.[11]

In view of what we have said, it would be a mistake to claim that the stage play is—as we ourselves, following common practice, expressed it at the outset—a *realization* of a corresponding purely literary work. For, on the one hand, two strata of the latter can in no way be "realized," i.e., the stratum

---

11. I have worked out the representation function that is effected in the stage play more thoroughly in the article "The Functions of Language in the Theater" [now in the Appendix, below; the article first appeared in *Zagadnienia rodzajów literackich* (Problems of Literary Genres) (Lodz, 1958), Vol. I].

of meaning units and that of represented (or here "Represented" [*repräsentierte*]) objectivities. The other strata, moreover, are also not "realized" but are only patterned on the corresponding strata of the purely literary work and hence are, with regard to it, entirely new formations. On the other hand, there appear in a stage play the structural differences we have discussed, which make it a *new* work with respect to the corresponding purely literary work. In the stage play we are thus dealing with a *different type* of work than the *purely* literary work. In spite of that, there is a close connection between a stage play and the corresponding purely literary work, provided that the latter exists at all, which—and this must be emphasized—need not necessarily be the case. It is precisely the identity of the non-realizable strata of the meaning units and the represented objectivities that in fact allows a *coordination* between these two heterogeneous works to be established and allows us to speak in *this* sense, but only in this sense, of "one and the same" drama in two different forms, that of the stage play and that of the purely literary work.

However, if the stage play is not a *purely* literary work, it is then a *borderline case*. The reasons for this are the following. (1) In a stage play we find a stratified structure analogous to that of a purely literary work, with the difference that new elements appear here and that some strata play somewhat modified roles. (2) The strata of meaning units and phonetic formations are also present in a stage play and have as significant a role as in a purely literary work. If one wanted to apply the expression "literary" to the stage play, one would have to include it among literary works, though not the *purely* literary. (3) In connection with the stratified structure, a polyphony of value qualities, which we earlier found to be essential for the literary work, is likewise present in the stage play. (4) Furthermore, the quasi-judgmental modification of the sentences spoken by represented persons is not lacking here. (5) Likewise, metaphysical qualities can be manifested in a stage play, and this manifestation usually has a much greater expressiveness than is possible in a purely literary work. (6) Finally, here, too, there is the particular structure of the sequence [of parts], and it conditions the various effects of the internal dynamics of the work.

These differences and similarities, therefore, lead us to regard the stage play as a *borderline* case of the literary work. At the same time the stage play constitutes a transition to works of a different type, which still show an affinity to literary works but can no longer be classed with them and stand, so to speak, between them and works of painting. These are the "pantomime" and the (silent) cinema.

§ 58. *The cinematographic drama* [*the film*]

LET US TURN NOW to an analysis of cinematographic drama. In fact, let us consider a certain ideal case where we are dealing with a completely "silent" cinematographic drama, one totally lacking in the usual "written" information.[12] On the other hand, we are interested here only in the *finished* drama and not its technical mode of formation. In particular, we are concerned with the relationship of a cinematographic drama to a purely literary work. Naturally, we will limit ourselves to the exposition of the basic structure of the cinematographic drama without going into numerous special problems.[13]

What does a cinematographic drama present us with? A discontinuous manifold of "images"[14] that conceals its discontinuity, each image being a reconstruction by photographic means of a visual aspect of a determinate object or objective situation. As these "images" succeed one another, they cause the

12. K. Lange is quite correct when he asserts that all this written information conflicts with the nature of cinematographic drama. The development of sound films can change nothing in this respect. (See K. Lange, *Nationale Kinoreform* [1918]—a work which I know only in part and at second hand.) I have analyzed the structure of sound films in the article "Le Temps, l'espace et le sentiment de réalité," *Revue internationale de filmologie*, I (1947), 127–41.

13. There is a voluminous critical literature concerning film which is largely dispersed in various professional periodicals. It was impossible for me to deal thoroughly with it. Of the writings known to me to date, Karol Irzykowski's book *Dziesiąta muza* (The Tenth Muse) (1924) is quite the best, if one turns to the core of Irzykowski's ideas and not to the frequently faulty formulations and concepts.

14. We will disregard the fact that these "images" are usually not reconstructions of multicolored aspects. Today's technical means make it possible to produce color films. Neutral images, however, have their own decorative value, which should not be overlooked in specialized investigations.

Immediately following the completion of this book, I wrote an "appendix" in 1928, concerning works of other art forms (painting, music, architecture). It was too large, however, to be included in the same book. In the course of time I have essentially reworked this appendix and have published it in Polish as three separate treatises. They are now collected in the second volume of my *Studia z estetyki* (Studies in Aesthetics) (Warsaw, 1958).

appearance of determinate objectivities just as paintings do, yet in a manner essentially expanded and altered, since in their succession and fusion they permit the appearance of temporally extended *events in their total concrete development.*[15] The latter is precluded in a "painting." In a cinematographic drama, however, there is neither the stratum of phonetic formations nor that of units of meaning, both of which appear in a literary work. Therefore, roughly speaking, only half the strata that are essential for the literary work remain. Consequently, it is *not* a literary work in a true sense. But it is not the number of strata alone that makes for the essential difference between a cinematographic drama and a purely literary work; rather, it is the fact that the ultimate constituent stratum in a cinematographic drama is exclusively the stratum of *visual aspects* and not the stratum of meaning units. In other words, here the *sole* constituting "material" is the *reconstituted* visual aspects, and they perform their constituting function by effecting the appearance of corresponding objectivities.[16] For this reason they attain decisive importance here. Things and people are given to us in the happenings quasi-perceptually, "from the outside," so to speak, and everything that we experience about them—indeed, everything they are—must have its basis in the manifold of reconstituted aspects. This leads to special technical difficulties and necessitates special artistic devices when what is to be represented is purely psychic occurrences of represented persons, since the meaning of their speech is inaccessible. In an entirely silent cinematographic drama those psychic occurrences which cannot be manifested in bodily modes of behavior and bodily

15. This is not contradicted by the fact that for aesthetic and technical reasons it is always only individual phases of events that are given; for these phases, too, are depicted in their entire course.

16. One should not forget here that the stratum of aspects in a cinematographic drama is not to be identified with the corresponding stratum of the literary work. In a literary work the schematized aspects are only held in readiness and are dependent in their constitution on the other strata of the work itself. In a cinematographic drama, however, they are not schematized in the same sense. The fact that they also undergo a schematization, or better, an alteration, follows from the changes that are introduced by the structure of the photographic apparatus. In particular, one should note the change resulting from the use of the one-lensed film apparatus, that is, the flattening of depth perspective. In principle, however, this can be removed by the use of stereoscopic equipment. Second, the aspects attain here a concrete development and as a result have their ontic basis in determinate, real objectivities and processes occurring *outside* the drama itself. In the article "Le Temps, l'espace et le sentiment de réalité," I have submitted the cinematographic drama to an in-depth analysis.

attributes are either altogether inaccessible (or, more precisely, they are not at all constituted) or are constituted only indirectly, in that they are determined by directly apparent situations. Thus their apprehension by the spectator always presupposes special subjective operations. In a silent cinematographic drama, then, limits of representation are set in this respect, though in other respects the limits are much broader, e.g., in comparison with the theater, where technical means are lacking. This limit in the representation of psychic occurrences also produces a certain shift in the center of gravity of psychic existence: the emotional sphere, and in particular those emotions, feelings, passions, etc., that are violent, powerful, and marked by a certain primitiveness and roughness, appears in the foreground; in contrast, the sphere of intellectual operations, the totally internal, subtle, self-absorbed, and inward-turning spiritual and mental life, is pushed into the background if not altogether removed. In connection with this, the range of metaphysical qualities that can be manifested in a cinematographically represented world is essentially narrowed.

It is not necessary, however, to view this as a deficiency of the cinematographic drama. Only one who considers it an imitation of the theater could feel this way. The fact is, however, that the cinematographic drama depicts only a *different* segment of existence, namely, all *events* (not merely "movements," as Irzykowski erroneously maintained) and things that can be depicted in *visual* aspects. At the same time, the concreteness of reconstituted aspects, as well as the possibility of making more accessible and more apprehendable through appropriate technical devices (e.g., enlarging the given "images") aspects which almost disappear in the normal course of perception, causes the various purely physical or bodily modes of behavior (or modes directly based on the bodily) of the objectivities (people, animals, things) which partake in the events represented to be depicted more distinctly than is possible with purely literary means. It is only that in a cinematographic drama the emphasis must be placed on *visual* events; if possible, the entire represented story must be developed only in them. Otherwise, as Irzykowski rightly stressed, the movies can lead only a parasitic existence with regard to the theater and to literature. On the other hand, it is precisely the concreteness of aspect reconstruction that is the reason for their appearing much more forcefully and becoming, to an incomparably greater degree than in a literary work, an inherent element of the play. And indeed, the artistic value of a cinematographic drama depends in the *first* place on the selection of reconstituted aspects, their decorative and other aesthetically relevant qualities, and only secondarily on the corresponding moments of the represented objectivities.[17]

One should not, however, go too far in this direction and consider the stratum of represented objectivities to be totally irrelevant or even expendable, since one cannot overlook the fact that it is part of the essence of an aspect to be an aspect of *something*. The idea of an "abstract" cinematographic drama— as Irzykowski called it—i.e., one in which the stratum of represented and depicted objects (things, persons, events) would be totally lacking, might be technically feasible; but it would be, not a mere modification of the cinematographic drama, but rather a completely heterogeneous type of work—even if it could be produced with the same apparatus.[18] If we agree that *both* strata are indispensable in a cinematographic drama, we would also have to agree that a *polyphony* of heterogeneous elements and corresponding value qualities is also present, even though here it is essentially poorer and simpler than in a purely literary work. The fact that the average naïve spectator is attuned almost exclusively to the events and things depicted does not contradict this.

To recapitulate: the cinematographic drama is *not* a *literary* work. In consequence of the fact, however, that in principle the same objectivities (with the above-mentioned limitations) are represented in it, that it does to even a small degree possess the stratum of represented objectivities, it is *related* to the literary work. If it is a work of art, it is much closer to literary works of art than are, for example, works of music or architecture, and it is likewise closer than works of painting and pictorial art. It is—if we dare say so—corrupted theater, which on the one hand has lost, as it were, the two linguistic strata but on the other hand, instead of using real objectivities for the function of reproduction, makes use exclusively of reconstructed and in some respects deconstructed [deformed] aspects as means of representation.

17. Credit for pointing this out is due to Irzykowski, in the book cited above; the concept of aspects, however, was unknown to him.

18. Irzykowski's position is remarkably shaky in this respect. On the one hand, he attacks the elimination of "content" (in his terminology) or—applying our concepts—the stratum of represented objectivities; on the other hand, he speaks with evident sympathy about the idea of "abstract" film without becoming conscious of the heterogeneity of the two kinds of "drama."

Like the literary work, the cinematographic drama can also be a work of art or merely an informative work or a scientific report (cf., for example, studies of bird flight, pictures for use in psychology, cinematography used for biology, medicine, etc.).[19] In this there is a new relationship between cinematographic drama and literary works. If it is a work of art, represented objectivities appear, not as real, but only as quasi-real; they appear only in the *habitus* of reality. They are also only purely intentional objectivities, and their pure intentionality is emphasized by the fact that the projected "images" are not real, ontically autonomous objects but only phantoms, which must first be interpreted by appropriate subjective operations as appearances of represented objectivities. The intentionality of represented objectivities is likewise unaltered by the fact that they are real things, people, and events that were photographed in the course of the film's production. For the objects which were photographed are, so to speak, not simply real objects. They perform here a function of reproduction and representation; they play a "role." And it is not the real objects as real objects but rather what is reproduced or represented by them (in accordance with the photographs that were made and the executed projection) which belongs as a stratum to the structure of the cinematographic drama. On the other hand, it is quite different when we are dealing with a scientific or informative film (e.g., the newsreel). Here the real things cinematographically photographed do not play any "role." They are photographed in their simple existence and essence. For whatever reason, they themselves are what we want to apprehend, in this indirect way, in their essence and occurrence. In contrast, purely intentional objectivities depicted by cinematographically reconstituted aspects now perform the functions of reproduction and representation in order to give us in an almost perceptual manner things and events that were once photographed.[20]

19. In comparison with our earlier usage, the term "literary work" will be used here in a broader sense. Cf. § 60.
20. It is clear that a very determinate conception of the structure of an "image" underlies the arguments of this section and is found throughout the text. In 1930, when this book appeared, it was entirely new. Since that time a number of studies of the image have been published in German, French, and English—from N. Hartmann's in 1932 to E. Gilson's in 1958—which are very close to the conception of the image, formulated almost at the same time, which underlies our discussion. The full text of my article, subsequently published in Polish ("O budowie obrazu" [The Structure of Paintings], 1946) was inaccessible to west

328 / THE LITERARY WORK OF ART

§ 59. *The pantomime*

A BORDERLINE CASE between theater and cinematographic drama is the pantomime. It is related to the theater
because in it, as in the theater, real objectivities are engaged in
functions of reproduction and representation and predetermine
manifolds of fully concrete aspects. With cinematographic drama
it has the common ground of lacking the two language strata, and
therefore it also undergoes a limitation of representability analogous to that of the cinema. At the same time, however, it also
differs from the cinema in that both the aspects and the movements and the mode of behavior of the "players" are formed
in such a way that the element of language lacking here is
replaced by other means. Pantomime counts, so to speak, on
saying, through the mimicry and gesticulation of the performing
personae, what could have been expressed more simply by words.
It is almost like a theater of the deaf and dumb. This is precisely
what does not occur in the case of cinematographic drama. Thus
the limits of representation in pantomime are much narrower
than in the cinematographic drama, since one does not have at
his disposal appropriately versatile technical means.

This much allows us to establish that there is a relationship
between the pantomime and literary works but no true affiliation.
We cannot go into the details of this.[21]

§ 60. *The scientific work; the simple report*

A MUCH MORE IMPORTANT borderline case of the literary
work is the scientific work. It differs in various respects from
literary works of art, even though it is relatively very close to it.
It shows a stratum structure that is altogether analogous to that
of a literary work, with the difference that elements of individual

European scholars, but a French résumé did appear in the *Bulletin of the
Polish Academy of Sciences* in 1946. To what extent one can speak here
of mere relationship or of influencing is something I cannot answer.

21. We should like to disregard the complication that arises from the
frequent confusion of pantomime with musical "accompaniment" (which,
for that matter, is incorrect, since it is a question of something other than
a mere "accompaniment"). The presence of musical elements is not
essential for pantomime. If they are present, we have a new type of art
work, which we do not want to analyze here in greater detail. The limits
of what can be represented are undoubtedly enlarged by the musical
factor.

strata, as well as their roles, are partially different. All of these differences are closely connected with the different kind of function that the scientific work plays in man's spiritual life. It consists of establishing cognitive results attained and transmitting them to other conscious subjects. It is precisely this function, however, that the literary work in our sense of the term cannot perform.

The differences between the two types of works in question are the following:

1. Sentences that appear in a scientific work are almost exclusively *true judgments*. They may be true or false, but, whatever the case, by their very essence they lay claim to truthfulness. Both the quasi-judgmental modification of assertive propositions and the analogous modification of all other propositions, which we have found to be characteristic of the literary work, are lacking here. Even when occasionally a purely "rhetorical" question happens to appear, one which in principle could be replaced by an assertive proposition, it still lays claim to being a *valid* question.

2. The structure of a scientific work naturally consists of purely intentional sentence correlates (almost exclusively states of affairs) and represented objectivities. But since sentences are here predominantly true judgments, the directional ray of the contained meanings passes through the content of the purely intentional sentence correlates so that the sentences refer to objectively existing states of affairs or to objects contained in them. Purely intentional states of affairs are in principle "transparent" and differ from objectively existing states of affairs only when we are dealing with false or at least doubtful propositions and, for that matter also, when the objectively existing states of affairs cannot yet be apprehended.[22] It would be a mistake to think that the objectivities represented in a scientific work perform a function of reproduction and that by virtue of this function it is only the sentences that refer to the portrayed ontically autonomous objectivities. This can indeed be the case, but not when the scientific work remains in its proper function; it is possible only in the particular form that is imposed on it

22. We frequently know that a proposition is false, and yet, nevertheless, we cannot apprehend the objective state of affairs that pertains to the corresponding true proposition. It remains unknown. But even as something "unknown" it differs from the known purely intentional state of affairs of the false proposition. The unknown state of affairs, naturally, must be unequivocally determined in some manner for it to be apprehended as "unknown."

when one construes it as a "conception" of the given author, as is frequently the case in, for example, historical treatments of philosophical works. It is only then that represented objectivities perform the functions of reproduction and representation, and in this regard the entire work approaches some literary works.

3. In a scientific work, in both the stratum of phonetic formations and the stratum of units of meaning, there may appear properties which, viewed in themselves, contain aesthetic value qualities and which, in conjunction with corresponding elements of other strata, produce a polyphony of value qualities. But while this, too, is not precluded in a scientific work, it is not at all necessary; for a scientific work, it is a dispensable luxury. A scientific work is not at all expected to have such properties. It is expected primarily to contain true propositions and to harbor such structural properties as will facilitate its function of cognitive exchange. Everything else must be subordinated to this central purpose. This, however, is precisely what is not only not essential for literary works, in particular literary works of art, but is in fact precluded for *genuine* works of art. The question of what the basis is for further particularities of the structure of scientific works and the question of the differences between them and literary works of art would be a subject for special extensive analysis.

4. Scientific works can contain, as a special stratum, manifolds of schematized aspects held in readiness, provided the sentences refer to objects that can appear in manifolds of aspects. If aspects are at all present in a work, however, they play an essentially different role in it than in a literary work of art. Namely, they come into play solely as useful and sometimes even indispensable auxiliary means for the transmission of cognitive results. The presence of decorative moments is thus entirely dispensable and in fact is frequently a hindrance.

Finally, the possible manifestation of metaphysical qualities is essential only when a given metaphysical quality is itself a subject of the cognitive result that is achieved and transmitted, or at least contributes to its transmission. In all other instances their manifestation is not only inessential but may also counteract the main function of a scientific work and is thus to be avoided.

Mutatis mutandis, the above may also refer to simple information or the simple report. We shall not go into these in greater detail.

§ 61. *Introduction*

IN OUR ANALYSES up to now we have treated the literary work as an objectivity *in itself*, and we have attempted to see it in its characteristic structure. We have considered it as something *detached* from the living intercourse of psychic individuals and hence also from the cultural atmosphere and the various spiritual currents that develop in the course of history. Only in those places where the literary work itself indicated subjective operations were we compelled to fall back on subjective elements. Now is the time to bring the literary work back, so to speak, into contact with the reader and introduce it into concrete spiritual and cultural life in order to see what new situations and problems arise as a result. This is also necessary since our observations have led us to the conclusion that the purely literary work is a formation that is *schematic* in various respects, containing "gaps," spots of indeterminacy, schematized aspects, etc. On the other hand, some of its elements demonstrate a certain potentiality, which we have attempted to suggest by the expression "holding-in-readiness" [*Parathaltung*]. Nevertheless, in the live intercourse we have with it during a reading, an individual literary work does not seem to exhibit any such spots of indeterminacy, schematizations, or any potentiality of aspects held in readiness.[1] The question therefore

---

1. This potentiality—which should be elaborated here—also shows itself in the thus-appearance of represented objects. This thus-appearance

arises: how does a literary work appear during reading, and what is the immediate correlate of this reading? We have already had occasion to indicate that a distinction should be drawn between the work itself and its concretizations, which differ from it in various respects. These concretizations are precisely what is constituted during the reading and what, in a manner of speaking, forms the mode of appearance of a work, the concrete form in which the work itself is apprehended. The next task before us is to describe the properties of the concretization of a literary work and to point out the relationships, on the one hand between the concretizations and the literary work, and on the other between the concretizations and the subjective experiences in which they are constituted.[2]

§ 62. The concretizations of a literary work and the experiences of its apprehension

WHAT DO WE HAVE IN MIND when we speak of a "concretization" of a literary work? Instead of directly answering this question, let us first distinguish these concretizations from subjective operations and, more generally, from the psychic experiences we have during the reading. The literary work we read or hear or see on the stage is—according to our previous analyses—a very complex structured object at which we direct ourselves in a manifold of interconnected conscious acts and other experiences which no longer have the special structure of acts. It is precisely because of the complexity of its structure and the heterogeneity of its elements that all these experiences and acts are of a very diverse nature and may be effected in various possible combinations and complications. These are, above all, various cognitive acts, such as perceptual acts, in which word signs or word sounds and phonetic formations of a higher order are apprehended (or perceptions of things and

---

is truly complete only when the aspects have passed from mere preparedness and schematization to actuality and concreteness. But this is possible only in the concretization of a work.

2. The "concretization" of a work is what W. Conrad presumably had in mind when he spoke of the "realization" of the work of art. However, he did not investigate this "realization" more closely. See "Der ästhetische Gegenstand," *Zeitschrift für Ästhetik und allgemeine Kunstwissenschaft,* III, no. 3 (1908), 480, passim.

persons that find themselves "on stage"),[3] meaning-apprehending acts that are based on cognitive acts, and, finally, acts of imaginative beholding of represented objectivities and situations and, if need be, of metaphysical qualities manifested in them. This imaginative beholding is, for its part, based on the first-mentioned acts. In perceptual acts, in which we apprehend the phonetic stratum (or in which reproduced objects are presented to us in a stage play), as well as in the imaginative beholding of represented objectivities, manifolds of concrete aspects are simultaneously experienced in the form of either perceptual or imaginational modifications. Indeed, if the reader submits to the work, exactly those aspects are experienced whose schemata were held ready by the work. Moreover, various experiences of aesthetic enjoyment are aroused in the reader,[4] experiences in which aesthetic values have their source and perhaps also attain explicit development. Finally, various feelings and emotions [5] are evoked by the reading in the mind of the reader (or spectator). To be sure, they no longer belong to that group of experiences in which the literary work is *apprehended concretely,* but they still are not without influence on its apprehension.

As we see, the situation that we find in the psychic subject during a reading is very complicated, and it would require special analysis [6] to dissect it thoroughly. As we have already noted, the complexity and variety of this situation is but a mirror image of the structure of a literary work. In a manner of speaking, in order to do justice to it, this structure requires us to perceive it not in simple and simply constructed total experiences but rather to develop a great range of various conscious acts and experiences. The complexity of a total apprehension of a work is such that the experiencing ego has too much to do at once, as it were, and thus cannot give itself equally to all the components of this total apprehension. Of the entire manifold of simultaneously experienced (or executed)

3. Strictly speaking, these are not simple sensory perceptions, but it would take us too far to elaborate on this. This matter is not of great importance for what follows.

4. See M. Geiger's splendid analyses in his "Beiträge zur Phänomenologie des ästhetischen Genusses," *Jahrbuch für Philosophie und phänomenologische Forschung,* Vol. I (1913).

5. See Max Scheler, "Zum Phänomen des Tragischen."

6. I have submitted all these facts to a detailed analysis in my book *O poznawaniu dzieła literackiego* (Lvov, 1937) [*Vom Erkennen des literarischen Kunstwerks* (Tübingen, 1968); English translation by Ruth Ann Crowley and Kenneth R. Olson, *The Cognition of the Literary Work of Art* (Evanston Ill.: Northwestern University Press, 1973)].

and interwoven acts and other experiences only a few are effected as central and with full activity by the ego; the rest, though still experienced and effected, are only "coeffected," coexperienced. In the process, there is constant change with regard to which component acts (or experiences) are central at any given moment and which are developed only "in passing," only marginally. Along with this change, however, there is also a change in the direction of our attention. Consequently, the parts and strata of the work being read that can be seen clearly are always different; the rest sink into a semidarkness, a semi-vagueness, where they only covibrate and cospeak, and, precisely because of this, they color the totality of the work in a particular manner. Another consequence of this constant change and the various ways we partake, as it were, of this or that experience is the fact that the literary work is never *fully* grasped in *all* its strata and components but always only partially, always, so to speak, in only a *perspectival foreshortening*. These "foreshortenings" may change constantly, not only from work to work but also in one and the same work; in fact, they can be conditioned and required by the structure of the given work and its individual parts. On the whole, however, they are not so much dependent on the work itself as on the given conditions of the reading. As a result, we can correctly grasp the work only to a certain degree—never completely. One might almost be tempted to say that one and the same literary work is apprehended in various changing "aspects." [7] The manifold of these "aspects" pertaining to one and the same reading of a work is at the same time of decisive significance for the constitution of a specific concretization of a literary work being read at a given time. Since these manifolds are generally different in two different readings, we see the way to distinguish individual concretizations of the work from the work itself.

Before we do that, however, a note of some importance: the wealth and complexity of subjective operations and experiences that are to be effected in the apprehension of a literary work require—if the reading and the apprehension of the work are to be at all successful—the apprehending subject to shield himself from all disturbing influences. Thus, there is usually an involuntary thrusting-aside and suppression of all those experiences and psychic states belonging to the rest of the given

---

7. W. Conrad also uses this word, without, however, indicating the situations presented here. See his "Der ästhetische Gegenstand."

reader's real world; there is as if a blindness and deafness to acts and events of the real world. During our reading we even try to push away, as possible distractions, events and concerns that in themselves are quite negligible (hence we look for a comfortable position, a quiet setting, etc.). This aloofness from our real surroundings leads, on the one hand, to the situation that the represented objectivities that are depicted constitute a separate world for us, one that is distant from actual reality; on the other hand, it enables us to assume an attitude of pure beholding with respect to the represented objectivities and to enjoy fully the aesthetic value qualities that appear in the work. It is because of this, among other things, that we achieve the specifically "aesthetic" ("beholding") attitude that is absolutely necessary for the apprehension of, and vital communion with, works of art.[8] Ultimately, therefore, the same wealth of experiences of apprehension that on the one hand contribute to the "perspectival foreshortening" of a literary work in a reading, and hence possibly to a distortion of its characteristic total form, do, on the other hand, contribute to appropriately viewing it as a work of art.

All these acts of apprehension and these experiences naturally constitute the condition under which a literary work can be vividly apprehended in one of its possible concretizations. Nonetheless, not only the work itself but each of its concretizations is different from these experiences of apprehension. Quite clearly there would be no concretizations if such experiences of apprehension were not effected, since concretizations are dependent on the latter, not simply in their mode of existence, but in their matter as well. There is, however, no reason to conclude on this basis that they are anything psychic or in any way an element of experience. This would be the same as saying that two objects, *A* and *B,* that are mutually dependent in their existence must *eo ipso* always be of the same kind or be related as part to whole! Between a concrete color and its concrete extension there is a much closer relationship than between a concretization of a literary work and the corresponding experiences of apprehension, and yet no one would say that color is extension or that extension is color or, finally, that extension is part of a given color. And just as a rainbow is not something psychic, even though it exists concretely only when a visual perception is effected under certain objective circumstances, so

8. Jonas Cohn takes an analogous position in his *Allgemeine Ästhetik* (Leipzig, 1901), pp. 32*n,* 35.

also the concretization of a literary work, though it is conditioned in its existence by corresponding experiences, has at the same time its second ontic basis in the literary work itself; and with respect to the experiences of apprehension, it is just as transcendent as the literary work itself.

We are not in a position here to give a comprehensive theory of consciousness and psychic existence or of the various possible relationships between conscious experiences and ontically autonomous and ontically heteronomous objectivities. It may, perhaps, suffice if we recall that every experience can, generally speaking, be apprehended only in the *reflection* or in the *living* of the act, and all things psychic only in *inner* perception (or, as M. Geiger says, in the *"Innewerden"*). If the concretization of a literary work were a real component of the conscious experience in question, or if it were something psychic, it too would have to be apprehended in this, and only this, way. Yet this is not true, either of a literary work itself or of any concretizations of literary works. And, in fact, no one turns his attention, while reading a work or while being a spectator in a theater, to his conscious experiences or to his psychic states. Anyone would laugh if we were to suggest that he do this. Only a theorizing literary critic could hit upon the bizarre idea of looking for the literary work "in the mind" of the reader.

§ 63. *The literary work and its concretizations*

Now THAT WE HAVE DISTINGUISHED, in the preceding section, the concretizations of a literary work from subjective experiences of apprehension, let us draw a line between the concretizations and the work itself.

We can deal aesthetically with a literary work and apprehend it live only in the form of one of its possible concretizations.[9]

9. Taken superficially, this statement seems to lead to a fundamental difficulty. For how can we contrast the literary work with one of its concretizations and apprehend it in a structure pertaining only to it and not the concretization if it is only apprehendable in the form that it assumes in an individual concretization? If there is no direct access, so to speak, to the literary work itself, there is a danger that all our analyses are suspended in air. We believe that the truth of our analyses will defend itself against such a charge. First, if we can, in fact, apprehend each individual literary work only in one of its concretizations, this concretization is not a cloak that impedes access to the work itself. The individual differences between concretizations already enable us to establish what

Namely, we are then dealing with it precisely in the form in which it expresses itself in the given concretization. Nevertheless, ultimately we do not turn our attention to the concretization *as such* but to the work *itself*, and we are usually not conscious of the difference between it and the respective concretization. Yet, in spite of that, it is essentially different from all of its concretizations. It is only expressed in them, it develops in them; but each such development (as long as it is not a mere reconstruction of the work) necessarily goes beyond it. On the other hand, none of these developments goes as far as the work itself, because of the usual foreshortenings mentioned above and also because of possible shifts in the elements of the work that are actually apprehended. The concretization not only contains various elements that are not really part of the work, though allowed by it, but it also frequently shows elements that are foreign to it and which more or less obscure it. These facts compel us to draw a consistent and detailed line of distinction between the literary work itself and its various concretizations.

1. In the purely literary work itself, word sounds appear as *typical Gestalt* qualities, which can be frequently and characteristically intermingled with manifestation qualities. In the concretization of recitation aloud (declamation), these *Gestalt* qualities are carried by concrete sounds and thus attain

---

belongs to the work itself and what pertains to the accidentally conditioned concretizations. Second, we are not examining a single work in its individuality but rather the content of the general idea of every literary work in general (cf. *Essentiale Fragen* [Halle, 1925] p. 52). We are thus not at all obliged to be bound by individual concretizations. But even when we attempt to apprehend a fully determinate literary work, it is possible to apprehend it in its pure form, so to speak. What, in fact, distinguishes the work itself from its concretizations? First, the fact that the spots of indeterminacy contained in the work itself are partially filled in a concretization. Second, the potentialities contained in the work itself (the aspects held in readiness, the metaphysical qualities) are transformed into actualities in the concretizations. Finally, the apprehension of the meaning units can be inadequate in the concretizations. In all these points, however, it is possible for the concretization to proceed in such a way that these differences disappear. Thus it can contain the filling of spots of indeterminacy and the transformation of potentialities into actualities, and, finally, it can adequately perform the concretization of the meaning units. In that case we obtain a very particular "concretization" of the work, which I have called (see *The Cognition of the Literary Work of Art*) a "reconstruction" of the literary work. Ultimately, with regard to the possibility of the results here given, one must note that in the text we are speaking of aesthetic involvement in the work, whereas the condition for the possibility of establishing our results is a theoretical, purely cognitive approach to the work.

expression and concrete fullness.[10] These concrete sounds have various other properties, whose range is prescribed or allowed by the form of the sound, which thus possibly has a *modifying*, but at any rate a supplemental, role with respect to the concretizations. These properties vary from case to case, and they (though not they alone) account for the difference between the individual concretizations of one and the same literary work. Their potential modifying action need not be limited, moreover, to the stratum of phonetic formations; it may also be expressed in modifications of other strata of the concretized work, and then it either leads to a *better* expression and a meaningful supplementation of other strata or produces obscurity and distortion in some elements of the latter (cf. "good" and "bad" declamations). In the first instance, the concretized work—if we take it as a pure work—can gain new aesthetic values which are strange but "suitable" to it; in the second, on the contrary, it can lose various values which according to its essence it should possess (more precisely, these values are not expressed).

2. In a concretization, word meanings and meaning contents of sentences can be intermingled, even in a fundamentally adequate apprehension, with meaning components that are unspecifiable and that change from case to case (e.g., if in a given region certain words have a specific local coloration of meaning which is, in a certain sense, "untranslatable").[11] Even if they produce no significant deviation in the stratum of meaning units of a given literary work, they can, in various respects, determine intentional states of affairs or represented objectivities, and, in particular, the "thus-appearance" of the latter, more closely or differently than these are predetermined by the work itself. Because of this, spots of indeterminacy that are necessary for the work itself may be partially removed, especially when, among the intermingled meaning elements, there are actualizations of moments of the potential stock of nominal word meanings appearing in the given work. If the intermingled meaning

10. A special modification occurs in the case of silent reading, where, first, the graphic element plays a role and, second, the word sounds are not perceived *in concreto* but are only imagined. We shall not concern ourselves with this at greater length.

11. That is, speaking more exactly, the meaning of this coloration is usually not made conscious separately and clearly, and it can be apprehended or intended only as one that is fused with the total stock of meaning, on the basis of a corresponding immediate experiencing. See H. Ammann's appropriate observations in *Die menschliche Rede* (Lahr i.B., 1925), Vol. I.

components produce deviations or more significant transformations of sentence meanings—in which case, naturally, one can no longer speak of adequate apprehension of the work's meaning stratum—there occurs what we usually call, somewhat inappropriately, an "alteration" of the whole work. What actually occurs here is either a shift in meaning which obscures the work or the conscious creation of a new work, one that is only more or less related to the original.

3. In a concretization, sentence meanings are really apprehended or intended. Thus they no longer remain in the form of a *loaned* intentionality, which is characteristic for the meaning stratum of the literary work itself, but are *taken over* by the reader from words (or sentences) and really *actually* intended. Naturally—to stress it once again—the intended meaning does not become something psychic because of this. It would be absurd to claim this.

4. The most radical difference between a literary work and its concretizations appears in the aspect stratum. From mere preparedness [*Parathaltung*] and schematization in the work itself, aspects attain concreteness in the concretization and are raised to the level of perceptual experience (in the case of a stage play) or imaginational experience (in a reading). In this, concretely experienced aspects inevitably transcend the schematized content of aspects held in readiness in the work itself by virtue of the simple schema's being filled out, in various respects, by concrete elements. As a result of these completions, which, to be sure, are prescribed to a certain degree by the schematized aspects (though they may still vary from case to case), any two concretizations of one and the same work must differ from each other. Moreover, the completions, and the changes taking part in them, may be so diverse in nature that it is hardly possible to foresee how a given specific concretization may be formed. And this is especially true for the further reason that every concretely experienced aspect of a represented object is analogous to only an abstractly excerpted segment of the entire content of the aspect of our respective total surroundings—a segment which is in fact immersed in the total aspect of these surroundings, is intermingled with it, and in various ways is functionally dependent on the "rest" of this content. Completions (fulfillments) and, connected with them, the displacements that occur within contents of aspects (even if they are minute) may, for example, cause the predominance of a type of aspect not prescribed in the work itself. Thanks to this, represented objects

may, for example, appear in a concretization in a form much more strongly rationalized than it is, in the work itself, *de facto* represented and made to appear [12] by aspects held in readiness. As a result, concrete aspects may contain entirely new decorative moments, which were not at all intended, so to speak, by the work, and may thus even impose a new style on the whole concretized work. Whether, in the event of such a sweeping transformation of the aspect stratum, the given concretization can still be considered a concretization of the *same* work, or whether it then expresses an entirely *new* work, is a matter that requires a separate, extensive analysis in each concrete instance. In any event, the identity of the work presented in various concretizations can be maintained only if the objectivities represented in it permit in their thus-appearance various styles of modes of appearance and if, at the same time, the change in the style of appearance does not effect the manifestation of metaphysical qualities predetermined in the work itself.[13] If these two conditions are not met, we are dealing with the concretization of a *new* work. If this [inappropriate] concretization is considered a concretization of the original work, we get a characteristic phenomenon of obscuration [of the work by one of its variants]. A literary work can be expressed for centuries in such a masked, falsifying concretization until finally someone is found who understands it correctly, who sees it adequately, and who in one way or another shows its true form to others. Herein lies the great role of literary criticism (or literary history) or—if we are dealing with the theater—of stage-directing: through it the true form of the work can again be expressed. Conversely, false

12. Strictly speaking, this appearance is really effected only in a concretization.

13. From this point of view one can start a discussion about whether a given performance of a play is "good" or "bad" and understand the full sense of this discussion. There are, of course, cases—indeed precisely where the above given conditions are fulfilled—where both parties to the argument are correct and the polemic is sterile. But even here the fundamental validity of both points of view can be indicated objectively. The subjective standpoint of some critics, who in principle consider their individual "impression" the sole distinguishing factor, certainly goes too far. The so-called subjectivity of criticism or literary history undoubtedly comes about only when the critics focus solely on the changing concretizations of the work. But this is precisely what is not necessary. Only a direct orientation on what is essential for the given work and an elimination of the manifold accidents of individual concretizations are required in order to emerge from a hopeless state of radical subjectivity. Basically, the radically subjective standpoint of literary criticism is mere naïveté.

interpretation, resulting from false concretizations, may obscure it.

Even though the change in style of the mode of appearance does not produce extensive transformations in the work and its identity is thus maintained, the style alteration which can still occur in concretizations nonetheless brings about a modification of the concretized work's total polyphony of value qualities. This opens up the possibility of the transformation of one and the same literary work in the course of the formation of its concretizations, the possibility of a "life" of the literary work itself. This possibility is obviously connected with transformations in the other strata of the concretized work. We shall return to this presently.

5. The concretization of a literary work is furthermore distinguished by the fact that a truly explicit *appearance* of represented objectivities occurs only here, whereas in the work itself they are only indicated and held in a state of potentiality by aspects held in readiness. A *fully* perceptual appearance, however, can be given only by the concretization of a stage play. Herein lies the previously indicated superiority of this kind of literary work.

6. In concretizations of works there comes a situation that may deceive us as to the essential nature of the literary work. Because of the transformations in the strata of phonetic formations, units of meaning, and aspects that occur in a concretization of a work, a number of spots of indeterminacy in represented objects are removed.[14] As a result, represented objects appear to us in concretizations in a much fuller form than they possess *de facto* in the work itself. Their constitution is taken one step further. In principle, however, they *cannot be completed* in *any* concretization; i.e., spots of indeterminacy will always remain in the represented objects. For it is part of the essence of purely intentional objects—as Edmund Husserl quite correctly observes, though without good reason he carries this

---

14. If the identity of the work is to be maintained, the limits of variability of the individual fulfillments that are prescribed by the moments constituted in the work may not be transgressed. This variability in the face of the maintained identity of the work is permissible only because the work is a schematized formation. When W. Conrad speaks of a sphere of irrelevancy in the "realization" of the work, he probably has in mind precisely this permissible variability of individual fulfillings, in both the stratum of aspects and the stratum of represented objects. But it is only when we have established the literary work as a schematized formation that we can understand that this sphere of irrelevancy is possible and allowed by the very essence of the work.

claim over to real objects—that they cannot be *fully* constituted in *any finite* series of constitutions. Now, the objects represented in a literary work are, according to their content, almost exclusively of the nature of real objects, which, as we have already established, can exist only as universally, unequivocally determined objects. Consequently, we are predisposed in the apprehension of represented objects in the concretization of a work to treat them as *fully* determined and to forget that we are dealing here with purely intentional objectivities. By doing this, we certainly distort the literary work; but it is only through this that the represented objectivities expressed in the concretization attain in their content an approximation to the nature of real objects so far-reaching that their power of suggestion increases to a high degree. We are then almost inclined to believe in their reality, and yet, due to the aesthetic attitude, we never believe this with complete seriousness.[15] It is precisely this disposition for a reality acceptance that never reaches serious consummation, that is always held back at the last moment, as it were, that forms the special nature of the aesthetic attitude and carries with it that unique stimulation we get from dealing with works of art in general and with literary works in particular. "Real," yet not real in earnest; breath-taking, but never as painfully so as in the real world; "true," and yet only "imagination." This attitude truly allows us to enjoy to the full the aesthetically valuable qualities of the work and gives us that unique delight that no real fact—even the "most beautiful"—can give us. The disposition for reality acceptance which, in the case of vital intercourse with literary works of art, takes place in their concretization, is indispensable for perceiving aesthetic values and would not be possible—only in the case of *literary* works, of course—without the quasi-judgmental modification of assertive propositions. If, as a result of any circumstance in which the concretization of the work takes place, we are forced to take at the outset the attitude that the represented events and objects deal with *purely fictitious* formations, which carry no trace of a

15. Naturally, an attitude is possible—especially in the case of a play performed in a theater—where a positive, unconditional acceptance of represented objectivities is effected (e.g., if children form the audience). But then we are dealing with a particular illusion, which does not permit the aesthetic values of the given literary work of art to be apprehended in its concretization. For this reason we believe that Konrad Lange errs in his conception of the essence of art, even though this conception at first seems to be very plausible. One would still have to examine in detail what he understands by "illusion." That would take us too far, however.

habitus of reality, then for us the work remains irrelevant, dead, dispensable; its polyphony of value qualities cannot develop, nor can the metaphysical qualities be manifested.[16] At the same time, however, every step beyond the mere *habitus* of reality toward the fullest reality acceptance, toward absolute illusion, makes an adequate expression of the literary work of art impossible in the given concretization.

7. Finally, we must mention still one more property of the concretization of a literary work, one that we have in fact already indicated. The particular order of sequence of the parts of a literary work is transformed in a concretization into a genuine sequence in phenomenal, concrete time. Here the literary work attains genuine *development*. Every concretization of a literary work is a temporally extended formation. The time span occupied by a given concretization may be greater or smaller according to circumstances, but it can never disappear. It is only thanks to this that the external and internal dynamics of the literary work of art achieve developed expression, whereas in the work itself they remain in a state of unique potentiality. Thus it is only in a concretization that those aesthetic values that are conditioned by the dynamics of the work or carried by them can be fully constituted.

§ 64. The *"life"* of a literary work in its concretizations, and its transformations as a result of changes in the latter

THE ARGUMENTS in the preceding section have opened the way for a new problem, which we might call the problem of the *life* of a literary work. Here the word "life" is used in a metaphorical sense, and therefore it would be advisable for us first of all to clarify the original meaning of this word, at least in its main elements. It is very difficult indeed to explain this meaning thoroughly, since the essence of life has not yet been satisfactorily established. Only a few indispensable observations in this respect should suffice to illustrate the situation in the case of a literary work.

16. If Konrad Lange has this situation in mind when he speaks of "illusion," then his position is certainly correct in principle.

The word "life" means two things above all: the *totality* of events happening to a living being from its beginning to its death, and, second, the "process" of becoming of these events, itself. If we take the word "life" in the second sense, it immediately becomes obvious to us that every "living" being *continues* as one and the same individual for a period of time. And as long as it exists at all, there can be no phase of interruption in its life. And conversely, too: if the life of an individual ceases, it ceases to be an individual. Life in this sense is a particular mode of existence of individuals of a determinate kind. Continuity of life, however, does not suffice to characterize it exhaustively, since "dead" things also continue for periods of time. We must thus add a second feature: every living being continually *changes* during its life (in the first meaning of the word). Whether this change *must* extend continuously over the entire life (as is claimed by some investigators, e.g., Bergson) may be left undecided. But again, this change as such is not characteristic of life: a *particular system* of changes must exist which, despite all the fortuities in which a given individual lives, remains typical for all living beings and establishes the "life" of an individual (in the first sense) as a typical and uniform *whole*. Every living being has a specific system of changes in which this being [*Wesen*] "develops" and which lead to a culminating phase where what was previously contained in embryo and in a particular actual potentiality [17] "develops" into what the given living being "essentially" should be. This culminating phase is in turn followed by a system of characteristic changes, in which there is a slower or faster (or altogether abrupt) reversal, a decay up to the moment of incapacity for life, to the moment of "death." The progression through these characteristic phases of change appears to us to be the essential element of life. Various circumstances in which a living being develops may of course prevent it from attaining one of its predesignated, so to speak, culminating phases, so that, unripe and prematurely atrophied, it draws closer to death; similarly, it is also possible for the life of an individual to be "cut short" abruptly by external circumstances. But the very fact that one can speak at all, with *justification*, of a "period of maturity" or of a different development of certain situations "than one would normally expect" indicates the cor-

17. One is reminded here of Heidegger's paradoxically formulated proposition: "Existence *is* its possibility" (see *Sein und Zeit* [Halle, 1927], pp. 42, 143; English translation by John Macquarrie and Edward Robinson, *Being and Time* [London, 1962]).

rectness of this conception of life. And still one more thing: the idea that whatever is living must necessarily be a psychic or even conscious being is a question that is at the very least highly questionable. Whether psychic or not, every living being has (or at least seems to have) emanating from it an active manner of reacting to forces working on it. This manner of reacting is totally different from the way "dead" things *passively undergo* change.[18] The essential elements of life indicated by us undoubtedly do not exhaust its nature. But they suffice for our purposes.

It is clear that the literary work cannot "live" in the strict sense of the term. The distinguishing elements, however, and the analogies should be established.

Once a given literary work has been written (conceived), it can exist without undergoing any changes even when many concretizations of it arise. There is nothing in the essence of the literary work itself that would necessitate change. The only thing that is necessary and visible on the basis of its structure is that at some point it has to *come into being*. For it is the stratum of meaningful sentences and, in particular, the manifold interconnections among the sentences that actually appear in a work (but these interconnections are accidental, in that others are possible for these same sentences [19] if they appear in a different order) which indicate subjective operations where sentences are formed and sentence complexes are established. As a purely intentional object, the literary work of art need not partake in the events of the real world and be drawn into their flow. But precisely because it emerges from the execution of subjective operations and hence lies fundamentally within the range of action of psychic individuals who can effect such operations, and because, at the same time, sentences that have been created do not necessarily have to appear in the form once given to them, the literary work can undergo changes without ceasing to be the same work. Indeed, these may be changes that are realized not only in the stratum of phonetic formations (as, e.g., in a "faithful" translation) but also in the units of meaning and thus in the strata that are constitutively dependent on them. Our daily praxis already convinces us that in a given work some sentences (and hence states of affairs) can be removed or

18. See M. Scheler, *Die Stellung des Menschen im Kosmos* (Darmstadt, 1928).
19. "These same sentences," but with the qualification that various modifications of meaning occur in their content owing to the change of order (see § 23, above).

replaced by other appropriately selected sentences without affect-
ing what is essential for the represented objects and events or
the polyphony of value qualities that is characteristic of the
given work. The changes may even go so far that, e.g., by de-
leting "unnecessary" sections, the given work may be made more
concentrated, strengthened in its internal dynamics, and therefore, if need be, "improved," without thereby becoming a different, other work.[20]

Here we come upon an essential problem, entirely different
in nature from the one we treated in Part II. There we were dealing with the essential basic structure of the literary work *in
general.* Here it is a question of what is essential or inessential
for a *very specific* literary work, taken in its *individuality,* which,
as a literary work, must contain the previously indicated basic
structure. Only very concrete investigations performed on a
specific work can determine what is part of its essence and,
therefore, how far changes of this kind can go without destroying the original work or without creating an entirely new work.
Regardless of how matters stand in individual cases, it is clear,
at any rate, that (1) all these changes can be brought about
only on the condition that appropriate subjective operations are
directed at them (so to speak "from outside") and (2) these
operations can be realized only in a concretization of a work.
The work *itself,* once it has been created, cannot in *any* respect
change *by itself,* cut off, so to speak, from its concretizations; it
can only *be* changed. This is already implicit in the fact that
none of its strata, nor it itself, taken as a whole, is an *ontically
autonomous* object. It is created, changed, and destroyed by appropriate subjective operations. For a literary work can even be
destroyed when the author undoes the already created work by
means of special intentional acts and simultaneously also destroys the physical conditions whose existence would enable
other psychic subjects to concretize the work already condemned
by its author to nonexistence.

If we observe that a literary work can undergo change only
on condition that it be expressed in a concretization, one can
speak of its "life" in a twofold and, in both cases, figurative
sense: (1) the literary work "lives" while *it is expressed in a*

20. See Max Scheler, "Formalismus in der Ethik," *Jahrbuch für
Philosophie und phänomenologische Forschung,* I (1913), 419; English
translation by Manfred S. Frings and Roger L. Funk, *Formalism in
Ethics and Non-Formal Ethics of Values* (Evanston, Ill.: Northwestern
University Press, 1973).

manifold of concretizations; (2) the literary work "lives" while it *undergoes changes as a result* of ever new concretizations appropriately formed by conscious subjects. Let us try, to begin with, to further clarify the first point.

Individual concretizations of one and the same work are, on the one hand, individual objectivities that have *no real* parts in *common* and hence form a manifold of *distinct* elements. On the other hand, they are still concretizations of *one and the same* work. However, this does not mean merely that they are more or less similar to one another; it means, above all, that they all have a special relationship to the work. We shall attempt to clarify this relationship in the next chapter. In addition, this manifold of concretizations is, generally speaking, temporally ordered; there are concretizations which develop earlier or later in time.[21] The distinctness and temporal discreteness of concretizations (in the case of one and the same reader) makes it impossible for a given concretization directly to cause changes in a temporally later one. If a change which occurs, for whatever reason, in a concretization C_n is to appear in a later concretization of the same work, a new factor, lying outside the work and its concretizations, is required: namely, a conscious individual who concretizes the work and who from his own experience knows the concretization C_n. If this factor comes into play, which—as we shall soon see—can happen in various ways, it is possible for later concretizations to take into account, as it were, changes occurring in earlier concretizations; nor is it precluded that retroaction may occur. In particular, we have the following possible situations in mind.

If we read the same work a number of times in succession (even if at long intervals), we usually remember more or less accurately the concretizations constituted in the previous readings and read *sub specie,* so to speak, of these earlier concretizations without being clearly conscious of which particular items in these concretizations are to be ascribed to the action of these concretizations and which are the adequate expression of the work itself (and "its" concretizations in a *narrower* sense). We can, e.g., have from the very beginning a certain attitude that is not quite appropriate for the given work and thus read it "falsely," i.e., we can develop concretizations that do not ade-

21. This does not mean that, of any two given concretizations of a work, one must always be "earlier" and the other "later." It is possible for two, or indeed many, concretizations to develop synchronously or to partially overlap in time.

quately express the work. We may form the habit of false read-ings; new concretizations, which of course inevitably produce modifications, thus carry all the traces of the first inadequate concretization. Only a change in the original attitude—whether caused by external circumstances or by the fact that in a given happy moment we are particularly susceptible to the peculiar nature of the work and attain a better understanding of it—can suddenly break off this connected series of concretizations and open up a new one which differs from the first in a number of critical features. Naturally, the series that is built on the first inadequate concretization can always contain in its later ele-ments new features, all of which lie in one *line*, as it were, and always represent a further development of the original tendency contained, as in embryo, in the first concretization. It is equally possible, however, for later concretizations to be ever fuller and more adequate expressions of the work or for various modifica-tions to occur within the framework of moments that are not unequivocally established by the work itself. The concretizations may then represent a continually progressing development of types allowed by the work, e.g., of decorative moments of the manifolds of aspects or of the completions of spots of indeter-minacy, and the like. Or again, there may be a change in the type that is allowable, etc. It is a known fact that every epoch in the over-all development of human culture has its own particular type of understanding, its own aesthetic and nonaesthetic val-ues, its specific predispositions to precisely one and not other modes of apprehending the world in general and works of art in particular. In some periods of time we are especially susceptible to specific aesthetic value qualities, while being blind to others. But when we are also capable of perceiving the latter in the works of art presented to us, the values characteristic for the given period are still closer to us. If the literary work, or the lit-erary work of art, were not a schematic formation, as it in fact is, it would also not be possible for there to be, in different eras, concretizations of one and the same work that could adequately, or at least in a manner allowed by the work, express its unique features and still differ variously and radically among them-selves. It is only the schematic nature of the literary work that makes this fact possible and understandable. But it is not always —as we have already established above—that the development of the manifold of a work's concretizations goes in such a direc-tion that the changes that occur in them stay solely within the bounds predetermined by the work. Frequently there are far-reaching deviations from the work and various phenomena of obscuration, which are closely connected to changes in the cultural atmosphere. They are also closely connected with other circumstances, however. Certain works of art, and, in particular, certain literary works of art, require appropriate *training* on our part if the developing concretizations of work are to be adequately expressed. This training can come about in various ways. In this way we also come to the circumstances in which still other factors than the ones mentioned above contribute to the mediation between the individual concretizations. These are, above all, verbal or written transmission of moments that are characteristic for the individual concretizations of a work to another reader, i.e., when one reader tells another of these concretizations or informs him of his own manner of apprehending the work.[22] All "critical" articles, essays, discussions, attempts at interpretation, historico-literary studies, etc., belong in this category and play the mediating role in the realization of ever new concretizations of the work. They train the reader to understand the work in a certain way and hence apprehend it in determinately conditioned concretizations; sometimes this training is good, but sometimes it is bad. Another instance of such mediation, i.e., in the case of a play, is the staging of a work by a director according to his understanding of it. It shows the spectators this work in a form that prescribes a manifold of specifically conditioned concretizations. Both the "repetition" of the performance and its imitation by other directors produce concretizations which are all guided not only by the first performance but also by that concretization of the work that was constituted in the director's reading (of the work). To be sure, in this case there is a shift in the interrelationships of the individual concretizations. One may say that it is the *performance*, which serves as a model, that undergoes concretization, and not the play itself. Within the total manifold of a work's concretizations, a special group is constituted whose members are closely interrelated. Gradually a tradition is developed of performing or understanding the given work in a certain manner, so that the reader is, from the beginning, under the influence of a "literary atmosphere" that has arisen in these various ways. This "literary atmosphere" introduces itself into the over-all cultural atmosphere of the time and maintains various functional relations with it. It has a tendency

22. Usually this report has the form of information concerning the work itself, since the informer is not aware of the difference between the work and its individual concretization.

to persist for some time. Only when the external circumstances of life are altered by some, e.g., political, event or when a strong individual appears who, either by the creation of novel works of art or by a novel interpretation of existing works, enters and drastically alters the current cultural atmosphere can there be a change in it. Concretizations of works that are constituted as a result of this change then assume a visibly different form. Of course, when we speak of a cultural atmosphere of an era, it is only a simplifying and stabilizing approximation. The atmosphere is changing continuously, if slowly, and, for the people of a given era, usually imperceptibly. In each period of time, moreover, it conceals disconnected and incoherent moments. Nevertheless, in the total manifold of intersecting currents, tendencies, attitudes, etc., a specific "trend of the times" can be clearly distinguished, one that is noticeable particularly in the style of the works of art created in a given period. On the other hand, one can ascertain certain lines of change occurring over the course of succeeding eras. Since, as we have already attempted to show, the concretizations of a literary work are dependent on the attitudes of the reader, they consequently carry in various respects the "traits of the times" and to a certain degree take part in changes of cultural atmosphere. As a result, the manifold of concretizations of one and the same work is ordered not only purely temporally, but it also indicates a factual order that is relative to the atmosphere of the given era. In this sense one can speak of development, unforeseen changes, declines, and renaissances. If one merely has in mind a gradually developing manifold of a work's concretizations, one can speak of the "life" of a literary work *in* its concretizations.

In spite of all the differences between the "life" of a literary work, understood in this way, and the life of a living being (which we cannot further develop here), there are also clear analogies. We will have to rest content with pointing out one of them. In its concretizations, the life of a literary work—especially if it is a work of art of the first order and not "stillborn" kitsch—shows phases in its course of development as sharply delineated as those that occur in the life of a psychic individual. There is a period (especially in ground-breaking works) in which the work cannot be fully expressed in its concretizations because the reader cannot yet fully understand it, a period of preparation, of containing in embryo, what later will be fully developed or at least can be developed. There comes a period when the number of concretizations does not merely grow, as the work is read by more and more people, but the work, in both the individual concretizations and the development of the total wealth of its aspects manifesting themselves therein, undergoes an ever more adequate expression—which is similar to man's period of maturity. In this manner the work simultaneously "experiences" the culminating point of its "success": it stands in the center of interest of a generation, it enjoys the valuation of all its features, it is valued, loved, and admired. Then, for whatever reason, the spiritual atmosphere of the time changes. The number of concretizations decreases, concretizations that are constituted are more and more inadequate, some of the aspects of the work are not concretized at all, a visible coolness appears in the relationship between the readers and the work, it can no longer excite them, it is increasingly more foreign to them and more impoverished in its concretizations, until it sinks and fades into oblivion: there comes a time where there are no concretizations of the work.

This general schema of the "life" of a literary work in its concretizations naturally can undergo various modifications in a given concrete instance. For long years the work may not "experience" any concretizations, and then comes a brief day of rapid popularity and the formation of diverse concretizations. It can last through a number of different spiritual eras and then undergo [a phase of] typically changing concretizations; it may "fade away" and then unexpectedly "experience" a period of revival, etc. What is important is that there really is a certain analogy to the life of a living being.

There is, however, a further analogy: just as a living being changes in connection with the lives of other living beings and under the influence of the real circumstances in which it finds itself in its individual life-phases, so there are changes in the concretizations of a literary work that are closely connected with the lives of psychic individuals and are influenced by the cultural atmosphere. Yet, at the same time, there is a significant difference here. By virtue of its organization and its ontic autonomy, a living being has its own mode of reacting to the influences of the external world; the source of its mode of reaction lies within itself. In contrast, the concretization of a literary work is not an ontically autonomous object. Thus it cannot "react" to cultural influences. It only *undergoes* changes, which correspond to the conscious acts from which it arises. And though the work itself takes part in its shaping when the reader is attuned to its apprehension and when this attitude essentially codetermines the constituting of the concretization (even though certain limits of variability of the concretization are predetermined from the standpoint of a more or less adequate expression of the work), it is still not at all necessary for this expression to occur, and thus the concretization may depend totally on the constituting subjective operations. If worse comes to worst, it would not be a concretization of the given work but a pure product of subjective operations: the first concretization of an entirely new work. This is caused precisely by its ontic heteronomy as well as by the discontinuity between a concretization and the work itself.

There is, however—as we have already indicated—still another "life" to a literary work. We say the work "lives" when it *itself* (and not merely its concretization, as in the above instance) *undergoes various changes* as a result of variously formed concretizations. How are we to understand this more precisely?

If there were no concretizations of a work at all, it would be separated from concrete human life as by an impenetrable wall. Concretizations constitute, as it were, the connecting link between the reader and the work and emerge when the reader approaches it cognitively and aesthetically. However, since concretizations are the only form in which the work can show itself to the reader in its full unfolding and are the only form in which he can grasp the work, and since, at the same time, every concretization contains, besides those elements which express the work, others which complete it and modify it in various respects, and, finally, since the overwhelming majority of concretizations express the work only inadequately, the development of a manifold of concretizations has a significant influence on the literary work itself: it undergoes various transformations due to the changes that occur in the concretizations. Obviously, this is possible only on the further condition that, as he reads, the reader (or the spectator in a performance) take a certain attitude toward the work; but this, after all, is most frequently the case and is altogether natural.

We have previously established that, just as the literary work arises from subjective operations, it can also be changed or even destroyed by analogous subjective operations. What we had in mind then were, above all, the operations in which, for example, the author (in preparing a "second edition") or the reader, with *conscious intent*, establishes a different connection between sentences or even introduces some new ones. In such cases the work is changed in a conscious, intentional manner. The literary work, however, can also be changed unintentionally. Such a change can occur when, in a simple apprehension of the work, the reader—as is usually the case—is not conscious either of the fortuitousness of a *given* concretization or of those points in which it materially and necessarily differs from the work, or, finally, of the concretization as something to be contrasted to the work itself. As a result, he absolutizes the given concretization, identifies it with the work, and in a naïve way directs himself intentionally to the work thus intended. Everything that pertains to the content of the given concretization is then ascribed to the work. Indeed, in this naïve manner of apprehending the work, the subjective operations of apprehension are simultaneously effected along with the simple categorical realization of the existence [*Setzung*] of the work thus intended. Hence the work is not sifted carefully, in a critical and cautious receptive attitude, to remove all the possible impurities, but instead is violated and altered. The changes may be of various kinds. The most far-reaching among them are those produced in the stratum of meaning units, because this stratum plays the greatest constitutive role in the work, and changes occurring in it evoke changes in nearly all the other strata. The most frequent changes to occur are those that depend on the actualization of a different part of the potential stock of meanings from the one that is predetermined by the context. However, word sounds or word signs can have meanings attributed to them that are entirely different from those belonging to the work, and these meanings can become fixed in the work itself.[23] But even if the changes in the structure of the work were not that far-reaching, the absolutization of a concretization i.e., where it is taken for the work itself, would produce changes in the latter. For every concretization—as we have already established above—necessarily goes beyond the literary work. Hence the work itself seems to be fuller and more substantial than it actually is. As a result of the inevitable, even if slight, inadequacy in expressing the work that appears in a concretization, the work changes imperceptibly in the hands of the reader. If we also observe that changes in individual concretizations have a tendency to become consolidated in subsequent concretizations, we will realize that the work

23. That this is possible at all stems from the fact that the connection between a determinate word sign (or word sound) and a determinate meaning is not a necessary unity but is rather only a linkage that is relative to a meaning-bestowing act or to other subjective factors.

itself, "living" in its concretizations, changes in consequence of these transformations, develops in one direction or another, takes on stylistic features which originally were only allowed by its structure, weathers crises of style changes or becomes atrophied, etc. In *this* sense the literary work itself "lives," as opposed to the "life" we discussed earlier, when we were dealing only with its concretizations. It has phases of magnificent development and perfection as well as phases in which, through impoverishment of the concretizations, it itself becomes more and more impoverished, etc. It is also possible for the language in which the work is written to lose its manifestation qualities for us because it is no longer a "living" language. In that case, some states of affairs are not developed at all and certain aspects cannot be held in readiness; consequently, corresponding objectivities cannot be depicted, and, at the same time, the work is poorer in some decorative moments and the like. The work may then die a natural death, so to speak, since at a given point in time it is totally foreign and incomprehensible to the readers, inasmuch as they are no longer capable of reaching its peculiar form and discovering the treasures that are dormant there. If the work is "written down," it is always possible in principle to nullify all the changes produced in it, provided there is someone who can "decipher" it. A work which is then "dead" can be reborn. Once we lose the original meaning of the text, it is impossible to restore the original work unless we reconstruct by some *other* means—e.g., by historical studies—the original correlation between word sign (or word sound) and meaning. If we succeed, however, with a meaning-adequate "deciphering" of the text, the original work reappears in its proper form, and all later changes in the work are cleared away and removed by appropriate subjective operations as "falsifications" and "misunderstandings." In fact here—despite prevailing opinion—the work is usually changed anew; it is only that the new changes return it to its original form. All these changes, however, must remain within the limits that are characteristic of every single work if the identity of the work is to be maintained. Here again there arises the important and difficult problem of how to determine these limits of change. We cannot solve this problem here. In the first place, because the essence of an object's identity is still not at all clear; second, because—as we have already indicated above —these limits can be determined only on the basis of apprehending the *individual* essence of a specific work. This transcends the subject matter of our investigation. But the general observation, that changes in a specific work must occur within such limits if its *individual* nature is to be maintained, is of little use for us until this individual nature is established for a specific work. New investigations, oriented in an entirely different direction and focusing on an entirely specific work, would be necessary here. What is important for our purpose is the basic fact that the literary work can undergo change without losing its identity. By this same token, the question posed at the beginning, as to whether the literary work is an ideal object, is again answered—negatively. What remains now is to determine as positively and precisely as possible the ontic position of a literary work.

14 / The Ontic Position
of a Literary Work

§ 65. *Introduction*

WE HAVE TRAVELED a long way. We have considered
the literary work in its various aspects and in its numerous structural features and have demonstrated situations that have succeeded in revealing its essential nature and clearly showing it in
its heterogeneity with respect to psychic experiences on the one
hand and ideal objectivities on the other. We believe that we
have uncovered in the literary work a unique sphere of specially
structured objectivities which are very important for various
reasons, and, among them, purely ontological reasons. Almost at
the end of our study we came upon the phenomenon of the "life"
of a literary work and the interrelations between the work itself
and its concretizations and, hence, its relation to subjective operations and experiences. After taking into account the entire
range of these issues, we see that a certain danger that was supposed to have been practically overcome arises anew: the literary
work, taken purely in itself, appears at first to be a totally rigid
formation, and, in this rigidity, it is also fully secured as regards
its identity. In isolation from all its concretizations and from the
subjective operations of apprehensions performed by the reader,
it appears to us as something so heterogeneous with respect to
subjective operations that every thought about its subjectivization or psychologization must from the outset be quite untenable.
After taking into consideration the situations that are produced
when the work is read by a number of readers, it again seems to
be threatened in its identity and in its proud heterogeneity with
respect to subjective experiences. In spite of all the differences

that we have established between it and its concretizations, it seems to dissolve in their manifold variety and to lose, thanks to the close ontic interrelations and interrelations of essence between concretizations and subjective experiences, its heterogeneity with respect to these experiences. Thus the old question crops up again: is not the psychologistic conception of the literary work right, after all? Would it not, instead of speaking of *one* literary work, expressed in many concretizations, be simpler and more correct to "reduce" the literary work to these various concretizations and simply consider it a theoretical, abstractly obtained fiction which does not "truly" exist? All that would exist then would be a manifold of "concretizations" which then, naturally, would be concretizations, not of anything identical, but merely of similar intentional correlates of corresponding manifolds of [conscious] acts. And would it not then be a mere difference of words to speak of "intentional correlates" instead of simply "imaginings" [*Vorstellungen*], as in a psychologistic conception? The conception of the literary work developed here may be finer and more subtle, and any talk of "imaginings" may still be very crude and primitive; but do they not ultimately come to the same thing, once we agree that the literary work can be "reduced" to a manifold of ostensible "concretizations" and, at the same time, assert—as in fact we have already done—that every single concretization necessarily belongs to the corresponding subjective experiences and exists if, and only if, these experiences exist?

Can the literary work, however, really be reduced to the manifold of concretizations? Is this not contradicted by the numerous differences we have shown between the work itself and its concretizations? Someone might answer us by saying that these differences exist only when at the outset one posits the idea of a literary work expressing itself in its concretizations, which is what has actually happened in our study thus far. But what guarantees for us the identity of the work with respect to all its concretizations, especially when it is conceded that the individual concretizations differ widely among themselves and that the reader very frequently absolutizes the concretization he has at the moment and believes that in it he has apprehended the work itself? And, in particular, if the work is read by different readers, what guarantee do we have of its identity, i.e., its *intersubjective* identity? And what is identical in that case? Might it not ultimately be shown that what is identical is nothing other than that which "evokes" the various concretizations, i.e., the "signs" on the paper that are perceived in the reading? But since these "signs" obviously cannot be that mysterious something which we call the "literary work" and with which we commune in the aesthetic attitude, it would perhaps be most correct to say that in the individual readings it is merely similar "concretizations" that arise and that it is only a special delusion or error if we all believe that we are reading one and the same work. Finally, if the literary work is only a formation of subjective operations, which cannot exist with ontic autonomy, the question arises, how does the work exist when it is not read by anyone? Is it not invalid hypostatizing to assert its existence also under these conditions? And even if it does exist in some manner, what constitutes its ontic basis if this basis is not to be the subjective cognitive operations?

At first glance, this whole complex of questions seems to refer to matters that are of interest only to literary theory, that is, matters that have no great significance for other disciplines, in particular for philosophy. Why, then, these difficult investigations and the effort to avoid, at all costs, the psychologistic solution? Such doubts are groundless, for here we come up against a question that is of fundamental significance for the theory of knowledge and especially for logic. For—as our arguments have shown—the scientific work is a borderline case of the "literary work," and the most important distinction between it and "literary works" lies in the fact that in scientific works sentences do not undergo any quasi-judgmental modification but are instead true judicative propositions. But regardless of whether they are true judicative propositions or not, they are, at any rate, *propositions*. If propositions are not ideal objectivities in the strict sense (as we hope to have shown), if they arise from special subjective operations, and if it is precisely this circumstance which leads us to doubt whether propositions so constructed possess intersubjective identity and a mode of existence that is heterogeneous with respect to subjective operations, then the above questions clearly refer just as much to the scientific work as to the purely "literary" one. And if this cannot validly be claimed for the literary work, the scientific work must also be deprived of this identity and this mode of existence and must likewise be reduced to a manifold of more or less varied "concretizations." What, then, could one say about the possibility of cognitively valuable science if the formations of scientific work were only "concretizations" of that kind, if the identity of the meaning of scientific assertions could be taken only *cum grano salis*, and if each one of us, in reading "a" scientific work, were, strictly speaking, dealing with *other* propositions, proofs, and theories? Is this not the direct path to skepticism, or at least to the admission that *intersubjective* knowledge is impossible? And, if strict communication is impossible, what would be the value of a science that is valid only for a single cognitive subject? For on what other scientific path can there be communication between cognitive subjects than by means of propositions?

Thus the dangers we are contending with here have an incomparably greater significance than the relatively unimportant matter of literary theory. Overcoming these dangers is of the greatest fundamental importance.

On the other hand, it is clear that if one could show that, despite their ontic relativity to subjective operations, sentences and complexes of sentences possess intersubjective identity and have a mode of existence that is heteronomous with respect to conscious acts and that enables them to exist even when—once they have been conceived—they are not thought or "read" by any conscious subject, then by that same token the intersubjective identity of the literary work as a *schematic* formation would be saved. For, as our analyses have shown, sentences form the constitutive element of the literary work, one on which all the other strata—with the exception of the stratum of phonetic formations and their determinate arrangement and with the exception of elements of other strata that are constitutively dependent on them—are ontically dependent. Therefore, if the intersubjective identity of the stratum of phonetic formation could not be established, the literary work "in itself" would, if one may so put it, indeed be poorer and more strongly relative to the momentary circumstances of the given reading than our analysis has shown; but this could no longer change anything in the existence and the intersubjective identity of the literary work—and hence also the scientific work.

Thus the problems that are now to be solved are the following: Are the sentences that arise from subjective operations intersubjectively identical? Do they also exist when they are not thought? What is their mode of existence and the ontic basis of their existence if they do exist?

§ 66. *The intersubjective identity of the sentence and the ontic basis of its existence*

IN THE STAGE OF ANALYSIS where we now find ourselves, there are two courses along which we can proceed: either the purely *phenomenological,* which refrains from accepting the existence of anything besides pure consciousness, or the *metaphysical,* which does not shy away from accepting the existence of other objectivities if there are justified motives for it and if the purely phenomenological approach does not suffice. If we wish to take the first course, we must examine now the phenomena and subjective operations of intersubjective linguistic communication among conscious subjects, as well as the effectiveness of this communication. In other words, we must show how it happens that, when two different conscious subjects apprehend a sentence, they apprehend a meaning that is *identically* the same [1] and how they can communicate with regard to this and become quite sure that this is truly the case. This course, however, would take us into the most difficult questions of the phenomenological theory of cognition, and totally new and extensive investigation would be indispensable. On the other hand, it would still only indicate a detour, since an ontic or metaphysical conclusion would have to be drawn only from the solution of the cognitive-theory problem. Thus, we will not follow this course, even though we fully see its validity. We also believe that our problem can be solved directly if we only succeed in finding the objective, ontically autonomous basis of existence of the literary work or of the sentences appearing in it.

First of all, we must distinguish between the basis of the *coming into being* of the literary work and the ontic basis of its *existence* (i.e., after formation). We have already found the former in the subjective operations the author executes when forming the work. They consist primarily of sentence-forming operations, though these, of course, do not exhaust them. The question now is, what do the sentence-forming operations do? Are they creative in a true sense, producing something totally

1. See Husserl, *Méditations cartésiennes,* (Paris, 1931), § 43, p. 77. [*Cartesianische Meditationen und Pariser Vorträge* (The Hague: Nijhoff, 1950); English translation by Dorion Cairns, *Cartesian Meditations: An Introduction to Phenomenology* (The Hague: Nijhoff, 1960), p. 91.]

new *ex nihilo,* and does what they produce have the same mode of existence as they? Both questions must be answered in the negative. In the process it will be shown what makes up the ontic basis of the literary work (or its constituent sentences) and what mode of existence applies to it. The subjective conscious acts in which the sentence-forming operations are executed are ontically autonomous objectivities. The created work and the created sentences are not ontically autonomous objectivities but only purely intentional ones. Nonetheless, the work (or the sentence) exists as soon as it is created. But it exists as an ontically heteronomous formation that has the source of its existence in the intentional acts of the creating conscious subject and, simultaneously, the basis of its existence in two entirely heterogeneous objectivities: on the one hand, in *ideal* concepts and ideal qualities (essences), and, on the other hand—as we shall see—in real "word signs." The only thing the sentence-forming operation (or the manifold subjective operations in which the literary work arises) can accomplish is—as far as the meaning content of the sentences is concerned—merely the *actualization* of the meaning elements of corresponding ideal concepts and the *formation* of these actualizations into *a unified whole.* Let us explain ourselves more precisely:

Earlier in our discussion we distinguished between word meanings and ideal concepts. A word meaning, we said, is nothing other than an *actualization* of the meaning contained in corresponding ideal, ontically autonomously existing concepts. Moreover, it is at any one moment an actualization of only a part of this meaning. This actualization and formation of a unified whole out of component parts is realized through sentence-forming operations whereby they immediately produce word meanings in the form in which they must appear as component parts of a determinate sentence or a determinate sentence complex. Through this actualization something new is undoubtedly produced: the meaning content of the sentence or the meaning content of a sentence complex. *Ideal concepts are not component parts* of these formations. They are as transcendent with respect to them as are subjective operations, and they are also transcendent with respect to the latter and remain beyond the reach of their influence. But they do constitute the ontic basis of sentences and the regulative principle of their formation. In consideration of their ideal meaning content, the conscious subject selects appropriate moments in them, brings about their ontically heteronomous actualization, and unites them into a new whole.

Along with the actualization of the meaning, there is at the same time an intentional concretization of word sounds and phonetic formations, so that the entire sentence (meaning-content and word-sound "expression") is thus created. The intentional formation of phonetic formations is different from the actualization of the meaning content of a sentence. We shall return to this shortly. Before we do, we must stress two things: (1) the fact that both ontic bases of the sentence or the literary work (the basis of its coming into being in subjective operations and the basis of its existence in ideal concepts) are transcendent with respect to it and, in particular, (2) that, in the actualization, the ideal meaning elements of a concept serve the author only as a model of the component parts of the actualized meaning content and that this fact decides the special, the unique, essence of the *ontically heteronomous* mode of existence of a literary work (or an individual sentence). The ontically heteronomously existing objectivity, as we have said, has no ontic basis in itself but rather refers to a different entity, indeed ultimately to an ontically autonomous entity. The intentional act of pure consciousness is not creative in the sense that it can create genuine realizations of ideal essences or ideal concepts [2] in an object that is intentionally produced by it. If it were creative in this sense, it could create genuinely real and *eo ipso* ontically autonomous objectivities. However, this is denied to it. Thus, in the forming of a sentence, it can produce only *actualizations* of ideal meaning contents of concepts and form them into new wholes (i.e., meaning contents of sentences). Moreover, these are actualizations in which no ideal, realized (i.e., having the ontic form of realization) meaning contents really [*reell*] inhere, that is, they are not immanent in the true sense that we find in the realization of ideal essences in *real* (and *ipso facto* ontically autonomous) objects. And similarly, if a purely intentional object (e.g., a "thing") is created by a conscious act, the intention contained in it is not capable of producing a *genuine* realization of any ideal essence.

In a strict, ontically autonomous sense, the intentionally created thing "is" not, e.g., "red." For it to be that, it would *really* [*reell*] have to contain a genuine realization of the essence "redness." It is precisely this inclusion, this immanence of the realization of an ideal essence in an objectivity, and, on the other hand, the realization itself, which the pure conscious act cannot produce. It never goes beyond the simulated quasi-inclusion described above, the quasi-realization which, on the one hand, re-

2. These do not permit any genuine realizations at all.

fers to the intentional *sic iubeo* of the conscious subject and, on the other, to the corresponding ideal essence. In this same sense, every sentence—taken according to its meaning content—refers to the sentence-forming operation of a conscious subject from which it is intentionally derived, as well as to the ideal concepts whose actualizations (but not realizations) constitute this sentence as components of its uniform total meaning.

However nonexistent a sentence or sentence complex may be in the sense of ontic autonomy, however unlikely it is that it will be found in the real world as a reality, it cannot be denied that *generally* it has an existence. It is not preposterous to accept its ontically heteronomous existence; but, conversely, it is preposterous to require of a meaning content of a sentence that it be real (possibly psychic) or ideal. It is incapable of being either one or the other. Anyone who is inclined to accept only ontically autonomously real or ideal objectivities must, for the sake of consistency, doubt the existence of sentences (and, by extension, sentence complexes, theories, literary works); at no time, however, can he make them into anything real or ideal. But then he must bear in mind that he thus also denies the possibility of science and negates his own thesis. In contrast, the person who concedes the ontically heteronomous existence of sentences must also admit *all* their ontically autonomous bases, and he cannot limit himself to accepting pure conscious acts. For just as a sentence could not come into being without sentence-forming operations, it likewise cannot exist ontically heteronomously without ideal concepts. This is, in fact, required, on the one hand by its characteristic ontic heteronomy, and on the other by the circumstance that it is a meaning-formation. The acceptance of ideal concepts, essences, and ideas may contradict so-called transcendental idealism, but transcendental idealism itself is untenable as long as it is contradicted by the very thing whose acceptance makes possible the principal discoveries and mainstays of transcendental idealism—the purely intentional object. For without ideal essences and ideas, purely intentional objectivities are impossible in the same degree as *real* objects taken in a *true* sense.

Just as the abandonment of ideal concepts makes word meanings, sentences, and sentence complexes impossible, and just as the idealization of the units of meaning of various degrees is as absurd and contradictory to the essential facts as is their psychologization, so, conversely, the acceptance of ideal concepts not only makes possible the recognition of the ontically heteronomous existence of sentences (and the derived intentional objectivities projected by them) but at the same time makes possible the acceptance of the intersubjective identity of sentences for different conscious subjects. It is only with reference to the meaning content of ideal concepts that the readers of a literary work can reactualize in an identical manner the meaning content of sentences given to them by the author. If there were no ideal concepts and, furthermore, no ideal qualities (essences) and ideas, not only would sentences or real and intentional objectivities be impossible; it would also be equally impossible to achieve between two conscious subjects genuine linguistic communication, in which both sides would apprehend an identical meaning content of the sentences exchanged. There frequently are misunderstandings between two speakers, and, practically speaking, they frequently cannot apprehend identically the same sentences. But with the existence of ideal concepts there is at least in principle the possibility that, by recourse to the corresponding objectivities and by apprehending at least part of the meaning content of the corresponding ideal concepts, each of the speakers succeeds in forming or reconstituting a sentence with a meaning content identical to the other's and hence understanding the sentence spoken by the other.

We believe that in this way we have overcome the danger of subjectivizing the literary work or of reducing it to a manifold of concretizations. But we have done so only by accepting the existence of ideal concepts. In order to fully justify the correctness of our position, we would need a theory of ideal concepts and their actualization in word meanings. This, however, would require a new and extensive study. To those for whom the acceptance of ideal concepts seems dangerous, who are inclined to assume a waiting attitude with regard to them, we can only suggest that they see in this acceptance a hypothesis without which neither the literary work as an identical objectivity opposed to all of its concretizations, nor the scientific work and intersubjective knowledge, nor, finally, the manifold concretizations of literary works could be accepted.

We must now complete our discussion of the formation and the existence of the phonetic stratum of the literary work.

§ 67. *The identity of the phonetic stratum of the literary work*

OUR PRECEDING ANALYSES have shown how great a role the phonetic stratum plays in a literary work. Thus it is necessary, after establishing the identity of the stratum of meaning units, to consider whether and within what limits the phonetic formations of a work are identical, in contrast to all their concretizations, and whether they can be identified as identical in the reading. Our previous distinction between the concrete phonic material and the "word sound" as a typical phonic formation will be helpful to us in this respect.

As we stated at the beginning of our analyses, only the phonetic *formations* of lower and higher order belong to the literary work itself. In this respect there is nothing to be changed in what has been said. There is only the question of how these formations are ascribed to the work and how their identity is evidenced in the work's manifold concretizations. The difficulty here lies in the fact that, in general, one cannot claim that word sounds— taken as meaning formations of this kind—are ideal essences or have their ontic basis in them. Word sounds are undoubtedly formed in the course of the development of a language and then become relatively established, so that in the space of rather long periods of time they are apprehended or intended, in linguistic intercourse and on the basis of concrete phonic material, as the same thing (and are themselves concretized). To a much greater extent this also applies to various phonetic formations of a higher order, which—especially in true literary works of art—can sometimes be unique and owe their origin to the author's creative powers. As something based on appropriately ordered word sounds, they are apprehendable without further ado and in an identical manner in the reading of the work as soon as the word sounds on which they are constructed are themselves apprehended in their identity. What is the situation, however, with the ontic basis of the identity of the word sounds and with the way their identity is evidenced in the individual concretizations of the work?

Let us assume that the author finds a manifold of word sounds in the living language in which he is writing the work. The assumption, then, is that the intersubjective identity of word sounds in the living language is assured.[3] By means of appropriate selection and ordering, the author intentionally incorporates these word sounds into the work during its creation, either in the manner of a simple oral *performance*—as, for example, in the case of folk songs—or by *fixing* them in writing, where it is again necessary to assume an intersubjective, established relationship between typical written word signs and the corresponding word sounds. By actually using phonetic formations (perhaps newly created ones), beginning with word sounds, the author determines, by means of a fixed intention, that precisely these phonetic formations and not others will belong to the given work. This intention in fact makes them as much an intentional component of the literary work as the other elements of the work. At the same time, it makes them external carriers of the word meanings that are actualized in conjunction with them. In this, the work is completed as an intentional formation. But now it must continue, *along with its phonetic stratum*, as identically the same. This is possible because there are ideas for everything that exists objectively. The word sounds that are actually expressed are an objectively existing entity in which the typical formations attain genuine concretization. The intention that causes the word sounds, in the sense of typical formations, to be components of the literary work produces at the same time an intentional concretization of the contents of the corresponding ideas of concretely expressed word sounds; this concretization is different from the ideas themselves and is only ontically heteronomous, but in them it has its ontic basis, which ontically founds the identity of the word sounds belonging to the given work, as opposed to all its concretizations. One of our difficulties is thus removed. Another matter, however, is the question of how word sounds, ontically founded in their identity, evidence their intersubjective identity when they are read by different subjects. The words actually expressed are created from the outset as intersubjectively identical formations as long as the given linguistic community continues to exist. Only a signal, as it were, is necessary for the reader to know that in a given case he is dealing precisely with these and no other words. These signals, which, as we have said, must be formed *typically*, are the *graphic* signs of *letters*. These typical letters, however, must be based on some individual, e.g., visually apprehensible, material. In other words, if it is not

3. The question of how this is possible is one of the most important problems of the philosophy of language. We cannot discuss it here, however.

simply meant to be given "orally" and, in this purely oral transmission, subjected to extensive changes, the literary work must be written down. In some real, fixed, relatively little-changeable material, the "letters" must be established as signals for the use of corresponding word sounds.[4] It is this appropriately formed real material which, along with subjective operations, ideal concepts, essences, and ideas, makes up the third, even though indirect, ontic basis of the literary work. Naturally, this basis is not sufficient for the ontically heteronomous existence of the work. The other two ontic bases must not only be present as well; they are, in fact, more essential for its existence simply because the relationship between the objectivities founded by them (i.e., the sentences) and the literary work is entirely different from the relationship between the typical letters or the concrete graphic material and the work. Whereas the sentences are genuine components of the literary work, neither the real graphic material nor the typical letters founded on it are an element of the literary work. As we have said, they are merely a *regulative signal* for the reader, informing him which word sounds he is to concretize in actual expression (as in recitation out loud) or in imaginative reconstruction (as in silent reading). This signal shows the reader the way, as it were, to apprehend the work in its phonetic stratum. Thus, although it is transcendent to the work itself, as well as to its concretizations, and has only a relatively fixed relationship to the word sounds, we can also see in it an indirect ontic basis for the work which makes possible the apprehension of an identical phonetic formation.

To be sure, this apprehension through the graphic recording of the work is assured only so long as "the same" signs are "linked" to the same word sounds; this, naturally, does not always happen, since this linkage is purely accidental and is relative to subjective acts of linking. If there is a change in the "pronunciation" of "the same" word, i.e., if for any reason there is a change in the word sound of "the" word, it is usually still linked to the same letters. The work is read and understood, but its phonetic stratum, and hence at least some of the work's elements which are constitutively dependent on the phonetic stratum, undergo various modifications. At first these modifications

---

4. Today the literary work can be fixed by recording it phonographically, without such "graphic signs" or "signals." This is not an essential distinction for us, however. In these cases, too, there exists a real object, the recording, in which the literary work finds its indirect ontic foundation.

occur, so to speak, only within the work's concretizations: with respect to the phonetic aspect, the work is apprehended incorrectly; there is still, however, the possibility of its adequate apprehension by recourse to the manner in which the given words "should" be pronounced. If, however, the reader ceases to be conscious of the fact that the "pronunciation" he uses is only an individual property that does not correspond to the author's "pronunciation," or the word sounds of his work, we have an instance of what we previously called the "absolutizing" of the work's concretization: with respect to its phonetic side, the readers read the work in such a manner that they intentionally think of the word sounds they use as belonging to the work itself, and in this way they therefore *change* the work itself. Then, if it is impossible to ascertain, even in an indirect way—say by historico-linguistic analysis—what the "proper pronunciation" of the given words should be (as, e.g., in the case of a "dead language"), the given literary work undergoes lasting change, which, in the light of the above-indicated central role of the phonetic stratum in the literary work, may be very far-reaching and may greatly affect the polyphonic harmony of the work's value qualities. And even though the work as a total formation remains the same, the identity of its phonetic stratum is then not assured to the same extent by its ontic bases as is the stratum of units of meaning in the recourse to ideal concepts. But even in the latter respect the work can undergo change—as we have already demonstrated. It may, for example, be impossible to have recourse to the corresponding ideal concepts, and the reader's absolutization of the individual concretizations of the work may cause some word meanings to be embodied in the work as actualizations of *other* ideal concepts than those in the original state of the work. In individual instances it may be difficult to prove the degree of these changes; but if, despite the changes worked in it, the work is to remain identically the same, it is nevertheless clear that the founding of the stratum of units of meaning in ideal concepts both protects the work ontically from subjectivization and makes it possible, at least in principle, to change it back to its original form.

This should certainly suffice to show that, despite the indisputable fact of its "life," the literary work cannot be psychologized.

15 / Concluding Reflections
on the Literary Work of Art

§ 68. *The literary work of art and the polyphonic harmony of its aesthetic value qualities*

IN CONCLUSION, it is incumbent on us to settle yet one more question relating to the literary work of art. In the course of our analyses we have frequently referred to the value qualities that are constituted in the individual strata of the literary work and that in their totality bring about a polyphonic harmony. The polyphonic harmony is precisely that "side" of the literary work that, along with the metaphysical qualities attaining manifestation, makes the work a *work of art*. In connection with this, the question may arise whether it is not simply this polyphonic harmony of value qualities that constitutes the literary work of art, so that the entire stratified structure that we have presented in all its details should be taken in the sense of a founding object which makes the establishment of a literary work of art possible but which in no sense belongs to it. The direct consequence of an affirmative answer to this question would be to take this polyphonic harmony not simply as a separate *stratum,* cutting across the entire literary work, as it were, but as a *separate object* with which we could deal only in terms of the aesthetic attitude and which would completely conceal from us both the complex stratified structure of the literary work—which would serve only to found that object—and the work itself. We would then have to begin our analysis anew in order to set forth the essence of the literary work of art thus formed. Our work thus far would then have to be considered as a possibly useful preparation but one that did not solve the real problem.

It seems to us that this viewpoint is false. A simple analysis of what is before us when we are dealing with a literary work of art convinces us of this. Certainly, if there were no aesthetic value qualities in the individual strata of the literary work, so that, as a result, no polyphonic harmony could be constituted, then the formation whose anatomy we have attempted to give would no longer be a work of art. This does not yet mean, however, that the polyphonic harmony of aesthetic value qualities is *itself* a work of art. It is only what *makes* the literary work a work of art (provided that the metaphysical qualities in the work are manifested), but it is fused with the other elements of the work into a close unit. It is something which stems both from the qualifications or the contents of the individual strata and from the close interconnection of the strata, and it is perceived as something dependent on the whole work. To put it more precisely, both the individual strata and the whole which arises from them show themselves—given, of course, an appropriate attitude on the part of the reader—in manifold aesthetic value qualities which, in unison, of themselves produce a polyphonic harmony. The fact, however, that the literary work of art shows itself in these value qualities does not cause any of its strata to disappear from the reader's field of view. Quite the opposite: what is given to the reader thematically, what first catches his attention, is—as we have already established—the stratum of represented objects, while the other strata are cogiven in a rather more peripheral manner. In contrast, the aesthetic value qualities are like a bright gleam that irradiates the represented objectivities and, at the same time, when experienced by us in aesthetic enjoyment, encompasses us in a special atmosphere and, depending upon the mood, either lulls us or grips and transports us. The point of departure for this subjective resonance, which is the subjective correlate of the experienced polyphony of value qualities, is always the presence of another stratum, but chiefly the object stratum, of the literary work. Finally, the aesthetic value qualities cannot be detached either ontically or purely phenomenally from their constitutive basis—from the corresponding elements of the individual strata. It is part of their essence that they are ontically dependent characters of something which carries them. Indeed they are, so to speak, doubly dependent, since they are not constituted in some hidden essence of something unknown, nor are they the direct properties of an objective carrier; rather, they are characters which have their constitutive basis in the intuitively given *properties* of an objectivity. As we have said, they cannot be separated, even phenomenally, from this, their constitutive basis. A determinate combination of objective properties or discernible elements must always be given or experienced for them to be intuitively established in the manner indicated above. In this way the polyphony of value qualities forms a closely interconnected whole with all the strata of the work, and it is exactly this whole with which we commune in aesthetic perception and enjoyment. This whole is thus the aesthetic object: the literary work of art.

Naturally, as with every objectivity in general, so also with the literary work of art, various subjective attitudes toward it are possible. One may, for example, read a given literary work of art with an altogether nonaesthetic attitude, e.g., when the work is being read by a psychiatrist who wants to determine, on this basis, the author's mental illness. In such an attitude the aesthetic value qualities are not only left out of account; they are even suppressed when they appear in an involuntary aesthetic contemplation. If we are dealing with a genuine and great work of art, however, we are forced into an aesthetic attitude by the very thematic apprehension of the work's object stratum, and we must make an effort—if we have any reasons for doing so—to resume a nonaesthetic attitude, e.g., one of pure cognition. The fact that in these cases we make ourselves blind to the aesthetic value qualities of the work of art only shows that we are not fair to it, that, instead of letting the total work of art work on us, we only single out a part which plays an aesthetically subordinate role in it; this does not indicate, however, that as a result we move from the literary work of art to another objectivity, which only "founds" it.

As our analyses have shown, manifold aesthetic value qualities are constituted in the various strata of the literary work of art. And it is precisely for this reason that there is considerable diversity among them, and only because of this diversity, in turn, can they form a polyphonic harmony. One can, of course, for the purpose of analysis, intentionally differentiate these qualities from the remaining elements and moments of the work and— if one wishes to—speak of a special stratum of the work. One should not forget, however, that it is precisely the diversity of aesthetic value qualities that does not permit them to merge into a fused sphere of homogeneous elements such as we find in the previously distinguished strata of the work. Naturally, they merge into a harmonious structure; but even though it is true that this harmony has its own completely new, "derived" Gestalt qualities, it is still a *polyphonic* harmony, an aesthetic expression (if we may use this term) of the stratified structure of the literary work. At the same time, this polyphony best shows that the ontic basis of the individual "voices" of this harmony lies in the individual strata of the literary work of art. On the other hand, the harmony of aesthetic value qualities constitutes a new unifying bond that binds even more closely the individual strata of the work, which, according to their essence, are already closely fused, and manifests anew the unity of the literary work of art despite the characteristic heterogeneity of its elements.

Thus a possible objection to our conception of the literary work of art is removed. Nevertheless, a certain validity must be conceded to it if it is turned in a somewhat different direction. In this way we can also avoid the danger of a possible error or misunderstanding that may arise on the basis of our present considerations. We have distinguished between the purely literary work as it exists in itself, independent of its concretizations, and these concretizations. Now, one must not forget that, taken in this isolation, the literary work is a *schematic* formation in which, moreover, various elements persevere in a characteristic *potentiality*. These two circumstances have as their consequence the fact that at least some, if not all, aesthetic value qualities and the metaphysical qualities in the work do not attain, themselves, *full development* but remain in a *latent state of "predeterminacy" and "holding in readiness."* Only when the literary work of art attains *adequate* expression in a concretization is there—in an ideal case—*a full establishment, an intuitive exhibition, of all of these qualities.* One may say that it is the nature of all of these qualities to exist in a true sense only in the concretization and in the case of the metaphysical qualities, only in the realization.[1] It follows, therefore, that the literary work of art constitutes an *aesthetic* object *only when it is expressed in a concretization.* Taken in isolation, apart from its concretizations, it is only a "work of art" in the sense determined by W. Dohrn in his book *Die künstlerische Darstellung als Problem der Ästhetik.* It is not the concretization itself which is the aesthetic object, but rather the literary work of art taken precisely as it is expressed in a concretization in which it achieves its full incarnation.

---

1. At first this seems to be trivial. But it does not apply to all objectivities, e.g., to ideal concepts and their actualizations in propositions or to ideal objects and ideas.

WE HAVE THUS COME to the conclusion of our study. We do not conceal the fact that, despite the broad range of our analyses, we have shown merely the main features, the basic structure, of the literary work. Various lines of inquiry require further investigation and completion. Our effort will be amply rewarded if the reader takes the results of this book as a point of departure for further investigations and if he succeeds, not only in carrying them on, but also in replacing any possible errors we have made with better insights. For after the years we have spent on the preparation of this book, we now know better than at the beginning of our study how infinitely difficult it is faithfully to grasp the literary work in its unique essence. The literary work is a true wonder. It exists and lives and works on us, it enriches our lives to an extraordinary degree, it gives us hours of delight, and it allows us to descend into the very depths of existence, and yet it is only an ontically heteronomous formation which in terms of ontic autonomy is a nothing. If we wish to apprehend it theoretically, it shows a complexity and many-sidedness that can hardly be taken in; and yet it stands before us in aesthetic experience as a unity which allows this complex structure to shine through. It has an ontically heteronomous existence that seems to be completely passive and to suffer defenselessly all our operations; and yet by its concretizations it evokes deep changes in our life; it broadens it, raises it above the flatness of everyday existence, and gives it a lovely radiance. It is a "nothing" and yet a wonderful world in itself—even though it comes into being and exists only by our grace.

APPENDIX

The Functions of Language
in the Theater[1]

I

§1. IN MY BOOK *The Literary Work of Art* I have concerned myself twice with the theater. Once in § 30, where I distinguished between the main text [*Haupttext*] and the stage directions [*Nebentext*] in the play, and in § 57, where I dealt with the stage play as a borderline case of the literary work of art. The main text of the stage play consists of the words spoken by represented persons, while the stage directions consist of information given by the author for the production of the work. When the work is performed on stage, the latter are totally eliminated; they perform their representing function and are really read only during a reading of the play. The stage play is a borderline case of the literary work of art, however, to the extent that, besides language, another medium of representation exists within it—namely, the visual aspects, afforded and concretized by the players and by the "decor," in which represented things and persons, as well as their actions, are depicted. Within the framework of my book there was insufficient space to discuss in greater detail the various and in part very complex functions of the linguistic formations which constitute the main text. Likewise, in the thirty years since the appearance of my book, as far as I know neither the linguists, like, for example, K. Bühler, nor the philosophers, like, for example, Nicolai Hartmann, have dealt at any greater length with this topic. Similarly, the literary critics, e.g., B. R. Petsch,[2] have

1. This appendix also appeared as a paper in *Zagadnienia rodzajów literackich* (Problems of Literary Genres) (Lodz, 1958), Vol. 1.
2. Cf. B. R. Petsch, *Wesen und Formen des Dramas* (Halle, 1945).

hardly noticed the problems existing here. Thus it seems necessary to indicate, at least sketchily, the various functions and modifications of language (more precisely, spoken linguistic formations) in the stage play.[3]

It will be useful at the outset to remind ourselves that every literary work is a two-dimensional linguistic formation. On the one hand, it contains four different, though closely interconnected, strata: word sounds, as well as phonetic formations and phenomena of a higher order; sentence meanings and higher units of meaning; schematized aspects; and, finally, represented objectivities. On the other hand, one should differentiate from beginning to end the sequence of parts (chapters, scenes, acts) and the specific quasi-temporal structure of the work. If a play is really performed on the stage, a stage play is constituted in which represented persons and things as well as the acts of the former are depicted, at least in some of their features, by means of visual aspects. In contrast, words or sentences which constitute the "main text" are presented to the audience in their concrete *phonetic* form by represented persons, i.e., by being actually uttered by the actors.

The whole problem of language in the stage play is based on the central fact that though the entire main text is an element of the world represented in the stage play and though, in particular, the articulation of individual words or sentences is a process effected in the represented world and is part of the behavior of the represented person, this does not at all exhaust the role of the statements expressed in the performed play since, at the same time, this role consists of performing the linguistic function of representation—which is still ramified in various ways—which must then remain closely connected to the other means of representation that are active in the play, i.e., the concrete aspects supplied by the actors.[4]

§ 2. Before we proceed in detail with the individual functions of the linguistic formations in a stage play, we must above all

3. In recent years two works have appeared in Poland dealing with related problems: S. Skwarczyńska's *O rozwoju tworzywa słownego i jego form podawczych w dramacie* (The Development of Verbal Material and Its Forms of Presentation in the Drama) (1951), and I. Sławińska's "Problematyka badań nad językiem dramatu" (Problems of Investigation of the Language of Drama), *Roczniki Humanistyczne*, Vol. IV (Lublin 1953–55). Both works contain a number of noteworthy observations.

4. One should not forget that the real players (men and "props") are not components of the stage play. They are merely psychophysical *ontic bases* of the play being performed, whose only components are the persons represented in it—the dramatis personae.

become aware of the various factors that compose the world represented in this play. It breaks down, in short, into three different domains, which, with regard to their mode of existence and their properties, are homogeneous components of one and the same world only in a manner of speaking. They should be distinguished with respect to the basis and the means of their representation. These three domains are:

1. Objectivities (things, people, events) presented to the spectator in an exclusively perceptual [5] manner through the acting of the actors or through the decor.

2. Objectivities presented, so to speak, in a twofold manner, first in perceptual depiction (in the same manner as the objectivities in [1]), and, second, through a linguistic mode of representation, where they are discussed on stage. The linguistic mode of representation forms here a completion of the depiction, especially as concerns the psychic states of the represented persons. Hence there must be harmony between these two modes of representation so that contradictory objectivities do not arise—though, naturally, various kinds of "poetic license" are allowed in a literary work of art.

3. Objectivities represented exclusively by linguistic means and thus not shown "on stage," [6] even though they are discussed in the main text. As regards their mode of representation, they seem at first glance to be entirely on the same level as objectivities in a purely literary work. On closer examination it becomes clear that the manner of their appearance is somewhat different because at least some of them stand in various relations to the objectivities shown on stage (where they then belong to the latter's broader environment) and in this way achieve a character of reality that is more suggestive than that of objects represented in purely literary works. If, in this case too, the unity of the represented world is to be maintained, the linguistic mode of representation of objectivities that are *absent* from the stage must also appropriately harmonize with those that are depicted. A special case of the group of represented objects that are at issue here may consist of all objects that are "past" in relation to objects shown as being "present" (thus, for example, past events,

5. The word "perceptual" cannot be used here without a certain essential reservation, and it should be understood only as a convenient shorthand expression. I do not have the space to elaborate on these issues, however.

6. I am using quotation marks, since, strictly speaking, it is a question of space *represented* by means of the stage. But the expression "on stage" is shorter and more convenient.

processes, as well as things and people that "once" existed). Among these, a special group of "past" objects may again be delineated (though it may at the same time be ranked along with the objectivities in [2]), i.e., those that belong to the past of the objects "now" appearing on the stage and yet *identical* with them. If, for example, in Ibsen's *Rosmersholm* we follow the "present" vicissitudes of Rosmer and Rebecca West and in the process always discover something new about the past of these two people, we become conscious of how it mingles increasingly with their "current" lot and indeed begins to dominate the events now taking place, until, finally, it forces the tragic decision. Represented merely linguistically, the past achieves in the tragic end of Rosmer and Rebecca nearly the same self-manifestation as their decision to take their own lives, which occurs directly "on stage." This, itself, is again intentionally determined only by the conversations of the two represented persons, but it is done in such a way that it seems as real and actually present for the spectator as the last words of the departing individuals.

§ 3. The various functions of the words "actually" spoken are connected to these three groups of represented objectivities. We should first mention the functions that occur, so to speak, "within" the represented world and leave for later the functions that are performed by words spoken "on stage" and directed to the audience.

Above all we have in mind here the function of the *representation* [7] of objectivities that are intentionally meant in the spoken

7. As will be clear from the following, I am distinguishing among representation, expression, communication, and "influencing" functions of linguistic formations (words, sentences, and complexes of sentences). A reader not closely acquainted with the history of these distinctions will probably first think of K. Bühler, whose *Sprachtheorie* (Jena, 1934) was disseminated quite widely, especially among linguists. In fact, however, analogous distinctions go back at least to K. Twardowski's *Zur Lehre von Inhalt und Gegenstand der Vorstellungen* (Vienna, 1894). Subsequently, E. Husserl in his *Logical Investigations* (1901) dealt extensively with "expression" [*Ausdruck*] and "manifestation" [*Kundgabe*]—in later terminology, "meaning" [*Bedeutung*] and "expression" [*Ausdruck*]—on the basis of which K. Bühler, in his article "Kritische Musterung der neueren Theorien des Satzes," *Indogermanisches Jahrbuch*, IV (Berlin, 1920), 1–20, then distinguished three main types of sentences: manifesting, releasing, and representing [*Kundgabe-, Auslösungs-, und Darstellungssätze*]. In *The Literary Work of Art* I have not only questioned some of Bühler's assertions (especially his concept of representation); I have also sought to investigate more closely the concepts of "expression" and "representation." Then in 1934 Bühler distinguished, in his *Sprachtheorie*, the three functions of expression, representation, and signaling [*Appell*]. Finally, in my essay "O Tlumaczeniach" (On Translations), in *O sztuce*

words by their meaning or by the meaning [of the sentence in which they occur]. According to the type of linguistic formation actually being expressed, these may be nominally projected objects (things, people, processes, events) or states of affairs determined by sentences which, for their part, serve for the representation of things or people. This mode of representation may be effected either purely "conceptually" or—as Husserl once said —"significatively," or it may occur in such a way that the intended objects are represented in evoked imaginational aspects.[8] This function of representation constitutes, to be sure, only a *completion* of the world represented in the course of the play, since the main work of representation is done here by the concrete aspects of objects shown on the stage (though in simply represented space). The merely complementary elements of the represented world may, however, be so important that without them the play would not only be incomprehensible but would also be bereft of the moments that are most essential for the dramatic plot. The difficulty of renouncing this linguistic mode of representation in a dramatic play and yet maintaining an artistically and materially complete whole is seen in the pantomime or the silent film. Nevertheless, the role and the part of this linguistic representation in the constitution of the represented world of various plays is still quite varied, and it would be interesting to investigate individual works (and authors) in this respect in order to determine more precisely the type of representational art utilized by them.

The second essential function of spoken words is the *expression* of the experiences and the various psychic states and events of the persons speaking them. These expressions, which are effected through the manifestation qualities [9] of the tone of speech, are inserted into the total expression function performed

---

Tłumaczenia (The art of Translation) (Wroclaw, 1955), I distinguished, in place of these three, five different functions of language, from which I took the above four.

8. In connection with this, we must become aware of the fact that the aspects that belong to a stage play are of a twofold nature: (1) those imposed on the spectator in concrete visual form through the actors appearing on stage, and through which represented persons and things appear to the spectator almost perceptually; (2) those held in readiness by the linguistic structures of the text and only suggested to the spectators. The spectator can concretize them more or less vividly, but only in a form the imagination will allow. Since objects depicted by aspects of this second type are joined in various ontic relations with those shown by means of the first, their depiction can achieve a degree of vividness that is very rare in purely literary works.

9. Cf. *The Literary Work of Art*, § 13.

by the speaker's gestures and facial expressions. Basically, it is a component of the total expression function and hence a process that is executed within the represented world, even though at the same time it contributes to the constitution of some of the components of this world. There are various connections between the linguistic expression and the remaining expression functions, which are more or less close, depending on the uniformity of the represented world.

Third, words and sentences spoken by represented persons perform the function of *communication*. In particular, what is said by a given person is communicated to the other person, the one to whom the words are directed. Living speech—insofar as it is used in its natural function—is always directed to another (a fellow man). Exceptions to this are the so-called monologues, whose function in this respect is still to be investigated but which have been limited in modern drama to the minimum precisely because they are thought to lack the function of communication.

A conversation between two persons deals very seldom with mere communication; it has to do with something more vital, i.e., with influencing the person addressed. In all the "dramatic" conflicts which develop in the represented world of a play, speech directed at someone is always a *form of action for the speaker* and basically has real meaning for the events shown in the play only if it really and essentially advances the developing action.[10] The form of the spoken word as a factor advancing the action will be investigated later. For the moment we wish only to stress that the function of influencing the person addressed and the other people taking part in the total action of the work is the main achievement of the speeches of represented persons.

§ 4. These four functions of speech in a play are only those functions which the spoken word performs *for and within* the

10. S. Skwarczyńska distinguished, among other things, the "dramatic function" of language in the "drama." As far as I understand it, this function constitutes a special case of the fact that words spoken in a play constitute a segment of dramatic action, i.e. that speaking is a process in the represented world. It is only from this standpoint that one can understand that spoken words "advance the action," as Skwarczyńska puts it. Besides this, Skwarczyńska distinguishes between the function of "indirect" and "direct" characterization of persons appearing in a play. In part this involves the expression, and in part the representation, of properties of persons through the meaning of the speeches and, finally, the consequences the spectator draws from the characteristic properties of speeches concerning the character traits of the speakers.

represented world. These are not all the functions of the spoken word in the stage play. One should not forget that the play is performed before an audience and is designed for that audience, and the words spoken by represented persons have still another (and for that matter different) function to perform with regard to it. Here we have a new perspective for investigation, one which, moreover, has already been treated a number of times in the critical literature.[11] Here I will restrict myself to comments which are absolutely necessary.

The theater is not only the stage but also the house and the audience that fills it. The world that is represented and depicted in a play forms a remarkable intentional superstructure and a reinterpretation of what *really* happens during the performance "on stage." During the "performance" (i.e., in the course of the individual "acts") the real stage is naturally always "open" to the audience in the house (once the curtain goes "up"). But the (in a certain sense fictitious) space represented "on stage," in which the action represented in the play develops, as well as the processes and events that occur during this action, can be treated and formed in two different ways: as if all of this were taking place in a world "open" to the audience or in one that is "closed" to it. With regard to the "open" stage, one can still distinguish two different forms of the represented world and the ways it is presented to the audience (i.e., the play of the actors and the design of the decor). We do this by seeing whether the "openness" of the stage (or represented space) is formed and designed for an audience seen merely as an aggregate of "spectators" or whether it is intended for people who are no longer simply spectators but are, at least to a certain extent, *participants* in what occurs "on stage." In the first case we have, e.g., pseudo-classical dramas as well as Shakespearean dramas—though in an acting style where the actor openly turns to the audience and treats it to a "performance" and a concert, as it were, without at the same time quite forsaking the attitude that he is "really" directing his speeches to another represented person. In the second case we are dealing with old Greek tragedies, which formed a kind of mystery play in which the audience took part.

It is only the modern "naturalistic" theater—designed for a mass of "spectators" who are perceiving it with an aesthetic attitude—which creates the fiction of a "closed" stage, i.e., one

11. Waldemar Conrad in particular dealt with this aspect of the theater in "Der ästhetische Gegenstand," *Zeitschrift fur Ästhetik und allgemeine Kunstwissenschaft*, III (1908); IV (1909).

which is actually open but where the acting is done as if the "fourth wall" were not missing and as if there were no spectators of the events taking place "on stage." The actor is supposed to give the impression that he is not seen or heard by anyone but the participants in the represented world with whom and to whom he is speaking. The entire represented world and everything that occurs in it is constituted as if there were no outside observers (i.e., observing from a spot outside the represented world): it, and everything in it, should be as "natural" as possible. In spite of this, this whole manner of composing the represented world and the actor's style is in fact tailored for an observer (but one who is thought of as being absent). This is due to the opinion that the highest art consists in giving the spectator "nature" in its nakedness, unchanged by the spectator's presence. Any modification of the behavior of individuals or of the course of events that is undertaken to produce an "effect" on the spectator is felt to be "artificial," "unnatural," a "falsification" of "nature." Thus the spectator, as someone known to the persons represented in the drama and taken into account in their behavior and their decisions, must be removed, since he would be an obstructive factor in the represented world. For that reason, the represented persons (and consequently the actor himself) must behave as if no one but the other represented people were observing them. Thus the "fourth wall" is closed fictitiously; and only when everything takes place as it would with the fourth wall closed can this wall be, in a manner of speaking, transparent. This is the highest art of producing effects through the appearance of not wanting to do so.[12] Likewise, the so-called impressionist drama is fundamentally "naturalistic," with the single difference that the nature being simulated consists of "impressions," of feelings experienced and enjoyed by all the persons in a scene.

Whatever the nature of the "open" or seemingly "closed" stage that we have in a stage play (or "performance"), we must still add to the above-mentioned functions of represented speech those which refer to the people in the house (in particular, the "spectators"). These are functions of communication and influencing that are *directed in a different* way from those discussed above. According to the nature of the "open" or (seemingly) "closed" stage that we have in the given stage play, these new functions run their course in a different way and also

12. This was, for example, the ideal of the theater for Stanislavski.

modify to a greater or lesser extent the course of the functions of the same words in their relation to specific elements of the represented world. In terms of the ideal of a "closed" stage, they should indeed run their course in such a way that they would evoke no interference in the performance of the latter functions. It may perhaps be said that one can never fully avoid such interference or that, if one were to succeed fully, there could then be no function of communicating with or influencing the spectator. Taking the matter purely empirically, one might perhaps agree that the complete removal of interference, or, to put it more generally, the modification of the "natural" course of speech and the spoken words by the functions directed at the spectators, hardly ever succeeds. If it is reduced to the bare minimum, however—e.g., in naturalistic drama, say, late Ibsen —it does not follow that the function of communication and influencing directed at the spectator must likewise be reduced to a minimum or to zero. The reason is that it is performed primarily through having the *actor*—even if he is not the represented person—attune himself more or less to the spectator and not merely show him the represented speech and thus merely impart its meaning but also act on the spectator. It is only that the nature of this action is altogether different from the action that the words spoken within the represented world have on the other represented person. For as long as it is *not* a mystery play we are dealing with, the influencing of the spectator consists of evoking in him an aesthetic experience and the experience of being moved by represented human vicissitudes, but not of evoking a linguistic answer, or any other answer, to the speaker. And, according to naturalistic principles, the strongest aesthetic influence on the spectator will be exerted precisely when the actor behaves as if he were quite unaware of the spectator's presence. Nevertheless, he does notice it, and he must take it into account, even if he does not show it.

Now, the great problem of forming the spoken word in the theater consists precisely in fulfilling, successfully and harmoniously, all of these functions in the very dissimilar situations (in the represented world and the auditorium) in which it is spoken and in terms of the different goals which the theater sets for itself in its various epochs, styles, and genres.

II

I WOULD NOW LIKE TO DISCUSS, in somewhat greater detail, the individual cases and modifications of the functions and forms in which the spoken word (or the represented speech) appears in a stage play.

§ 1. I have already established that words spoken by a represented person in a situation signify an *act*[13] and hence constitute a part of the action, in particular in the confrontations between represented persons. They do so primarily because they are spoken in a determinate spot of represented space (e.g., the lover's room), in a determinate moment (of represented time), and in a determinate phase of development of the action, with a certain disregard, at the same time, for the fact that this is occurring in the real space of a real stage. Second, because they are spoken in this and no other way and because they have precisely the content they actually have. All of this is essential for the spoken word. Only from this does it follow that it is directed to some other determinate person, that it acts on that person in a given way, and that thereby a certain step is made in the development of the action of the "drama." Without this actual articulation of the words, the action being developed in the play would not only be poorer by a part, but it could also develop in a different way. The latter occurs in connection with the fact that the articulation of the words may have various consequences according to the way in which the spoken words perform their functions within the represented world. This, however, does not depend merely upon what these words are; it also depends on what component they constitute of the total behavior of the given person and what role they play in it.

With respect to this last circumstance, the words of individual characters in the play may be formed in various ways. Or, taking the matter from a different point of view, once they are formed in a given way, the question arises of what their relation is, as component parts of the speaker's behavior, to the totality of that person's behavior. Do they closely enter into it,

13. Whether this act always "means" something, i.e., whether it plays a more or less important role in the action, is another question, indeed a central question of dramatic composition. In a "good" drama every word which is an act without "meaning" is dispensable and, therefore, if it does appear, is a flaw in the composition.

or are they a relatively minor factor in it or something entirely accidental? Are they appropriately adapted to the other behavior patterns of the given person, thus harmonizing with them, or are they in more or less stark contrast with them (e.g., as when a mild and well-bred person suddenly speaks harsh and brutal words to someone who has done nothing to him)? In both cases, but especially in the case of contrasts, one must ask whether and to what extent the manifestation of such contrasts by the over-all situation or by the previous phases of the action is appropriately prepared and grounded or whether it appears as something which does not permit itself to be materially grounded in the represented world. Finally, is this merely a consequence of an error in composition, or can it be explained by the desire to work on the spectator in a certain manner? Is it part of a specific style of composition pertinent to a special work? One can consider the relation between the over-all behavior of the represented person and the words spoken by him from another vantage point, however, i.e., by asking whether this behavior (in facial expressions, movements, etc.), as it is formed by the actor in a *given performance*, harmonizes with the words being spoken? Is it attuned to them, or does it conflict with them in any way? In other words, one asks whether the actor's acting is (intentionally or unintentionally) good or bad.

Words that are spoken, i.e., in the *concrete* manner in which they are uttered in a performance in a given play, may perform their expressive function with greater or lesser efficiency. This may depend on the tone of the delivery (which is predominantly the domain of the actor).[14] But this tone in turn depends (at least to some extent) on both the content of the words spoken and the syntactic structure of the given linguistic formation.[15] It would take us too far from our main subject if we were to go into details. A broad field of linguistic phenomena has to be investigated here. Among the general aspects, however, under which the function of expression must be considered are whether the expression is "sincere," "honest," "true" or, contrariwise, "mendacious" or "insincere" or whether, at the very least, the speaker does not intentionally or unintentionally conceal or cover up something he does not want to betray. Connected with this is the

14. Though this tone may be determined by the text of the play, it is realized fully only in the actor's performance.
15. The poet must have a feel for the syntactic form and the words in which something is said if he is trying to express something both definite and fundamentally ineffable.

question of whether it is "natural" or "artificial" and whether this is intentional (on the part of the represented person or the actor) or unintentional (due to the actor's failure), and so on.

As I have noted, the spoken word can be a form of *acting on* whomever it is directed to, and sometimes on those who are merely witnesses to what is said. Some form of such action occurs in every conversation, because the words that are spoken evoke at least certain experiences of understanding in the person addressed. However, one must distinguish among various forms of "conversation," of which we would like to contrast, in summary fashion, only two. The first, which hardly appears in a "drama"—or, more precisely, a stage play—constitutes, so to speak, "calm" (frequently purely theoretical) conversation, in which the speakers merely share certain facts which do not affect them emotionally. The other constitutes conversation which is basically a form of argument or conflict between the speakers. Thus it is simply a question of either converting the other person to the (theoretical or practical) position held by the speaker himself or of moving him in some way (e.g., by evoking appropriate feelings, desires, or acts of will) to a given mode of behavior and, in particular, to a mode of action which the speaker finds desirable. The suppression of an activity may also be part of the desired mode of behavior. Here we are speaking of "active" discourse. For that matter, "active" discourse seems to be the "normal" form of discourse in the stage play. In it we see the speaker genuinely influencing the person addressed.

The influencing of the person addressed may be attained either by the content of the speech or by the manner, and particularly the tone, in which something is said, or, finally, by both. As far as the content of the speech is concerned, it can act on the person addressed through what it refers to or through what is determined by its meaning, as well as by the manner in which it does this. What is communicated to the other, i.e., what is being spoken about, may refer either to a fact in the external world of both speakers or to something existing within the speaker himself (or in the person addressed), e.g., a decision that one imparts to the other, or a feeling that one nurtures, and so on. In any event, if it is to move the other person in any way, it cannot be entirely inconsequential but must play some role or have some importance or meaning for him; otherwise it will leave him quite "cold." If he is to be moved—and in a manner intended or at least in some way desired by the speaker—the form of the presentation, i.e., the way it is "worded," cannot be altogether arbitrary. It can, for example, be clear or unclear, complicated or simple, ambiguous or unambiguous, direct and "straightforward" or convoluted and veiled. Each manner of speaking is characterized by its own effectiveness. This is not to say, however, that it will always evoke the same sort of effect on the person addressed. There are numerous modifications, depending on the person and, especially, on his state of mind. Even the "clearest" words may seem unclear to him, especially in relation to what is intended, and thus may not evoke the expected verbal or merely emotional answer. But even the situation in which the given words are expressed in a certain formulation can essentially modify their "real" action. The poet, therefore, must take these circumstances into account and correspondingly form the words of the speaker.

The kind and the degree of influence depend perhaps in equal measure on the manner in which the words are *expressed*. It has been frequently and correctly observed that *C'est le ton qui fait la chanson!* One could object that the tone always expresses only the psychic states of the speaker and is of no importance in acting on the person addressed. It remains to be seen whether the tone always succeeds in truly expressing these psychic states. What is more, we must consider whether there are not modifications of tone that are not at all, or not primarily, designed to express something about the psychic state of the speaker. To decide this with any certainty, one would have to have a full compilation of the possible modifications of the "tones" of speech, which, as far as I know, no one has yet attempted. I, too, can give but a few examples. Thus, one can speak in a "violent" or a "calm" tone. One can speak "mildly" or "sharply," "considerately" or "inconsiderately," "kindly" or "condescendingly," or, in contrast, "humbly," "respectfully," in a "friendly" or a "hostile" tone, "candidly" and "frankly" or "suspiciously" and "insincerely," "confidingly" or "openly," and so on. One can ask someone for something "importunately" or, in general, speak "importunately." One can refuse a request very "considerately" or do it in an "inconsiderate," "brutal," or "coarse" way. Depending on whether one speaks to another in a "friendly" or "courteous" manner, one can win him over or make him refractory, one can make him well-disposed toward oneself or, conversely, make him unfriendly and hostile, and so on. If one takes into consideration not only the manner of speaking in the conversation but also various kinds of address, e.g., a speech at a public meeting, a sermon, or an exhortation before battle, one again finds another series of modes of speech which affect the listener in a particular way. It may also be granted that in every such mode of speech something of the speaker's soul is expressed (with greater or lesser clarity and purposefulness); in all this, however, the role of the manner in which the words and sentences are expressed is not exhausted. For the point in question is: what are the further consequences of the expression? And, in connection with that, can the expression be applied, more or less intentionally, to a determinate end?[16] Here one must assert that the person with whom one is speaking is always sensitive to a greater or lesser degree to the speaker's tone and to what is expressed in it. Under the impression of the experienced or consciously apprehended tone, he reacts in a corresponding manner of behavior, part of which is also his verbal answer. If, e.g., one speaks "courteously" with someone, the courtesy may certainly also be only the expression of a spiritual quality of the speaker; most frequently, however, it is a social form whose purpose is to evoke a correspondingly favorable attitude in the interlocutor. Similarly, when one rebukes someone in a "sharp" tone, this is done primarily not to communicate the speaker's dissatisfaction or anger but to have the person recognize his actions as being incorrect and to change them accordingly. In most cases, therefore, where a psychic state is expressed verbally or mimetically, its function in social intercourse is not so much that of an objectivity to which we are attuned in an expressly cognitive way; rather, it is something noticed in passing which stimulates us to further action. The act of answering (including the verbal one) also evokes an analogous reaction on the part of the first interlocutor, so that in the course of the (active) conversation there occurs a psychophysical joining of the two speakers and an interplay of answering reactions and of the experiences, thoughts, feelings, desires, etc., manifested in them. Hence there is *one* conversation process of argument, conflict, or collaboration between speakers. These speakers and the psychic changes occurring in them constitute only a relatively dependent factor in this process.

This is the situation if the mutual influencing of the speakers occurs directly during the conversation. But there are also indirect consequences of the conversation, or of the spoken words, which occur only a certain time after the conversation. These later consequences can also be intended by the represented

16. Often one conceals one's feelings and speaks quite "calmly" simply to put the other person in a friendly mood.

person's speech. In particular, these can be, among other things, other discussions between the characters, so that the entire play presents a chain of human vicissitudes developing through the conversations. The existing "dramatic" literature, with its extraordinary wealth of different forms of human intercourse in speech acts, can best inform us of the manifold functions of speech in human life. What we have noted above must suffice for now. It will be necessary, however, to add one more observation, which points in a perhaps unexpected direction.

There is a special consequence of the fact that men speak to each other and, in doing so, manifest their own thoughts and experiences; this is the self-influencing of the speaker by his "expression" of himself. First of all, our thoughts, and frequently our decisions as well, ripen in the speaking. They unfold in the words that are uttered and take on developed form in them. To be sure, this can also occur in "silent" thought; nonetheless, speaking with another is a kind of thinking "out loud" which we ourselves hear and of which we can be much more conscious than when we merely think something to ourselves without having to externalize it in verbal form. Second, we feel much more at ease when our speech and the thought developing in it can be effective—if it is understood by the other person and if it can incline him toward a certain action or conviction. For it to be effective, however, it must be perfected in verbal form; it must unfold in individual parts, clarify itself, justify itself, and in this way attain persuasive power and impact. In speech we become clearly conscious of matters which frequently slip away from us in the "silent" life [of thought] and which, like uncompleted acts, burden our intellectual and moral conscience. This is therefore the first form of *self-influencing* by speaking with another person: our thoughts, and we ourselves, ripen. This becoming-conscious that is achieved in speaking often has the effect of suddenly making one sensitive and awake to one's own errors, thus inducing one to make the first step toward an internal transformation which, without this self-expression, would perhaps not as easily be attained. Expressing ourselves before another person frequently liberates us: the heretofore unexpressed, which lay heavily on the soul, now falls away; after a long and dogged silence something that was concealed from us enters, through conversation, into the bright light of day and is cast aside like wornout clothes without any particular exertion. By speaking with another person, we not only reveal ourselves to him—be he friend or foe—but to ourselves as well. And this frequently unties our hands and warms our hearts. In opening ourselves up to someone else, we open up the possibility of an intimate communion with the other person which we could perhaps not achieve without the mutual expression. This is the reason why our love is unripe and incomplete as long as it does not find some verbal expression, no matter how laconic. But basically this concerns all our feelings and attitudes: whether friendship or enmity, admiration or contempt, they want to be expressed, and only in this expression do they attain their ultimate fulfill-ment. In their fulfillment, however, the definitive formation of the given person is also effected; he, too, is ultimately formed, or he matures into a good or bad figure. In a play we are funda-mentally witnesses to this sort of maturation of a person, though it need not necessarily be understood as positive growth or im-provement. If, for example, we follow Peer Gynt's fate, we see how, in the various situations and discussions, he slowly ripens in his peculiar empty soul until at the end, in his last form, he is revealed to be barren. In a life of silence, without the frequent verbal encounters with other people, without the consequences of every discussion and the action effected in each discussion, he would not have been able to discover himself and to arrive at his tragic truth.

§ 2. These, then, are the various forms of language as a kind of act and occurrence in the stage play. In all of these forms it appears as a manifold of *meaningful* formations whose consti-tution, unfolding, and actual expression is the already discussed participation of (represented) speech in the development of the action of the "drama." At the same time, these formations in-tentionally project, in accordance with their content, a manifold of objectivities and, therefore, essentially contribute to the con-stitution of the world represented in the play. In this respect they perform the same function as, generally speaking, all the lin-guistic formations in literary works; and if they differ from the latter, the reason is simply that in a stage play they are not the only (and perhaps not even the main) means of representation. As a result, they have to construct within the limits of the repre-sented world only what is not or cannot be constituted and shown by means of concrete visual aspects realized by the actor. From the *sense* of the conversations conducted "on stage" we learn, primarily, various things about the spiritual life of the persons represented that are not or cannot be expressed either by their physical or their verbal behavior and that are frequently indis-pensable for the formation of their personalities. On the other hand, we also learn about objects and events that cannot be depicted in the space represented "on stage" and in the time represented in the course of the play. This essential completion of the represented world has the result that everything of which we (as spectators) are witnesses constitutes only a small segment of what forms the full represented world in the given play. Therefore, what is directly depicted not only acquires intelligibility but also fullness of life and concreteness, without which there could be no complete people or events in the play but merely—if we may use the term—"backdrops." Without these "backdrops," however, all the rest that is projected merely verbally could never attain the vividness and fullness of appearance that is possible in the theater. It is here that we see the decisive role of nonverbal representation in the play.

§ 3. This is the role and the mutual relationship of the two different means of representation taken, so to speak, from the purely anatomical standpoint. At the same time, we see in it the role of both of these means of representation in relation to the spectator who attends the theater and who finds and perceives in it a work of art of a very special sort.

On the surface of it, the functions that are to be fulfilled by the main text of the play with respect to the spectator are the same as those of the words spoken by a represented person to an interlocutor; they are the same representing, expressing, communicating, and influencing functions of language. Nevertheless, the essential difference between the spectator and the (represented) interlocutor to whom the words are directed causes the role of these same words to be essentially changed for the spectator. The reason is that, first of all, the spectator finds himself *outside* the world represented in the play; second, he is not a partner in the conversation nor does he partake in the dramatic action; finally, he is a spectator, who, while perhaps not exclusively, exists primarily in an aesthetic attitude during the performance and is attuned to the apprehension of the work of art or to the constitution of the aesthetic object that is constructed on the basis of this work. From this dissimilarity arise, so to speak, various postulates of what the same words in the main text are supposed to accomplish in their manifold functions with respect to, on the one hand, other represented persons and, on the other, the real spectators. From the differences in these postulates there also arise various requirements, directed at the formation of the spoken words, which must be met if these postulates are to be fulfilled.

We have touched on one case of the dissimilarity of these postulates in our discussion of so-called naturalistic drama. Words spoken by represented persons are to be formed in as "natural" a way as possible and are to be directed exclusively to the interlocutor. Thus they must be adapted according to the situation in which they are spoken and to the effect they are to have on the person to whom they are directed. At the same time, they are to be heard by the "spectator" in the audience and are to make an impression [17] on him in order to evoke in him the corresponding phase of the aesthetic experience and to "please" him. What is supposed to evoke in the interlocutor, on the basis of his understanding, a feeling of, e.g., fright and a defensive attitude is meant to be understood by the spectator merely in its meaning content and its expression content and is to be apprehended in its artistic function, so that the result will be an aesthetic reaction and, in particular, pleasure or displeasure. If fear, anger, and a defensive reaction were to arise in the spectator, there would be no aesthetic apprehension. From the very beginning, the spectator must keep a certain emotional distance between himself and what is said and what occurs in the represented world so that he will not feel threatened in the same sense as the addressed represented person or respond in the same way. Yet these different effects are to be evoked by *the same* spoken words. It would seem that, if they were really the same *in every respect*, they could not produce reactions so dissimilar in two different witnesses to the conversation. Something in them must be different for the spectator and for the represented person; otherwise the difference between their action on the spectator and on that person would be, not simply incomprehensible, but impossible. If the words spoken "on stage" are formed according to naturalistic requirements, the difference being sought cannot inhere in any property of the phonic side of the given linguistic formations or in any moment of meaning, since the spectator is supposed to apprehend these formations in precisely the same features and even in the same functions as the represented persons in represented space. The only difference still possible is in a different ontic character of the words spoken by the represented person. That is, for the represented persons, these words have the character of reality, i.e., they see the expression

17. I am disregarding the case where the play is a mystery in which the audience gathered in the theater is to take some active part. I am thus limiting myself solely to the cases where the audience observes the play, with an aesthetic attitude, as a work of art.

of these words as a fact in their common (represented) world, the one to which they themselves belong. The spectators in the audience, on the contrary, observe the spoken words and the fact of their being spoken only as something "represented," as something portrayed by artistic means but not actually existing in the real world. It is precisely to avoid this that the words actually spoken by the actor are identified with the represented, merely "acted" words; i.e., the spectator must overlook, so to speak (or in a certain sense "forget"), that the words of the represented person belonging to the represented world are "in reality" actually spoken by the actor and have validity only in the merely represented world of the given play.

A different kind of abstraction is at issue in all nonnaturalistic plays. Here the words (linguistic formations) belonging to the main text of the play gain certain attributes that enable them to work aesthetically on the audience in the house, i.e., to put it crudely, to appeal to them. The speeches of the individual represented persons are, for example, spoken in verse or intoned in a certain manner which, in terms of the given work or the dominant fashion (or style) of the given epoch, makes them "declamation" and not "natural" speech. The represented persons in turn behave as if they do not notice that these verses and declamations are often not at all appropriate to the situation.[18] Instead of quickly coming to an understanding about the situation, making their decisions, and acting on them in order, for example, to avoid a calamity, they frequently deliver long tirades, reply to them with equally long, artistically embellished speeches, and act as if this were quite appropriate and natural— all this to please the spectator. In the old theater, these tirades were, moreover, not at all directed at the interlocutor; on the contrary, the actor simply turned to the audience with various facial expressions and gestures designed to let them know what he was doing and experiencing, while the other represented persons in the same represented space were apparently not at all obliged to see and understand what was happening. The "natural" expressive functions of speech were hindered or generally nipped in the bud, since the intonation of verse did not permit their development. The musicality of verse indeed often interferes with the meaning of speech by disregarding and even

18. This occurs to a much greater extent in modern opera, where the "heroes"—participants in a bourgeois drama, e.g., *Madame Butterfly* —do not seem to be at all aware that they are continually singing when they should be simply speaking.

counteracting the accents required by syntactic functions. In other words, sentence melody is frequently interrupted by verse melody, and the latter is not subordinate to the former. Naturally, this need not be so; if it is the case, however, it is only an expression of what different demands are placed on the main text of a play by those functions which are attuned to the audience and, on the other hand, by those functions which the linguistic formations of the main text are to perform within the represented world. The art of the great dramatists consisted of creating works in which—though they are not "naturalistic"— there is a certain harmony between the different claims placed on the linguistic formations of the text. But it is merely a harmony and never a complete elimination of the differences in the creation of linguistic formations for the audience and for the represented persons. Their "unnaturalness" is then reduced to a minimum, but it still always requires a certain willingness to ignore it on the part of the represented persons, as long as they are still treated as members of a "natural" (though understandably merely represented) world. Still another case is possible if the represented persons can be taken from the very beginning as fictitious, purely poetic characters who may be expected to behave just as "unnaturally" in their linguistic context as in the other aspects of their psychophysical life (e.g., the characters in Wagner's *Ring* or Shakespeare's *Tempest*). Just as their external appearance, their physical attributes, or, more generally, their characters are, from the very beginning, straight from the world of "fable," so also their verbal behavior can be altogether different from the "natural" functions of speech. The entire represented reality is then formed according to the principles of aesthetic effect on the public in terms of a certain artistic style, and the formation of represented speech must be (or, more simply, is) subordinated to this fundamental principle. One must then find only those forms of phonic and semantic text formation that will assure that language functions can be realized in the verbal intercourse of these fictitious people as well and that, therefore, the possibility of mutual verbal communication and mutual interaction of the "heroes" is continued. It would take us too far if we were to go into details. But it must be stressed that we have here a broad and interesting field of investigation in individual theatrical works, one which initiates us into the arcana of the extraordinarily manifold art of language formation in the service of the theater and its artistic and aesthetic operations.

Selected Bibliography

This Selected Bibliography is based on the fullest Ingarden bibliography to date, "Bibliografia prac Romana Ingardena 1915–1971," compiled by Andrzej Półtawski, in *Fenomenologia Romana Ingardena* (Warsaw, 1972), pp. 19–54. The Polish bibliography notes the different editions and translations and also the critical reaction to Ingarden's work. It deals only with Ingarden's philosophical works, excluding his publicistic work, his youthful literary efforts, his many articles on cultural and pedagogical subjects, and his theater criticism. The items are arranged in chronological order.

"Über die Gefahr einer Petitio Principii in der Erkenntnistheorie." *Jahrbuch für Philosophie und phänomenologische Forschung*, IV (Halle, 1921), 545–68.

"Intuition und Intellekt bei Henri Bergson, Darstellung and Versuch einer Kritik." *Jahrbuch für Philosophie und phänomenologische Forschung*, V (Halle, 1922), 285–461.

"Essentiale Fragen." *Jahrbuch für Philosophie und phänomenologische Forschung*, VII (Halle, 1925), 125–304. Also published separately as *Essentiale Fragen*. Halle, 1925.

Über die Stellung der Erkenntnistheorie im System der Philosophie. Halle, 1925.

"Bemerkungen zum Problem Idealismus-Realismus." *Festschrift, Edmund Husserl zum 70. Geburtstag gewidmet. Jahrbuch für Philosophie und phänomenologische Forschung, Supplement* (Halle, 1929), pp. 159–90.

Das literarische Kunstwerk: Eine Untersuchung aus dem Grenzgebiet der Ontologie, Logik und Literaturwissenschaft. Halle, 1931.

"Edmund Husserl: *Formale und transzendentale Logik*." *Kantstudien*, XXXVIII, no. 1–2 (1933), 206–9.

"Der logistische Versuch einer Neugestaltung der Philosophie." *Akte des VIII Internationalen Kongress für Philosophie in Prag*. Prague, 1934.

"Vom formalen Aufbau des individuellen Gegenstandes." *Studia Philosophica, Commentarii Societatis Philosophorum Polonorum,* I (Lvov, 1935), 29–106.

"L'Essai logistique d'une refonte de la philosophie." *Revue philosophique,* Year 60, no. 7–8 (Paris, 1935), 137–59.

O poznawaniu dzieła literackiego (The Cognition of the Literary Work). Lvov, 1937.

"Wandlungen in der philosophischen Atmosphäre in Polen." *Slavische Rundschau,* IX, no. 4 (Prague, 1937), 224–33.

"Der Mensch und die Zeit." *Travaux du IX* Congrès International de Philosophie (Congrès Descartes),* VIII (Paris, 1937), 129–36.

"Das ästhetische Erlebnis." *II* Congrès International d'Esthétique et des Sciences de l'Art,* I (Paris, 1937), 54–60.

"Das Form-Inhalt-Problem im literarischen Kunstwerk." *Helicon,* I, no. 1–2 (The Hague, 1938), 51–67.

"De la poétique." *Bulletin International de l'Académie Polonaise des Sciences et des Lettres, Classe de Philologie—Classe d'Histoire et de Philosophie,* no. 1–10 (Cracow, 1945), pp. 36–39.

"De la structure du tableau." *Bulletin International de l'Académie Polonaise des Sciences et des Lettres, Classe de Philologie— Classe d'Histoire et de Philosophie,* no. 1–10 (Cracow, 1945), pp. 39–42.

O budowie obrazu (The Structure of Paintings). Cracow: Polish Academy of Sciences in Cracow, 1946.

"Quelques remarques sur la relation de causalité." *Atti del Congresso Internazionale di filosofia,* I (Rome, 1946) 573–77.

"Quelques remarques sur le problème de la relativité des valeurs." *Actes du III* Congrès des Sociétés de Philosophie de langue française* (Brussels-Louvain, 1947).

"Le Temps, l'espace et le sentiment de réalité." *Revue internationale de filmologie,* I, no. 2 (Paris, 1947), 127–41.

Spór o istnienie świata (The Controversy over the Existence of the World). 2 vols. Cracow, 1947–48.

Szkice z filozofii literatury (Essays on the Philosophy of Literature). Lodz, 1947.

Studia z estetyki (Studies in Aesthetics). 3 vols. Warsaw, 1947–70.

"Quelques remarques sur la relation de causalité." *Studia Philosophica, Commentarii Societatis Philosophorum Polonorum,* III (Cracow, 1948), 151–66.

"Les Modes d'existence et le problème 'idéalisme-réalisme.'" *Library of the Xth International Congress of Philosophy,* Vol. I. Amsterdam, 1948.

"Des différents conceptions de la vérité dans l'oeuvre d'art." *Revue d'esthétique,* II, no. 2 (Paris, 1950), 162–80.

"Kritische Bemerkungen zu Husserls *Cartesianische Meditationen.*" In *Edmund Husserl, Gesammelte Schriften,* Vol. I: *Cartesianische Meditationen und Pariser Vorträge,* pp. 203–18. The Hague, 1950.

"O tłumaczeniach" (On Translation). In *O sztuce tłumaczenia* (The Art of Translation), pp. 127–90. Wroclaw, 1955.

"La Valeur esthétique et le problème de son fondement objectif." *Atti del III° Congresso Internazionale di Estetica, Venezia, 3–5 Settembre 1956,* pp. 167–73. Turin, 1957.

"Über die gegenwärtigen Aufgaben der Phänomenologie." *Archivo di Filosofia, I: Compito della Fenomenologia,* pp. 229–41. Padua, 1957.

[Immanuel Kant's] *Krytyka czystego rozumu.* Polish translation by Roman Ingarden, with an introduction, of Kant's *Kritik der reinen Vernunft.* 2 vols. Warsaw, 1957.

"The Hypothetical Proposition." *Philosophy and Phenomenological Research,* XVII, no. 4 (1958), 435–50.

"Die Asymmetrie der ursächlichen Beziehung." *Festschrift für H. Conrad-Martius: Philosophisches Jahrbuch der Görresgesellschaft,* pp. 100–110. Munich, 1958.

"Von den Funktionen der Sprache im Theaterschauspiel." *Zagadnienia rodzajów literackich,* I (Lodz, 1958), 65–91.

"Bemerkungen zum Problem des ästhetischen Werturteils." *Rivista di Estetica,* III, no. 3 (Padua, 1958), 414–23.

"L'Intuition Bergsonienne et le problème phénoménologique de la constitution." *Congrès Bergson,* pp. 163–66. Paris, 1959.

"Edmund Husserl zum 100. Geburtstag." *Zeitschrift für philosophische Forschung,* XIII, no. 3 (Meisenheim-Glan, 1959), 459–63.

"Über den transzendentalen Idealismus bei E. Husserl: Husserl et la pensée moderne." *Akten des II Phänomenologischen*

Kolloquiums, Krefeld, 1956, pp. 190–204. The Hague, 1959.
Also in French, *ibid.,* pp. 204–15.

"Le Problème de la constitution et le sens de la réflexion constitutive chez Edmond Husserl." *Husserl, Cahiers de Royaumont,* III (Paris, 1959), 242–64. Participation in the discussions, *ibid.,* pp. 66–67, 88–89, 188, 233–34, 269–70, 329–30, 373.

O dziele literackim. Polish edition, revised, of *Das literarische Kunstwerk.* Translated into Polish by Maria Turowicz. Warsaw, 1960.

"Notes sur l'objet de l'histoire de la philosophie." *Diogène,* no. 29 (Paris, 1960), pp. 130–41.

"Raccourcis de perspective du temps dans la concrétisation de l'oeuvre littéraire." *Revue de metaphysique et de morale,* LXV, no. 1 (1960), 19–51.

"The General Question of the Essence of Form and Content." *Journal of Philosophy,* LVII, no. 7 (1960), 222–33.

"L'Homme et la nature." *Atti del XII Congresso Internazionale di filosofia, Venice, 1958,* II, 209–13. Florence, 1960.

"Aesthetic Experience and Aesthetic Object." *Philosophy and Phenomenological Research,* XXI, no. 3 (1960), 289–313.

"Nature humaine." *Actes du XIᵉ Congrès des Sociétés de philosophie de langue française,* pp. 220–23. Montpelier, 1961.

"A Marginal Commentary on Aristotle's *Poetics.*" *Journal of Aesthetics and Art Criticism,* XX, nos. 2 and 3 (1960–61), 163–73, 273–85.

Issledovanija po Estetike (Investigations in Aesthetics). Russian translation by A. Ermilov and B. Fedorov of selected articles from *Szkice z filozofii literatury* and *Studia z estetyki,* Vols. I and II. Moscow, 1962.

"Prinzipien einer erkenntnistheoretischen Betrachtung der ästhetischen Erfahrung." *Actes du IVᵉ Congrès International d'Esthétique,* pp. 622–31. Athens, 1960–62.

"Poetik und Sprachwissenschaft." *Poetics, Poetyka, Poètika* (First International Conference on Poetics), pp. 3–9. Warsaw, 1961.

"Bemerkungen zum Problem der Begründung," *Studia Logica,* XIII (1962), 153–76.

"Edith Stein on Her Activity as an Assistant of Edmund Husserl." *Philosophy and Phenomenological Research,* XXII, no. 2 (1962–63), 155–75.

Time and Modes of Being. English translation by Helen R. Michejda of §§ 1–3, 8–15, 25–28, and parts of § 31 of *Spór o istnienia świata* (see above). Springfield, Ill., 1964.

Untersuchungen zur Ontologie der Kunst. Tübingen, 1962.

"Le Mot comme élément d'une langue." *Thinking and Meaning: Entretien d'Oxford 1962. Logique et Analyse,* n.s. V (Brussels, 1962), 212–16.

Z badań nad filozofią współczesną (Investigations in Contemporary Philosophy). Warsaw, 1963.

Der Streit um die Existenz der Welt. 3 vols. Tübingen, 1964–65.

"Artistic and Aesthetic Values." *British Journal of Aesthetics,* IV, no. 3 (1964), 198–213.

"Husserls Betrachtungen zur Konstitution des physikalischen Dinges." *Colloque de l'Académie Internationale de Philosophie des Sciences, Fribourg, 1963. Archives de Philosophie,* XXVII (1964), 356–407.

"Das schöpferische Verhalten des Autors und das Mitschöpfertum des Virtuosen und der Zuhörer." *Aspecten van Creativiteit, Verhandelingen voorgedragen in een zitting ter herdenking van het 50-jarig bestaan van het Bureau voor Muziek-Auteursrecht BUMA, 16 december 1964,* pp. 29–33. Amsterdam, 1964.

Przeżycie—dzieło—wartość (Experience—Work of Art—Value). Cracow, 1966.

"Werte, Normen und Strukturen nach René Wellek." *Deutsche Vierteljahrschrift für Literaturwissenschaft und Geistesgeschichte,* XL, no. 1 (1966), 43–55.

"Einige ungelöste Probleme der Werttheorie." *Orbis Scriptus: Festschrift für Dmitrij Tschizewskij,* pp. 365–73. Munich, 1966.

"Jean Hering (1890–1966)." *Philosophy and Phenomenological Research,* XXVII, no. 2 (1966–67), 308–9.

O poznávání literárniho dila. Czech translation by Hana Jechova of *The Cognition of the Literary Work* (1937). Prague, 1967.

"Betrachtung zum Problem der Objektivität." *Zeitschrift für philosophische Forschung,* XXI, nos. 1 and 2 (1967), 31–46, 242–60.

Vom Erkennen des literarischen Kunstwerks. Greatly enlarged German edition of the Polish *O poznawaniu dzieła literackiego* (1937). Tübingen, 1968.

"Die ontische Fundamente der Verantwortung." *Akten des XIV Internationalen Kongress für Philosophie, Wien, 2–9 September, 1968*, I, 235–42. Vienna, 1968.

"Das Problem des Systems der ästhetisch relevanten Qualitäten." *Actes du Ve Congrès International d'Esthétique, Amsterdam, 1964*, pp. 448–56. The Hague, 1968.

[Edmund Husserl's] *Briefe an Roman Ingarden: Mit Erläuterungen und Erinnerungen an Husserl* [by Roman Ingarden]. *Phaenomenologica*, Vol. XXV. The Hague, 1968.

Erlebnis, Kunstwerk und Wert: Vorträge zur Ästhetik 1937–1967. Tübingen, 1969.

"Ästhetik und Kunstphilosophie." *Akten des XIV Internationalen Kongress für Philosophie, Wien, 2–9 September, 1968*, IV, 214–19. Vienna, 1969.

"Le Concept de philosophie chez Franz Brentano." *Archives de Philosophie*, July–September and October–December, 1969, pp. 458–75 and 609–38.

"Z rozważań nad wartościami moralnymi" (Reflections on Moral Values). *Rozprawy filozoficzne* (Towarzystwo Naukowe w Toruniu. Prace Wydziału Filologiczno-filozoficznego), XXI, no. 2 (Torun, 1969), 105–17.

"The Physicalistic Theory of Language and the World of Literature." *Yearbook of Comparative Criticism*, II (1969), 80–98.

Über die Verantwortung: Ihre ontische Fundamente. Stuttgart, 1970.

Innføring I Edmund Husserl Fenomenologi. Norwegian translation by F. Christiansen of the German text of lectures delivered in Oslo in 1967. Oslo, 1970.

"Co jest nowego w ostatniej pracy Husserla?" (What Is New in Husserl's Last Work?). *Studia Filozoficzne*, no. 4–5 (65–6) (1970), pp. 3–14.

"Künstlerische Funktionen der Sprache: Ein Ausblick." *Sprachkunst*, I, no. 1–2 (1970), 20–31.

"Bemerkungen zu den Bemerkungen von Profesor Zofia Lissa." *Studia Filozoficzne in Übersetzungen*, no. 4 (1970), pp. 351–63.

"Gastvorlesungen von Roman Ingarden, Amsterdam 14 März, 1969." *Bulletin international d'esthétique*, V, no. 14 (Amsterdam, 1970) 5–7.

U podstaw teorii poznania, Część pierwsza (The Bases of Cognitive Theory, Part I), Warsaw, 1971.

"Ausgangsprobleme zur Betrachtung der kausalen Struktur der Welt." *Philomates: Studies and Essays in the Memory of Philip Merlan*, pp. 398–411. The Hague, 1971.

"Die vier Begriffe der Transzendenz und das Problem des Idealismus bei Husserl." *Analecta Husserliana: The Yearbook of Phenomenological Research*, I (1971), 36–74.

"O badanjach filozoficznych Edith Stein" (The Philosophical Researches of Edith Stein). *Znak*, Year 23, no. 4 (202) (1971), 389–409.

"Bericht über meine Studien zur Ästhetik." *Contemporary Philosophy: A Survey*, IV (Florence, 1971), 106–10.

The Literary Work of Art. English translation by George G. Grabowicz of *Das literarische Kunstwerk*. Evanston, Ill., 1973.

The Cognition of the Literary Work of Art. English translation by Ruth Ann Crowley and Kenneth R. Olson of *Vom Erkennen des literarischen Kunstwerks*. Evanston, Ill., 1973.

Investigations into the Ontology of Art: Music, Painting, Architecture, the Film. English translation of *Untersuchungen zur Ontologie der Kunst: Musikwerk, Bild, Architektur, Film*. Evanston, Ill., forthcoming.